TREES

of Britain and Ireland

History, folklore, products and ecology

EDWARD MILNER

Published by the Natural History Museum, London

First published by the Natural History Museum,
Cromwell Road, London SW7 5BD

ISBN 978 0 565 09295 5

DESIGNED BY Mercer Design, London

REPRODUCTION BY Saxon Digital Services

PRINTED BY Toppan Leefung Printing Limited

FRONT COVER: weeping ash, Fraxinus excelsior © Photolibrary Ltd.

BACK COVER: from top left clockwise – strawberry tree, *Arbutus unedo*;
sawfly larvae on hazel; hawthorn, *Crataegus* ssp., all © Edward Milner/ACACIA
Environment; wild bee, *Andrena* spp. © Stuart Roberts; sycamore, *Acer
pseudoplatanus* © Edward Milner/ACACIA Environment; shaggy bracket fungi,
Innonotus hispidus © UKM/Ian Kimber.

THE TREE
COUNCIL

Contents

1 Introduction

IN 1992 MY INTEREST IN TREES LED ME to produce a series of documentary programmes for Channel Four TV entitled *Spirit of Trees*. In these, I tried to show the work of scientists and activists who were pursuing diverse lines of enquiry and campaigning to raise interest and concern about the conservation of trees and the restoration of woodland. To accompany the series I wrote *The Tree Book*, starting from the research for the programmes. Initially the whole project concentrated on trees in Britain and Ireland but for some topics, such as record trees and unusual trees, I widened the approach to include California, Socotra and China, pursuing what presenter Dick Warner referred to as 'the complexity of the relationship between us human beings and these giant plants'.

Since the early 1990s the range of books specifically about trees in Britain has increased enormously. There is an extensive literature about all aspects of woodland (in particular by authors such as Rackham, Peterken and others) but in 1992 I wrote that 'most books on trees are written by foresters', and that they were mostly concerned with identification and little else. This was true at the time, but in fact things had already begun to change. Several authors have subsequently referred to the Great Storm of 1987 as the stimulus for their deep personal interest in trees, and memorable personal narratives about trees, such as those by Colin Tudge, Roger Deakin, Ben Law and Richard Mabey, have since been published to considerable public acclaim. Several other books of spectacular photographs of trees have been published by Tree Register of the British Isles (TROBI) (Johnson, 2011), Thomas Pakenham, Archie Miles, Herbert Whone, Andrew Morton and others, while Fred Hageneder has produced a series of interesting books investigating mainly the spiritual aspects of trees (see References).

OPPOSITE **Fine aspen tree at Corrieshalloch Gorge, Ross-shire.**

In this book I have concentrated on our native trees, and look at those aspects of trees that tend to be missed out of many other tree books, including history, ecology, management and folklore. How our native trees will fare in the future under the conditions brought about by climate change is a matter for speculation, but I hope that some pointers may become evident from the baselines explored here. My purpose is to promote an appreciation of the intrinsic worth of our trees as multi-faceted living entities each with its own nature and place.

Outline of the book

In the first three chapters I introduce some general information about the life of trees; the origin of trees and their basic biology and life history; an explanation of which trees I am including and why; and some indication of the relationships between trees and other organisms that have evolved over hundreds of millions of years. This is followed in Chapter 4 by portraits of each of our native tree species in alphabetical order from alder to yew, with some like whitebeams and willows grouped together. For each tree there is an account of its distribution, ecology and history, followed by the uses of the tree and its products, folklore associated with the tree and an account of the network of other organisms that depend on the tree and indicate its place in the ecosystem.

Following the tree portraits are some unifying themes. In Chapter 5, I describe the historical management of trees – coppicing and pollarding, fruit production and hedges – followed by newer uses such as the production of biomass to burn for electricity generation, and the use of trees for the restoration of contaminated land. In Chapter 6 I discuss the folklore traditions relating to trees in different parts of these islands, while in Chapter 7 I discuss the future of our native trees and their associated other organisms in the context of climate change, and under threats such as the globalisation of pests and diseases, the proliferation of deer and the possible introduction of genetically modified trees.

At the end of the book there are tables of information and data about native trees, including a checklist, biological characteristics, and lists of associated insects, fungi and diseases. These are followed by a list of references and other sources, and a glossary.

What is a tree?

Everyone knows a tree when they see one, but to define the word precisely is not easy. What is the difference between a tree and a bush, or a tree and a large shrub? Certain features are generally agreed: a tree is woody, more or less erect, at least in favourable circumstances, usually single-stemmed and for many authors 'able to exceed 6 metres (20 feet) in height' (Mitchell, 1991). But some do not reach this height and yet are clearly trees, and perhaps the most important feature of a tree is that it looks like a tree! So an

oak is a tree and heather is not a tree, but where is the dividing line? I have tried to define a tree as a woody plant with (potentially) a proportionally large main stem, which is more or less rigid. When the wind blows across the scrubland, bushes bend and sway from the ground up, but the main trunk of a tree stays more or less rigid, though the branches may sway. I like this point because it seems to me there is a very interesting category of small, even minute, trees right down to 'God's bonsai', the tiny dwarf willows that grow on the tops of our mountains. Spindle, alder buckthorn and juniper usually grow in the form of bushes, but as photographs in this book show, all can occur as perfectly acceptable trees. I have had to draw a line somewhere; dogwood and guelder rose are excluded as shrubs or bushes, rather than trees, but I have no doubt that some readers will know of individuals of even these species that would qualify as 'genuine' trees.

The history and biology of trees

Trees are very ancient in origin. They have dominated the vegetation of the planet since long before the dinosaurs, and first appeared in the Devonian period around 365 million years ago. Their life strategy of using strong woody stems to hold up many leaves to manufacture food on a large scale has clearly been a great success. The first modern-looking trees were wind-pollinated gymnosperms, which are represented today by conifers, gingko and cycads. However, within about the last 100 million years these have been overtaken and in warmer zones largely replaced by flowering trees or broadleaves (angiosperms), many of which have evolved together with pollinating and seed-distributing organisms, especially insects, but also mammals and even reptiles.

Worldwide there are today about 700 conifer tree species, most of them restricted to the northern temperate zone and tropical mountains. These have largely been displaced at lower altitudes by broadleaved trees, of which there are thought to be around 30–40,000 species, out of a total of around 250,000 species of flowering plants. The vast majority of all tree species occur in the tropical forests, where there can be hundreds of species in a single hectare, but there is also an enormous diversity in the oldest undisturbed temperate forests such as those in western China. In Britain we have an extremely limited tree flora largely because, as recently as 12,000 years ago, most of our landmass was covered

LEFT Sycamore trees thrive in
exposed situations such as here
in Glencoe, Scottish Highlands.

with ice and the rest with treeless tundra; today's trees have mostly arrived here since the ice melted.

The life-cycle of trees is as diverse as that of any other group of plants, but generally, after the germination of the seed, it takes a number of years for a tree to reach sexual maturity and develop its full-grown form. Conifers, like other wind-pollinated plants such as grasses, tend to have small, insignificant flowers, as do the wind-pollinated broadleaves. However, many broadleaves have developed brightly coloured blossom or flowers that offer both pollen and nectar to visiting animals such as bees and flies, which may consume these products but also transfer them from tree to tree thus pollinating the flowers.

Once the flowers have been pollinated and the ovules fertilised, seeds and often the ovary and surrounding tissues, develop and grow into fruits. In fact there are two separate processes that botanists have noted. One is the physical arrival of pollen, which in some trees, such as apple, is in itself sufficient to stimulate the growth of the fruit (although not necessarily the seeds). Then there is fertilisation, the fusion of the genetic material of the pollen with that of the ovum, leading to the production of offspring with genetic material from both parents. So fruits sometimes have viable seeds but not always.

In many plants, including some trees like hawthorn, apple and oak, fruits are attractive as food. This leads to another relationship, that of trees with fruit-eating animals and insects, which then act

as dispersal agents. Some trees hold onto their fruits until they are eaten; in other cases such as oaks and crabapple the fruits fall when ripe. Large numbers of fruits are destroyed by being eaten but others are stored, by birds or mice for example, and some of these germinate. In other cases the seeds germinate after they have passed through the gut of the animal or bird. Very few of our trees have seeds that remain viable for very long in the soil, unlike some flowering plants such as foxglove whose seeds may remain viable for decades.

Large seeds like acorns have substantial food reserves, allowing them to develop roots to anchor them in dense vegetation before they begin to manufacture their own food by photosynthesis. Other tree seeds, like those of birch or willow, are tiny and must start photosynthesis within a day or two of germination. In all cases, forming an early association with mycorrhizal fungi may be the key to the success of the young trees. These are the fungi that develop around or sometimes within the cells of the tree roots. The fungi are able to extract mineral elements from the soil and convert them into compounds that the seedling needs, while the fungi benefit by absorbing sugars that the seedling has manufactured from the energy of the sun by photosynthesis.

What is a species?

A species is usually defined by zoologists as a single interbreeding population, though botanists find this definition is unworkable. One reason is that some plants have a tendency to double or triple the number of chromosomes; apparently this alone can give rise to intermediate forms. In some trees (and other plants) this seems to be connected with the fact that they have been cultivated for thousands of years. I have tried to use the word tree when 'species' is problematic. The main trees in which this is relevant are willows, *Salix* spp., elms, *Ulmus* spp., whitebeams, *Sorbus* spp., and fruit trees, *Malus* spp., *Pyrus* spp. and *Prunus* spp.

Willows interbreed. The pollen of several native species will fertilise the female catkins of other native species giving rise to hybrids, some of which are fertile and may then pollinate or be pollinated by one of the parents, and so on. Various introduced willows also interbreed with native species; Stace (2010) lists over a hundred different hybrids. As a result there are effectively many intermediate forms between native willow species and introduced species. In elms, apart from wych elm, sexual reproduction is rare and selected trees have been widely planted from cuttings taken from individual trees, while in whitebeams new forms arising from cross-pollination sometimes become self-replicating clones through the production of seeds that are viable without having been fertilised. This phenomenon is called apomixis. The genetic make-up of fruit trees is also complex; recent investigations at Cheddar Gorge and other limestone sites near Bristol have revealed several new forms (Rich *et al.*, 2010).

What is a native tree?

This apparently simple question is complicated. It is normally accepted that there is a flora and fauna of a territory that occurs naturally, i.e. without human intervention. In Britain this is more complicated as much of the country was covered in ice-sheets as recently as the last glacial period, which ended around 11,000 or 12,000 years ago. Since then a good deal of recolonisation has taken place. Like other trees birch had been present here before the last glacial period, and as the ice melted seeds blew in on the wind. Birch then reproduced by seed with its spread following the retreat of the ice (see pollen maps p.15). That's about as native as you can get, although around 10,000 years ago birch itself was effectively a new arrival, as were Scots pine, juniper and some willows.

Hornbeam and beech arrived far more recently, if the pollen record is to be believed, but again, they presumably arrived on the wind. Basket willow is more problematic; it may have been brought here by human migrants 'before 1500' (Hill *et al.*, 2004),

RIGHT Mature birches showing variation in habit due to genetic diversity. Dunkeld, Scotland.

ABOVE A mature white willow, *Salix alba*, growing at a spring near Long Melford, Suffolk.

RIGHT Sheep have restricted aspen to inaccessible cliffs in much of Scotland.

as was sweet chestnut, *Castanea sativa*. In their PLANTATT (Attributes of British and Irish Plants) database of British flora, Hill and his co-authors have summarised current thinking and refer to two categories of non-indigenous plant species. These are known as archaeophytes (which arrived before the year 1500) and neophytes (which arrived since 1500), as opposed to native plants, which were still here (in 'refugia') or arrived by natural means after the last glacial period. Among trees, most archaeophytes are fully naturalised (i.e. they now occur in otherwise natural plant communities without human intervention) but some, like walnut, are not. Neophytes include trees such as horse-chestnut, Sitka spruce and lodgepole pine.

Essentially, this book concerns itself with native wild trees, whether species or varieties, in their natural habitat. To make this manageable I have restricted myself to native trees and archaeophytes (while excluding those, like walnut, which have not become completely naturalised in the sense of successfully competing with the native flora in natural situations). I have also excluded all neophytes, with one exception: sycamore, which I regard as a special case (see p.133), and today is clearly naturalised all over these islands, whatever its origin.

The origins of both basket willow and crack willow are uncertain, but they are apparently archaeophytes, arriving long before 1500, and naturalised along waterways, reproducing and spreading in competition with the native flora.

For cultivated trees such as apples and pears I have decided on a case-by-case approach. Many fruit cultivars were brought here at different times, but since their flowering strategy (being self-incompatible) results in new varieties occurring all the time, many unique 'sports' have arisen here from chance cross-pollination and can be found in hedgerows, on wasteland and at woodland edges. They may not be separate species, but they are unquestionably native. Some of these 'pippins', such as Bramley's Seedling, have been cherished and used by orchard growers as recognised cultivars and spread by cuttings and grafts.

English elm is something of a mystery: 'it is not certain that it is an archaeotype. If it occurs outside Britain and Ireland there is no evidence as to which way it travelled' (Oliver Rackham, pers. comm. 2009). Plot's elm, Exeter elm, Huntingdon elm and others are now thought to be sports of unknown origin, some of which have been widely planted from cuttings.

I have generally omitted cultivated varieties of other native trees, except in a few cases in which the origin is known and native, such as fastigiate yew. In peri-urban areas, in addition to the native holly *Ilex aquifolium*, there is a wild hybrid (Highclere holly, *Ilex* x *altaclerensis*), which results from cross-pollination with an introduced species (*I. perado*) that is widely planted by horticulturalists. It is evident that the idea of a native species includes a range of possibilities; effectively, some trees are more native than others.

9

2 The history of our native trees

FROM THE AVAILABLE GEOLOGICAL EVIDENCE we now know that most of the landmass of these islands was covered with ice for the 10,000 to 15,000 years up to the beginning of the present warmer period known as the Holocene. It should be remembered that Britain was still connected to the rest of Europe at this time and other details of the coastline may have been significantly different at the time. A little after 11,000 years ago the climate began to change, the ice began to melt and gradually trees began to spread. How do we know this? Largely this is based on evidence from pollen cores in the mud of lakes and other wetland areas.

Pollen studies

Pollen is so well preserved in peat and in lake sediments that the grains can be extracted and identified, while the deposits can be dated from stratigraphy and using a radiocarbon technique. Professor J. Birks of the University of Bergen in Norway has combined evidence from studies made at 135 sites 'all with satisfactory radiocarbon chronologies' (Birks, 1989). The sites are not evenly distributed, and in some areas such as south and east England the sites are fewer due to paucity of good pollen sediments, but the data was sufficient to produce maps showing the spread of species over time for a large number of species (including many trees) for the whole of Britain and Ireland. The maps are more accurate and detailed for wind-pollinated species, which produce large amounts of naked pollen grains. They are far less complete for insect-pollinated species, which produce larger, often sticky pollen grains in smaller quantities that are only likely to fall near their parent tree.

For the wind-pollinated species, their presence or absence can be determined easily, giving a fairly good idea about when they first arrived. The interpretation of pollen data for reconstructing the vegetation as a whole is more difficult. Traditional interpretations have been questioned by writers such as Vera (2002), who has suggested for example that high counts for both oak and hazel indicate not dense woodland but open woodland or even grassland dotted with trees. He has pointed out that hazel produces little pollen when well shaded, while inside a wood even oak pollen would be unlikely to travel far on the wind. The absence of both types of pollen might therefore be evidence of dense forest.

ABOVE Evidence of old forests can be found underneath peat deposits. These old pine stumps are at Loch Droma, Highland.

OPPOSITE Ancient oaks and hollies at Staverton Thicks, Suffolk.

There is also the likelihood that some of the movement of useful species was the result of deliberate human activity; people would have planted many tree species like hazel, oak and cherry where they needed them, as people do today. We know that trees such as apple and pear, basket willows and some elms were brought here for planting from elsewhere in Europe, so their presence in the pollen record from particular sites is not easy to interpret.

The maps in the box feature indicate the generally accepted patterns for the spread of eight tree species throughout these islands. Pollen from all these trees appears in sufficient quantities and consistently enough for the maps to be reasonably reliable. Beech has been excluded as it reached these shores much more recently than the others; the earliest reliable pollen data occurs as late as 3,000 years ago.

Dendrochronology

Dendrochronology is the science of precise dating, using the counting of tree growth-rings, which first provided an accurate and generally agreed calibration for carbon dating. Tree rings differ every year, thicker in good years and thinner when growing conditions are poorer. There may be various reasons for this – lower temperatures, less sunshine etc.

The first scientist to notice that tree rings gave consistent patterns and could be counted to give accurate dates of tree growth was A. E. Douglass, who used the technique in 1904 by confirming the age of a pine log with the man who had felled it. He later established a pine chronology for the American Southwest that went back over 2,500 years. Subsequently, much longer chronologies, back to about 7,200 years ago, were established for very old (living) bristlecone pine trees in the White Mountains of California. These counts were used to calibrate radiocarbon dating, and correlation tables were drawn up.

The application of this technique in Europe proved much more difficult. There are no long-lived trees with complete sets of rings like the bristlecone pines, but the technique was applied to oak, an approach greatly helped by the examination of large numbers of semi-fossil 'bog-oaks' in Ireland. While individual oak logs were rarely more than about 300 years old, a long series of overlapping records was put together, reaching back more than 7,200 years, confirming a similar series worked out in Germany. Since then work has established series for oak in several other European countries.

The British team that pioneered this work is based at the Palaeoecology Centre in Queen's University, Belfast. By the mid-1980s a complete chronology was in place, based on Irish oak. As

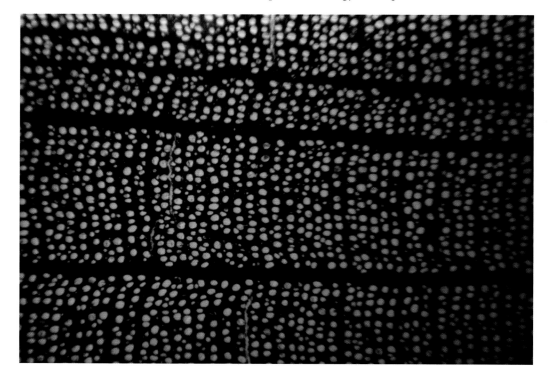

RIGHT Oak tree-rings under the microscope. The older part of the tree is towards the right edge of the image.

a result the team have been able to date precisely oak logs, building timbers and other oak relics.

Dendrochronological analysis of an Irish archaeological site, the Corlea 1 Track Co Longford, indicated that the timbers were felled in late 148 BC or early 147 BC, while those used for the English Sweet Track on the Somerset Levels were felled very much earlier, in late 3807 BC or early 3806 BC.

Tree-ring data provides precise information about environmental events, including atmospheric dust-veils, now understood to have been caused by major volcanic eruptions often thousands of miles away. Several periods of extremely narrow growth-rings have been found, some of which coincide with ice deposition levels in the Greenland ice-cap that show increased (acid) pollution, suggesting that the effects of major eruptions were felt worldwide.

LEFT Semi-fossil bog-oaks and bog-yews dug up from under peat in central Ireland.

LEFT The Sweet Track: this ancient timber track laid across a bog on the Somerset levels was discovered by and named after a local farmer. Excavation revealed a causeway constructed of cleft oak planks with hazel and alder pegs, and some pieces of elm, ash and holly (Coles and Orne, 1981).

Pollen mapping

In the maps, the shading shows the side of the line which the species had reached by each date, while the arrows are to give extra clarification of the direction in which the trees spread. A broken line is used when dates have had to be estimated due to a lack of proven information. The darker line gives the distribution around 6,000 years ago for each species.

ALDER There are many very early records of alder: wood and catkins dating from over 10,000 years ago have been found in Yorkshire, and it was present and locally abundant along the mid-Wales coast more than 8,900 years ago. Before that, alder pollen occurs in small amounts at many sites but consistently at just a few. Alder pollen and fruits are buoyant and remain viable for over a year, which complicates the interpretations; small amounts of pollen could be recorded at sites some way from an actual alder population – for example having been washed down a river to a lake far below. By 7,500 years ago alder had expanded inland in England and Wales, though in Ireland it was still confined to the northeast until 7,000 years ago. It finally reached the extreme north of Scotland by about 5,300 years ago. The pattern is erratic and later studies have suggested that the spread of alder was much more patchy, both in time and space, than that of other species, due to its association mainly with wet places, and its floating seeds.

ASH Pollen records show that ash was present in southern and central England in low but consistent amounts between 7,000 and 6,000 years ago. It then spread slowly northwards to Scotland and westwards to Ireland, where it probably replaced hazel on calcareous soils, and its pollen values also increased in England during the next 2,000 years.

BIRCH (a) (3 spp.) Pollen of birches has been found in some places dating back 13,500 years, but it is thought to have become very rare or even extinct between 11,000 and 10,200 years ago. Birch spread from the east, starting just over 10,000 years ago and was already well established everywhere by 9,500 years ago.

ELM Wych elm had reached southern England by 9,500 years ago, spreading quite rapidly west to eastern Ireland; its spread north to Scotland was slow, probably because of the acidic soils and more unfavourable climate. By 6,200 years ago it had become a regular if minor component of woodland as far north as Caithness. There was a dramatic decline for a period between 5,500 and 5,000 years ago, but this did not affect its range within these islands, and elm populations recovered later.

HAZEL Hazel was established around the shores of the Irish Sea before 9,000 years ago, though how this happened is not clear. It has been suggested that dispersal agents including birds, rodents and even humans may have been responsible, but fresh hazel-nuts can float in freshwater or seawater and still retain viability for at least 30 days, suggesting that water may be a more likely dispersal agent.

LIME (b) (2 spp.) Lime was present in southern England 7,500 years ago and gradually spread into central England and parts of Wales, becoming a major component of the forests, as in mainland Europe. Lime never reached the extreme southwest of England but reached its northernmost limits in the Lake District around 5,500 years ago; this coincides geographically with the residual native populations of *T. cordata* today in the Lake District and Upper Swaledale.

OAK (c) (2 spp.) Oak spread up the western seaboard of Europe from 10,500 years ago, reaching southwest England by 9,500 years ago and southeast Ireland soon afterwards. The trees spread rapidly throughout these islands over the next 1,400 years, but did not reach the north of Scotland until about 6,100 years ago.

SCOTS PINE (d) Pollen data shows that pine was present widely but locally in southern England by 9,000 years ago. In the next 500 years it spread north to the Lake District and the northern Pennines. It was already present in Ireland over 8,800 years ago, but not in Wales, suggesting that the Irish populations had an independent origin, possibly from Iberia. Pine expanded in northern Scotland between 8,500 and 8,000 years ago in the Loch Maree area, either from an independent refuge, from Scandinavia or as a result of expansion from Ireland. There were massive declines in both the Irish and the western Scottish pine populations around 4,000 years ago, leading ultimately to the extinction of pine in Ireland between 2,000 and 1,000 years ago. In both Scotland and Ireland large areas of pine forest were replaced by extensive blanket bogs, though the reasons for the decline there or its extinction in England are not clear, but may have been influenced by human intervention (burning).

Various other species are present in some pollen samples but not enough to enable maps to be drawn. However, scattered pollen records of several tree species can be traced in some places right back to the earliest birch dates – willow, rowan, juniper, poplar or aspen, holly and cherry among others. Yew and holly first appeared very early, around 9,000 years ago. Hawthorn first appeared around 7,000 years ago. Hornbeam did not appear until around the same time as beech, about 5,000 years ago, and then only in very small numbers; it seems to have first become common and widespread only by about 1,000 years ago.

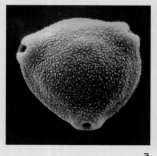

a

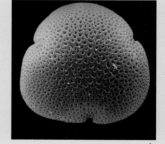

b

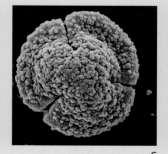

c

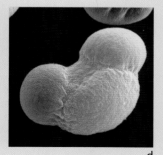

d

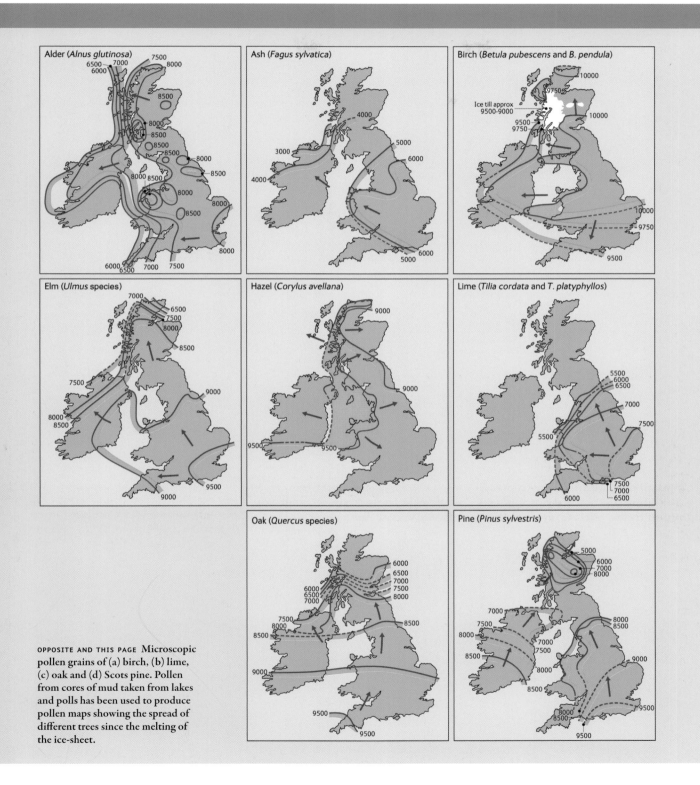

Alder (*Alnus glutinosa*)

Ash (*Fagus sylvatica*)

Birch (*Betula pubescens* and *B. pendula*)

Ice till approx 9500-9000

Elm (*Ulmus* species)

Hazel (*Corylus avellana*)

Lime (*Tilia cordata* and *T. platyphyllos*)

Oak (*Quercus* species)

Pine (*Pinus sylvestris*)

OPPOSITE AND THIS PAGE Microscopic pollen grains of (a) birch, (b) lime, (c) oak and (d) Scots pine. Pollen from cores of mud taken from lakes and polls has been used to produce pollen maps showing the spread of different trees since the melting of the ice-sheet.

3 Trees in the web of life

Trees act as pegs, fountains, oceans, pipes and dams, their work ramifying throughout the whole economy of nature. They hold up the mountains. They cushion the rain-storm. They control the floods. They maintain the springs. They break the winds. They foster the birds.

COLLIS, *The Triumph of the Tree*, 1951.

THE SIGNIFICANCE OF TREES TO LIFE on the planet is difficult to overestimate. Trees had a major role in making the diversity and success of life on land possible, although the full complexity of their contribution today is still not fully understood. For hundreds of millions of years they have extracted carbon dioxide from the atmosphere and fixed it in a stable form, at the same time releasing oxygen into the atmosphere. The air we breathe is dependent on trees, and the fuel we burn is largely derived from the fossilised remains of ancient trees.

Trees absorb and use sunlight to transpire water from their leaf surfaces, thus cooling the air, while drawing water up from the soil through their roots. The roots of trees begin much of the process of weathering of rocks, and then provide a structure that holds the soil so it is not washed away. Trees themselves hold large amounts of water as well as carbon.

In many places trees line riverbanks and prevent their erosion, and they drop foliage, fruits and branches, which all contribute nutrients to water and soil below. They create shade, and as forests or woodland they provide shelter from the extremes of climate; the canopy of even a single tree can reduce heat loss at night and prevent soil overheating in the day. A forest can be as effective as a range of mountains in causing precipitation. Trees maintain air humidity, which benefits many other organisms. They filter out airborne particles and build soil fertility. Like all green plants, trees manufacture simple sugars from water and carbon dioxide using

chlorophyll and the energy derived from sunlight. But whereas a single herbaceous plant may produce a few hundred grams of organic matter in a year, a large tree may gain a thousand times as much. A hectare of growing woodland may sequester carbon from the atmosphere sufficient to generate 10 to 15 cubic metres of organic matter (biomass) in a year.

Trees, fungi and microbes

In recent years the significance of fungal relationships with higher plants has become clearer. We now know that all trees and most other plants form active associations in the soil between their roots and mycorrhizal fungi. This is generally a mutualist relationship: plants provide organic material in the form of sugars, while fungi draw minerals from the soil (or the virgin rock) and make them available in soluble form. In many of our trees (oak, beech, birch etc.) the association is with

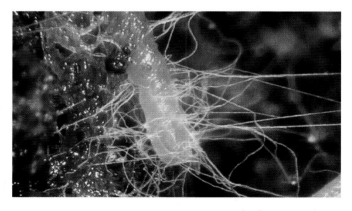

OPPOSITE Ancient small-leaved lime coppice stool on a steep bank at Keld, north Yorkshire.

ABOVE Strands of ecto-mycorrhizae around a tree root; the fungus gains sugars while providing the tree with minerals from the soil.

17

Trees and woodland as habitat *by Dr George Peterken*

Dr George Peterken, formerly of the Nature Conservancy, is the author of *Woodland Conservation and Management* (the standard work on the subject), *Natural Woodland* and *The Wye Valley*.

Trees have several distinctive functions in the ecology of a woodland. They create shade and shelter other organisms from the wind. They reduce total rainfall at ground level – light showers evaporate from the leaves and never reach the ground – and concentrate what does reach the ground around the bases of tree trunks, down which the rainfall flows. Trees also contribute directly to the soil with the decay of tree trunks, branches, leaves, flowers and fruit.

The woodland environment favours a distinctive assemblage of plants and animals. The shade excludes many strongly growing herbs and reduces the vigour of the rest. As a result, while the ground vegetation consists of a mixture of species, it includes some that almost require shade to survive and others, like bluebells, which make use of a short growing season before the tree canopy unfurls. Other plants survive for decades as dormant seeds in the soil (the persistent seed bank) while growing conditions are unsuitable. They spring to life when, for example, a tree dies and more light gets through, but retreat again to dormancy when the space is occupied by a thicket of saplings. The ground flora has few grasses, but often many kinds of broad-leaved herbs often with showy flowers.

Trees also form a structure on which plants and animals can grow. Mosses and liverworts commonly grow around the base of the larger trees, or dead branches, where they use the rainwater running down the tree trunk and stay above the accumulation of leaf-litter on the woodland floor. Lichens, which can stand more drought, can cover the trunk and can grow luxuriantly even on the smallest branches.

Animals use the physical structure provided by trees for shelter. Woodpeckers excavate holes, magpies and rooks nest in the upper branches, and other birds nest in the foliage or in the thickets of saplings. Squirrels construct dreys in mature trees, dormice nest in hazel bushes, and both badgers and rabbits excavate the ground under the roots of big trees, while bats favour the protection afforded by hollow branches or tree trunks.

Trees that are blown over drag up their roots on one side, leaving a hollow on the other, and some trees can survive this better than others (see Table 2). The fallen trunk collects leaf-litter as it is blown around the wood in winter, while the hollows may fill with water from the subsoil. It has been calculated that the entire area of soil in a natural woodland will be turned over once every 1,000 years by tree-fall alone. When coarse woody debris falls into streams this creates a multitude of micro-habitats – miniature waterfalls, pools, shallows, eroding banks and shoals, and the decaying wood itself is held in a variety of situations, encouraging different decomposers. Logs and

ABOVE **Ferns and mosses growing on a living oak branch provide a habitat for many tiny organisms.**

smaller branches can impede the drainage of whole areas, creating damp conditions; fallen timber and small branches on seepages are an important but underappreciated woodland habitat. Wherever they are allowed to lie, dead trees form a source of plant nutrients and energy – fuel for the whole woodland ecosystem.

ectomycorrhizae, where the fungal threads form a sheath around individual roots, but do not penetrate them. These fungi tend to develop large fruiting bodies, which disperse spores to a fresh host. We know these fruiting bodies as mushrooms, toadstools, bracket fungi and truffles.

Another type of fungal association is known as arbuscular mycorrhizal. In this relationship one or more members of a special group of soil fungi called Glomeromycota actually grow inside the root cells of their host-plant (Redecker, 2005). Such associations are now known to be extremely widespread among flowering plants including most tropical trees and some temperate ones, as well as many crop plants. Glomeromycota are strange fungi that produce spores asexually, but have no known sexual reproduction or aerial fruiting bodies; apparently their entire existence is underground in the soil.

Recently it has been discovered that there are also many benign fungi that grow within the leaves and stems of plants including trees, although their precise role inside plant tissues is less well understood. They can be seen when some trees die and almost immediately a mass of fungal fruiting bodies appear from many points, and close examination of recently fallen leaves shows a mass of tiny fungal fruiting bodies. In the living tree these internal fungi may contribute to the defence of leaves against herbivores. The fungal bodies themselves are protected by the tissues of their plant host from insects or other organisms that could otherwise prey on them.

Other fungi are harmful to plants, including trees. These are the parasitic fungi. Some, like rusts and cankers, cause minor damage such as leaf scars and spots, but others can be much more dangerous and even fatal – Dutch elm disease is one of the best known of these. Saprophytic fungi play a vital role in the breakdown and recycling of organic matter and are common among dead leaves, on dead wood and on other decaying parts of trees. Whereas many of the mycorrhizal fungi are generally associated with particular tree species, most of these saprophytic species are much less specific. Like the ectomycorrhizae they often produce fruiting bodies, some of which have familiar mushroom shapes. Others are in the form of blisters, powdery encrustations or even soft coralline structures. Some fungi are apparently benign while the tree is alive, but when it dies are already in position to become saprophytic. One example is shaggy bracket, *Inonotus hispidus*, on ash trees.

Trees also have beneficial associations with other organisms such as root-nodule bacteria (see alder, p.30), and indirectly with nitrogen-fixing bacteria in the soil. None of our native trees are members of Papilionaceae (legumes), a large family of plants including clover, gorse and many tropical trees, all of which have root nodules through which nitrogen is fixed (i.e. made available in soluble compounds) from the atmosphere.

Trees and plant-feeders

Every part of a tree is food for one sort of organism or another. Roots, bark, sapwood, cambium, heartwood, branches, twigs, buds, leaves, flowers (including pollen and nectar) and fruits are all the specific foods (and in some cases shelter) for plant-feeders (herbivores). Some herbivores, such as those that use leaves as food, may become so numerous that occasionally entire woods can be defoliated in a few weeks. In addition, the sap that runs oozing from wounds to the trunk or limbs of trees is food for flies, while rot holes and rainwater pools in the crook of branches support their own specialist organisms.

Mammals such as deer and wood mice eat foliage, fruits and seedlings, while many birds eat fruits or just the seeds, as well as using trees for shelter and for nesting. Because there are so many

insects feeding on trees, birds and other carnivorous species live on or inside trees and specialise in feeding on these herbivores. In this way a complex web of interactions develops.

Foliage-feeders

Some trees are attacked by far more herbivores than others. Table 4 shows the numbers of species of different groups of invertebrates known to be associated with each tree genus. Kennedy and Southwood (1984), referring to insects only (excluding mites), sought to explain these differences in terms of the relative abundance of the tree species involved, and certainly oak, birch and willow are the most abundant of native trees. They are also among the trees that have been here the longest – they were three of the earliest colonisers. Hornbeam and beech only appear in the pollen record in the last few millennia compared with holly or hazel, which have been here more than twice as long. But in that case why do hazel and holly have so few insects attacking them? The fact is that some trees appear to be more palatable than others, due to several factors, which must include leaf chemistry, fungal associations, or physical features such as hairy leaves (which may be an effective defence against caterpillars) or spines (which deter mammalian browsers).

Many plant-feeders, such as gall-inducing mites, flies and wasps, and various leaf-mining and leaf-rolling insects, tend to be specialised and adapted to attack a single host-plant or a group of related host-

ABOVE Young roe deer browsing hazel shoots at Gait Barrows National Nature Reserve, Lancashire.

LEFT Spectacular caterpillar of the emperor moth, *Saturnia pavonia*, on goat willow leaves.

plants. However, the caterpillars of many moths are polyphagous – that is they will eat the leaves of a variety of broadleaved trees (and of other plants). All the main broadleaf trees are attacked by these insects, while more specialised caterpillars (those restricted to particular trees) are more limited in number. On both willows and oak a similar proportion of caterpillars (25%) are restricted to the host genus, while for other native trees the proportion is much lower, typically around 10–18%. However, for the two gymnosperms, pine and juniper, the numbers are higher 70% and 67% respectively. The differences are similar when data for all plant-feeding invertebrates are compared (see Table 4, column 8). Every tree species has some plant-feeders specifically associated with it, although the numbers are very small for some trees like box and holly, and these chemically armoured trees (usually slow-growing, hardy species) appear to be totally avoided by the polyphagous plant-feeders.

In May 2008, Queen's Wood (north London) suffered a major attack of the polyphagous green oak tortrix, *Tortrix viridana*, caterpillars, and almost all the oak, hazel, hornbeam and wild service trees were heavily defoliated. The wild cherry was hardly affected, while holly remained completely untouched. Like many other plants, trees 'have evolved various strategies to defend themselves against herbivores and pathogens' (Frost *et al.*, 2008), some of which 'are induced... in response to herbivore feeding'.

The most frequent is to change their leaf chemistry by increasing the amounts of phenolic compounds in the leaves, making them less palatable or less digestible to herbivores. Trees like oak put out leaves in spurts, gradually increasing the tannin load through the season, and research on hawthorn has shown that damage to early season leaves can affect the composition of leaves produced later in the season. These changes have an energy cost to the tree and there may be trade-offs between additional resource use and the losses that may be caused by an attack. Some caterpillars generally occur early in the season (often in large numbers), while other species appear (often in smaller numbers) later in a typical summer. These differences reflect varying ability to digest leaves of different chemical composition, but the caterpillars themselves may become gradually stressed later in the season, and then may attract predators and parasitic wasps in late summer.

For other specialised insects the actual abundance and size of their host trees is significant. The rare hoverfly *Hammerschmidtia ferruginea* requires fallen aspen trunks or branches of at least 15 cm (6 in) diameter; this is just one of numerous species that require substantial populations of living trees and cannot survive without them. The gall-midge *Schmidtiella gemmerum* needs substantial stands of juniper, and fragmentation of its habitat on the South Downs has affected it badly, so that it has become

How different insects feed on living trees

The most familiar way for a caterpillar to eat leaves is by chomping through each one a slice at a time; this just requires sharp jaws and a big mouth to ingest the pieces of leaf. Smaller species can actually tunnel inside the leaf and eat it from the inside (leaf-miners) while keeping out of reach of parasites and predators, though in some species once they get near maturity they emerge and feed normally on the leaf surface, sometimes spinning a cover or rolling the leaf to protect themselves. Another group of plant-feeders have needle-like mouthparts that they jab straight into the leaf or stem and then suck the sap out; these are the plant bugs (Hemiptera), including leaf-hoppers, scale insects and aphids. Aphids often need to suck a great deal of sugar-laden sap to get enough protein, and the excess oozes out of them as honeydew.

Some sawfly larvae, and some caterpillars such as those of clearwing moths, burrow into the growing (cambial) layer of tree trunks, branches or twigs between the woody part and the bark. Gall-formers (which include mites, flies, wasps and other tiny insect larvae) cause the tree to grow extra tissue, which both protects them and provides them with food.

extinct in places where juniper patches have become too small or too widely separated. In both these cases minimum sizes of tree populations have been estimated for conservation planning.

Pollen-feeders

Another large group of plant-feeders, especially bees, flies, beetles and butterflies, is associated with tree flowers. Pollen and nectar are concentrated foods (providing sugars and proteins), which many adult insects depend on, especially early in the season. Most of these flower-feeders (including many butterflies and bees) appear to be very catholic in their tastes and visit many sorts of flower, but others may be much more selective.

Chambers (1946) studied the pollen loads of several species of wild bees of the genus *Andrena* for three summers and found that each species had very different pollen preferences, that this choice changed through the summer, and that the pattern differed from year to year depending partly on the weather. In all three years, several species started by visiting just fruit trees (apple, pear and plum) early in the season but switched to hawthorn blossom as soon as it was available, while they all took pollen from wild flowers at some time in the summer. Hardy *et al.* (2007) studied the pollen and nectar requirements of a range of butterflies and found that many species had a preference for the pollen of their larval host-plants; in other words the adults returned to the same host-plant that they had fed on as caterpillars.

Published records of insects visiting tree flowers are very limited and tend to be anecdotal. Side (1955) listed insects he had seen visiting wayfaring tree, *Viburnum lantana*, over three days and nights in 1952 – by far the largest number were beetles. St Mark's flies, *Bibio marci*, are well known to visit Plymouth pear, while danceflies (Empididae) have been noted visiting bird cherry and wayfaring tree. Hoverflies, which can digest pollen, are known to visit a wide variety of tree flowers including even wind-pollinated species such as hazel (Alan Stubbs, pers. comm.), but the few studies of pollen-feeding insects have been restricted to rare species (of major conservation interest) or those relevant to agriculture. Observations suggest that floral options from locality to locality and weather conditions have a major effect on both the presence and effectiveness of pollinators (Buchmann and Nabhan, 1995.). The current alarms about the decline of many honey-bee colonies has stimulated more interest in research about pollination and pollinators, but until now it has been a neglected field.

LEFT Wild bees like *Andrena* spp. are more efficient pollinators than honey-bees as pollen sticks to their hairs and is not mixed with saliva and rolled into balls.

Keystone species

This term was introduced by ecologist Robert Paine (1969) to describe species whose influence was much greater than their numbers or biomass would predict. He found that *Pisaster ochraceus*, a species of starfish, controlled the numbers of a mussel *Mytilus californianus*; without the starfish the mussel numbers expanded and overexploited the habitat.

In woodland environments major trees fit these criteria (in numbers if not in biomass) and should be considered as keystone species – the removal of trees changes the habitat completely, and in damper and colder parts of these islands can result in the land reverting to peat-bog. As the main primary producers, trees provide resources for the entire ecosystem, not only living foliage, fruits etc., but also from the decomposition of dead leaves, bark and wood. Trees do vary enormously in their degree of interactivity with other species (high interactivity being a feature of keystone species according to Paine's definition) but the removal of major tree species clearly has an enormous destabilising effect. The best examples are oak, beech, alder and Scots pine, each of which dominates particular habitats. In the Scottish Highlands aspen has come to be regarded as a keystone species, with a wide range of specialist insects being dependent on there being sufficient numbers of aspen trees.

The association of trees and insects has hardly been studied from the point of view of the trees concerned; in other words what insect populations are required for optimum pollination to occur? Orchard growers plant crabapple trees among cultivated fruit trees because they provide copious pollen. Some fruit tree varieties may produce very little of their own pollen; after all they have been selected for the qualities of the fruit, not for the production of pollen or nectar. The productivity of fruit trees is very much affected by the number and efficiency of the pollinators, and orchard growers pay beekeepers to bring their hives and station them among or near the trees during blossoming. In fact, some wild bees are much more efficient pollinators than either honey bees or even bumble bees, both of which moisten the pollen and carry it as a compact load, whereas *Andrena* spp. are much less tidy and get pollen grains on the hairs all over their legs and abdomen making 'brushing off' far more likely at every flower they visit. The implication is that a wide range of wild flowers and other wild trees are needed for a full complement of wild bees to thrive, and this is the best way to promote optimum pollination.

Seed dispersal

Many trees attract birds and mammals to disperse their seeds. Fruits are eaten by birds and mammals, mostly for the flesh, and as they then move away they deposit the seeds in their droppings, often far from the original tree. There is some specialisation among these fruit-eaters or frugivores (Snow and Snow, 1988). Some birds prefer certain fruits, partly influenced by the size of individual fruits and whether or not they are small enough for the bird to swallow whole. Other birds, such as finches, are actual seed-eaters; they destroy the

BELOW Early flowering trees like blackthorn provide nectar for many insects including peacock butterflies, *Inachis io*, which are well known as harbingers of spring.

BELOW Missel thrush feeding on rowan berries. Passing through the gut of a bird greatly enhances the germination rate of many berries, and explains the distribution of rowan.

seeds, as squirrels do with acorns, although squirrels may bury some undamaged ones. The numerous insects that attack either fruits or seeds are often more specialised; some attack the fruit of several different trees but most are restricted to one or two similar fruits such as apple and pear, while some weevils are restricted to particular nuts such as acorns or hazel-nuts. From the point of view of the tree these fruit and seed-feeders are almost entirely damaging, and in bad years they can destroy an entire crop.

Lichens, ferns and bark-lice

Trees provide a physical presence and structure, which provide support and shelter to many species of plants (epiphytes) and animals (e.g. bark-lice). Bark varies from smooth (beech, rowan) to rough (oak, elm) and from relatively acid (oak) to more base-rich (elm, maple, elder). Some barks hold a good deal of moisture (elm and elder) and others far less (beech, rowan). Lichens prefer rough, base-rich, damp bark, and the loss of elms has had a major impact on many lichen species. In damper

LEFT Ancient ash coppice-stool covered with a multitude of ferns, mosses and flowering plants provides a rich habitat for many other organisms. Lismore Island, Argyll.

western areas rainfall compensates for acid bark, apparently by leeching acid out. Some of the best places for lichen diversity are on western coasts from Horner Wood, Exmoor to Rassall Ashwood in Wester Ross.

Mature, over-mature and ancient trees

When trees become mature they may last for a long time in a more or less stable state with little sign of change. A large sycamore just outside the village of Boot in Eskdale in the Lake District looks virtually the same today as it did when my father photographed it just after the Second World War and I first saw it as a boy (see sycamore, p.134). Oaks last even longer before they become 'over-mature' and begin a long, slow decline. They often lose their top branches and gradually settle into a squat shape very like ancient pollards. The trunk begins to rot away and the tree becomes hollow – thereby actually becoming stronger and more stable. The tree that has reached this stage is particularly attractive to various specialised insects including numerous rare beetles.

In the last 20 years or so the importance of ancient trees for conservation, landscape and cultural history, has begun to be recognised. The Ancient Tree Forum is a thriving body with large numbers of enthusiasts over the country who have documented over 50,000 ancient trees, and campaigns to protect them are more and more successful against the depredations of local authorities and unsympathetic landowners.

Mast years

For centuries it was well known that some trees, such as oak and beech, only produced fruits very irregularly. In the mid-nineteenth century, European foresters noticed that abundant flower buds are only formed on beech during hot, dry summers, and during the period 1811 to 1922 the greater mast years in Europe apparently followed years of summer drought (see Table 2, column 12). Others suggested that frost in late spring was the determining factor. The phenomenon of mast years was studied by Professor D. Matthews (1955), who examined the Forestry Commission's records for beech seed availability in the years 1921 to 1950. He found that during the period studied there were 10 mast years, 14 years of moderate crop and 6 years with a total failure.

The good mast years were irregular, and there were never two consecutive good mast years, so Dr Matthews tried to find out under what weather conditions masting occurred. There appeared to be no correlation with the weather of the masting summer but when he analysed temperatures in the season preceding the masting he found that high July temperatures correlated well with good crops of beech mast in the following year. Three of the four anomalous years could be explained by late frosts in early May, which could have destroyed flower buds. Summer temperature and rainfall did not correlate directly with mast production, but only with the following year's crop. He concluded that high temperatures, low rainfall and much sunshine during July in the year before fruiting, and the absence of late frosts in the fruiting year, are the conditions necessary for masting, while recognising that even in the best mast years the quantities of fruit produced on individual trees varied a good deal.

These conclusions have been applied to other trees and explain masting in oak fairly well. Horticulturalists are familiar with a similar effect in fruit trees, and under natural conditions many trees appear to be more or less influenced by the phenomenon; warm, damp conditions tend to induce the laying down of more flower buds, resulting (in the absence of late frosts) in a larger crop in the subsequent year. Why do trees do this? Scientists now think that this irregular cropping means that while an entire crop may be destroyed by predators in normal years, bad years may have some influence on reducing the numbers of predators. Then, in mast years, the total production of seeds may overwhelm the predators

ensuring that at least some seeds manage to germinate and survive. In the future this strategy may be critical if native oaks are to survive the presence of grey squirrels.

Dead and decaying trees

The phrase 'dead wood' has unfortunate negative connotations in contemporary parlance, implying that it is something that should be removed or cut out lest it hold back the thrusting energy of youth and hamper maximum growth. Old and dead trees are tidied up and cleared away instead of being allowed to rot, whether standing or fallen, with the result that the rich array of insects, birds and other creatures that depend on such habitats find it increasingly hard to survive. Yet studies in places where dead trees are allowed to rot naturally have revealed that for the whole plant and animal community trees are just as important when they are dead as they are when alive; in ancient woodland perhaps 20% of all organisms (excluding micro-organisms), and up to 80% of all beetles depend on decaying wood.

Hollow trees are often the most stable ones, but many trees sometimes shed branches unexpectedly. Health and safety legislation, as well as some unfortunate accidents to members of the public, have resulted in this now being a matter of serious concern to land managers. The best approach that is now adopted in woodland open to the public seems to be to carefully manage public access – where possible by re-routing paths for example – so as to minimise the danger of accidents while at the same time causing as little disturbance to the natural environment as possible.

LEFT Big trees are vital to the ecosystem even when they die; many fungi, plants and animals contribute to recycling the nutrients they release as they decompose.

Why dead and decaying trees are important *by Dr Keith Alexander*

Dr Keith Alexander is the author of the most comprehensive report on invertebrates in dead and decaying wood in Britain and Ireland (2002).

The relationships between dead and decaying trees, invertebrates and fungi are determined by the fungal species rather than the tree species. With heartwood-decaying fungi, there are three main types: brown rots (called red rots by entomologists), white rots and soft rots. There are different species of fungi which decay dead woody tissues of heartwood and sapwood, and yet others that exploit dead wood in branches and twigs.

Brown rot is caused by the fungus breaking down the cellulose component of the wood and leaving the lignin as a brittle brown-orange-red colour. The commonest brown-rot heartwood-decaying fungi are chicken-of-the-woods, *Laetiporus sulphureus*, in broadleaves and *Phaeolus schweinitzii* in conifers. *Laetiporus* is most often found in the heartwood of oak, cherry, pear and plum, but may also be found in willow, yew, sweet chestnut and even occasionally in hazel, alder, beech and apple.

White rot (where lignin is broken down leaving mainly cellulose) is chiefly caused by the *Ganoderma* and *Inonotus* fungi and, again, these may use a range of hosts. *I. hispidus* is the main heartwood-decay species in ash and apple, while on oak the most common species is *I. dryadeus*. An individual oak tree may contain a brown-rotting fungus, *Laetiporus,* and various white-rotting fungi e.g. *I. dryadeus* and *Ganoderma*, at the same time.

The majority of these fungi are normally only active in dead woody tissues and few have any ability to cross into living tissues, and even then generally under exceptional circumstances such as a tree suffering from stress. So I would argue that the use of the term 'attack' is incorrect, as the fungi are merely nourishing themselves by feeding on tissues that are no longer used by the living tree itself.

Invertebrates in dead wood respond to the type of fungal decay, and to them the tree species is largely irrelevant. Brown rot and white rot each support characteristic suites of invertebrate species, so the brown-rot specialist insects tend to be associated with oak, for obvious reasons.

Oak heartwood is full of polyphenols (tannins etc.) and other chemicals that make it more durable and slow to rot. But that does not stop fungi from colonising the dead heartwood tissues, it merely slows them down. *Laetiporus* apparently specialises in decomposing such durable woods, so the advantage to the tree is presumably in controlling rates of decay and not allowing fungi to get carried away and remove too much wood too quickly.

Freshly dead or dying (undecayed) wood is more specifically distinctive (primarily chemically) and used by more specialist invertebrates, and these tend to be more directly associated with the particular tree species. Thus there are elm bark beetles and oak bark beetles. There are also specialised 'soft-rot' fungi, which occur in freshwater but can colonise damp patches on standing trees or fallen trunks.

Scarce fungi tend not to support any specialist invertebrates as the host is too unreliable to support viable populations. Scarce fungi are therefore eaten by generalist invertebrates rather than specialist ones.

LEFT **Chicken-of-the-woods, *Laetiporus sulphureus*, a common woodland fungus found on both living and dead wood.**

Ecology of trees

Trees, like all plants, show preferences for certain conditions and sites. They are not randomly distributed but occur in well-defined habitats and have definable geographic distributions, although these may vary over time. Like other organisms, populations of trees have a range of genetic potential; they are genetically diverse. This allows them to make use of the changing environment in which they are growing or into which they are able to advance. It also determines how well they compete with other species in those environments. For many years, Professor Philip Grime's team at Sheffield University investigated the relationship between the potential and field success of different plant species and developed theories to explain them (see box feature p.27). The idea of what he calls 'ecological strategies' are now accepted by scientists in many fields of biology. This concept has been used to interpret many other ecosystems including highly complex ones such as the species-rich tropical forests and coral reefs.

Ecological strategies of trees

Based on the work of Professor Philip Grime (retired), Director of the Unit of Comparative Plant Ecology at Sheffield University (Grime et al., 2007).

LEFT Coastal scrub subjected to salt spray on the western side of Lismore Island, Argyll: hazel, aspen, rowan, wych elm and even oak (left).

By recording details of the occurrence of every species of plant over a very large number of representative sites in the countryside, and by conducting germination and growth experiments under standardised conditions in the laboratory, the research team built up a database of basic biological information about the habits of every (common) native species. This is known as autecology. From this data they have been able to interpret the ecological strategies of plants (including trees) growing in the Yorkshire area, and compare them in a standardised way. Trees are more complicated because the strategy of the seedlings may be very different from that of the full-grown tree.

Three extreme features of habitats are recognised: (1) environmental stress (frost/high temperature, wind, drought/flooding), (2) disturbance (rivers in torrent, landslips, trampling and destruction by grazing/browsing, many human activities) and (3) availability of nutrients (soil conditions etc.).

In the triangular diagram opposite, each point is the extreme of one feature, and trees are placed in the triangle according to their ecological strategy. The extremes are exemplified as follows:

1. Stress-tolerators.

These species are able to survive a maximum environmental stress (poor soil and extreme climatic conditions, resulting in low plant production). They are typically slow-growing, hardy species, which can survive in chronically harsh conditions and include yew, juniper, dwarf birch and mountain willows and (as seedlings) rowan and holly.

2. Pioneers or 'weed' species.

These species tolerate a maximum disturbance of the environment (periodic total or part destruction of the plant as by storm/fire damage, flooding, heavy browsing). These species, whose strategy is to colonise disturbed ground, typically produce vast numbers of tiny seeds and colonise new habitats (examples are birch, alder and willows, and (as seedlings) black poplar and birch.

3. Competitors.

These species thrive and outgrow others under conditions of maximum nutrients and favourable conditions such as rich soil, shelter etc. These trees are the most competitive ones best able to make use of favourable conditions by growing very big, shading out other species and then living for a long time (examples are oak, beech and hornbeam, and (as seedlings) ash and beech.

Because of their longevity, most trees (excluding specialists like dwarf willow and dwarf birch) are to some extent intermediate by combining different characteristics in varying strengths and so do not reach the extremes that some other types of plants do. Partly this is because they are ecologically flexible, having the ability to adapt their form to the variable conditions they encounter. Juniper grows on heathland in the south of England as well as high on Scottish mountains. Some trees like oaks and pines growing near their altitude limit overlap with extreme stress-tolerant species, and adapt their growth habit to be more like the stress-tolerant species. *Krummholz* pines and oaks are a good example of this.

In severely disturbed conditions, such as the floodplain of a mountain torrent, trees such as willows hang on and do little more than survive until conditions improve (such as when the river changes course), when they grow tall and upright again.

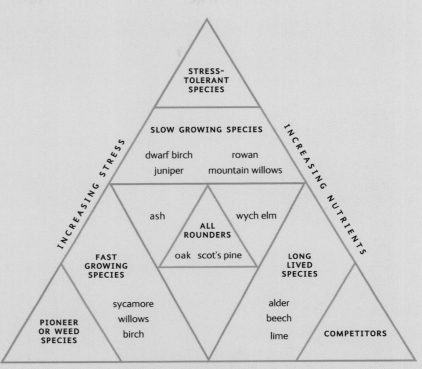

Some trees use different habits to achieve their strategy. Trees with wind-distributed tiny seeds (birch) or slightly larger seeds (sycamore, ash) are adapted to make use of disturbed or periodically damaged habitats. Where the soil is good, sycamore and elder thrive; where the soil is drier or more base-rich, ash thrives; where the soil is very poor and conditions are harsher, pine and mountain willows do well.

Other trees like arbutus, hazel and many willows positively thrive on being uprooted, disturbed and broken off by torrential floods. Their resilience and re-rooting of broken

ABOVE A simplified version of Grime's triangular model as a basis for identification of the ecological strategies of trees. Some mature trees exhibit different strategies at different stages in their growth from seedling to sapling to mature tree.

branches is a different strategy for making use of periodically disturbed habitats.

Thus, from the triangular diagram the spread of different strategies among native trees begin to have a recognisable pattern.

4 Portraits of native trees

ALDER *Alnus glutinosa* L. Gaertn

> **Birch family**: Betulaceae
>
> **Also known as**: Also known as aller, alls-bush, Irish mahogany or fearnóg (Irish), gwernen (Welsh), fearna, drumanach (Gaelic). In ancient Irish law, a 'commoner' (Neeson, 1991) (see p.185).
>
> **Biological Flora**: MacVean (1953)

With its dark green, stiff, strongly veined and serrated leaves borne on reddish stems and its dark fissured bark, alder is a characteristic tree of wet places, marshes, floodplains, stream sides and land liable to seepage or flooding. It normally grows to around 12 m (40 ft) and can reach more than twice that height at sheltered sites, but also frequently occurs in hedges. It has been recorded at an altitude of over 500 m (1,600 ft) in Scotland. A hardy tree, alder occurs naturally throughout these islands north to Sutherland. When planted, it grows well as far north as Shetland. Alder was one of the earliest trees to recolonise Britain after the last glacial period; the pollen record indicates its presence in isolated areas of Britain more than 8,500 years ago, and in parts of Scotland some time before Scots pine. It is regarded as native in all parts of the country except Orkney and Shetland, being particularly common in Wales. The size of both leaf and catkin has been found to decrease from south to north and east to west across the British mainland. In winter alder buds are characteristically bluish or purple. In spring, vast quantities of alder pollen are released into the wind from purplish-green catkins from late February to early April (contributing to early spring hay-fever) well before the leaves appear. At least some trees are not self-fertile and need pollen from other trees to fertilise the female flowers.

The female catkins (or cones) are green at first but become black when ripe, releasing their seeds into the wind; some land on water and float. The cones stay on the tree for nearly a year. The average number of seeds is around 60 and it has been estimated that there are around 4,000 catkins on an average tree, producing a total number of seeds of about 250,000. This number is probably exceeded among native trees only by some willows, aspen and birch. Seedlings survive waterlogging, and indeed they may require wet ground for up to a month after germination, but they cannot survive under the surface of waterlogged soil. They require high levels of light, humidity and oxygen, which restrict their natural establishment to gravel and mud on riverbanks. Established saplings can thrive on well-drained soil. Mature alder woods do not provide conditions suitable for successful regeneration and alder seed does not survive to form a persistent seed bank.

ABOVE Alder catkins in February, long before the leaves appear, giving the trees a purplish look.

OPPOSITE An ancient alder pollard, one of many in Glen Achall, Ross-shire near Ullapool.

LEFT An alder root-nodule caused by the bacterium *Frankia* sp., about twice natural size, with a section of some nodule.

Pure alder damp woodland or carr occur in many parts of the country but especially in East Anglia, while alder/ash and alder/birch woods occur naturally in the Highlands of Scotland but only occasionally elsewhere. Alder can be grown easily from seed and can also be propagated vegetatively over 400 years ago. John Evelyn recommended taking 2–3 ft (0.6–1 m) 'truncheons' in the autumn, 'binding them into faggots', and keeping them with their ends in water before planting them in the spring.

All alders fix atmospheric nitrogen by means of root nodules (see above) containing a filamentous bacterium, a species of *Frankia*. Once the growing tree is infected with this bacterium it has a great advantage for colonising very poor and waterlogged soil, and the nitrogen content of a seedling may double between February and May (Grime *et al.*, 2007). Alders have been used successfully to reclaim spoil heaps (see p.182) and other industrial waste sites, where they add fertility to the soil, so allowing other species to become established. The twigs are also known to accumulate metals such as gold from some soils.

Alder trees effectively delay erosion of riverbanks (and have long been planted for this reason) but ultimately may be fatally undermined, particularly where the local rock is soft or the river is prone to torrential flow. Alder is also resistant to salt spray although it does not apparently occur in coastal scrub, and it is used successfully to create coastal windbreaks.

LEFT The intense green foliage of alder trees lining the Achall River in the Scottish Highlands.

The uses of alder

When first cut, alder wood turns reddish-orange, although the colour soon fades. In Ireland the wood was traditionally used for making shields, its colour being interpreted to mean alder was the 'tree of war'. The wood is light and soft but resilient, and historically was used for clogs (being a poor conductor of heat), and for scaffolding poles and staves for herring barrels. It is a popular wood for wood-turning, although it was probably not used for the backs of Stradivarius violins as has been alleged (Mabberley, 1997).

Alder timber is particularly resistant to decay under water and, like elm and pine, it was used in cities such as Bristol and Edinburgh for piping the first municipal water supply as well as for piles under bridges and houses (Grigson, 1960). Alder timber is still sometimes used for coastal groynes, sluice-gates and other structures along water-courses.

Alder survives uprooting and storm damage well. When coppiced, alder wood can be used to produce fine charcoal, which was historically much in demand for making gunpowder, about 1 tonne of wood giving enough charcoal to manufacture 1 tonne of gunpowder. Alder was planted for this purpose in some places

TOP Alder trees in winter, lining a stream near Woking in Surrey.

ABOVE Traditional well-dressing picture in a Derbyshire village; alder 'cones' are used for the black colour.

31

such as Killarney, Ireland and Waltham Abbey, north London. In some places there are ancient alder pollards (Glen Achall in Ross and Cromarty, Geltsdale in Cumbria etc.), but it is not clear what the purpose was, as the foliage is unpalatable to domestic animals. The catkins and bark give a black colouring known in medieval times in England as 'a poor man's dye', and alder bark has been used in tanning for reddening leather.

ABOVE Alder leaf beetle, *Chrysomela aenea.*

ABOVE Leaf-pustule galls on alder caused by the mite *Eriophyes laevis.*

Folklore

Known as 'black knobs', the alder cones are used to provide the black colour in pictures at traditional well-dressings - annual events in Derbyshire villages at which local wells are garlanded. In Worcestershire there is an old tradition that carrying a piece of alder wood in a pocket safeguards against rheumatism. There are few medicinal uses for alder – Grigson (1960) knows of none, though he goes on to say that 'early reference books say the whole plant is astringent, and in the last century it was used as a substitute for quinine in allaying fevers'. A decoction of alder bark was used as a gargle and for treating burns in Norfolk, and for piles and 'heart trouble' in Co. Cavan. The cones were also claimed to be used as a treatment for gout (Vickery, 1995).

Alder is common in Ireland where strangely it was thought unlucky to pass the tree on a journey (O'Suilleabhain, 1942), (almost inevitable in such a boggy country one would think), but possibly because swampy land was a hideout for bandits. Otherwise Grigson concludes that 'not much emotion has gathered around the alder'.

Alder in the ecosystem

At least 26 species of larger fungi are known to be associated with alder, including the alder milkcap, *Lactarius obscuratus*, and the alder bolete, *Gyrodon lividus*, both fruiting bodies of ectomycorrhizae. The catkins sometimes produce strange tongue-like growths, which are caused by the ascomycte fungus *Taphrina alni*, related to the pathogen that causes witches' brooms on birch and hornbeam, while other *Taphrina* spp. produce leaf wrinkling (*T. tosquinetti*) and yellow leaf blisters (*T. sadebeckii*). A pathogenic fungus *Phytophthora cambivora* can cause dieback and leaf yellowing; in the 1990s its spread appeared to be a major threat but since then its impact has been patchy. Dead alder branches attract saprotrophic (specialised to live on dead wood) fungi such as the blushing bracket, *Daedalopsis confragosa*, the alder bracket,

Inonotus radiatus, and the delicate, reddish-orange alder goblet, *Cibaria caucus*.

Alder foliage is fairly unpalatable to domestic animals and deer (coppiced alder needs less protection than hazel), but relatively attractive to invertebrates, with 315 plant-feeding insects and mites recorded, of which 48 are restricted to alder (see Table 4). This puts it seventh in the list of native tree genera, below oak, willow and birch, but above ash and black poplar.

At least nine species of eriophyid mite and one gall-midge attack the leaves, while caterpillars of two tiny moths tunnel in the stems and main leaf-veins (*Epinotia tetraquetrana* and *Heliozela resplendella*). The shoots are mined by other insects including a tiny black weevil (*Anoplus roboris*), several other very small moths such as *Coleophora serratella* and three species of leaf-eating sawflies, which produce 'shot-holes' and other leaf damage.

A more common cause of extensive leaf damage (skeletonisation) is the beautiful metallic green leaf beetle, *Chrysomela aenea*, which is normally found on alder but has also been recorded from goat willow and birch. Moths associated with alder include the alder kitten moth, *Furcula bicuspis*, and the spectacular white-barred clearwing, *Synanthedon spheciformis*, the caterpillars of which bore under the bark of alder and birch trees. The extraordinary yellow and black caterpillar of the so-called 'alder moth', *Acronicta alni*, is found more commonly on most other broadleaves, while the so-called 'alder fly', *Sialis* spp., has no particular connection at all; the adults settle on most waterside plants – its larvae are aquatic and carnivorous.

The small seeds of alder (which can float for several weeks) are extracted from the cones by birds, including tits, *Parus* spp., siskin, *Spinus spinus*, and, in Scotland, the crossbill, *Loxia curvirostra*. In terms of its ecological strategy (see p.27) alder is a stress-tolerant competitor of wetlands, recovering well from disturbance and damage, including uprooting, and successfully shading out other species.

ALDER BUCKTHORN *Frangula alnus* Miller

Buckthorn family: Rhamnaceae

Also known as: Also known as black dogwood and butcher's prickwood, and breuwydden (Welsh).

Biological Flora: Godwin (1943)

Alder buckthorn, like the related common buckthorn, *Rhamnus cathartica*, is a multi-stemmed bush of 4–5 m (13–16 ft), which grows into a small tree of about 5 m (16 ft). It does not have spines, and has a loose canopy. A strongly gregarious species, it is typically found on light soils, often with alder, at the edge of both base-rich fens and acid bogs. It is also found in limestone scrub and as undergrowth in open woodland, and generally on a wider range of soils than common buckthorn.

Alder buckthorn is frequently found at the edge of damp areas especially in scrub bordering fens, but does not survive well on drier soils or under a dense canopy of other trees. It occurs in open woods but is shaded out by developing tree growth such as oak during a normal process of succession. Alder buckthorn is distributed throughout much of England and Wales and at scattered localities in Ireland and southwest Scotland, and occurs much further north in Scandinavia.

The papery bark is greyish-brown with numerous small corky warts; when scraped the inner layers are bright crimson and sweetish when chewed. It contains glucosides including frangulin, which has been used in herbal medicine as a gentle purgative, and even dispensed as 'Aperient Fruit Lozenges', as well as being used externally against headlice.

Young shoots are velvety with tiny hairs. The leaves are thin, alternate, with at least six pairs of parallel veins and without the serrated edge of the related buckthorn *R. cathartica*, and they turn clear yellow and red in autumn. The flowers, which both appear later and survive longer than those of common buckthorn, are attractive to bees and hoverflies, and valuable as late summer sources of nectar. If insect pollination fails the flowers are self-fertile.

The berries (which change from green to red and then to almost black when ripe) are attractive to some birds including cuckoos (Link, 1889, quoted by Snow & Snow), but often drop freely on to the ground in December and may be eaten and stored by mice; the fruits and seeds float for at least a week and may be distributed by water. They also remain viable for at least three years and possibly longer. Either due to mice or from undisturbed natural falling, seedling establishment below existing bushes can be very dense –

up to 100 per square metre (Godwin, 1943). Alder buckthorn's characteristics suggest that it should be common in hedges, but this has not been documented.

The uses of alder buckthorn

The wood burns slowly and produces high quality charcoal, which is both light and very flammable. Until the 1940s the fast-burning powdered charcoal was used for fuses; alder buckthorn was planted for this purpose in the New Forest and at Wicken Fen in Cambridgeshire in the 1920s according to Pearson (1945). During the Second World War the Women's Timber Corps was charged with finding

BELOW Full-grown alder buckthorn tree showing open habit, Hampstead Heath, London.

RIGHT Waxwing eating alder buckthorn berries.

BELOW RIGHT The tissue moth, *Triphosa dubitata* (above) and the brimstone butterfly, *Gonepteryx rhamni* (below) feed on the foliage of alder buckthorn and common buckthorn.

natural stands in the countryside, to augment the supply! The bark and berries have been used to produce a powerful purgative and liver tonic in folk medicine (as late as the 1940s this was an official drug in Germany). A yellow dye can be extracted from the leaves and bark, a green dye from the unripe fruit, and a dark bluish-grey dye from the ripe fruit. In Europe the seeds have been used to produce a burning oil, while the shoots have been used to make besoms and in basketry.

Folklore

The red colour under the dark bark is claimed to have a spiritual significance whose origin is lost in history, while 'the spirit of alder buckthorn' is sometimes invoked to control anger and depression, possibly through its purgative properties.

Alder buckthorn in the ecosystem

The orange leaf-rust *Puccinia coronata* attacks both alder buckthorn and common buckthorn, and alder buckthorn also suffers terminal dieback caused by coral-spot fungus, *Nectria cinnabarina*. Goats are particularly partial to the foliage of alder buckthorn, but otherwise it is little browsed. Just 33 plant-feeding insects have been recorded (fewer than are known from common buckthorn). These include the green caterpillars of the brimstone butterfly, *Gonepteryx rhamni*, which feed on the leaves, as do the smaller green larvae of the tissue moth, *Triphosa dubitata*. Larvae of two tiny moths mine the leaves, and the buds are damaged by a gall-midge (*Continaria rhamni*) while the psyllid (jumping plant-louse) *Trichochermes walkeri* causes leaf-roll on both alder buckthorn and common buckthorn. A majority of the insects which feed on alder buckthorn occur on both two trees, alder buckthorn and common buckthorn.

ASH *Fraxinus excelsior* L.

Olive family: Oleacae

Also known as: Also known as uinseann (Gaelic), uinnius (Old Irish), fuinnseog , onnen (Irish), funinnseog (Welsh), ask (Norse), esh (northern England); the scientific name *excelsior* means 'higher' or 'tallest', distinguishing it from the introduced manna ash, F. *ornus*. In ancient Irish law, ash is one of seven 'noble' trees. Place names: Ashford, Askrigg, Monyash, Aspatria.

Biological Flora: Wardle (1961)

Ash is one of the most widespread trees of Britain and Ireland, being recorded from more 1 km squares than any other tree apart from hawthorn (National Countryside Survey, 2007) and in more 2 km squares than any other tree apart from oak (Botanical Society of the British Isles, www.bsbimaps.org.uk/atlas). Ash is the fourth commonest tree species in woodland, and is recorded from more hedges than any other tree except hawthorn. According to the pollen record ash was one of the later arrivals after the last Ice Age and had not spread across the whole of England before about 6,000 years ago. Today its natural distribution covers the whole of Britain and Ireland as far north as Caithness, and it has been successfully planted in Orkney and Shetland. It is particularly well adapted to the British environment and has spread faster than most other trees.

A relatively short-lived tree, normally to about 180 years, under the right conditions ash can reach an extreme height of 38 m or nearly 125 ft (the champion tree according to the Tree Register of the British Isles, TROBI). Folkloric tradition suggests that in many places it was the tallest local tree, although today it rarely grows more than 15–18 m (50–60 ft), and it can survive as a wind-pruned shrub in very exposed situations. Ash will colonise poor and disturbed soils where few other trees will grow and it ascends to 450 m (1,500 ft) near Braemar, and 585 m (1,900 ft) in Snowdonia, but does not often occur naturally on acid soils. A full-grown tree can produce up to 100,000 wind-dispersed seeds every second year; the majority are consumed by small mammals or predated by caterpillars, but others may remain for several years in the seed bank.

On moist, well-drained, base-rich lowland sites ash is fast-growing, with the highest nutrient uptake of any native tree (Grime *et al.*, 2007). It is drought-resistant but the leaves are sensitive to late frost. The seedlings thrive in disturbed soil and are moderately shade-tolerant, often growing up vigorously towards the light through ground vegetation, which helps protect the seedlings from browsing deer. Like hawthorn, ash saplings can survive intermittent browsing for years, growing up only when grazing pressure is lessened. Ash is often found growing together with hazel, especially on heavy soils, and in woodland is sometimes replaced by field maple in better-drained places. On some base-rich soils pure ash woods can form on limestone, such as the Rassall ashwood above Kishorn, Wester Ross.

LEFT Mature ash tree at Rassall, Argyll, the northernmost pure ash-wood in Britain.

'Oak before the ash there'll be a splash, Ash before the oak there'll be a soak.' In spite of the popular rhyme, apart from aspen, the ash is nearly always the last native tree to come into leaf, usually in mid- to late May (see also oak). According to an old German folk tale, witches eat the buds on their way to Walpurgisnacht (May Eve) so that the trees do not come into full leaf until St John's Eve (Midsummer Eve). In the autumn, ash is often the first tree to drop its leaves and, as its foliage is relatively sparse even in midsummer, a rich ground flora is able to grow up under native ash trees.

Ash trees are usually dioecious (having male and female flowers on separate trees), but are variable, with some trees bearing male, female or bisexual flowers, sometimes in different years. The clusters of male flowers are purplish and turn yellow when the pollen is shed; the female clusters are pale green. The flowers appear before the foliage and the tree thrives in a windy temperate climate, both pollination and seed dispersal being by wind. Around 100,000 elongated winged fruits are borne on an individual tree, often staying on the tree well into the following season. In winter the tree is easily recognisable by the even patterning of the bark and matt black buds on the branches.

About 5% of seeds will germinate after one winter if chilled, but most do not do so for at least two winters, and experimentally seeds have been shown to remain viable for at least six years. Under natural conditions, predation of the fruits by birds, small mammals and caterpillars can destroy most of the crop. In experiments, batches of 50 seeds were sown in small areas of woodland soil; every one was eaten by voles and mice (Wardle, 1961).

Ash is grown commercially for timber, and it coppices and pollards vigorously. Cutting is traditionally done on a 12–20-year cycle, producing good quality roundwood and (historically) winter fodder (Spray, 1981). Ancient ash stools and pollards can be seen in old woods and wood-pastures; Rackham has estimated an ash stool 2.4 m (8 ft) across to be approximately 800 years old – very much older than uncut trees.

A number of varieties of ash are valued, perhaps the most celebrated being the weeping form, *pendula*, which is said to have originated from a tree found in the eighteenth century by the vicar of Gamlingay, in Cambridgeshire.

The uses of ash

Ash produces one of the best timbers of all Britain's native trees, very strong and flexible. John Evelyn advised 'every prudent Lord... should employ one acre of ground with Ash to every twenty acres, since in as many years it will be more worth than the land itself'. The value of ash timber has, for centuries been recognised as next in value to oak. The Anglo-Saxons used ash wood to make spears and shield handles, and subsequently it has been the wood of choice for tool handles, furniture, sports equipment, walking sticks, tent-pegs, oars, gates, wheel-felloes, tennis rackets and the frames and shafts of diverse vehicles from horse-carts to cars. Ash wood can be steam-bent and retains its strength; it is still used to make some traditional lobster and crab pots. Before the development of light alloys, ash wood was used for the construction of the body frame of Morgan cars and for aircraft wings, including the Sopwith Pup (First World War) and the Mosquito fighter-bomber (Second World War).

Young shoots of coppiced ash have been used in the past for animal fodder, though this is sometimes held to be a cause of diminished milk yields, and may cause butter to become rank. According to John Birkett, a farmer in Little Langdale, Cumbria, the trees are still sometimes lopped during hard winters to provide winter fodder for sheep. Historically, ash has also had another link with sheep as, on account of its alleged health-giving properties, ash was considered the 'proper wood' for a shepherd's crook.

Ash wood burns well, giving out little or no smoke and producing ash rich in potash; it produces excellent quality charcoal. Culpeper recommended ash leaves to cure an adder's bite, while decoctions of them in white wine 'helpeth to break the [gall] stone and expel it, and cure the jaundice'. Ash bark contains a

LEFT The production line for Mosquito fighter-bombers during the Second World War; the airframe was made of ash and lime.

bitter glucoside fraxin and the antioxidants fraxetin and quercetin, as well as tannin. Historically it was a substitute for cinchona bark for treating malaria, and it is still used as a constituent of anti-inflammatory medicines. The leaves have diuretic and laxative properties, while ash keys (fresh or pickled) are claimed to be a remedy for flatulence.

Folklore

Known in Scandinavia as *'yggdrasil'*, individual ash trees would be hailed as guardians of particular settlements, a tradition of ancient Ireland as well (see Chapter 6, p.185), where ash leaves or keys were carried to bring good luck and protect against witchcraft. Ash sticks dating from the first century, have been found on Anglesey (see www.druidry.org) and are thought to have been used as druidic wands. On Dartmoor, ash keys are known as 'Keys of Heaven', and Irish tradition has it that doctors should always carry an ash wand. It is claimed that ash makes the best firewood and will burn well even when green, which has been a cause of wonder – *'Burn ashwood of green/'tis fire for a Queen'*. In fact dry ash does not burn as well as some other timbers such as pine. It was believed that anointing with ash sap and a first bath by an ash fire would protect and strengthen the newborn. Gilbert White (1789) describes a procedure to cure a child of rickets by passing it naked through the cleft trunk of a pollarded ash. Ash had a reputation in medieval times for curing warts; pins used to prick the warts were then pushed into the bark and left there, while the charm was repeated: 'Ashen tree, ashen tree, pray buy these warts of me'. A ritual involving a split ash rod was even claimed to cure impotence. The burning of ash faggots at the midwinter festival is an old pagan tradition and the cue for revelry around Christmas (often associated with wassailing, see p.65).

Sprigs of a famous shrew-ash (a tree in which a live shrew has been immolated) in Richmond Park were supposed to cure various ailments in the nineteenth century; the present tree was planted in 1994 (but without a sacrificial shrew!). Ash is also believed to afford protection against snakes; 'nothing kills an adder faster than an ash rod'. Ash leaves are used for love divination and in Saxon times the ash replaced birch as the maypole. An ash 'money tree' (see p.191) stood until recently below Malham Cove. On the Isle of Man, ash trees are thought to safeguard the purity of springs, while in parts of the south of England schoolchildren carried ash twigs in their pockets on Ash Wednesday – and those who did not had their feet stamped on by others. It was said that ash trees produced no seed in the summer of the year when Charles I was beheaded, and subsequently the occasional absence of ash keys was taken to foretell bad times – at least for the royal family.

Three of the five legendary ancient trees of Ireland were ash (see p.187), and around AD 600, after King Aed Slain was murdered, these trees were felled to symbolise the triumph of Christianity over paganism. Lucas (1963) found that after hawthorn ash was the most frequent 'companion of a holy well', and the stumps of numerous great ash trees (succeeded by replacement saplings) can still be found at many holy wells across Ireland.

Ash in the ecosystem

Few large fungi are known to be associated with live ash and it is thought not to have any ectomycorrhizal associations. However, there are records of two ectomycorrhizal fungi near ash trees: the tawny bolete, *Boletus moravicus*, and the delicate *Amanita battarrae*. The spectacular shaggy bracket, *Inonotus hispidus*, is parasitic on the trunk of the tree. Dead ash wood is often colonised by the strange black globules of King Alfred's cakes, *Daldinia concentrica*. Like many others, this fungus has specific insects that feed on it; in this case a tiny beetle, *Platyrhinus resinosus*. Two other ascomycetes are common: tiny black fruiting bodies like pustules on dead wood, *Cryptosphaeria ennomia* and eruptive cankers sometimes of spectacular size (*Nectria galligena*, which can be up to 1 m or 3 ft across) on the living trunk. Other disfiguring growths are primarily due to a bacterium, *Pseudomonas fraxini*. A number of other fungi such as the powdery mildew, *Phyllactinia*

ABOVE King Alfred's cakes, or coal fungus, *Daldinia concentrica*, whose strange globular fruiting bodies are commonly found on dead ash or beech wood.

ABOVE The spectacular stag beetle, *Cervus cervus*, whose larvae burrow in dead ash logs (and some other broadleaves).

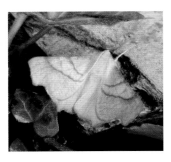

ABOVE Dusky thorn, *Ennomos fuscantaria*, whose foodplant is ash.

LEFT Spectacular fruiting bodies of the shaggy bracket, *Inonotus hispidus*, which is gradually hollowing out a living ash tree.

ABOVE The common ash leaf-roll gall caused by a plant louse, *Psyllopsis fraxini*.

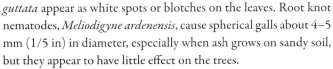

guttata appear as white spots or blotches on the leaves. Root knot nematodes, *Meliodigyne ardenensis*, cause spherical galls about 4–5 mm (1/5 in) in diameter, especially when ash grows on sandy soil, but they appear to have little effect on the trees.

Ash has only 155 associated plant-feeding invertebrates (oak has more than four times as many), fewer than most widespread trees, possibly due in part to ash's relatively late arrival here. The most characteristic insects associated with ash trees are perhaps the ash bark beetles (*Hylesinus* spp. and *Leperisinus varius*), which make familiar 'ash-rose' gallery patterns under the bark similar to those made by *Scolytus* spp. on elm. The ash bud moth, *Prays*

fraxinella, begins by mining leaves but then moves on to bore the twigs and is regarded by foresters as a serious pest, as is the ash scale, *Pseudochermes fraxini*. Other leaf-mines found on ash include the minute tunnels of a tiny fly, *Aulagromyza heringi,* and at least two species of tiny moth. Caterpillars of the dusky thorn moth, *Ennomos fuscantaria*, feed on ash leaves and twigs, and a variety of mites, aphids, bugs and gall-midges all feed on or induce galls on the leaves and fruits. Flower galling, which can affect whole trees, is caused by the tiny gall-mite *Eriophyes fraxinivorus*, while the common rolled leaf-edge (often turning purple) is caused by *Psyllopsis fraxini*, a plant-louse; other common galls include those caused by gall-midges such as *Dasineura fraxini* on leaves, and misshapen fruits by the gall-mite *Aceria fraxinivorus*.

Ash trees will colonise both dry and damp, base-rich soils and when established are very vigorous and competitive. Although relatively short-lived they are rarely overtopped by other trees but in woodland may be replaced gradually by longer-lived trees such as oak and beech.

ASPEN *Populus tremula* L.

> **Willow family:** Salicaceae
>
> **Also known as:** Also known as the common or trembling aspen, aspen poplar, asp (medieval), fel aethnen (Welsh), crithean (Gaelic), crann creathach (Irish). Place names: Aspley Guise, Stonham Aspel.

Aspen (or 'trembling poplar' as its scientific name suggests) was one of the first trees to spread after the last glacial period along with juniper, birch and small willows; earlier than hazel or even pine. It is a fine, erect, fast-growing, short-lived woodland tree that reaches 31 m (100 ft), which always grows as a stand or clonal group by suckering. Individual ramets (stems) may be short-lived but the clones are very long-lasting, possibly being thousands of years old. Aspen occurs far north of the Arctic Circle in Scandinavia, south to the Mediterranean, and east to China and Japan. It is found all over Britain and Ireland including the north and west of Scotland, Orkney and Shetland (where it is often restricted to cliffs inaccessible to sheep), though it never occurs abundantly. Aspen ascends to 700 m (2,300 ft), chiefly on cliffs, but it is not part of montane scrub. It is associated with birch woodland, especially in Scotland where it sometimes forms extensive pure stands of many clones, 'although it has been estimated that there are only 21 aspen-dominated woods that exceed 1.5 ha in extent' (Mackenzie, 2010).

Aspen is widespread on all types of soil (including lowland clays). It is discouraged by shading, but can withstand periodic waterlogging and survives harsh conditions of wind and salt spray and survives well in coastal scrub. Like other poplars it is somewhat susceptible to drought. The bark is usually smooth, pale and yellowish, becoming fissured in aged trees, although this varies between clones.

Aspen is a strangely overlooked species, unfamiliar to the general public, but regarded by many tree lovers as our most beautiful native tree. Its almost round and bluntly serrated leaves, constantly moving, are an unmistakable sight (and whispering sound), much admired by artists and poets. Gerard Manley Hopkins fell in love with the tree, and was saddened by the loss of an aspen grove at Binsey, near Oxford: *'My aspens dear, whose airy cages quelled/Quelled or quenched in leaves the leaping sun/All felled, felled, all are felled'.*

Since aspen clones survive felling, it is assumed the stumps and roots were also removed. Some authors believe he was actually

RIGHT **Beautiful autumn colour of aspen in the Scottish Highlands (see also picture on p.4).**

referring to a grove of black poplars, and a single black poplar was recorded by the Forestry Commission close to the site in 1952.

The constant movement of the foliage, like that of black poplar, is caused by the flattened and very flexible leaf stems. This may be an adaptation to windy conditions by dissipating energy throughout the canopy. Aspen is also particularly attractive in autumn as the leaves of some clones turn a bright shade of yellow and others a deep burgundy red, which adds splashes of vivid colour to the greens and browns of Scottish pine forests.

As with all poplars, aspen is dioecious (having separate male and female trees), the catkins of both sexes appearing well before the leaves. In many clones flowering does not commence until the trees

are 10 or 12 years old (unlike willows that begin flowering much younger), and only occurs at intervals of several years. Even then aspen apparently sets very little seed; in many places this is because surviving aspen clones are too far apart for pollination to occur naturally. Experiments by Worrell *et al.* (1999) have shown that seed production can be enormously increased by artificial pollination.

The tiny seeds are normally only viable for a few days (although experiments have shown they can be stored and remain viable) and, like those of native black poplar, require bare soil or mud to germinate and are very sensitive to drying out.

Aspen suckers vigorously, like wild cherry, and a clonal group develops from a single seedling. Each trunk may only stand for 50–100 years before dying, but the root systems are long-lived, and fire-resistant. Aspen was cut like coppice in England, encouraging the emergence of fresh suckers, but the tree does not produce coppice shoots.

The uses of aspen

Aspen wood, like poplar, is a very light, cheap and long-lasting timber, and can be used for fuel although it burns poorly. According to Rackham, in medieval times it was used to make clogs and arrow-shafts. It has been used for veneer and plywood, for matches and for lightweight boxes for fruit and vegetables, while in North America and Scandinavia it is widely used for pulp and paper-making, its narrow fibres with low lignin content being particularly suitable for making high-grade paper. As a poor conductor of heat it is used for seats and lining of saunas. Aspen also has considerable potential for reclaiming polluted or heavy-metal contaminated soils (see p.182).

BELOW **Bright red catkins of male aspen.**

Like other poplars and willows the leaves and bark contain salicin, a bitter glucoside first isolated in pure form by a French chemist Henri Leroux in 1829, and subsequently used to produce aspirin. A similar but sweeter compound (populin) is present only in the leaves and bark of aspen, but seems to have little effect in discouraging plant-feeding insects, red deer or sheep. The bark and inner bark have both been widely used for their medicinal and nutritive qualities, and in Norway aspen is still traditionally pollarded to provide animal fodder.

Folklore

The constant movement of the foliage may have been a cause of the numerous folkloric associations of aspen with witches, death and the underworld. Altogether it is widely regarded as an unlucky tree; in parts of Wales and Scotland, tradition has it that aspen can never rest because of the (unlikely) claim that it was accursed – even hated as 'the tree on which Christ was crucified'. In the Highlands and the Hebrides the wood is thought to be associated with bad luck and is never used for anything to do with fishing or farming, or used as firewood. As with some other 'unlucky' trees there is at the same time a contradictory tradition of using aspen branches to cure fever. Grigson, however, offers a rather cynical postscript: 'If the timber had been tougher, harder, more durable and more valuable, perhaps the legends would have been different.'

Aspen in the ecosystem

Aspen is associated with a rich variety of fungi including the large edible boletid, *Leccinum aurantiacum*, and the ascomycete *Taphrina johansonii*, which causes bright yellow bulges on the flowers. The aspen bracket, *Phellinus tremulae*, first reported in Scotland only in 2000, is found on standing trees and recently fallen ones; it is parasitic but may take several years to kill a tree. Aspen bark is unusually base-rich, and because of this the tree also attracts many species of lichen.

Altogether over 230 species of plant-feeding insect are recorded on aspen, nearly twice as many as on the related black poplar, and many of them are restricted to or mainly feeding on aspen. Among the most spectacular of these insects are the large poplar longhorn beetle, *Saperda carcharias*, and also *S. populnea*, whose larvae cause swellings and distortions in stems, and the hornet clearwing moth, *Sesia apiformis*, whose caterpillars mine the stems; all three are also found on native black poplar. Several species of long-beaked weevils, *Dorytomus* spp., feed on the catkins. Aspen leaves are mined by tiny black-and-orange leaf beetles, *Zeugophora* spp., as well as several sawflies and numerous small moths. A leaf-rolling weevil, *Byctiscus populi*, the dark-bordered beauty moth, *Epione parallelaria*, and the light orange underwing, *Archiearis notha*, are all rare and attractive species which are entirely or largely dependent on aspen foliage.

Spectacular red or green cauliflower galls on stems (especially in Scotland) are caused by a mite *Aceria populi*, while two gall-midges, *Harmandia globuli*, whose bright red, thimble-shaped galls can be seen on the upper sides of the leaves in June and July, and *Syndiplosis petiole*, which causes swellings on the leaf petioles, are also restricted to aspen. Other species cause all sorts of deformations, swellings, pouches and pustules on both twigs and leaves. In the Highlands especially, new records of gall-formers and other plant-feeding insects on aspen are being recorded frequently as entomologists study these previously neglected trees.

Dead aspen wood has its own suite of specialist insects, especially in Scotland. Aspen is unusual in developing a thick, damp, oily layer of decaying sap-filled wood just below the bark – much more than in other trees, and this attracts a suite of rare insects, among them the spectacular and rare aspen hoverfly, *Hammerschmidtia ferruginea*.

The ecological strategy of aspen is complex. The seedlings are pioneers that colonise damp soil (even in cold conditions) where there is good light. The mature tree is not overtopped by other trees and by means of its persistent root system survives environmental stresses such as storms or heavy snow and, to a limited extent, drought, as well as insect attack, better than many other trees. Aspen is very susceptible to grazing and has declined over recent centuries due to the introduction of sheep and the increase in deer numbers (which effectively prevent regeneration). In remote Highland glens there are still a few relic areas of boreal forest with large aspen stands and dead aspen wood.

In Scotland aspen is now a conservation priority species (Cosgrove *et al.*, 2005) and the subject of a Biodiversity Action Plan; it has been found that for satisfactory conservation of the full invertebrate fauna substantial stands of at least 4.5 hectares (11 acres) of aspen are required. In the Highlands a major project now aims to fully document the tree and its associated organisms, and to protect existing stands while selectively replanting aspen using genetically diverse stock raised from root cuttings. This work is now being promoted by the Highland Aspen Group (www.scottishaspen.org.uk).

BELOW The rare aspen hoverfly, *Hammerschmidtia ferruginea*.

BOTTOM LEFT Rarely seen fruiting bodies of the fungal pathogen *Taphrina johansonii* on aspen flowers.

BOTTOM RIGHT Rare aspen weevil, *Byctiscus populi*, now the subject of its own biodiversity action plan.

BEECH *Fagus sylvatica* L.

> **Beech family**: Fagaceae
>
> **Also known as**: Also known as boc, bece, beace (Anglo-Saxon), fea (Irish), ffawydden (Welsh) and crann faibhile (Gaelic). Derivative place names include Buckhurst Hill, Bechetts Green, Bookham.

Julius Caesar wrote that 'there is no beech timber in Britain', on the strength of which it was long assumed that the beech arrived with the Romans. However, the pollen record shows that beech first became established in England about 5,000 years ago (Godwin, 1984). Its natural distribution is thought to be restricted to four main areas in the southern half of England (see Rackham, 2006, p.363). In recent centuries this 'most lovely of all forest trees' (Gilbert White, 1789) has been widely planted outside its natural range and today regenerates from seed as far north as Caithness.

Beech is a fast-growing tree that thrives on an exceptionally wide range of well-drained soils as long as it has sufficient moisture, but being shallow-rooted it is very susceptible to drought and wind. It is generally a lowland tree but can be found growing at 650 m (2,000 ft) at Garrigill in Cumbria (where it was planted), and even higher in Scandinavia. It is typically associated with lime-rich soils of southern England such as on the Chilterns, where it is often the dominant tree species, but it also occurs widely on sands and gravels such as in Ashdown Forest and at Burnham Beeches.

Beech is characterised by its smooth grey bark on the massive trunk, and can often reach 30 m (100 ft). Planted specimens have reached 46 m (150 ft) in Scotland. Its dense green foliage casts such heavy shade that beneath it few plants can grow, and in beechwoods there is often little else at ground level except the familiar carpet of beech mast and the exceptionally persistent leaf-litter. The leaves are smooth edged (unlike the leaves of hornbeam), and there is a particularly marked difference between smaller, stiffer sunleaves and larger, softer shadeleaves. On young trees (and hedges) the dead leaves remain on the branches until the following spring. Normally beech trees do not produce suckers but they have been observed to do so occasionally (in Epping Forest and at Kew Gardens).

While beechwoods and copses, especially along ridges and on high ground are regarded as one of the characteristic elements of the traditional English landscape, traditional management has more often involved pollarding. Extensive areas of wood-pastures with pollarded beeches (probably cut mainly for firewood) can be seen at Epping Forest and Burnham Beeches; in previous centuries these woods together with hornbeam coppice woods were probably the source of much of London's firewood.

Beech is monoecious (having separate male and female flowers on the same tree). The diminutive green flowers appear in April – females first – at the same time as the leaves. Pollination is by wind. Beech trees first produce viable seed only when at least 28 years old, although 60 years seems more typical; once started, trees are known to continue flowering for at least 200 years.

The annual production of seed or beech mast varies enormously, with heavy production in periodic 'mast years' (see p.23). Most seeds are eaten by predators, but any that do survive germinate the following spring, after their deep dormancy has been broken by winter chilling. The seeds are susceptible both to waterlogging and to drying, reducing their viability. John Evelyn warned that beech seeds must be preserved 'from Vermin, which are very great Devourers of them'. In central Europe, beech mast is consumed by large mammals, such as wild boar. In England the ancient tradition of 'pannage', allowing domestic pigs to roam in woods for a period in the autumn, used to be practised in some beechwoods as well as in oakwoods.

Beech seedlings are fairly shade-tolerant and will regenerate under the shade of other trees but seldom under beech itself. As a result, in suitable conditions beechwoods tend to expand as pure stands until aged trees collapse, only then can young seedlings thrive.

In southern England beech has been used as a small-timber tree since the Bronze Age, and a pollarding tradition is very long established and has now been revived (especially at Burnham Beeches) as the significance of ancient pollards for rare insects and fungi has now been recognised. Historically, beech was even coppiced in some areas, such as the Chilterns, although it does not respond as well as other trees to this treatment. As a standard tree in a coppice system it was also unsatisfactory, casting too deep a shade for the coppice below, yet it was grown in this way in some places.

A number of varieties are well known to gardeners, including several different 'copper' beeches such as var. *purpurea, ziata* etc., and also both contorted and pendulous forms; Hilliers Nurseries (1981) lists 13 decorative cultivars.

OPPOSITE Fine planted beech trees at Keswick, Cumbria. As the climate changes, the north of England may become part of their 'natural' range.

The uses of beech

Beech wood is white, or reddish if grown on very rich soils, and very heavy when newly felled. It is close-grained, hard and smooth, but it is brittle and can split and twist when dried and so is not used as a building timber. It 'endures best under water or in waterlogged soil' according to Grigson, although this is rarely mentioned by modern authors. The piles under Winchester Cathedral and some of those under the old Waterloo Bridge were made of beech. Beech wood burns well and makes fine charcoal; in Scotland beech chips are burnt to smoke herrings.

The Latin word for beech, *fagus*, may be derived from the Greek phagein (to eat), and in Europe beech mast (when available) was eaten in times of famine and war. In France, the nuts are still sometimes roasted as a coffee substitute and the ripe nuts yield a cooking oil, while the cake left after pressing the oil can be fed to cattle. Beech wood ash is rich in potash, while the bark yields beech tar, which can be used as an antiseptic.

Folklore

For such a large and widespread tree, there is very little recorded folklore associated with beech in England, apart from it being thought 'proof against lightning'. In continental Europe it is much the same, as the only records of it having a cultural significance are prehistoric – some beech wood items having been found in Iron Age burials. In Nottinghamshire there is a tradition of children threading beech nuts to make necklaces, while in Hampshire it is said that children sometimes pick fresh beech leaves to eat. Traditionally, beech has long been considered to possess only limited medicinal properties. Culpeper recommends beech leaves as a cooling agent to alleviate swellings, and advises boiling them to make a poultice.

Beech in the ecosystem

Few plants can survive in heavy beech shade; the exceptions are pale plants with little or no chlorophyll. Ghost orchid, *Epipogium aphyllum*, bird's nest orchid, *Neottia nidus-avis*, and the unrelated yellow bird's nest, *Monotropa hypopytis*, all occur mostly under beech and parasitise the mycorrhizal fungi on the tree roots (Foley and Clarke, 2005), as does toothwort, *Lathraea squamaria*, although this plant is more often found under hazel

Numerous species of ectomycorrhizal fungi associated with beech produce conspicuous fruiting bodies. These include two russules, *Russula mairei* and *R. fellea*, a milkcap, *Lactarius blennius*,

Bodgers in the Chilterns

Beech is a very good wood for turning and steam-bending, and it is used for making chairs, tool handles, kitchen utensils and sports equipment. In the nineteenth century Windsor chairs became very popular; the seats were made of elm (which resists splitting) but otherwise beech was used. What started in the late seventeenth century as a cottage industry using wood from yew, ash, walnut and apple became industrialised and the beechwoods around High Wycombe were managed under the 'Chiltern selection system' to produce a continuous supply of medium-sized, straight timber for mass production of chairs and tables. By the mid-nineteenth century whole communities of 'bodgers' actually lived in the woods making legs and backs for chairs, while assembly of the finished articles was completed in large workshops in the town. The name Windsor chair (first referred to in 1724 by Lord Percival) apparently derives from the town being the main distribution centre for the local furniture industry.

LEFT *Traditional bodgers – makers of furniture parts – in Chiltern beechwoods c. 1925.*

the summer truffle, *Tuber aestivum*, and the delicious wood blewit, *Lepista nuda*, while the spectacular brackets of *Ganoderma applanatum* grows on live trunks of beech. Other fungi attack dead beech wood. These include the porcelain fungus, *Oudemansiella mucida*, shaggy scale-head, *Philiota squarrosa*, and the beech bracket, *Pseudotrametes gibbosa*, which characteristically harbours green algae growing on its upper surface. Yet others, such as beech mast candlesnuff, *Xylaria carpophila*, and the beech leaf bonnet, *Mycena capillaries*, live on decaying beech mast.

A serious disease of commercial plantations, beech bark disease, is caused by a parasitic fungus *Nectria coccinea*, carried by felted scale bug, *Cryptococcus fagisuga*, which produces what look like flecks of white wool that stick to the bark; heavy infestations can make trees look as if they are whitewashed. Treatment is by scrubbing with soapy water. In hot summers strip-cankers such as *Biscogniauxia nummularia* may cause damage that looks like lightning strikes on beech trunks.

Beech foliage is not particularly palatable to plant-feeding insects (see p.21, Table 4, line 12). It has more associated beetles than other native trees apart from oak and willows, but fewer other insects. Three insects are regarded as major pests: a leaf-wrinkling weevil, *Rhynchaenus fagi*, the seed-eating beech seed moth, *Cydia fagiglandana*, and the beech woolly aphid, *Phyllaphis fagi*. The extraordinary caterpillars of the lobster moth, *Stauropus fagi*, are most often found on beech, while the caterpillars of the barred hook-tip, *Watsonalla cultraria*, feed exclusively beech leaves. At least four other tiny leaf-mining moths are restricted to beech, including *Stigmella tityrella*, which excavates beautiful S-shaped tunnels between a pair of leaf-veins, while the tiny mite *Acalitus stenaspis* curls the edges of leaves. Yellow nail-galls and reddish vase-galls on the leaves are both produced by gall-midges, *Hartigiola annulipes* and *Mikiola fagi* respectively. The kernels of beech mast are eaten by squirrels and particularly dormice, as well as by many common woodland birds.

In its ecological strategy, beech is one of the best examples among British trees of a forest competitor; in good conditions it will dominate and shade out most other trees and ground plants except early spring flowers. Even on thin soils its wide, shallow root system takes up water extremely efficiently, denying moisture to other species. Beech trees are susceptible to windthrow, which they can survive if allowed to, and drought. Beech is also highly vunerable to damage by grey squirrels, which kill the apical buds of young trees (Ray Hawes, National Trust, pers. comm.)

TOP The charateristic nobbly boles of an old beech pollards at Kenwood, north London.

ABOVE Wood blewits, *Lepista nuda*, a gastronomic delicacy, often appears under beech trees.

RIGHT Nail galls on a beech. leaf caused by the gall-midge, *Hartigiola annulipes*.

BIRCHES *Betula* spp.

> **Birch family:** Betulaceae
> Silver birch *Betula pendula* Roth
> Downy birch *Betula pubescens* Ehrh.
> Dwarf birch *Betula nana* L.
>
> **Also known as:** Also known as beith (Gaelic), begh (Irish),
> bedwen (Welsh) and ribbon tree (Lincolnshire). In ancient Irish
> law, one of seven 'commoners' (see p.185). Derivative place
> names in England include Birkenhead, Berkhamstead etc. In Ireland,
> many names include 'beagh', 'behagh' etc., meaning birch land.
>
> **Biological Flora:** Atkinson (1958); de Groot *et al. (B. nana)* (1997)

Silver birch is a particularly beautiful tree, especially the tall, slender forms, although the architecture of both tree birches is very variable. The foliage is particularly attractive; the masses of tiny leaves move in the lightest breeze, and in autumn the flickering greens, yellows and gold produce a uniquely delightful effect. Our three native birch species were some of the earliest trees (after juniper and some willows) to colonise these islands after the last glacial period, possibly having survived with pine in small, northwestern refugia. The pollen record shows birch, including dwarf birch, occurring over virtually all but the furthest south and west by 9,500 years ago.

Silver birch freely hybridises with the downy birch, with which it can often be confused. Ennos *et al.* (2000) reported that genetic studies cannot conclusively separate all populations of the two species from numerous intermediate forms, although in theory downy birch has a double set of chromosomes. Both trees grow predominantly on poor acid soils (being pioneer species) with *B. pubescens* tending to favour damper sites. Both trees are relatively

BELOW Ancient birch near Nedd, Sutherland.

short-lived, rarely surviving much more than 100 years in England but generally longer in the Highlands. Downy birch tends to have a rounded crown and, although it can reach 20 m (66 ft), it rarely does so, while silver birch more often grows taller and straight, reaching nearly 30 m (100 ft) under favourable conditions.

Dwarf birch, *B. nana*, is a rare, slow-growing mountain species that is found in peaty, often damp conditions on exposed acid soils up to 860 m (2,800 ft), (Glen Cannich) rarely reaching more than 30 cm (1 ft) in height. It occurs mainly in the Highlands of Scotland (and two localities in northern England) but at scattered localities and often in small numbers, probably representing the relic fragments of a much wider distribution (De Groot *et al.*, 1997) reduced especially by grazing pressure from deer. In Scandinavia under less grazing pressure it grows much bigger and forms dense thickets. Dwarf birch is very frost-tolerant and survives well under the protection of winter snow, and it may live much longer than its larger relatives. It is also notable for its diversity of mycorrhizal associations, some of which produce aerial fruiting bodies (including five milkcaps, *Lactarius* spp. and five agarics, *Amanita* spp.).

The two larger birches are slightly less hardy than dwarf birch. Silver birch ascends to at least 600 m (2,000 ft) in the Highlands, downy birch to 774 m (2,500 ft). The most northerly natural

LEFT Dwarf birch, *Betula nana*, one of the hardiest of our native trees.

birchwood in Britain is at Berriedale, on the island of Hoy, Orkney, and consists mainly of downy birch. These two birches, and their hybrids, form woodland above and beyond the limits of oak in the north and west of Scotland, although not apparently in Cumbria where (possibly due to browsing pressure from high sheep numbers) there are oakwoods at a higher altitude than birch.

Birch is the second most common broadleaved tree in English woodlands, and the commonest in Scotland where there is sometimes an absence of competing tree species apart from sallows, *Salix caprea* or *S. cinerea*. On good soil and less exposed sites it may be gradually overtopped and replaced by other trees such as oak. The growth habit is extremely variable from tall stately standards to rounded low-growing forms more like bushes, which form a component of the woody scrub that grows above the main tree-line on mountains. Silver birch is a frequent component of mountain woodlands and heaths on poorer, acidic soils, while downy birch is often found in wetland communities with alder and willow.

Birch trees are monoecious (having male and female catkins on the same tree) and start flowering when they are only 5 to 10 years old. Both silver birch and downy birch produce quantities of wind-distributed pollen from male catkins in April. The female flowers are only receptive to pollen (see p.14) for a few days. After successful pollination the vast quantities of tiny winged seeds are ripe by August and shed mainly from September onwards. Seed production of individual trees can be prodigious – at least a quarter of a million – and is less variable than in mast trees like oak and beech. After a few weeks of chilling to break their dormancy, the viability of birch seed is high. Research has shown that most seeds typically fall within 50 m (165 ft) of the tree, although this may be greater at the most exposed sites. Some seeds may remain viable in the soil for a few seasons but not longer.

Birch seeds can germinate in well-lit situations on the thinnest rocky soils, scree, acidic peat-bogs and disturbed ground in woodland. On pure mineral soil, such as that uncovered by retreating ice, birch seeds can become established very soon after mosses and nitrogen-fixing herbs have begun the process of 'sweetening' the substrate, making it less acid and holding more nutrients and organic matter. Birch seedlings are hardy and survive some shading but are susceptible to both drought and grazing. In the Highlands birch can grow up through juniper, which protects it from deer browsing. In dwarf birch seedling

RIGHT The clouds of tiny birch seeds reach gutters and even window-sills in towns; a pioneer species it can colonise such places as if they were rocky crags.

FAR RIGHT Birch plantation from selected seed at Dunkeld, Scottish Highlands.

growth is very slow; in Scotland reaching no more than 3 cm (1 in) in the first year! Birch responds well to coppicing and both silver and downy birch can be managed to produce coppice wood, but compared with other trees the stools are relatively short-lived. Dwarf birch alone can reproduce vegetatively by layering, especially when overgrown by moss.

The uses of birch

Birch timber has been said to be fit only for use in plywood, upholstery framing and a few domestic items such as brooms. Evelyn dismissed it as 'of all other, the worst of timber'. Grigson claims that birch 'makes poor timber', but then he too admits that 'where other trees are scarce, the uses have been manifold, as in the Highlands'. In fact, birch timber's toughness is comparable to that of ash, and it is also a most attractive wood when turned. It was formerly used to make vast quantities of hard-wearing bobbins, spools and reels for the Lancashire cotton industry, and in the last few years the use of birch wood has been revived for furniture, window frames and flooring.

Traditional broomsticks or besoms are made from birch branches with a hazel handle, and birch brushwood is cut for use on racecourses. Less well known is the use of birch sap, which is tapped from the trunk in early April; about 75 litres (16½ gallons) can be obtained from a single large tree. In Eastern Europe this is a major source of sugar and it is also fermented to make beer and wine; in 1986 production in Russia was recorded as 42,700 tons (Mather, 1990). Birch-sap wine was Prince Albert's favourite drink, according to Queen Victoria's diaries. Silver birch wine is produced commercially at Moniack Castle near Inverness; annual production has increased from 9,000 bottles in 1990 to 25,000 bottles in 2009. Green birch poles were employed until the 1850s to stir molten copper, thus preventing the formation of copper oxides and resulting in a purer copper being produced.

Birch bark has been used as a famine food, and it contains a resinous essential oil betulin, which has anti-flammatory properties. In the absence of oak bark, birch was used in the Highlands for tanning, and the production of birch tar. A distillate of the tar can be used as an insect repellent. Birch produces very good charcoal, and has been used as an alternative to alder for making gunpowder. Birch tea, made from young leaves, contains vitamin C and flavanoids and has anti-oxidant properties. Herbalists have recommended such infusions to treat gout and rheumatism and even to dissolve kidney stones.

Since birch is expanding rapidly in contemporary disturbed landscapes, such as waste lots and disused railway land, Rackham has suggested that it should not normally be planted for conservation or amenity purposes since it appears anyway, and that the expansion of economic uses for the tree and its timber should be encouraged.

Folklore

The name birch may be related to the ancient Sanskrit 'bhurga' ('a tree whose bark is used for writing upon'); pieces of birch bark inscribed with Buddhist writings have been unearthed in Afghanistan and dated at around 1,800 years, making them some of the earliest such texts ever found.

In various parts of England there was an ancient tradition of using birch branches to decorate churches for Whit Sunday. The young growths represented the renewal of life, while the rustling of the leaves represented the sound of the Holy Spirit descending. This tradition was known from Shropshire and last recorded at Frome, Somerset, in 1994 (Vickery, 1995).

Apparently, birch is traditionally the tree to make the best maypole; Grigson suggests that this is due to the belief that it had magic power to ward off evil spirits. In Ireland birch was regarded as a protective tree against fairies and the Evil Eye, and birch branches were used to 'beat the bounds' of a parish to expel any evil spirits and 'beat the devil' out of miscreants. In medieval times, a bundle of birch rods was carried in front of the magistrate on his way to court, thereby combining a symbol of authority with a means of correction; this tradition endures on the Isle of Man today.

At the same time birch is believed to have life-giving properties, symbolises love and fertility and 'is widely associated with birth and young children' (Mac Coitir, 2003). In Scotland, birch kindling was used for a ritual fire at the first spring sunrise, the traditional start to the warmer half of the year, and was hung over doors on Midsummer Eve.

Birch in the ecosystem

That birch is able to thrive on almost pure mineral soil is largely due to its many mycorrhizal associates, several of which produce attractive fruiting bodies, although in some situations seedlings die, apparently before they are able to develop an association with a fungus. More species of fungus are recorded as being associated with the three birches (4,000) than with any other native tree. Of these, perhaps the most familiar is the poisonous fly agaric, *Amanita muscaria*, with its bright red cap. Others specific to birch include the tawny grisette, *Amanita fulva*, several species of *Russula* including the birch brittlegill, *R. betularum*, and the (brown) birch bolete,

Leccinum scabrum. The yellow rust *Melampsoridium betulinum* attacks the leaves of all three birch species. On dead trees a bracket called the razor-strop fungus, *Piptoporus betulinus*, is common, as is the tinder or hoof fungus, *Fomes fomentarius*, originally a northern species that has now spread to southern England.

Birch trees are host to one of the most familiar types of plant-gall – the clumped masses of twigs looking like dense birds' nests that are known as witches' brooms. These are caused by the fungus *Taphrina betulina* on downy birch and the closely related *T. turgida* on silver birch. A mature birch tree can have as many as a hundred of these growths. Sparrows and other small birds sometimes use them as nest sites. A related but much rarer fungus, *T. betulae,* causes nothing more serious than yellow or reddish spots on the leaves.

Occasionally enormous cankers occur high up on the trunk of birch trees. These are probably caused by *Nectria galligena*, which is the commonest canker agent of hardwood trees and affects many species including apple, ash and aspen. A strange gall shaped like a large turnip can sometimes be found on birch roots; this is caused by a soil bacterium, *Agrobacterium tumefaciens*.

Various researchers have reported that birches have inducible chemical defence mechanisms that partly deter browsing and, later in the season, can restrict insect damage (De Groot *et al.*, 1997). The living parts of birch trees are in fact eaten by a wide variety of both vertebrates and invertebrates (caterpillars of at least 317 moths and butterflies alone!). Sheep, deer, hares, rabbits and voles all eat birch leaves, and black grouse consume the buds, while red deer, horses, cattle and squirrels strip the bark, and voles, woodmice and small birds such as redpoll and siskin plunder the seeds.

With over 600 plant-feeding insects and mites recorded from birch, only oak and willow have more (Table 4). Many of these species feed on other broadleaved foliage as well, but at least 143 (24%) are restricted to birch and of these many are only recorded from one birch species but not the other. A host of organisms cause small deformities on birch leaves and twigs – nail-galls, pustules, swellings, crinkles and blisters of all sorts. A version of 'big-bud' is commonly seen; this is caused by one of at least seven species of birch gall-mite, *Acalitus calycophthirus*, while gall-midges such as *Semutobia betulae* frequently cause distortion to the fruits and fruit-scales, although they appear to have little effect on the overall health of the trees.

Over 50 different species of insect have been found mining the leaves of birch, often producing beautiful patterns on the leaf. Mostly these are tiny moths (such as *Lyonetia clerkella*, which is

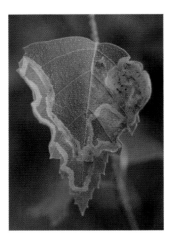

ABOVE A net-winged beetle, *Pyropterus nigroruber*, whose larvae feed on birch bark.

ABOVE RIGHT Larva of the sawfly, *Cimbex femoratus*, which feeds on birch foliage.

RIGHT Leafmine of tiny caterpillars of the micro-moth, *Lyonetia clerkella*.

FAR RIGHT The common green oak tortrix, *Tortrix viridana*, found on birch foliage and most other broadleaf trees.

also found on most rosaceous trees, and *Stigmella lapponica*), while others are very small weevils and sawflies. Two leaf-miners, *Swammerdamia passerella* and *Stigmella nanivora,* are specific to dwarf birch, which is also attacked by polyphagous moorland moths such as the northern winter moth, *Operophtera fagata.*

A smaller group of birch specialists are familiar leaf-eating species. The dark, spotted caterpillars of the black and white argent-and-sable moth, *Rheumaptera hastata*, spin individual leaves of birch, bog myrtle, *Myrica gale*, and some willows into a protective cocoon. Caterpillars of the spectacular large red-belted clearwing moth, *Synanthedon culiciformis*, and the Welsh clearwing, *S. scoliaeformis*, bore into the bark, while in the Highlands, caterpillars of the beautifully marked Kentish glory moth, *Endromis versicolora*, eat the leaves (and also those of alder). Two other insects commonly seen on birch are the red and green birch shieldbug, *Elasmothethus interstinctus*, and the yellowish grubs of the large birch sawfly, *Cimbex femoratus*, the latter being a pest of commercial birch plantations.

Ecologically, the larger birches are among the best examples among British trees of relatively short-lived pioneers that can be successful in harsh, cold conditions. Birch puts relatively little energy into protecting itself from unwanted infection, or the foliage being grazed, but by dispersing clouds of tiny seeds can colonise disturbed ground, bare rock and even crevices on buildings very easily. Birch has spread in recent times, especially in urban and suburban areas. 'During the twentieth century birch has perhaps benefited more than any other tree from disturbance in the environment, expanding its (self-sown) range in many environments' (Rackham, pers. comm.).

Once established, its ecological effect on mineral soils is enormous, while its 'soil-sweetening' effect of drying out and reducing the acidity of wet, moorland soils promotes the establishment of other tree species' (Ashmole, 2006). Like alder, birch has been used to reclaim spoil heaps in mining areas and on fly-ash from power stations where little else will grow. Perhaps it should better be termed a general 'habitat-sweetener', as birch also forms dense thickets with willows (providing cover for small mammals and birds), while the leaf-litter that builds up (unlike that of pine) provides a habitat for a wide range of invertebrates on the most unpromising gravel or scree. Together with some mountain willows dwarf birch is one of the few woody plants able to survive the sub-arctic conditions of the high plateaux in the Scottish Highlands.

BIRD CHERRY *Prunus padus* L.

Rose family: Rosaceae

Also known as: Also known as hagberry or hackberry, from the Old Norse heggr, ceirosen (Welsh), and fiodhag (Gaelic), but there is apparently no name in Irish

Biological Flora: Leather (1996)

Bird cherry is a small deciduous tree with strong, tannin-smelling, peeling bark, normally growing only to about 4–5 m (13–16 ft) or even lower as a shrubby many-stemmed bush, but capable of reaching 19 m (60 ft). It occurs naturally in the northern half of Britain (except Orkney and Shetland), the far northwest of Ireland, and in most of Wales and Norfolk; elsewhere bird cherry cultivars have been widely planted especially as street trees. Bird cherry ascends to over 640 m (2,000 ft) in the Lake District and the Scottish Highlands. Bird cherry is the most northerly and most montane species of *Prunus* (Leather, 1996).

Bird cherry favours damp, sheltered, stream-side sites on mildly acidic or base-rich soils and survives light shade. The dense foliage is often bright green, each leaf with a red petiole. Bird cherry usually occurs as a dense clonal group, and it also coppices well. It is common in upland ashwoods and on limestone pavements and similar sites such as at Buttertubs near Hawes; in East Anglia it grows with alder, while at Loch Lomond it grows as an understorey tree in oak woodland.

The tree is tolerant of a variety of stresses, including drought and frost, but not salt spray. Young saplings are grazed by both rabbits and voles, but the leaves are unpalatable to domestic animals especially goats; possibly for this reason it is sometimes used for hedging.

The leaves have a serrated edge (unlike alder buckthorn with which it can be confused) and about nine pairs of veins, although

BELOW **Bird cherry in flower, Glen Affric, Scottish Highlands.**

on the underside of the leaves the veins have a more reticulate appearance. The attractive white flowers are packed in elongate racemose inflorescences (horizontal or drooping, unlike wild cherry whose blossoms are upright) containing 10–40 individual florets, which can be almost as abundant as on hawthorn. They have a slightly fishy smell (due to trimethylamine), which attracts mainly small flies (six species reported), as well as some bees and at least four species of beetle. The flowers are protogynous – meaning that the female parts mature before the stamens and pollen – and are self-fertile (unlike related trees such as apple), automatic self-pollination occurring quite frequently once the stamens ripen. The bitter fruit ('hags', 'hacks', 'hackers' or 'hog-berries') about 6–8 mm (¼–⅓ in) across, resemble small sloes in appearance. Seed is set in most years but bird cherry is a mast tree; there is an interval of one to three years between heavy crops. The seeds enter a deep dormancy that is only broken by prolonged chilling (or, in nurseries, stratification).

The uses of bird cherry

As a small tree the hard, heavy red wood is only available in small sizes but is easily worked and takes a high polish. The shiny, pea-sized, dark purplish-black fruits are bitter-tasting due to small quantities of hydrogen cyanide. This disappears with boiling and the 'hags' can be used to make sharp jams and jellies. Infusions of the bark have been used as a general tonic. A green dye can be obtained from the leaves, and dyes varying from grey to green from the fruit.

Folklore

In the northeast of Scotland, bird cherry is looked on as a witch's tree (Gregor, 1889, quoted by Vickery, 1995), and the wood is only used as firewood.

BELOW **Mature bird cherry clone, Inchnadamph, Sutherland.**

Bird cherry in the ecosystem

Various ectomycorrhizal fungi are known to be associated with bird cherry, including the scaly earthball, *Scleroderma verrucosum. Dermea padi*, a canker-forming fungus that sometimes infects the branches, and a number of pathogenic fungi such as a small bracket *Heterobasidion annosum* and the rust *Pucciniastrum padi* have been recorded on the branches and leaves. Other causes of leaf spot, wilt, canker etc. are bacteria such as *Pseudomonas mors-prunorum.*

The diversity of insects associated with bird cherry is low, but the foliage is particularly attractive to a small group of leaf-eating insects, some of which can occur in very large numbers. Infestations of the tiny bird-cherry oat-aphid, *Rhopalosiphum padi*, may permanently damage terminal shoots (causing tighter tree architecture). The gregarious white and black caterpillars of the tiny bird-cherry ermine, *Yponomeuta evonymella*, in their silken festoons can completely defoliate whole trees in early spring, but the trees produce new foliage a week or two later and show no permanent ill-effects. The abundance of these insects varies enormously from year to year.

The leaves are frequently galled by mites and tiny flies; the erineum (patch of hairs) on the underside of the leaves is caused by the gall-mite *Eriophyes paderineus*, and the small red nail-galls by *Phyllocoptes eupadi*. A few other insects are restricted to bird cherry; these include a yellow aphid, *Myzus padellus*, and a sawfly, *Pristiphora retusa*, whose green larvae feed on the leaves.

One small brown weevil, *Furcipus rectirostris*, with a spectacularly long and elegant rostrum or beak, feeds on the fruits, which are sometimes infected with a fungus, *Taphrina padi,* that causes them to develop as misshapen 'pocket plums'. Observations in the Chilterns by Snow and Snow (1988) showed that thrushes most frequently take bird cherry fruit, with robins and warblers taking most of the rest. Bird cherry is a northern species. Ecologically, it thrives in cold conditions, often on poor, mineral soil near streams. As it is shade-tolerant, it also occurs as an understorey tree in woodland.

BOTTOM LEFT Nail galls caused by the mite *Eriophyes padi* can cover the surface of bird cherry leaves.

BELOW Bird cherry ermine moth, *Yponomeuta evonymella*, whose caterpillars can defoliate whole trees.

BOTTOM RIGHT Bird cherry blossom being pollinated by a tiny dance-fly, *Empis* sp.

BLACK POPLAR *Populus nigra* ssp. *betulifolia* (Pursh) Wettst

Willow family: Salicaceae

Also known as: Also known as willow poplar, cotton tree, water poplar, a' chaitheann (Gaelic). Derivative place name: Poplar (on the River Lea, East London); the name derives from the Greek 'papillo' to shake.

The native black poplar is a massive tree growing to 38 m (125ft), exclusively occurring in wet places by rivers and streams. Characteristically the trunk is deeply furrowed, often with massive burrs and irregularities, and the large lower branches curve downwards. The tree occurs naturally in England and Wales as far north as a line from the Mersey to the Humber, with a few trees being found along the River Tees. Natural populations can be found on various river floodplains in southwest England, along some rivers in East Anglia and along some rivers in central Ireland. Possibly because they seem little affected by air pollution, black poplars have been widely planted in some large towns such as

BELOW **Massive bole and deeply furrowed bark of the native black poplar (see also picture on p.200).**

Manchester. Black poplars have also been planted in Aylesbury Vale (although why this was done is not known), but as with urban planting these trees are almost exclusively male specimens of European *P. nigra* stock, or of hybrid poplars, *P. x serotina,* with only some indigenous *P. nigra* ancestry. The female trees are less popular in an urban setting as they produce masses of fluffy fruits.

Like other poplars and willows, the black poplar is dioecious with spectacular flowering and fruiting, with scarlet male catkins briefly creating a wonderful effect in April, before shedding clouds of tiny pollen grains into the wind. Some nectar is also produced and insects such as hoverflies are often seen to visit the catkins, so some insect pollination may occur.

There are very few places where both sexes of the native tree can be found growing near one another, so natural regeneration (uncontaminated by non-native pollen) takes place only very rarely. When viable seeds are produced (around the end of June), they will only germinate if they land on bare, wet soil (eroded banks, or islands in rivers) and the resulting seedlings must stay moist until the leaves fall in October. Flooding, drought and shade are all fatal and the seedlings are also unable to develop in competition with other vegetation. Modern management of rivers has practically eliminated the required habitat so that natural regeneration is prevented.

This is unfortunate because, as Rackham explains, 'our black poplars are evidently the last shadow of the vanished floodplain wildwood'. The trees do sometimes regenerate vegetatively: fallen branches or trunks can take root in the mud and suckers can grow up from roots damaged by rivers in flood. Black poplars are known for having very large, vigorous root systems and certainly could be a major threat to buildings and drains if planted inappropriately close to them, but this combination of factors has resulted in a major decline of the trees, and regeneration of pure strains has almost ceased. The conservation of local genetic stock of the native trees is now accepted as an important conservation priority.

Black poplars pollard well, and are very easy to propagate vegetatively, the traditional method being by making long cuttings or 'truncheons' about 2 m (6½ ft) long in autumn, and planting these in damp soil in the spring.

The uses of black poplar

Being massive trees with such a distinctive shape and large bosses protruding from the trunk, black poplars have been used as natural landmarks or boundary markers in river valleys. They have been used in some places as hanging trees. Poplar timber is light, absorbs

The Aston on Clun poplar

In England, a famous black poplar known as the Arbor Tree stands at a junction in Aston on Clun in southwest Shropshire, grown from the cutting of an earlier tree that was blown down in September 1995. It is permanently decorated with flags attached to long larch poles, which are renewed every Oak Apple Day (29 May) during a local carnival. Records show that the pageant used to be much more elaborate, with a procession of historical characters including Diana, goddess of Nature, St George of England and St George of Ethiopia. This ended with a mock wedding festival commemorating that of squire John Marston and his bride, Mary Carter, in the 1780s, but possibly following an earlier festival, which celebrated the restoration of the monarchy in 1660, and even further back to a local fertility rite. Cuttings from the tree as 'fertility charms' were traditionally given to newly wedded couples in the village, although this custom has been suspended due to excessive demand from outside the village (see p.190).

shock and resists splintering, and is heat- and fire-resistant. It was traditionally used for clogs and for flooring, in oast-houses and in servants' quarters (it was said that, in case of accidents such as the upsetting of oil lamps, it would not burn!). Black poplar wood was traditionally used to make wooden shields and to line the floors of carts, and for timber-framed buildings. An analysis of the distribution of the trees in Norfolk shows that the majority of trees occur close to farms, kilns, mills, smithies and malthouses (Barnes *et al.* 2009).

The very pale, yellowish-white wood has been used for veneers. It turns well and makes attractive bowls and has been used for artificial limbs, packing cases, pallets, interior shelving, toys, plywood and light baskets for soft fruit. Hybrids of black/balsam poplars were planted in East Anglia during the 1960s for the production of matches and the bark has been used as a (poor) substitute for oak bark in tanning leather. Today, fast-growing hybrids of *P. nigra* are being tested for biomass production on a short-rotation coppice, where it can produce as much as 16 tonnes of timber per hectare per annum.

Folklore

According to Greek mythology, black poplar resulted from Phaeton's fatal attempt to drive Apollo's chariot across the sky. Phaeton's sisters made such a nuisance of themselves mourning his death that the gods on Mount Olympus decided to change them into black poplars.

John Evelyn recommends the use of black poplar leaves for winter cattle feed and claims that the juice of poplar leaves is an effective cure for ear-ache, while the buds, when crushed with honey, are good for sore eyes. According to Geoffrey Grigson, an ointment was made in medieval times using poplar buds as the main ingredient. This was used for treating inflammation, bruises and gout, and was popular with the handlers of prize-fighters. Culpeper claims that 'drops from the hollows of this tree take away warts, wheals and other breaking out of the body', and modern herbalists associate the tree with cures for arthritis and a variety of other ailments. Less sought after are the fallen male catkins, which – according to Grigson – 'look like fat red grubs. Not surprisingly they have been called Devil's Fingers, and are supposed to bring ill-fortune if picked up'.

Black poplar in the ecosystem

A number of fungal fruiting bodies are found under and on poplars; the rare but edible slate bolete, *Leccinum duriusculum*, an ectomycorrhizal associate, is apparently restricted to the genus *Populus*, while a common, bright yellow blister gall on the leaves is caused by a parasitic fungus, *Taphrina populina*. Since 2000

FAR LEFT Devil's fingers, the fallen male catkins of a native black poplar. There is an old belief that it is unlucky to touch them or pick them up.

LEFT The strange spiral deformation of the black poplar petiole caused by the aphid, *Pemphigus spyrothecae*.

blackening and dieback of shoots in damp summers appears to have been caused by a parasitic fungus *Venturia populina*, which weakens trees making them more susceptible to other diseases such as poplar leaf spot, *Marssonina brunnea*. Mistletoe occurs very rarely on native black poplar although it is common on hybrid poplars (see p.67).

Black poplar is closely related to aspen, but has far fewer plant-feeding insects that are specifically associated with it. The large green caterpillars of the poplar hawk moth, *Laothoe populi*, can sometimes be found on most poplars and willows including native black poplar. Two spectacular moths on poplar in the south of England are the wasp-like hornet moth, *Sesia apiformis* (although it is usually found on hybrid trees), and the red underwing, *Catocala nupta*, which also occurs on willows, while two other characteristic insects are the poplar grey moth, *Acronicta megacephala*, and a brown leaf-hopper, *Idiocerus fulgidus*.

The tiny larvae of the poplar cambium fly, *Phytobia cambii*, make long tunnels, which damage the wood for veneer use (it also attacks aspen and willow). A variety of swellings, spirals and blisters of leaves and petioles are caused by gall-aphids (such as *Pemphigus bursarius*, *P. spirothecae* and *P. populi*), some of which are commoner on Lombardy poplars or hybrid trees. Poplar is their primary host but the alternate generations of these aphids are found on various marsh plants such as fool's parsley, *Aethusa cynapium*. Larvae of the palisade sawfly, *Stauronematus compressicornis*, graze the leaves within a dry 'palisade' of wood particles cemented together with dried saliva. The leaves can also suffer from a condition known as 'gold leaf' caused by the fungus *Ascomyces aureus*, which can sometimes be so abundant as to make a single tree look as if it has been sprayed with gold paint.

Ecologically, native black poplar is a pioneer of mud banks and other waterlogged ground, surviving flood and damage but being relatively short-lived. Unlike the alder (which occurs in very similar habitats) black poplars can 'remind us of the splendour of the medieval countryside' (Rackham). A small band of enthusiasts around the country search out local trees, campaign for their conservation and actively promote special planting schemes; this has now been endorsed by the Forestry Commission. Until recently DNA analysis has been conducted under the European Forest Genetic Resources Programme (EUFORGEN), for which black poplar was one of four pilot species. The conservation strategies for black poplar are discussed in some detail by Cooper (2006), and now DNA fingerprinting of black poplar clones is available from Forest Research, and this is advised where new planting is envisaged so that less common clones may be given priority (A'Hara *et al.*, 2009).

BLACKTHORN, SLOE *Prunus spinosa* L.

Rose family: Rosaceae

Also known as: Also known as dreenan, draoighneach, draighean (Irish), droigheann dubh (Gaelic), draenen ddu (Welsh); the fruits – sloes, slones, bullums.

This spiny member of the genus *Prunus* grows as scrub and in woodland edges extending as far as the north coast of Scotland and the Outer Hebrides. It is generally found only at low altitudes, although in Cumbria it thrives at 500 m (1,600 ft), where it has presumably been planted. Blackthorn occurs on a wide variety of soils except the most acid, and is very tolerant of salt spray – occurring in coastal scrub where it is sometimes grazed and wind-pruned down to dense masses no more than 30–40 cm (1–1 ¼ft) high.

While it normally occurs in a shrubby form, blackthorn can grow to a tree of 4 m (13 ft). It suckers profusely and because of this can effectively invade grassland, subsequently contributing to the process of vegetational succession by providing shelter for seedlings of trees such as oak, ash and hazel, which in due course shade it out (see oak, p.58).

The flowers, in dense, brilliant white inflorescences, appear in early spring before the leaves. They have a mild fragrance and are visited by insects, especially bees, the female parts becoming mature before the stamens. Unlike many rosaceous trees blackthorn may be partly self-fertile. The familiar black sloe, an astringent fruit with a large, hard seed, is often bluish in appearance when ripe due to the presence of wild yeast, *Saccharomyces paradoxum*. Fruiting varies considerably from year to year; this may be related to the abundance and effectiveness of pollinators that are influenced by the weather from year to year.

The uses of blackthorn

The dried leaves have been used to make 'Irish tea', and even smoked as a substitute for tobacco. The astringent qualities of the fruits have been used as a remedy for various complaints from sore gums to kidney stones and as a general tonic. Collections of sloe stones have been found at Neolithic sites; they may have been buried to sweeten them after picking. Sloes are popularly made into sloe gin and rather acidic jams and jelly (Phillips, 1983), and the best results are thought to be obtained if the fruits have endured frost while still on the tree.

Folklore

The dense heavy wood of this spiny tree is understood in Ireland to symbolise fierceness and physical protection; it is used to make walking sticks and shillelaghs (Irish cudgels). At the same time there is an ambiguous element to this belief; the wood is simultaneously considered 'unlucky'. Nevertheless, at Sandwich, Kent, a long tradition holds that the mayor has a black knotty stick (of blackthorn wood) as a symbol of power, and as recently as 1994 a new mayor was presented with a staff of office selected from a local hedgerow. As with hawthorn, tradition has it that the blossom is not to be taken indoors. Flowering often coincides

OPPOSITE **Blackthorn foliage with fruits (sloes), and lichens, _Usnia_ sp.**

BELOW **Blackthorn in flower, Cockfosters, North London.**

with cold weather known as 'blackthorn winter' – a bad time for planting 'anything of a tender nature' – but the right time for sowing spring barley.

Blackthorn in the ecosystem

Blackthorn survives browsing by large mammals; deer or sheep may prune the bushes severely without killing them. Nearly 200 invertebrates, especially caterpillars, feed on the foliage (over 180 moth and butterfly species are recorded). The total for the three native species of _Prunus_ is over 380, about the same as _Populus_ (see Table 4). The plant-feeders include caterpillars of the emperor moth, _Saturnia pavonia_, and in southern England the brown and scarcer black hairstreak butterflies, _Thecla betulae_ and _Satyrium pruni_. _Thecla betulae_ also occurs on blackthorn growing in south-west Wales and on The Burren in Ireland. One species, now extinct, that fed mainly on blackthorn was the black-veined white butterfly, _Aporia crataegi_, which used to be widely distributed in southern Britain in the nineteenth century. Around 1925 it mysteriously disappeared in spite of the abundance of blackthorn, and it has not been seen in Britain ever since.

Among the commonest and most widespread micro-moths on blackthorn are several gregarious species of the family Yponomeutidae such as the orchard ermine, _Yponomeuta padella_, and the hawthorn moth, _Scythropia crataegella_, but caterpillars

Rosaceous trees

Bird cherry is a member of the large worldwide rose family Rosaceae, which includes about 100 genera and nearly 3,000 mostly temperate species, many of them trees or shrubs but including many wildflowers and fruits such as strawberries and blackberries. Compared with other tree families, the Rosaceae have diversified relatively recently (originating around 40 million years ago) and they have evolved together with a variety of specialised insect pollinators, as well as both bird and mammal seed dispersers. Some genera such as *Sorbus* continue to diversify rapidly (see whitebeams, p.141).

Rosaceous plants have regular, usually hermaphrodite flowers, which are often scented, and they are characterised by their main parts, such as petals or sepals, existing in groups of five. The fruits are often juicy and attractive to birds (those fruits which stay on the tree) and mammals (those fruits that tend to drop to the ground).

The Holocene history (since the last glacial period) of our rosaceous trees is not well documented, chiefly because their waxy pollen occurs only sparingly in sediments.

of most general plant-feeding moths are recorded as well. Like other *Prunus* species, blackthorn is often abundantly galled. Perhaps the most familiar galls are the irregularly swollen fruits or 'pocket plums', caused by a fungus, *Taphrina pruni,* whose spores are spread by the plum mite, *Eriophyes padi,* which itself causes leaf pustules along the leaf midrib. Bud-galls are caused by a gall-midge, *Asphondylia pruniperda.* A hard, flat cushion in the bark may be caused by a gall-mite, *Acalitus phloeocoptes,* the swollen leaf midrib by another midge, *Putoniella pruni,* and common leaf-edge pustules by yet another mite, *Eriophyes prunispinosae.* Leaf-rolling is caused by some micro-moths or the larva of a small sawfly *Nicronematus monogyniae,* while aphids are quite commonly present, with at least eight species recorded, including *Rhopalosiphum nymphaeae* (also found on wild cherry). Relatively few insects occur on both these *Prunus* species, but more often on other broadleaved trees.

Sloes are eaten by birds, usually in November and December (haws tend to be consumed before sloes), but they are at the upper limit of size that can be swallowed by blackbirds and thrushes, and are generally too large for robins and starlings, which both peck the flesh. Sloes are also eaten by mammals, including badgers and foxes. The hawfinch devours the seeds of fallen fruit. Blackthorn is extensively planted for hedging, and then incidentally provides good nesting cover for small birds and shelter for migrants.

The ecological strategy of blackthorn is similar to that of common hawthorn. It is a stress-tolerant competitor, marginally less tolerant of harsh conditions than hawthorn, but reproducing mainly by extensive suckering. The role of blackthorn in nurturing groves of newly established trees (oak etc.) in grassland has been discussed at length by Franz Vera (2002 etc.), who proposes the idea of a cyclical process: grassland > thorny scrub (blackthorn) > oak/hazel woodland > closed canopy forest > opening created by fall of trees > expanded clearing becoming grassland > thorny scrub > etc. While some aspects of this succession have been challenged by various writers such as Kirby (2003), it is indisputable that blackthorn can play a role in the ecological succession from grassland to woodland by providing protection from grazing animals for seedlings of trees such as oak and hazel.

FAR LEFT Wind and sheep-pruned blackthorn in coastal scrub, Lismore Island, Scotland.

ABOVE LEFT A characteristic gall of blackthorn, pocket plums are caused by the fungus, *Taphrina pruni.*

LEFT Leaf galls on blackthorn are caused by the mite *Eriophyes prunispinosae.*

BOX *Buxus sempervirens* L.

> **Box family:** Rosaceae
>
> **Also known as:** Also known as bocs (Welsh), bosca (Irish) and bocsa (Gaelic). Derivative place names: Box Hill, Boxworth, Boxford. Staples (1970) lists many similar examples throughout southern England, although some 'box' examples may not refer to box trees.

Box is a small tree up to 6 m (20 ft), often occurring in the wild as a multi-stemmed clonal group with characteristic yellowish trunks and dense foliage above. There has been some dispute as to whether it is really a native species, but box pollen from 6,500 years ago has been found at Ellerside Moss in Lancashire, while charcoal from box has been found in Iron Age camps near the south coast. There are also several records of preserved box artefacts and even 'clippings' (!) dating from the Roman period. It is now thought that box is native in southern England, occurring naturally in a few scattered sites in beechwoods and scrub on south-facing chalk or limestone slopes; elsewhere its occurrence is probably the result of planting, but it may have been present but subsequently become extinct. At Boxwell in Gloucestershire there is a dense wood of pure box merging into a beechwood; its origin is uncertain. At Box Hill in Surrey there are stands of box/yew woodland with occasional emergent ash trees.

The evergreen leaves (notched at the tip) stay on the branches for about four years. They have a bitter taste and a distinctive odour. Box is one of the oldest and most widely planted ornamental garden plants in Europe, possibly partly due to the unpalatable leaves which discourage browsers. Box hedges are also good shelter for small birds.

The tiny greenish and (to most people) sweet-smelling flowers occur in clusters, a terminal female flower being surrounded by a number of male flowers. The flowers are visited by various insects

BELOW Multi-stemmed box tree at Box Hill, Surrey.

but are also self-fertile. The fruit is a small three-horned capsule, which when ripe snaps open throwing out the six small black seeds. These do not appear to grow successfully immediately under the mother trees, and they may need to be transported away by wood ants or washed away by rainwater before successful germination can result; the resultant seedlings are notably shade-tolerant.

The uses of box

Box combs bear no small part
In the militia of the feminine art
(JOHN EVELYN, 1664)

Box wood is yellow, extremely hard and fine-grained and much prized for woodworking small, accurately turned items such as chessmen, mathematical instruments, flutes, small pulley blocks, small moving parts in the textile industry and, for centuries, combs! It is still the preferred medium for wood-engraving as it is both easy to work and hard-wearing. The celebrated nineteenth-century naturalist and engraver Thomas Bewick claimed that one

of his blocks made of boxwood was still sound after nearly one million impressions!

Box wood has been coppiced for centuries for firewood and to produce high quality charcoal, small pieces of which have been found associated with Neolithic camps on the South Downs. The frequency of 'box-' or 'bex-' in place names is thought to reflect the high value placed on locally planted box, because at many of these places there is no sign of natural stands, and today it is restricted to gardens and planted around war memorials. According to Grigson, box used to be far more common in the south of England before centuries of over-harvesting took their toll, but there is little evidence for this. The wood has now become so scarce that the Society of Wood Engravers has been forced to plant its own box grove for future use. A National Collection of over 90 box cultivars is maintained by the National Trust at Ickworth Park, near Bury St Edmunds. Box leaves contain several toxic alkaloids (buxine, parabuxine and parabuxonidine). Infusions of bark and leaves are used for their medicinal qualities; they have been used in small quantities to as a purgative, a sweat-inducing agent, for the treatment of venereal disease and for de-worming horses. In France the leaves are used as mulch in vineyards.

Folklore

In some parts of England box is associated with funerals and was used to decorate graves, and even for lining coffins (Staples, 1970). In Lancashire and Cumbria, box sprigs are sometimes still provided for mourners at a funeral, who then take them and drop them into the grave (Vickery, 1995). Perhaps this is why it is

ABOVE LEFT Box-bug, *Spanioneura fonscolombii*, one of the few insects resistant to the toxins in box leaves.

LEFT Tiny yellow flowers of box; they are slightly scented and attract small flies as pollinators.

thought unlucky in some places to cut a box tree down, or bring box indoors; 'bring box into the house, take a box out'. In France and Poland Roman Catholic worshippers carry sprigs of box to church on Palm Sunday, a custom that is maintained at French and Polish churches in Britain.

Box in the ecosystem

Box may be browsed intermittently by deer in hard winters, but it is generally avoided by rabbits, and is not touched by other browsing animals. Only a few small fungi are known to be specifically associated with living box, although it may be attacked by parasitic species including box rust, *Puccinia buxi*, on leaves, which causes yellow dieback of leaves that gradually turn purplish-brown. In 1997 there was a serious outbreak of an unknown disease of cultivated box at a nursery in Hampshire. Dark brown spots appeared on the leaves, black streaks on the stems and there was severe defoliation; the cause was a previously unknown fungal pathogen finally described in 2002 and named *Cylindrocladium buxicola*. This has already become a serious pest of plant nurseries; so far no effective treatment has been found, and strict quarantine measures and incineration of all parts of the infected plants together with sterilisation of the adjacent soil are now standard precedure. A few saprotrophic fungi are associated with box, including the delicate box parachute, *Marasmius buxi*.

The toxins in the leaves evidently make box unpalatable to most insects (even common broadleaf feeders) and fewer herbivorous species feed on box than on any other native trees apart from strawberry tree. An unusually high proportion (nearly 50%) of those that have been found are restricted to the tree – their scientific names give a clue to this – in other words, they are highly specialised plant-feeders that are able to counter the box leaf alkaloids.

Yellowish leaf blisters are caused by a box gall-midge, *Monarthropalpus flavus*, while white waxy deposits and a thickening of leaf-tips into a small cabbage-gall (which can be abundant on individual plants) is caused by tiny psyllid bugs, *Spanioneura buxi* or *S. fonscolombii*. The thickening of the flower buds into small galls is caused by the gall-mite, *Eriophyes canestrinii*. The box psyllid, *Psylla buxi*, galls leaves on planted box but has not been recorded from wild trees. Ecologically, box is a (slow-growing) competitor on base-rich soils, but only as an understorey tree. It might also be termed a survivor or a defensive tree (like some other understorey species such as spindle and buckthorn), having developed strong chemical defence against insect attack.

BUCKTHORN *Rhamnus cathartica* L.

> **Buckthorn family:** Rhamnaceae
>
> **Also known as:** Also known in country areas as common or purging buckthorn, crossthorn, waythorn, hartsthorn, ramsthorn, ramh-druighean (Irish), sgitheach (Gaelic) and rhafnwydden (Welsh).
>
> **Biological Flora:** Godwin (1943)

This rather thorny, multi-stemmed shrub with sparse foliage grows into a spindly tree with a dense crown growing to 4–6 m (13–20 ft) but sometimes reaching nearly 10 m (33 ft). Buckthorn strongly prefers lime-rich soils and, while never common, is distributed in open woodland and hedges throughout much of lowland England and southern Scotland, with scattered records from parts of Ireland where calcareous rocks occur. It is intolerant of shade and does not occur in dense woodland. It ascends to over 335 m (1,000 ft) on

BELOW Mature buckthorn tree in an old hedge near Henley-on-Thames.

limestone in Yorkshire. Together with alder buckthorn and grey willow it also forms a component of a very different vegetation type, fenland carr, as at Wicken Fen in Cambridgeshire.

The leafy shoots that grow in opposite pairs often end in a spine, while the leaves are oval with a dull green surface and only two pairs of main veins (unlike alder buckthorn). The leaves are sometimes pinkish, becoming yellow or brownish (not red, unlike alder buckthorn) before falling. Where branches touch the ground they can take root (layering) and this characteristic is used by gardeners for propagation. Buckthorn is dioecious, having male and female flowers on different trees, the strongly scented yellowish-green flowers growing in tight clusters. Counts have shown that female (fruiting) individuals tend to outnumber male (non-fruiting) individuals by about six to one. Various bees and some flies have been recorded visiting the flowers. The fruits (drupes), each containing three or four seeds, turn from green to black on ripening. Counts have been made, and in 1932 a single tree was recorded as bearing 1,455 fruits! Buckthorn is a rather gregarious plant, very often occurring in hedgerows, supposedly due to bird dispersal, but in fact the fruits are actually less popular than most other berries and are only eaten later in the autumn when they are already dry and shrivelled. In a test with blackbirds and a song thrush, buckthorn was the least palatable out of 11 fruits including rose-hip, hawthorn and elder. The foliage is generally refused by cattle, although goats and sheep (and probably deer) will browse on it.

The uses of buckthorn

Buckthorn wood is hard and dense but little used. The bark and unripe fruits can be used to produce a yellow dye for paper, and the ripe fruits to produce a green pigment ('sap or bladder green') used by water-colourists; even the last overripe fruits can produce a red dye.

Folklore

The black shining berries look innocent, but don't try eating them. They were employed as 'a mighty and muscular purge for men and animals'. Quantities of buckthorn seeds were found in ancient latrine pits at St Albans Abbey – it is not clear whether its use was primarily medicinal or penitential. The bitter juice contains two active ingredients, the glycosides rhamnocathartin and rhamnin, as well as a sugar, rhamnose).

When the berries are boiled with honey and then diluted a gentler purgative can be produced. It is sometimes marketed as

LEFT **Clusters of the ripe black fruits of buckthorn at Gait Barrows, Lancashire.**

'syrup of buckthorn' and used for treating animals, although it is apparently no longer commercially available.

Buckthorn in the ecosystem

The range of fungi known to be associated specifically with live buckthorn is limited although, like other rosaceous trees, it surely has various ectomycorrhizal associations. Orange specks on the leaves are caused by crown rust, *Puccinia coronata*, a powdery mildew, *Sawadaea bicornis,* is also common, as is a 'tar-spot', *Rhytisma* sp., which disfigures the leaves. Relatively common woodland fungi such as Jew's ear, *Auricularia auricula-judae*, and the delicate scurfy twiglet, *Tubaria fufuracea*, are both saprophytes on dead buckthorn wood. Only 46 species of plant-feeding invertebrate have been recorded (of which just 9 are restricted to *Rhamnus* – a further 20 occur on buckthorn and alder buckthorn only but not on other trees). This may be partly due to the tree being uncommon and less abundant than other trees. Buckthorn is the major food plant of the brimstone butterfly, *Gonepteryx rhamni*, and because of this the tree is now frequently planted in conservation areas and nature reserves. Looper caterpillars of three geometrid moths are also found only on buckthorn foliage; the green larvae of the tissue moth, *Triphosa dubitata* (also on alder buckthorn), the brown-and-cream larvae of the brown scallop, *Philereme vetulata*, and those of the dark umber, *Philereme transversata*, which can be mistaken for the first two, as there are two colour varieties – a green one and a brown-and-cream one!

Thickenings and rolling of the leaf-edges are caused by a psyllid bug, *Trichochermes walkeri* (common only in the south of England), while a common leaf erineum with blade thickening above is caused by a gall-mite, *Phyllocoptes annulatus*. At least two aphids, *Aphis mammulata* and *A. nasturtii*, are restricted to *R. cathartica*, as are some of the tiny caterpillars, which mine the leaves, such as *Bucculatrix franutella*. Ecologically buckthorn is an understorey tree or hedgerow competitor on base-rich soils, its chemical defences apparently making it unappealing to many plant-feeding insects.

CRABAPPLE *Malus sylvestris* L. Miller and
DOMESTIC APPLE *Malus pumila*

Rose family: Rosaceae

Crabapple also known as: crab, scrab, wilding, bittersgall, gribble, sour grabs, scrogg, cranfia-uill (Irish) and crabys (Welsh). (Gaelic) and rhafnwydden (Welsh).

Domestic apple also known as: ubhall (Gaelic), crabys (Welsh), cranfia-uill (Irish). Strangely, in ancient Irish law apple was considered one of seven noble trees (see p.185).

The crabapple (the scientific name means 'woodland apple') is a small to medium-sized, somewhat thorny tree usually with a dense, rounded crown. It normally grows to no more than 5–6 m (16–20 ft) but is recorded as reaching 17 m (56 ft), and it ascends to an altitude of 380 m (1,250 ft). It occurs across the whole of Britain and Ireland but less commonly in the northern half of Scotland. Crabapple trees usually occurs as isolated individuals in various types of woodland, in hedges and in scrub. This may possibly have evolved as a defence from insect attack, but how this extreme non-gregarious distribution is achieved is not known. Crabapple seeds may germinate only after passing through the gut of a bird or a mammal. In eastern England crabapple is scattered through almost all types of woodland at roughly one tree for every 10 hectares (Rackham), and is sometimes regarded as indicating ancient woodland. Many small woods therefore have only a single individual (or none at all), although in the woodlands of the Lake District crabapples are more frequent, often being found next to the sites of old charcoal-burning pitsteads. Occasionally crabapple is gregarious (the New Forest, Bluebell Wood in north London), but it can be mistaken for the trees arising from domestic apple pips. Crabapple is identified by having completely hairless flower-stalks (pedicels) and hairless, shiny undersurfaces of the leaves.

The domestic apple has no thorns and larger leaves, usually with downy hairs on the undersurface at least on the veins. It can grow to at least 24 m (78 ft) (Morden Park), but is usually a small tree of no more than 4–5 m (13–16 ft) as a planted tree, and exists in the wild as pippins of uncertain parentage. Apple trees are very variable – over 2,000 varieties are known in England alone and over 7,500 worldwide. Apple and pear were among the earliest plants to be domesticated, a process which probably resulted from selection and breeding in

RIGHT **Ancient crab-apple tree at Craxdale Hall, Durham.**

ABOVE Crabapples will turn yellowish once they are ripe and then drop to the ground. They are eaten by large mammals such as wild boar and deer.

LEFT Wild apple woodland in the Tienshan Mountains, Uzbekhistan.

the mountains of central Asia around 10,000 years ago (see p.171). Charcoal and seed impressions on pottery have been found at sites in Europe dating from the Neolithic period (up to 4,000 years before present). In more recent times Henry VIII had apple varieties brought from different parts of Europe for his orchards at Hampton Court (which unfortunately have not been retained).

Following DNA analysis it is now understood that the cultivated apple originated from the wild Asian or Almaty apple, *Malus sieversii* L., which forms natural woodland on rocky hillsides in central Asia (Juniper and Mabberley, 2006). Most of the different characteristics of familiar apple varieties – whether suitable for eating or for cooking, maturing at different times, and varying resistance to disease – are present among fruits in the wild groves of *M. sieversii* (see p.171).

Crabapple blossom is pinkish, and produces copious nectar and abundant waxy yellow pollen. The flowers appear in May, slightly later than those of wild cherry, but before the main woodland canopy fully emerges, providing an important early source of pollen and nectar for bees and hoverflies that avoid shade. Both crabapple and domestic apple are normally self-sterile, and depend on insects for pollination. Because of this need for cross-pollination (out-crossing) apple trees are very diverse; the prized cultivated varieties each arose from single parent trees originating by chance (see p.171). Crabapple fruits or crabs are like a smaller version of a domestic apple, yellow to

red and sharp-tasting. Partly because of their size and that they fall to the ground when ripe, it is thought they are adapted primarily to dispersal by large mammals including wild boar and deer (Snow and Snow, 1988), and in central Asia by porcupines. Even domestic pigs are known to shake apple trees and eat the fruit (Paul Hand, pers. comm.). All apples are a popular food for birds, that can damage commercial crops; some seed-eating birds eat the pips from fallen fruit.

The uses of crabapple and domestic apple

As the abundance of commercial apple crops is often limited by the number and efficiency of pollinators, single non-native crabapple trees are often planted at intervals in commercial orchards as an extra source of pollen and attraction for additional pollinating insects. Crabapple pollen does not result in viable apple pips but does succeed in stimulating the growth of the tissue below the flower, which becomes the flesh of the fruit.

Apple wood is of excellent quality; it is uniform in texture and when dried slowly is suitable for the most delicate woodworking, such as wood-engraving and fine carving. It is also extremely hard and tough; before steel replaced it apple wood was often used for working parts of corn-mills and other machinery. It has been used for making set squares and other drawing instruments, and before the softer beech became popular, for furniture. Apple wood makes fragrant firewood and high quality charcoal, and a yellow dye for wool can be produced from the bark.

'An apple a day keeps the doctor away' is an old saying with some truth in it. The fruits are extremely nutritious, containing vitamin C, several organic acids, salts of potassium and soda, organic phosphates and other compounds of calcium, magnesium and iron. The bark and roots contain phloridzin and quercetin, while the seeds give amygdaline and an edible oil. Crabapples produce excellent jelly and wine; Grigson recommends that two or three crabs improve a cooked apple dish such as apple tart. Most of the health benefits of domestic apples – such as improving the digestion – apply to crabapples, although they are often too sour to eat raw. Verjuice, a fermented bitter brew from crabapples, 'was used by medieval cooks as we would use lemon juice' according to Phillips (1983).

Folklore

The name crabapple may be derived from the idea of the tree being crabbed, or 'of awkward character', which gives the wrong (i.e. sour) fruit. The folklore associated with apples is extensive and diverse (Vickery, 1995), and the tree appears in various folk tales. One strand is to do with determining true love and the suitability of marriage partners. 'Throw apple pips into the fire while saying the name of your love; if the pip explodes then the love is true; if not, the pip will quietly burn away'. There are also sayings about

unsatisfactory unions such as 'she had searched the orchard through and through until she found the crab'. Unseasonal flowering is thought to be unlucky or even a harbinger of death.

In October each year, apples and other fruits are celebrated at the Apple Festival, when the National Fruit Collection at Brogdale is open to the public. There are now similar events organised to promote old apple varieties and traditional fruit-growing in various parts of the country (see www.fruitforum.org).

Apple in the ecosystem

Apple trees are attractive to a wide variety of insects and pathogens, as apple growers everywhere find; it seems as if domestication of apple – as with some other crop plants – has resulted in a concentration of its enemies. Fireblight, caused by a bacterial pathogen, *Erwinia amylovora*, is a pest of cultivated apples (more serious on pears) and can destroy a whole orchard in a single growing season. It is spread by insects, birds and wind, entering the trees at any injured surface of leaves or branches.

Irregular knobbly swellings on roots, trunk or branches are caused by colonies of a woolly aphid *Eriosoma lanigerum*, and more serious damage is done to the bark by a canker-forming fungus *Nectria galligena*. A variety of mildews, fruit scabs and fruit rots affect all apples, caused by ascomycete fungi, while dead branches are sometimes infected by *Rutstroemia rhenana*, which produces beautiful tiny orange-brown flat cups. Apple scab disease

Wassailing the apple

The tradition of 'wassailing the apple' or 'apple howling' (around Christmas) was associated with cultivated apple. Jugfuls of cider were thrown at the trees, while shotguns and pistols were fired into the branches to the accompaniment of shouts of 'Hail to thee, old apple tree!' (Wilkes, 1972) and general merriment ensued, supposedly to guarantee a good crop the following summer. This tradition was apparently strongest in cider-growing areas such as Devon and Somerset and has been revived by cider companies in recent years.

RIGHT This old engraving was first published in the *Illustrated News* in 1854.

ABOVE A hedgerow wilding, arising from a discarded pip, Lyndhurst, Hampshire.

is caused by the fungus *Venturia inaequalis* (which also affects other rosaceous trees), and the fruits can be scarred by activities of the apple rust mite *Aculus schlechtendali*.

In total 271 invertebrate plant-feeders are recorded from apple and crabapple, of which 30 are restricted to *Malus*. Several are major pests. As commercial orchards are usually monocultures, with hundreds of genetically identical trees all growing together, insects that may be rare and cause little damage on wild crabapple can decimate commercial orchards. Among this host of small insects and mites are at least 21 species of leaf-miner, such as the apple-leaf skeletoniser, *Chloreutis pariana*. Galls include leaf pustules containing mites, *Phyllocoptes goniothorax,* and various forms of leaf-rolls and swelling caused by aphids, mites or the apple leaf-curling midge,

Dasineura mali, an orchard pest. Several insects have the potential to become pests, damaging the developing fruit or, at the very least, causing defects that render the fruit unmarketable. The codling moth, *Cydia pomonella*, is a scourge of apple growers worldwide, and other orchard pests include the apple sawfly, *Hoplocampa testudinea*, apple-grass aphids, *Rhopalosiphum insertum*, and finally the apple blossom weevil, *Anthonomus pomorum*, identified as the most important pest of organic apple orchards in UK.

Ecologically, crabapple is a stress-tolerant competitor, which can survive well as an understorey tree in woodland. The ancestors of domestic apple are generally squat, medium-sized trees, which can establish themselves on bare rocky slopes and eventually form whole woodlands up to considerable altitudes in the mountains of central Asia. There they are well able to resist harsh winter storms and snowfall, and in the summer both high temperatures and drought stress.

Mistletoe

Mistletoe, *Viscum album* (drualas in Irish, draoidh-lus Gaelic, uchelfor Welsh) is a hemi-parasitic, epiphytic plant that occurs on a wide variety of deciduous trees, especially cultivated apple and other rosaceous trees, hybrid limes and poplars. It is rare in most of Britain but common in its main stronghold in Worcestershire/Gloucestershire/Somerset, a major fruit-growing area. Orchards suit its habit particularly well as it is light-demanding and does not occur within woodland. This may explain why it is found more commonly on hybrid limes (which are planted in sunny places) than on native limes which are woodland trees.

Mistletoe is dioecious, and the female plants bear the only native white berries of any woody plant. It supports at least eight plant-feeding insects, of which three are restricted to the plant. These include the tiny black and white mistletoe marble moth, *Celypha woodiana*, whose green caterpillars mine the leaves. This moth is now a UK BAP priority species. A jumping plant-louse, *Psylla visci*, is restricted to mistletoe, as is the tiny brown weevil *Ixapion variegata*, a recently introduced species.

The white berries are particularly well adapted for bird dispersal as the seeds are surrounded by a sticky jelly that resists digestion so that the seeds

readily stick to any branch where they land in the bird droppings. Mistletoe berries are taken mostly by mistle thrushes (which will defend the plants from other birds) and migrant blackcaps, but less frequently by other fruit-eating birds, some of which appear not to recognise the white berries as food.

It is claimed that mistletoe has had a major cultural significance since ancient times. This is thought to be in part due to its distinctive forked branching, and evergreen foliage. There are Norse, Greek and Roman mistletoe traditions. In Britain the folk customs may result from the 're-invention in the eighteenth and nineteenth centuries of the remnant of an ancient fertility tradition' (www.mistletoe.org.uk). Because of the connection with paganism, mistletoe has often been banned from churches. The tradition of kissing under the mistletoe may be of Celtic origin; in various parts of the country there is also a tradition of keeping a sprig until Shrove Tuesday or for the whole year 'to keep evil spirits away' (Vickery, 1995). There are now campaigns to promote mistletoe traditions and to conserve the plants, while new festivals are being invented or old ones revived. Examples include the Tenbury Wells Mistletoe Queen and National Mistletoe Day in early December.

ABOVE **Mistletoe is common in old apple orchards, especially in the west of England, here growing on a traditional variety, Lord Lambourne.**

A herbal tea made from mistletoe leaves is claimed to improve blood circulation and liver condition, as well as having other health benefits.

RIGHT The rare, red-belted clearwing moth, *Synanthedon myopaeformis*, whose caterpillars bore under the bark of old fruit trees especially apple and pear.

FAR RIGHT ABOVE The noble chafer, *Gnorimus nobilis*, a spectacular beetle of old orchards.

FAR RIGHT BELOW Caterpillar of the major orchard pest, the codling moth, *Cydia pomonella*.

ELDER *Sambucus nigra* L.

> **Honeysuckle family**: Caprifoliaceae
>
> **Also known as**: bore, boor or bour tree, battery, dog-tree, ellhorn, trom (Irish), ysgawen (Welsh) or craobh fhearna (Gaelic). Place name: Yelverton (Devon).
>
> **Biological Flora**: Atkinson & Atkinson (2002)

Elder is a small, generally short-lived tree that grows to 10 m (33 ft). The weak branches are often arching, while the overall shape is rounded and irregular; in some exposed places it can form a dense circular bush like sallow. The trees age rapidly, but genuinely ancient specimens can be found in some exposed situations. The yellowish-grey bark is soft, gnarled and deeply furrowed, and usually covered in mosses and lichens, which give a venerable appearance; older trees can frequently become hollow. The natural distribution covers the lowlands of mainland Britain and Ireland (it is planted in Orkney and Shetland), ascending to 470 m (1,500 ft) (possibly planted) in Cumbria. Elder is usually found on nitrogen-rich soils and disturbed ground, such as around rabbit warrens, where it is often associated with stinging nettle, *Urtica dioica*. It also occurs with hawthorn. Its natural habitat is on alluvial floodplains and woodland edges where there is rich, disturbed soil, and it is unable to establish itself from seed in an existing sward. Mabey dismisses elder as nothing more than a 'jumped up weed', noting that it is most common on urban wasteland and old rubbish dumps.

When crushed the soft leaves have an unpleasant smell; they are nitrogen-rich and experiments show that when fallen they decay extremely rapidly, only nettle decomposing faster.

The abundant sweet-smelling inflorescences are made up of around 700 florets, each producing copious nectar, which attracts bees, wasps and hoverflies as well as some beetles and flies. Not all the florets are pollinated so there are usually fewer fruits than florets. The berries are very attractive to birds, ripening in August immediately after viburnum fruits and before haws are available. They are a particularly popular food with starlings, but Snow and Snow (1998) found that more bird species (both seed dispersers and seed eaters) feed on elder than any other fruit, partly because the fruit appear so early in the season. Subsequently, viable seeds can persist in the soil for many years.

The uses of elder

Evelyn's comment that 'A very considerable fence may be made of elder' seems a little optimistic as the stems are rather brittle; perhaps he meant a hedge? In fact, today when elder occurs in a hedge it is regarded by Hedgelink (see p.179) as evidence of neglect. Historically the hard, close-grained, yellowish wood was used for small machine parts, for butchers' skewers and for carving small objects. The pith was used in the past by entomologists to pin out insect specimens, while there is a tradition (which may still occur in country areas) that children remove the pith and use twigs to make pea-shooters or toy guns.

All parts of the plant contain essential oils. Analysis of dry elder flowers has produced as many as 79 different compounds, some of which repel insects. Experiments have shown that the spruce bark beetle, *Ips typographus*, reacts negatively to elder extracts, and some gardeners use ground-up leaves as a natural pesticide. Dried elder leaves can be used as a tobacco substitute. The bark, root and leaves can all be used as a diuretic; elderflower water is used as a skin cleanser and is commercially sold as *Eau de Sureau*. Commercial elder vineyards exist in various parts of the south of England and Wales from Kent to Pembrokeshire. Elder flowers and fruits are used to make increasingly popular wines and cordials, elderflower pressé etc., while the dried fruits can substitute for currants and are used to make a peppery relish known as pontack sauce. In the Forest of Dean the flowers are dried and used to make 'ellum blow tea', which is claimed to be a cure for various ailments but especially coughs colds and flu.

Folklore

'Elder is one of the most enigmatic plants in the British Isles' (Vickery, 1995). There are conflicting traditions about elder from different parts of Britain and Ireland, including the Isle of Man. In northern Europe elder was regarded as being the home of a female spirit, and in various parts of England there is a tradition that elder is not to be cut down without 'asking the Old Lady's leave'. It is widely seen as a fairies' and witches' tree, a symbol of evil; it is thought very unlucky to cut elder down, burn it ('you will see the Devil'), or bring the blossom into a house.

OPPOSITE **Bole of mature elder, possibly an old coppice-stool, one of the fastest-ageing native trees.**

At the same time it is valued for its protective and medicinal qualities. In Ireland a self-set elder tree near a house is considered lucky as it protects from witches and lightning. In some places it is said to be the tree from which Judas Iscariot hanged himself – "the proof being the ugly smell of the leaves". The flowers or berries are taken, but it is thought 'advisable to ask the tree's permission first'. Elder is traditionally used to ward off flies, for example by planting near a cowshed, and for curing warts. A fresh branch can be used to control swarms of bees, and it is claimed that with the appropriate incantations it can protect milk or even cure warts. The presence of elder trees in remote areas is often evidence of former habitation.

RIGHT **Blossom on an unusual pollarded elder at Hatfield Forest, Essex.**

Elder in the ecosystem

Elder foliage is not grazed by rabbits, and thrives around their warrens. Three species of ascomycete fungus attack the leaves. These include *Cercaspora depazeoides* and *Phoma sambuci-nigrae,* which cause dark spots on the leaves. Jew's ear, *Auricularia auricula-judae,* a gastronomic delicacy, is a specialised wood-rot fungus most commonly found on elder wood (as well as buckthorn). Few insects are associated with elder, just 41 being recorded (of which 17 are restricted to the tree) possibly because the leaves are too nitrogen-rich for most general plant-feeders. The flower stems are commonly infested with a black aphid, *Aphis sambuci,* that also congregates around buds and on new shoots. A gall-mite, *Epitrimerus trilobus,* rolls the leaf-edge, while a gall-midge, *Placochela nigripes,* produces bud-galls on the flowerhead. The leaves are occasionally mined by a tiny agromyzid fly, *Liriomyza amoena,* and can be damaged by small nocturnally feeding sawflies, *Macrophyla* spp., all restricted to elder. A tiny black and white moth, *Phlyctaenia coronata,* whose caterpillars spin a web on elder leaves in late summer, is also found on viburnum.

Widely dispersed by birds, both as seeds scraped off the bill and passing through the gut, elder is a competitor on nitrogen-rich soils where it is apparently not replaced by taller species. At places like old sewage beds or human habitations it can form a pure stand of woodland, probably succeeded by other trees but not for many years. Although somewhat shade-tolerant it is short-lived but may be directly replaced by its own seedlings.

TOP The tiny crowned phlyctaenia moth, *Phlyctaenia coronata,* whose caterpillars are restricted to elder foliage.

ABOVE Black spots on elder leaves caused by the ascomycete fungus, *Phoma sambuci-nigrae.*

LEFT Elder blossom attracts many hoverflies, Syrphidae.

ELMS *Ulmus* spp.

> **Elm family:** Ulmaceae
>
> Wych elm *Ulmus glabra* Hudson
> English elm *Ulmus procera* Salisb.
> Smooth-leaved elm or East Anglian elm *Ulmus minor* Miller
>
> Also: '*Ulmus plotii*' Druce, Plot's elm or Lock's elm; local elms such as Huntingdon elm, Exeter elm etc.. and another group (Jersey elm, Wheatley elm and Cornish elm), sometimes known as *U. sarniensis*, are probably all varieties of *U. minor*.
>
> **Also known as:** Also known by many local names such as chewbark, wychwood *(U. glabra)*, and Warwickshire weed, elven *(U. procera)*, leamhán (Irish and Gaelic), llwyfen (Welsh). Many place names are associated with elm (e.g. Shipton-under-Wychwood in Oxfordshire).

Elms are 'the most complex and difficult trees in western Europe, and the most intimately linked to human affairs', according to Rackham, who has written extensively on the subject in his book, *History of the Countryside*. Wilkinson (1978), Richens (1983) and others have devoted whole volumes to these much-loved trees. While wych elm is generally accepted as a species, the other elms are perhaps better understood as an aggregate, or collection of genetic forms, partly because they rarely set seed and are propagated vegetatively. There has been considerable disagreement between taxonomists about elms, and these disputes have only been partially clarified by recent genetic studies.

Coleman (2000) has made some genetic researches into *Ulmus*. From nearly 100 *Ulmus* samples collected from various parts of England and the Edinburgh area, he found that there was a genetic continuum between wych elm and East Anglian elm, *U. minor*, indicating the presence of hybrids and intermediate individuals. Some of these hybrids were apparently fertile. However, he concluded that 'elm taxonomy appears to be further from reaching a consensus than at any time in the last 400 years'. As regards *U. plotii* (Plot's elm), he concluded that it was not a separate species but a single clone. He did not find it growing anywhere in woodland and all the '*U. plotii*' trees he sampled were genetically so similar that they were clearly derived from a single parent individual and had apparently been spread by the planting of cuttings and rooted suckers.

RIGHT **Mature wych elm at Glen Moriston, Scottish Highlands, beyond the present range of Dutch elm disease.**

As a result of other DNA studies Gil *et al.* (2004) have suggested that English elm, *U. procera*, may be a single clone. They suggest that cuttings may have been 'transported by the Romans from Italy to the Iberian peninsula, and from there to Britain for the purpose of supporting and training vines. Its highly efficient vegetative reproduction and inability to set seeds have preserved this clone unaltered for 2,000 years'. Goodall-Copestake *et al.* (2004) have made genetic studies of 535 samples of elm across Europe (of which, however, only 20 were from the UK) and recognised two indigenous species: *U. glabra*, and *U. minor* Mill. emend. Richens *sensu latissimo* (which is taxonomists' jargon for 'in the widest sense'). Under this interpretation of the extremely variable *U. minor* (which would now include both *U. plotii* and *U. procera*) there were both suckering strains and strains reproducing by

seed – all very complicated! *U. minor* and *U. procera* are therefore thought to be part of a genetic continuum, but are not clearly defined species. The others, such as Plot's elm, Exeter elm and Huntingdon elm are now believed to be genetic 'sports' or planted cuttings from individual and unique parent trees.

Without the benefit of genetic evidence, botanists have generally used three main groups of elms identifiable in the field, and in the account below this tripartite division is used, based largely on features of their leaves. *U. minor* has smaller leaves (less than 7 cm/2¾ in long), which are slightly rough on the upper surface, while those of both *U. procera* and *U. glabra* feel like sandpaper. *U. procera* produces pollen but not viable seed, while *U. minor* flowers and may produce viable seed very occasionally. Both *U. minor* and *U. procera* sucker profusely and generally occur as clonal groups.

On the other hand, wych elm, *U. glabra*, does not sucker, but does produce fertile flowers which are largely wind pollinated although some insect pollination is possible, and it produces abundant viable seed (less in the north). It is regarded as a native tree that occurs naturally in woods and beside streams, especially in hilly districts, while the natural disribution of *U. minor* (as a native tree) is probably restricted to East Anglia, the East Midlands and the easternmost part of Kent.

English elm, *U. procera*, was widely propagated and planted, and because of its viable pollen it may very occasionally have hybridised with the native wych elm.

Elms are predominantly lowland trees, growing 40 m (130 ft) tall in some places on deep, well-drained soils. Although English elm does grow successfully up to an altitude of 460 m (1,500 ft) in Derbyshire. Wych elm is more stress-tolerant and is found in mountain valleys in Scotland and ascending to 400 m (1,300 ft) in Yorkshire and in montane scrub as high as 530 m (1,700 ft) in Atholl, while it also thrives as a component of coastal scrub on exposed cliffs as far north as Mull and Skye.

Wych elm flowers are purplish-red, about 2 cm (¾ in) long (see p.7), and appear in bunches in February or March, well

OPPOSITE A fine pair of mature wych elms at Lochinver, western Scotland.

RIGHT Wych elm in coastal scrub on Lismore Island, Argyll.

before the leaves. The flowers have two styles surrounded by four or five stamens with purple anthers. The fruits are just over 2 cm (¾ in) long, consisting of a single seed surrounded by a continuous membrane, making possible effective wind dispersal. Heavy crops (mast years) occur only every three years or so, but normally most of the seeds disappear, probably eaten by mice and birds. The seedlings that do emerge are more shade-tolerant than ash, and tend to grow in ashwoods and with lime in ancient woodlands.

Historically, elms were much coppiced and regularly pollarded (known as 'doddle trees' in Cambridgeshire). In the Yorkshire Dales at least, and possibly elsewhere on poor soils, this was done to provide fodder for animals in hard winters (Spray, 1981), although the practice began to decline around the beginning of the nineteenth century (Fleming, 1997) when root vegetables may have replaced the dried elm leaves as winter fodder. In some places, enormous old pollards could still be seen in the early 1990s, such as in upper Swaledale (by 2008 only one or two dead stumps remained). Fleming estimated that most of these old hulks dated back to the fifteenth or sixteenth centuries, the biggest ones possibly earlier, the oldest being over 600 years old when they died.

Drawings from the nineteenth century suggest that enormous elm pollards of great age dotted the country, many of them well known. Lees (1874a, b) claimed that 'the Wych elm has powers of endurance almost equal to that of the oak', although he admits that it does age and start to decay 'earlier than any tree except the willow'. Among the greatest examples he saw were Piff's Elm, near Tewkesbury; the Rotherwas Elm, near Hereford; and the three 'monstrous boles' of an elm in Oakley Park in Cirencester. He claims that farmers in some places used great hollow elms as storerooms or even pigsties. There is nothing left of these great trees today, although as recently as 2009 one or two old hulks could still be found in Swaledale.

Dutch elm disease and the elm decline

Until the 1960s fine English elms dominated many lowland landscapes, but then they were progressively attacked by a particularly virulent disease carried by bark beetles, *Scolytus scolytus* and *S. multistriatus*. There had been epidemics of Dutch elm disease (not its country of origin but first investigated by Dutch scientists) in the 1920s and 1930s, which killed many trees. The pathogen was identified as a parasitic fungus, *Ophiostoma ulmi*, previously known as *Ceratocystis ulmi*, which grew threads inside the trunk of the tree resulting in a clogging of the vessels that transport water up

ABOVE **A mature elm infected by Dutch elm disease, Camden Road, London 2009. The tree has since died.**

the trunk from the roots. This causes desiccation and subsequent death of the leaves.

In the early 1970s a new strain of the disease arrived from North America on imported logs. It spread rapidly, killing 100% of trees in many places, and in less than a decade most of the English elms had

LEFT The last great elm hulk, Marrick Priory, Swaledale.

In recent years a fungus, *Phomopsis oblonga,* has invaded the bark of dying wych elms, and may begin limiting the populations of bark beetles. Some strains of the very variable *U. minor* have proved resistant to Dutch elm disease, so that in some places such as East Anglia occasional groups of full-grown elms survive today. In the light of this recent experience researchers have reassessed historical data and the pollen record; several earlier epidemics of disease that look suspiciously like that caused by *O. novo-ulmi* were recorded in the nineteenth century (Rackham, 1986). Much further back, around 5,800 years ago, the pollen record throughout northwest Europe shows a major reduction in elm, referred to as the Elm Decline, coinciding with evidence of the rapid expansion of cereal crops and an agricultural way of life. Some writers have suggested that the reduction of elm in the pollen record meant that the trees were cut down, but as Rackham points out, this is unlikely; it would have required such a vast collective effort by humans that it is an insufficient explanation. Pollen production may have been reduced because of pollarding and coppicing, but a major episode of a viral infection imported from Europe is a more likely major factor in the Elm Decline.

The uses of elm

For over 5,000 years elms have been felled for timber and coppiced, mainly for fuel in many parts of the country. The earliest Neolithic trackways, such as the Sweet Track in Somerset dating from 3,806 BC (dated precisely from the oak planks), provide evidence of the early use of elm timber wood, although it was only a minor component of that construction. Elm wood is of medium weight (that of *U. glabra* is denser) and strength, but it distorts easily and has to be seasoned carefully. It bends well ('wych' comes from Middle English 'wyche', which means pliant; nothing to do with witches), and has high tensile strength at right-angles to the grain, resisting strains that split other timbers. Giraldus Cambrensis, a twelfth-century writer, claimed that the Welsh shortbow was always made of elm, and it was used as an alternative to yew even in England.

In former times elm was second only to oak as a construction timber, English elm being particularly durable for exterior use, especially in wet conditions. Before metal pipes were made, elm was one of the few timbers used for water-pipes since, according to

been killed. Investigations showed that a different fungus, *O. novo-ulmi*, was responsible, spread mostly by the larger beetle, *S. scolytus*, and attacking all native elms, although *U. glabra* with its greater genetic diversity and normal reproduction by seed was less affected than the others. The fact that the English elm was clonal meant that whole groups of trees were vulnerable to the pathogen (as was the potato in Ireland when late-blight caused the total destruction of the crop). In the 1970s it was estimated that altogether more than 25 million elms died. As the disease did not kill the roots, the profusely suckering elms did survive, some of them since growing large enough to produce (sterile) flowers before succumbing again to the disease. In some woods where elm must have predominated as recently as 50 years ago, all that remains now are thickets of saplings. Even in some of the worst affected areas some individual trees still survive – these are presumably from more resistant elm clones.

Grigson, 'the portion in the well did not decay easily, the portion above the ground did not split when the water froze'. Many towns had elm water mains, including Bristol, Southampton, Liverpool, Hull and Edinburgh. In some places straight-trunked elms (with the side branches removed) were grown specifically for this purpose (Coleman, 2009). Old elm water-pipes survive in some places and are occasionally disinterred during building works. Elm piles were laid under bridges and buildings, including those under the old Waterloo Bridge, and elm wood was used for coastal groynes, canal engineering (such as locks) etc.

While shipbuilding employed mostly oak, elm wood, when available, was much in demand for keels, rudders and the bottoms of canal barges, in the fishing industry for trawler boards, in the countryside for the hubs of cart-wheels, and also for coffins. Elm was formerly used a great deal for furniture, such as settee frames and sculpted Windsor chair-seats, and in decorative turnery, although unseasoned wood is sometimes attacked by the furniture beetle, *Anobium punctatum*.

Folklore

Ironically, the introduced 'English' elms were seen as part of the quintessentially English landscape, East Anglian elms appearing in numerous paintings of traditional country scenes such as those of Constable and Cotman. In fact, not everyone was convinced of the tree's beauty; there was 'a certain enlarged weediness about the elm', which 'lacked a strong character except in full foliage'

(Grigson), and unfortunately 'would accompany man on the way to meet his Maker' (in an elm-wood coffin).

Vickery relates country rhymes from Warwickshire and from Guernsey suggesting that the first appearance of elm leaves indicated the time for sowing barley, although which species of elm this refers to is not clear. In Bedfordshire, for 30 or 40 years in the mid-nineteenth century, an elm planted at the burial site of a celebrated murderer was visited by sufferers of ague, who would nail strands of hair or nail-clippings to the tree (Vickery, 1995).

The bark of elm was boiled in water to produce a treatment for burns and boiled in milk to treat jaundice, and the inner bark was chewed to cure a sore throat. Richens dismisses them all as ineffective, but harmless. In some places elm is associated with the Feast of the Ascension and in some Staffordshire villages elm branches are still occasionally carried around in procession as what was probably the relic of an ancient fertility rite. At Lichfield, elm boughs were used to 'beat the bounds' of the parish until the demise of local elms forced a substitution.

Elm in the ecosystem

Clearly the significance of elms in the ecosystem has been greatly reduced by Dutch elm disease and many of the plant-feeding invertebrates and fungi specifically associated with elm (66 out of a total of 284 invertebrates) have disappeared or become very scarce indeed. Less choosy species have moved to other trees. Both the two bark beetles (*Scolytus* spp.) have apparently become virtually extinct in large parts of the country (although isolated elms continue to

LEFT Water-pipes made from straight wych elm trunks, recently excavated in Edinburgh.

contract the disease), and the balance of beetle/pathogen/tree is unstable, although there is always a possibility that genetic resistance to the disease may develop, or that a virus strain may affect the fungus causing its effect to decline. Commercial claims about disease-resistant elms are not yet proven.

Unlike beech, birch and oak, elms are not associated with ectomycorrhizal fungi, which produce the characteristic fruiting bodies such as boletes and milkcaps. Elms are associated with microscopic fungi known as arbuscular (branching or shrub-like) endomycorrhizae, which penetrate the cells of the rootlets.

When so many elms died over a relatively short period, several dead-wood fungi became very common, although they have since declined. They include edible species such as the common oyster mushroom, *Pleurotus ostreatus*, and the dark, orange-brown velvet shank, *Flammulina velutipes*, the poplar bracket, *Oxyporus populinus*, and the giant bracket, *Rigidoporus ulmarius*. One fruiting body of the giant bracket near Kew Gardens reached 4.8 m (16 ft) in circumference and 316 kg (696 lb) in weight, thereby gaining entry to the *Guinness Book of Records*.

Two celebrated butterflies use elm as their main foodplant and have been affected by the disappearance of elm trees. The large tortoiseshell, *Nymphalis polychloros*, has disappeared altogether and is now extinct in Britain, but the white-letter hairstreak, *Strymonidia w-album*, has made a successful recovery by adapting to live on the leaves of elm suckers. The white-spotted pinion moth, *Cosmia diffinis*, is one of several elm-feeding species which has suffered a major decline.

Caterpillars of at least 10 species of tiny moths (micro-lepidoptera) mine the leaves of elm, e.g. *Stigmella lemniscella*, as does the tiny elm flea weevil *Orchestes alni*. Aphids colonise the leaves and curl them over; the elm-currant aphid, *Eriosoma ulmi*, on *U. minor*, and a related species, *E. patchiae*, on wych elm. Other aphids produce spectacular galls, including *Eriosoma lanuginosum*, which causes a large pouch-gall to develop from a whole leaf; this turns grey at first, and then bright red or purple. A gall-mite (*Tetraneura ulmi*) produces a fig-gall on *U. glabra*; infestations may be so heavy as to result in thousands of these small growths on the foliage, while the leaves of *U. procera* are commonly covered with pustules caused by the gall-mite *Eriophyes ulmi* (now called *Aceria ulmicola*). The leaves appear to survive these attacks; perhaps heavy

LEFT AND ABOVE Lethal damage caused by infection from the galleries or tunnels excavated by the elm bark beetle, *Scolytus scolytus*.

TOP The edible velvet shank fungus, *Flammulina velutipes*, growing on a dead elm.

infestations of mites protect the leaves from other defoliators? Certainly larger caterpillars are rarely found on galled leaves.

Wych elm seeds are known to be predated by birds such as greenfinch, and probably also by mice. The trunks of mature elms may have rot-pockets that provide an important habitat for saproxylic flies. Seepages or 'sap-runs' are common and the bark can develop a 'wet breadcrumb' consistency on which the larvae of these species depend, but, as with other insects associated with elm, these have now become very rare. Historically, elms were also one of the most frequent host trees for the stag beetle, *Lucanus cervus*, now most commonly associated with ash. Elm bark is fissured, rough, water-retentive and naturally alkaline, making it a good habitat for lichens; over 200 species have been recorded.

Ecologically, elms compete well on deep, well-drained soils, dominating and overtopping most other trees, although not so exclusively as beech or hornbeam as they do not cast such dense shade. However, their susceptibility to disease makes these statements provisional. Since the epidemic of Dutch elm disease, English elm has been restricted to a limited role of recurrent competitor in gaps, new saplings arising from the extensive live root system. Wych elm competes well with other trees even under environmental stress such as in exposed, cold situations and when subjected to salt spray, but is never abundant in woods.

TOP LEFT The elm leaf-bug, *Riboutiana ulmi*. It uses its piercing mouthparts to suck elm sap.

ABOVE LEFT Mine of the tiny moth, *Stigmella lemniscella*. The caterpillar is green.

LEFT Massed pustule-galls on elm leaves caused by the mite, *Aceria ulmicola*.

FIELD MAPLE *Acer campestre* L.

Maple family: Aceraceae

Also known as: maple, English maple, whistle-wood, dog oak, 'oak', or ketty-keys. It is called gweniolen (Welsh), but there are no names for the tree in Irish or Gaelic. Derivative place names include Maplestead (Essex) and Mappledore (Wiltshire).

Biological Flora: Jones (1945b)

Field maple is a common, medium-sized tree, a late arrival compared with most of our native trees. It is a lowland species found in woodlands and hedgerows throughout England and Wales, increasingly rare north of Shropshire and Lincolnshire, but occurring as far north as Northumberland, particularly on base-rich soils. It is often associated with ash and hazel, preferring drier soils than ash. It is thought to be introduced in both Ireland and Scotland, where it is scarce, but has been successfully planted as far north as Durness on the north coast of Sutherland.

Field maple can reach 17 m (56 ft) in the open, and 25 m (82 ft) in woodland, but is better known when coppiced or pollarded. Ancient maple coppice stools up to 4.5 m (15 ft) across have been reported by Rackham. Old maple pollards can be found at ancient wood-pasture sites such as Hatfield Forest. Field maple is fairly shade-tolerant and often occurs as an understorey tree, more rarely

in pure stands; it is not a pioneer species and is not present in the early stages of establishment of woodland. In autumn the foliage turns a bright yellowish-green. As it resists pollution well, it has been (and still is) planted in towns, but does not do well at coastal sites as it is susceptible to salt spray.

BELOW LEFT **Mature field maple; Great Missenden, Buckinghamshire.**

BELOW **An aged field maple growing in an abandoned hedge near Henley-on-Thames.**

ABOVE LEFT **Field maple flowers.**

ABOVE **An eighteenth century harpsichord, traditionally made from field maple wood.**

The paired leaves are five-lobed with blunt ends, downy when young and dark green when mature. The hermaphrodite flowers are small and pale yellowish, with five sepals and petals, and eight stamens. Some trees have only male flowers, but others have been observed to change sex over several seasons. Various small insects such as danceflies, *Empis* spp., and small bees, *Andrena* and *Halictus* spp., pollinate the flowers. Maple is a mast tree; seed production varies from year to year. The paired fruits are winged samaras (similar to sycamore keys only smaller), and vary in quantity.

Field maple seeds need prolonged chilling to break their dormancy and do not germinate for 18 months. Seedling viability is variable and seedlings 'seem to be rather uncommon' (Jones, 1945). Once established the seedlings are shade- and drought-tolerant (even surviving under beech), and apparently are not very palatable to mammalian browsers.

The uses of maple

Maple is much used for hedging, and has long been coppiced for firewood and for fencing stakes. Maple wood is very even-grained, heavier and darker than sycamore. It has long been popular with wood-turners (bowls, spoons and cutlery handles) and cabinet-makers, especially for very fine articles as it can be worked so thin as to be almost transparent. According to Evelyn, 'The timber is far superior to beech'. Since it takes a high polish, it is also an excellent veneer wood. It has good sound qualities and is used for musical instruments such as harpsichords, drums, violins, guitars and double bass. It was traditionally used for the backs of violins (though not from maple grown in England). In ancient times, maple wood was used for making harps, examples of which have been found in Saxon barrows, including at the Sutton Hoo ship treasure, near Woodbridge, Suffolk. Like many members of the maple family, *A. campestre* produces sweet sap in the spring, which can be used for making wine, maple syrup or sugar. The wood burns well and produces fine charcoal.

Folklore

Culpeper recommended decoctions of the leaves or the bark for 'strengthening the liver', but otherwise there are few medicinal uses or folk beliefs associated with field maple. Like alder, maple seems to have 'raised little emotion' among country people. In some areas (Suffolk, Nottinghamshire) in places where oak was scarce, maple leaves were worn on Oak Apple Day; consequently in these places field maple was known as 'oak' or 'oak-apple' (Vickery, 1995).

Maple in the ecosystem

Maple seeds are eaten by mice, and the seedlings are devoured by snails. Few macrofungi are known to be associated with the living tree. Conspicuous white patches on the trunk are caused by a parasitic fungus, *Dendrothele acerina*, while a powdery mildew, *Sawadaea bicornis,* causes pale blotches on the leaves.

A feature of maple that often puzzles observers is the occurrence of the lines of small holes in the trunk that look as if they have been drilled by a draughtsman; in fact these are caused by the sap-sucking activities of woodpeckers (which also attack lime, elm and occasionally oak trees).

A total of 86 plant-feeding invertebrates have been recorded as associated with field maple, which puts it in the middle range of tree species (see Table 4). Some are specific to *A. campestre*, while others are also found on the related sycamore, *A. pseudoplatanus*. Among those restricted to field maple are several species of aphid e.g. *Drepanosophum acerinum*, several leaf-mining micro-moths and a small leaf-mining sawfly, *Heterarthrus healyi*. Masses of tiny red pustules or nail-galls are often seen on the leaves. These are caused by a mite, *Aceria aceriscampestris*, while the sparser yellow or reddish rounded galls in the angle of veins are caused by another species, *A. macrochelus*. Moths whose caterpillars feed on maple leaves include the reddish plumed prominent, *Ptilophora plumigera*, and the mocha, *Cyclophora annulata*. One very rare wood-boring beetle, *Gastrallus immarginatus*, is associated with field maple trees in Worcestershire.

The ecological strategy of field maple is intermediate; it is a specialised competitor on drier, base-rich and neutral clay soils. The seedlings, like the tree itself, are fairly shade- and drought-tolerant, and do not establish well outside woodland.

TOP Pustules caused by the mite, *Aceria aceriscampestris*.

ABOVE Scarce plumed prominent moth, *Ptilophora plumigera*, whose caterpillars occur on field maple and sycamore in chalk areas of southeastern England.

LEFT Stool of old field maple coppice at Hatfield Forest, Essex. The rows of marks on the bark are caused by sapsucking woodpeckers.

ABOVE Mine of the tiny sawfly, *Heterarthrus wuestneii*, frequently found on field maple leaves.

81

HAWTHORNS *Crataegus* ssp.

Rose family: Rosaceae

Hawthorn *Crataegus monogyna* Jacq.

Midland hawthorn *Crataegus laevigata* (Poiret) DC

Also known as: may or may-bush, whitethorn, quickthorn or quicken, bread-and-cheese tree, moon-flower, sgeach gheal (Irish), sgitheach and droigheann (Gaelic), draenen wen (Welsh). The fruits are known as haws, aglets, cuckoo's beads, butter-haw, heathen-berry, pixie pears, cuckoo's beads or chucky cheese.

Hawthorn is one of the most widespread and ubiquitous trees in Britain and Ireland, capable of reaching 15 m (49 ft) in woodland but more usually occurring as a small tree or large shrub up to about 8 m (26 ft). The common hawthorn is a tree of hedges (overwhelmingly the commonest woody component of hedges, mainly due to planting) and woodland edges especially on base-rich soils, and surviving as a shrub under heavy shade. Midland hawthorn (or woodland hawthorn), less spiny and with simpler leaves, is a somewhat shade-tolerant woodland understorey tree.

BELOW **Old hawthorn growing on the limestone pavement above Kirby Stephen.**

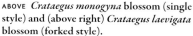

ABOVE *Crataegus monogyna* blossom (single style) and (above right) *Crataegus laevigata* blossom (forked style).

RIGHT Hawthorn shieldbug, *Acanthosoma haemorrhoidalis.*

It is common in southern and eastern England, especially on heavy clay soils, but scarcer in Wales, Scotland and Ireland.

Common hawthorn can be extremely slow-growing in exposed situations or when otherwise stressed; at present it ascends to 610 m (2,000 ft) in Cumbria, tenaciously surviving possibly for centuries on rocky cliffs. Although the twigs are spiny, the foliage is grazed by deer and rabbits but is not very palatable to cattle. In grassland, hawthorn saplings may establish themselves and survive for many years while being constantly nibbled; as with blackthorn, a (deer) browse line is often visible on hawthorn at the edge of thickets. When grazing pressure is then reduced it may begin to grow vigorously. The seedlings are not shade-tolerant so hawthorn apparently cannot grow through covering vegetation as ash and birch will.

Hawthorn flowers first appear in late April or early May (i.e. before the woodland canopy has fully emerged), with *C. laevigata* blossom (and leaves) preceding those of *C. monogyna* by up to two weeks. In both cases the flowers give off a heavy fragrance with a hint of fish (due to the presence of trimethylamine), which attracts a wide range of insects including flies. In the wild the petals tend to be white to pale-pink in colour, while horticulturalists have tended to select varieties with pink or even red flowers. The two species are distinguished largely by the structure of the flowers, *C.*

monogyna generally having, as the name suggests, a single style, and *C. laevigata* (usually) having two styles. Neither is self-fertile.

The red fruits or haws ripen by late August or September and may stay on the tree until the following spring. Haws vary considerably in size, and are one of the most important bird fruits, for both migrants and residents. Snow and Snow recorded individual hawthorn trees being defended by pairs of mistle thrushes. As with other bird-dispersed fruits, hawthorn seeds probably germinate better after passing through an avian gut. Haws are also attractive to seed-eaters like finches, which destroy the seeds. Haws are eaten by small mammals such as voles, mice and squirrels, which probably destroy most of the seeds.

The seeds require chilling (overwintering) to break their hard-coat dormancy, followed by warm moist conditions, and they generally do not germinate for at least 18 months; however, no persistent seed bank has been reported. In orthodox ecological theory (Tansley, 1939) hawthorn is important in the early stage of a natural succession from grassland to secondary woodland. By protecting the seedlings of trees such as oak from grazing, common hawthorn contributes to the establishment of woodland, but under conditions allowing a normal succession it is subsequently shaded out as a full woodland canopy develops (but see blackthorn, p.56). On disturbed ground such as abandoned arable fields hawthorn can form pure stands, which can last for decades, there being no immediate source of other tree seeds. When full-grown, hawthorn has a characteristically dense, tangled crown, much used by nesting birds from finches to hawks.

The uses of hawthorn

Hawthorn was widely planted for hedges, especially during the Enclosures about two hundred years ago, and in some places has been pollarded (probably for firewood) in wood-pasture. Some ancient pollards can be seen at Hatfield Forest.

Like other rosaceous wood, hawthorn is hard and tough, the scientific name *Crataegus* being derived from an Ancient Greek word κράτος τό, meaning strength. Yellowish to pink in colour, it is used for fine work of various kinds, including veneer and cabinet work, and for making fine boxes, tool handles, mill-wheel teeth, mallets and the ribs of small boats. Because it is so fine-grained and even, it has been used for fine wood-engraving. It also burns well and makes excellent charcoal.

For centuries haws and hawthorn flowers have been used to produce a variety of jellies, wines, liqueurs, ketchups and teas. The haws are known in some places as pixie pears, cuckoo's beads or chucky cheese; dried and ground-up they have been used to adulterate flour. 'Bread and cheese' (the fresh leaves) is still eaten by children in some parts of England and makes a palatable addition to a salad; the name may date from a famine in 1752, when it is said that colliers in the Bristol area were reduced to eating hawthorn leaves from the hedgerows.

Medicinally, bark, flowers and fruits are astringent, containing several flavonoids including crataegin and quercetin. Culpeper recommends pounded or bruised and boiled seeds as a cure for various internal pains, probably because both seeds and the dried flowers have the property of reducing blood pressure. Compote of fresh fruits can be used as a cure for diarrhoea. Hawthorn tea made from either dried leaves or berries is still available commercially and is recommended by herbalists for various heart conditions.

Folklore

Hawthorn or may has perhaps more connections with ancient beliefs and traditions than almost any other tree. From research by the Folklore Society conducted in the 1980s in England, nearly a quarter of all reports of 'unlucky' plants referred to hawthorn, more than twice as many as any other tree. Hawthorn is thought to have powerful supernatural associations (for good or evil) in many cultures.

As the name suggests may blossom is strongly associated with May Day (Beltaine), the farming festival when both fertility and production are thought to need protection. The full blooming of hawthorn blossom at the beginning of May in the Gregorian calendar (May Day was on what is now 12 May) used to signify the beginning of summer. In some places the May Queen, garlanded with the blossom still parades at village festivals.

Throughout the country areas of Ireland hawthorn is still believed to be the home of the fairies or the 'little people', and hawthorn (or quickthorn) is the most frequent tree found guarding a holy well (Lucas, 1963). Pilgrims hang items of clothing on such trees when taking the holy water – in some cases to offer thanks for healing. In some parts of Ireland farmers erect a May bush of hawthorn by the farm gate to protect their dairy herd. In other parts of Ireland May boughs (of hawthorn) are erected outside houses, encouraging the fairies to bless the house at such a sensitive season.

In both Ireland and England many country people consider it is unlucky to bring may flowers into a house (possibly because it attracts flies?). But then in other parts of England hawthorn blossom may be deliberately brought inside, to cure sickness. Historically, some of these traditions have been suppressed by the Church, while in other cases the traditions were Christianised, or just accepted as harmless. In England objections to May traditions in the eighteenth century were more political: overt interest in 'the Virgin Mary's tree' aroused the suspicion of covert Roman Catholicism and therefore of political dissent.

Hawthorn in the ecosystem

A characteristic fungus found growing under hawthorn is the rather phallic-shaped fruiting body of the ectomycorrhizal thimble morel, *Verpa conica*, which has a white stem and a dark brown cap. The tiny orange cup-shaped fruiting bodies of the parasitic *Monilinia johnsonii* are rarely found, although in spring the greyish wilting of leaves caused by this fungus is often seen. Two rusts, *Gymnosporangium* spp., are also common, and hawthorn is susceptible to fireblight, *Erwinia*

The Glastonbury thorn (and the Appleton thorn)

At Glastonbury, there are several trees called the Holy Thorn. The original tree is supposed to have grown from Joseph of Arimathea's stave: he arrived in ad 63 and it is claimed that he thrust it into the ground on Wearyall Hill above Glastonbury. It sprouted and grew into a tree, which bloomed 'miraculously' near Christmas, as well as normally in the spring. (Similar stories elsewhere claim other sacred trees as having 'arisen from a saint's staff stuck into the ground' etc.) The phenomenon was also connected with Christ's crown of thorns, even though *Crataegus monogyna* does not occur naturally in Palestine. Successive trees have been derived from cuttings. One stands in the grounds of the ruined abbey, another outside the parish church. The one on Wearyhill was unfortunately vandalised in late 2010, although the stump is sprouting vigorously. From the tree outside the parish church, the unseasonal flowers are clipped and sent to the Queen to decorate her table at Christmas. There are other specimens at Wells, at Bath and at Appleton Thorn in Cheshire, and now at various arboreta. At Appleton, the

tree is claimed to be a descendant of an original cutting taken from Glastonbury to Cheshire about 1178 by Adam de Dutton, a Crusader knight who made a pilgrimage to Glastonbury to give thanks for his safe return from the Holy Land. At Appleton an annual 'bawning' (decoration) ceremony takes place on the third Saturday in June every year. The Glastonbury thorn is featured in *Spirit of Trees*, No.5.

ABOVE A holy thorn, outside Glastonbury parish church, grown from a cutting like all other examples of the tree.

amylovora, although it is resistant to honey fungus, *Armillaria* spp. The foliage of hawthorn is particularly palatable to insects (over 400 invertebrates are recorded of which just 58 (14.5%) are restricted to *Crataegus* spp.), especially caterpillars (233 species recorded). In the southern half of Britain among the most characteristic are the gregarious, silk-spinning larvae of the hawthorn webber moth, *Scythropia crataegella*. At least 25 micro-moths are known to mine the leaves, as does the tiny weevil *Ramphus oxyacanthae*. While heavy insect infestations of the foliage are sometimes seen, hawthorn has been shown to be able to change its leaf chemistry in response to damage, and by this means discourage further insect attack (Edwards and Wratten, 1985).

The commonest galls on hawthorn are those caused by mites; the green-becoming-brown leaf pocks by *Aceria crataegi* and the leaf margin rolls by *Phyllocoptes goniothorax*. The hawthorn button-top gall, which affects the terminal shoot is caused by the gall-midge *Dasineura crataegi*. Larvae of several insects are commonly found in the developing berries, including the hawthorn berry fly, *Anomoia purmunda*, and a tiny weevil (*Neocoenorrhinus aequaticus*). Other insects frequently found on hawthorn include

a spectacular longhorn beetle, *Anaglyptus mysticus*, the large hawthorn sawfly, *Trichiosoma tibiale,* and the hawthorn shieldbug, *Acanthosoma haemorrhoidale*.

The ecological strategy of common hawthorn is a stress- and disturbance-tolerant competitor. Midland hawthorn is intermediate; it is shade-tolerant competing well as a long-lived understorey tree in woodland.

RIGHT A medieval woodcut showing the Holy Thorn and Joseph of Arimathea.

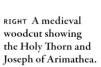

HAZEL *Corylus avellana* L.

> **Birch family:** Betulaceae
>
> **Also known as:** hale, hasketts, nuttall, woodnut, hales, hezzel, coll (Irish), calltunn (Gaelic), colleen (Welsh). In ancient Irish law one of seven noble trees.

Hazel was one of the first group of trees to spread through Britain and Ireland after the last glacial period, preceded only by juniper, birch, aspen, some willows and pine. Since then it has spread to all parts of Britain and Ireland including the Northern Isles of Scotland. Hazel favours base-rich soils, and often forms pure stands. These can still be seen in parts of England and on some coastal slopes in the west of Scotland. It ascends to around 640 m (2,000 ft) at Atholl, and forms a low scrub vegetation on exposed limestone, such as on the Burren in the west of Ireland. It is also common in coastal scrub on exposed slopes, such as those on the west coast of Mull.

Hazel grows as a small, relatively short-lived understorey tree to 12 m (40 ft) in oak and ashwoods, but is rarely allowed to reach its full height as it has been coppiced nearly everywhere. Without cutting, hazel trees live to around 100–150 years, but coppice stools over 1,000 years old are known. Hazel is sensitive to shading and neglected stools stop flowering and die out in dense woodland. In many places hazel stands are now moribund and only where coppicing is maintained continue to thrive.

Hazel responds vigorously to damage and uprooting. It does occasionally produce suckers (in Leigh Woods in Bristol), and on steep slopes it may layer – those branches touching the ground putting out roots. When hazel stools are banked up with soil (plashing), they will produce extra roots and these rooted sections can be removed and used to propagate the tree. This method

BELOW Ancient uncoppiced hazel, Glen Lochay.

dates from medieval times, or possibly earlier. Hazel occurs very frequently in hedges (fourth most frequent after hawthorn, ash and oak), but only rarely (19th most frequent) as an emergent hedge tree.

The bark of hazel is smooth and coppery-brown. The leaves are quite similar in shape to those of the elm, with a pronounced apical point, but they are soft and furry to the touch. They may be purplish when they first appear (loaded with anthocyanins probably to protect against plant-feeding insects), but they then turn green and in autumn can turn bright yellow, often giving hazel woods a spectacular appearance in October and November.

Hazel is wind pollinated. The male flowers are catkins, known in some country areas as 'lambs' tails', appearing earlier than any other flowers and shedding pollen as early as January. The female flowers are very diminutive, with characteristic crimson threads that are the stigma and styles from a tiny group of flowers.

Seed production is variable; hazel is a masting tree (see p.23). This can be deduced by reference to the document dated 1337 quoted by Rackham (1986) from Kimbolton, Cambridgeshire that the annual value of nuts in the park was 6s 8d 'when they happen'. While similarly attractive to small mammals (such as dormice, squirrels and woodpigeons), the seed strategy of hazel is different from that of oak, as the nuts require a deep dormancy to be broken by cold before they will germinate. However, in neglected coppice, even when they do appear, most nuts are taken by predators and few survive to germinate. Hazel does succeed in reproducing itself by seed in damper western woodlands (observation by the author in Cumbria and at Watersmeet, north Devon) but Rackham fears that due to nut predation by grey squirrels this no longer happens in most parts of England; where hazel seedlings do appear they are browsed by deer. From being one of the most abundant trees in Britain a few millennia back, over much of England the future of hazel as a naturally regenerating tree is now uncertain.

The uses of hazel

Hazel rods and sticks, being particularly splittable, pliable and tough, have been used for a wide variety of products since Neolithic times. Even today traditional woodsmen cut hazel coppice for over 100 different items from this tree, including traditional hurdles, thatching spars and net stakes, and to make 'mattresses' to shore up riverbanks and as part of coastal defences (see p.181). Today, where hazel is still coppiced, demand for many traditional products such as hurdles and even thatching spars exceeds supply (see also p.176).

ABOVE Ancient coppiced hazel, Nedd, Sutherland.

Hazel coppicing is now expanding in some areas as a result of increased enthusiasm for countryside skills, and coppicing courses such as those run by the Bill Hogarth Memorial Apprenticeship Trust (BHMAT) in north Lancashire are oversubscribed (Oaks and Mills, 2010). Hazel-nuts were a major food in prehistoric times and are still very popular; hazel-nut butter (like peanut butter) is available from health shops today.

Folklore

In Ireland, hazel was known as the Tree of Knowledge, while in medieval England it was a symbol of fertility. According to Grigson, the hazel is a magical tree here and throughout most of Europe, and is 'protected by elves'. It is the sacred tree of the Celts; in medieval England it was a symbol of fertility. Nine hazel trees surrounded the mythical Connla's Well in Ireland, but this was unusual, as hazel is not among the 10 trees most often found at holy wells in Ireland according to Lucas (1962-3).

Many country beliefs are associated with hazel. A hazel rod (or a bundle of hazel twigs, carried by many Irish emigrants) was thought to protect against evil spirits, 'abduction by fairies', and (outside Ireland) snakes. In some places it was believed that a hazel twig or cluster of (ideally three) nuts was lucky and, if tied to a horse's mane, would protect the animal from magic. Hazel is claimed to be the proper wood for making a wand, but the catkins are unlucky and should not be brought into the house. Hazel hurdles keep sheep in and at the same time allegedly protect them from magic. Hazel-nuts are carried as charms or to ward off rheumatism ('an elf-shot illness'), while in Scotland a double nut (St John's nut) was supposed to have particular power, and was thrown at witches. The use of hazel for dowsing is thought to have been introduced in the sixteenth century by German miners. A hazel rod may indicate not only water, but treasure and even criminals – as a sort of folk lie-detector. Hazel 'nitches' - bundles of sticks - are carried by villagers of Great Wishford on Oak Apple Day (see p.185).

Hazel-nuts had such strong pagan significance that they needed Christianising – this was done in Normandy by giving the nuts (of the closely related species, *C. maxima*) the name Philibert, from an early Christian martyr. Filberts from France have been widely planted in Kent (where they have become known as 'Kent cobs') and elsewhere, replacing the native hazel. In Ireland, times of prosperity were commonly referred to as 'times of many hazel-nuts'. At Kingston upon Thames, hazel-nuts are ceremonially cracked (in church) on Cracknut Sunday (Michaelmas Eve).

The hazel-nut harvest has traditionally been an occasion for carousing and unconstrained behaviour (the more so because it did not happen every year), with crowds invading the woods. The owner of Hatfield Forest complained in 1826 that 'under the pretence of gathering nuts, the idle and disorderly men and women of bad character from Bishop's Stortford... are afforded an opportunity for all sorts of Debauchery' (Rackham, 2006). Various traditional rhymes attest to the dangers of 'nutting' expeditions during which young ladies of virtue could be led astray.

Hazel in the ecosystem

Two ectomycorrhizal fungi are commonly associated with hazel, the fiery milkcap, *Lactarius pyrogalus*, and a small bolete (*Leccinum pseudoscabrum*), which is sometimes mistaken for brown birch bolete, *Leccinum scabrum*. Dead hazel branches are attacked by a number of fungi including the brown blobs of hazel woodwart, *Hypoxylon fusum*, and the spring hazelcup, *Encoelia fufuracea*, and it is known to be associated with the summer truffle, *Tuber aestivum*. Hazel gloves, *Hypocreopsis rhododendri*, a curious brown laminate fungus characteristic of hazel (and blackthorn) is restricted to some Scottish Atlantic coastal woodlands and is sufficiently rare to be the subject of a species action plan under the UK Biodiversity Action Plan (BAP). The pale toothwort, *Lathraea squamaria*, parasitises the roots of hazel.

Hazel catkins provide some of the earliest pollen and are visited by hoverflies such as *Melangyna quadrimaculata*. Later, the young foliage is particularly palatable to browsing mammals (coppice stools have to be protected from deer), but the tree is only moderately attractive to foliage-feeding invertebrates (311 species recorded, of which only 31 are restricted to hazel), perhaps partly protected by its hairy leaves. However, in woods attacked in early spring by defoliating caterpillars such as green oak tortrix, *Tortrix viridana*, or the winter moth, *Operophtera brumata*, even

BELOW Fruiting bodies of the ectomycorrhizal fungus, *Leccinum carpini*, usually associated with hazel.

BELOW Flowers of toothwort, *Lathraea squamaria*, a strange plant with no green leaves that parasitizes the roots of hazel and beech.

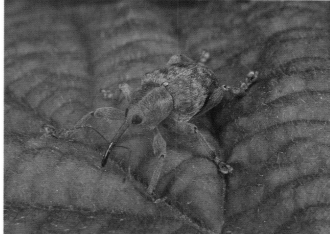

ABOVE Sawfly larvae on hazel foliage, *Croesus septentronialis*.

ABOVE RIGHT Hazel nut weevil, *Curculia nucum*.

RIGHT Second flush hazel leaves after early season defoliation by green tortix caterpillars, *Tortrix viridana*.

hazel is attacked, producing 'shot-holes' in the leaves. Hazel (and alder) are both sometimes seriously defoliated by more selective feeders such as caterpillars of the nut bud moth, *Epinotia tenerara*, which attacks catkins and leaf buds. Caterpillars of the scalloped hazel, *Odontopera bidentata*, are in fact rarely found on hazel, but more often on other broadleaf trees.

Hazel is sometimes infested by a bud-gall similar to big-bud in blackcurrants, caused by a gall-mite, *Phytoptus avellanae*, while other gall-inducers attack both the leaves (a gall-midge: *Contarinia cybelae*) and the male catkins (a mite: *Phyllocoptes coryli*). The developing nuts are attacked by a beautiful small weevil with an extremely long rostrum or beak, *Curculio nucum*, which is sometimes a pest in commercial nut-orchards, although grey squirrels, *Sciurus carolinensis*, are more serious and widespread pests and can destroy the entire crop. The ecological strategy of hazel is intermediate; it is a disturbance-tolerant survivor, growing very fast on rich soil (at the edge of floodplains) without shade, but being overtopped by denser-canopied and taller species where these are present. Hazel is less specialised than either birch (a pioneer) or beech (a competitor) and survives disturbance better than either. In Scotland, Atlantic hazel woodlands are now a conservation priority for the Atlantic Hazel Action Group.

HOLLY *Ilex aquifolium* L.

Holly family: Aquifoliaceae

Also known as: holegn (Anglo-Saxon), holm, cuileann (Gaelic), cuilin (Irish), celyn (Welsh). Place names: Hollinsend (Sheffield), Hollingworth (Cheshire), Hollins Clough (Dovedale) and many hollins. In ancient Irish law one of seven noble trees.

Biological Flora: Peterken and Lloyd (1967)

One of the earliest trees to colonise these islands after the last glacial period (although its pollen occurs only sparsely), holly is found on a wide variety of soils from very acid to slightly alkaline on chalk or limestone up to altitudes of about 600 m (2,000 ft) in the Lake District and up to 776 m (2,500 ft) at Coire of Bonhard in the Scottish Highlands. In most mountain areas scattered trees are a common sight on rocky hillsides. It is found considerably further north in Scandinavia (to 64°N), where it is restricted to the coast as it is, surprisingly, susceptible to hard frost. In southern Europe it is limited by high summer temperatures and is restricted to mountain areas. Holly occurs naturally in oak and hornbeam woodlands, normally growing up to about 10 m (33 ft), while individual trees can reach at least 23 m (75 ft) in some places (e.g. Staverton Thicks, Suffolk).

Holly is also sensitive to both drought and waterlogging but tolerates exposure, wind and salt spray, shade, browsing and frequent cutting (see below). It also survives air pollution well and has been much planted in towns where (prior to the Clean Air Acts in the 1950s) it survived heavy depositions of soot; in some places it even developed a deciduous habit.

Holly trees are dioecious, both male and female trees bearing small white flowers (in late spring) that produce a small amount of nectar, which attracts honeybees, bumblebees and some hoverflies. Some trees have been observed to change sex over time. The trees

BELOW **One of the famous old holly pollards at Stiperstones, Shropshire.**

ABOVE Holly survives salt spray well; this bush is growing on a west coast cliff on Skye near Elgol.

RIGHT Mature holly by a stream at Wrynose Pass, Lake District, arising from a seed probably deposited by a bird.

first flower after about 20 years, but maximum production of berries on the female trees is not until around 40 years, and then heavy fruiting generally occurs only in the mast years. In the New Forest these are thought to coincide with mast years for beech. Although toxic to humans, the red berries, each containing up to four seeds, are an important source of winter food for many small birds as they tend to stay on the tree longer than most other fruits, even after frost.

Individual bushes can be defended by pairs of mistle thrushes in hard winters; in Yorkshire these birds are even known as the 'hollin cocks'.

The seeds only germinate in the second or third year due to dormancy but may germinate sooner if they pass through the gut of birds. The prickly seedlings are very shade-resistant and can survive even under beech. In the wild, holly has proved a useful tree to farmers because of its palatability, its vigorous response to cutting including coppicing, as well as its frequent suckering, layering and the natural rooting of detached twigs

In the south of England native holly is sometimes replaced by a hybrid Highclere holly (*I.* x *altaclerensis*), which results from bird dispersal of seeds from cross-pollination with Canary Islands holly (*I. perado*), introduced by horticulturalists.

Holly is often found in old hedges dating back before 1700, especially in lowland parts of the west of England. At some places such as Dungeness and Epping Forest there are pure holly stands. A general increase in holly within woodland across the south of England has been noted in recent years; this has been interpreted as evidence of increased nutrient levels in the whole ecosystem.

The uses of holly

In spite of their prickly leaves, holly seedlings are grazed by deer, while the upper foliage of mature trees is less spiny and can provide palatable and highly nutritious fodder for domestic animals. Before hay and turnips were used for winter feed (Radley, 1961), holly was coppiced and pollarded for this purpose, especially on the gritstone areas of the southern Pennines (Spray, 1981). During hard winters holly is still pollarded in parts of Cumbria. In medieval times hollies were probably planted for this purpose and traces of these small holly 'hags' or 'hollins' (wood-pastures of holly pollards) 'are a feature of mountain regions' (Rackham, 2006). There are many ancient pollards (both holly and rowan) in wood-pasture at Stiperstones in Shropshire, while at Staverton Thicks some ancient hollies have even shaded out aged oak pollards. With this diverse and localised history in mind, ancient hollies should perhaps always be afforded a high conservation priority.

Holly wood is white, heavy, very fine-grained and even, but it can distort when dried, so it is generally only used for small items, and for situations such as tackle on ships where it is constantly wetted. It is easily worked and has been used for block printing of textiles and by artists for woodcuts. Holly wood stains and polishes well and is prized for inlay work on decorated furniture. It can even be stained black and used as a substitute for ebony. Other products include chess pieces, hammers in harpsichords, billiard cues, walking sticks and even a substitute for box by wood-engravers. In medieval Ireland it was used for chariot shafts, arrows and shillelaghs (cudgels).

Rabbit-breeders use a holly stick for the animals to gnaw; the sap acts as a tonic. When boiled and fermented, the bark makes birdlime, a sticky substance used to trap small birds. Beating with holly or the application of powdered berries are both supposed to be remedies for chilblains. Young leaves contain ilicin, a bitter alkaloid; this is released by boiling and the brew has been recommended as a cure for colds, bronchitis, jaundice and rheumatism. A few berries swallowed whole can act as a strong purgative.

Folklore

There are more varied local folk beliefs and traditions associated with holly than most other native trees (see Howkins, 2001). In Ireland it is regarded as unlucky to cut down a holly tree at any time, as 'it is an abode of fairies'. In Norfolk and Worcestershire hedge-cutters avoid trimming holly. In North Wales it is said that holly is allowed to grow tall in hedgerows to discourage witches (although the National Countryside Survey, 2007 found very few hollies as hedgerow trees in Wales), but 'it should not be grown near the house'. In some parts of Wales it is even said to be 'unwise' to sweep a chimney with a holly branch.

In England, on the other hand, possibly from Anglo-Saxon rather than Celtic tradition, holly *was* planted near houses to ward off lightning, witches and other evils. Holly is claimed to be associated with ancient midwinter (Howkins, 2001), and as long ago as the Middle Ages records show that holly branches were incorporated into Christmas celebrations in both churches and houses, the scarlet berries warding off evil, while the thorns were supposedly a reminder of the Crucifixion. In some parts of England hanging up a holly branch that had previously adorned a church was believed to bring good luck. In much of England and Wales it is considered unlucky to bring holly into the house before Christmas Eve and occasionally (in Derbyshire and Dorset) even to do so at Christmas. In parts of Cornwall holly is still used for a Christmas tree instead of spruce, as was generally the case until the Second World War. In the Forest of Dean it is said that miners would only take an oath on the Bible if they were holding a holly stick at the same time.

Historically, alcohol was often sold at fairs and markets under holly trees (a lucky place perhaps?): the frequency of public houses being called the Hollybush or just The Bush may reflect early licensing arrangements.

Holly in the ecosystem

No particular major fungi are specifically associated with live holly. Holly shoots are sometimes distorted by fasciation, a malformation caused by the bacterium *Corynebacterium fascians*, and the leaves are blackened and killed by attacks of the fungal holly blight,

ABOVE Hollens were small plantations of holly for use as fodder in hard winters; in areas like the Lake District often all that remains is the name.

Phytophthora ilicis, first reported at Crowborough, East Sussex, in 1989. The damage caused is apparently only temporary, and affected branches generally recover.

Apart from birds, few other organisms are associated with holly, only strawberry tree and box having fewer associated invertebrates. The alkaloid ilicin apparently protects holly from most invertebrate foliage-feeders. Of 32 species recorded, just two are restricted to *Ilex*. These two are both common and widespread; the holly leaf-miner fly, *Phytomyza ilicis*, sometimes causes the whole leaf to change colour from dark green to bright yellow or red, while the holly aphid, *Aphis ilicis*, is a black species, which sometimes attacks buds and young leaves causing strong leaf-curl. Holly aphid is often found on hedges where the holly is pruned and has produced young growth out of season.

In May and June the bright, yellowish-green caterpillars of the holly blue butterfly, *Celastrina argiolus*, can be found as far north as the Scottish border feeding on the developing berries. Eggs laid on male trees also hatch into caterpillars, but in the absence of berries are assumed not to survive. The holly blue alternates its generations with a secondary host-plant such as ivy, *Hedera helix*. Larvae of the smaller holly tortrix moth, *Rhopobota naevana*, are found on both holly and blackthorn, while the so-called holly weevil, *Ropalomesites tardyi*, is normally associated with ivy.

The ecological strategy of holly is as a long-lived and extremely shade-tolerant pioneer (even surviving under beech), which has evolved protection against invertebrate attack and to some extent from browsing by mammals. When browsing is reduced, holly can grow into a competitor, being capable of overtopping even oak in some circumstances.

TOP Wolf's milk, *Lycogala epidendrum*, a strange ascomycete fungus growing on a dead holly branch.

MIDDLE Discoloured blotches caused by the holly leaf-miner, *Agromyza ilicis*.

BOTTOM Caterpillars of the holly blue butterfly, *Celastrina argiolus*, are found on holly but more often on ivy.

HORNBEAM *Carpinus betulus* L.

Birch family: Betulaceae

Also known as: Also known as ironwood, hardbeam and oestrwydden (Welsh), but there are no Gaelic or Irish names.

Hornbeam is a relative newcomer to Britain, first appearing in the pollen record only around 5,000 years ago; its natural distribution extends from the southeast of England to Bristol and the southeast corner of Wales and no further north than the Wash. Over much of this area it has apparently replaced lime in woodland during the last few millennia. Hornbeam has also been widely planted elsewhere. Superficially, hornbeam looks like beech, growing up to 32 m (105 ft). The leaves are rougher to the touch, with a serrated edge and (often) paired veins. The trunk tends to be fluted or even

oval in cross-section, and less 'tidy' than beech bark. Hornbeam leaves turn orange-brown in autumn (more uniformly than birch), often giving a beautiful effect in those woods where it is the most abundant tree.

The trees throw as dense a shade as beech, and can effectively stifle all smaller plants except spring flowers such as bluebells and wood anemone. Hornbeam is 'usually dominant, if it occurs at all. It grows on a wide range of soils but predominantly acidic clays' (Rackham). Hornbeam is what he terms 'highly gregarious', not because of suckers like wild cherry, but arising from abundant seed that apparently (among tree seed) has unusually high viability. In Essex hornbeam forms pure stands of woodland.

Hornbeam timber is unsuitable for construction purposes, but it burns well, and so the trees have generally been coppiced (often with oak standards), or pollarded in wood-pasture, and it is quite rare to find full-grown hornbeam trees that have been allowed to grow naturally.

An elegant upright or fastigiate form (probably introduced in the nineteenth century from Europe) is much planted in urban streets. Hornbeam makes an excellent dense hedge, and is little damaged by deer, although in early spring grey squirrels do considerable damage by stripping patches of bark. In ancient woods there are often hornbeams along the edge, possibly grown up from earlier planted hedges. Hornbeam survives uprooting well, continuing to grow from prone trunks.

The flowers are small but numerous in pendent catkins and are wind pollinated. The fruits have membranous wings and hang in untidy bunches before carpeting the ground beneath the trees. The seeds have deep dormancy characteristics and require prolonged chilling before germination. Most seedlings under full canopy last a very short time before they suddenly disappear, possibly eaten by woodmice or slugs, although far more survive in open areas such as recently coppiced areas. Where the seedlings are established they can grow slowly for many years until released by an opening in the canopy due to tree-fall.

The uses of hornbeam

Hornbeam wood is harder than box and exceedingly tough and heavy, blunting saws more quickly than oak, but it is

LEFT **Old hornbeam pollard with witches brooms,** *Taphrina carpini*, **at Hatfield Forest, Essex.**

ABOVE The hornbeam seedling is fairly shade-tolerant, but it requires light to grow more than a metre or so.

RIGHT Grey squirrel damage on a hornbeam tree, Queens Wood, north London.

a poor, irregular timber and not used for construction. It is highly resistant to wear and has been used for industrial flooring as an alternative to maple, and historically for mill cog-wheels, pulleys, mallets, billiard cues, skittles, dominoes and butchers' chopping blocks. It is also still used for musical instruments, especially for the internal mechanism in pianos and harpsichords.

The prime use of hornbeam wood was as firewood. According to John Evelyn, hornbeam wood burns 'like a candle' and in the London area until the mid-twentieth century provided much of the fuelwood and ordinary charcoal for the capital. Abandoned hornbeam coppice can be seen in many woods around London. Hornbeam is popular with horticulturalists as it can be shaped and trained or pleached into decorative hedges and barriers.

Folklore

In Britain there is no record of folkloric associations for hornbeam (which may often be mistaken for beech), but elsewhere in Europe it is associated, somewhat fearfully, with deep and dark forests. Together with oak it is a dominant tree in the densest parts of the Bialowieza Forest in Poland, the only remaining habitat of the European bison, *Bison bonasus.*

Hornbeam in the ecosystem

Macrofungi associated with hornbeam include two ectomycorrhizal species, a milkcap (*Lactarius circellatus*), and a small bolete (*Leccinum pseudoscabrum*, which is also found under hazel), as well as an edible boletid (*Krombholziella carpini*), and the beautiful red, but inedible, *Russula lucteotacta.*

Like birch, hornbeam bears witches' brooms (caused by a fungus, *Taphrina carpini*), sometimes as many as 50 or 60 to a single tree. Several saprotrophic fungi are restricted to the dead wood, including the strange dark pustules of an ascomycete (*Melanconium stromaticum*), 'which exude masses of black spores like lava-flows from tiny volcanoes' (Spooner and Roberts, 2005).

The plant-feeding invertebrate fauna associated with hornbeam is rather limited (155 species of which just 14 (9%) are restricted to hornbeam). In some years the foliage can be badly damaged by common defoliating caterpillars like those of the green oak tortrix, *Tortrix viridana*, or the winter moth, *Operophtera brumata*, but the trees then produce a second (minor) flush of leaves in late June, although growth of the tree is presumably reduced for that season.

Hornbeam leaves are sometimes deformed and swollen along the midrib and other veins by gall-mites (*Aceria tenellus*, *A. macrotrichus*) and gall-midges (*Zygiobia carpini*). At least 15 species of leaf-miners attack hornbeam, of which four are fairly common (*Phyllonorycter esperella*, *P. tenerella*, *Parornix carpinella*

and *Stigmella carpinella*); all of these and the leaf-hopper *Oncopsis carpini* are most frequently found on hornbeam. The small, winged hornbeam fruits are attractive to birds, and when fallen are eaten by small mammals such as woodmice.

The ecological strategy of hornbeam is as a strong competitor. Under good growing conditions of deep, fertile soil and sheltered location it will (eventually) shade out most other species except beech and oak, a characteristic it shows more clearly in the lowlands of central Europe.

BELOW Abandoned ancient hornbeam coppice with a carpet of bluebells in springtime; once the canopy develops very few plants can grow in the heavy shade later in the season.

JUNIPER *Juniperus communis* L.

> **Cypress family:** Cupressaceae
>
> **Also known as:** mountain yew, saffern, safin, aittin, samha (Gaelic), crann fir or aiteal (Irish), merywen (Welsh). Place names: Attadale (Wester Ross), Savanaghanroe (Ulster), Juniper Green (near Edinburgh).
>
> **Biological Flora:** Thomas *et al.* (2007)

One of the first trees (together with birch) to become established after the last glacial period, juniper occurs naturally throughout Britain (including islands as far north as Shetland) and to the west of Ireland, especially in upland areas where it ascends to over 1,000 m (3,200 ft) and is a major component of montane scrub. In some areas juniper occurs in lowland calcareous grassland. The erect or spreading form (subspecies *communis*) can reach 9 m (29½ ft), but more often only grows to 3–4 m (10–13 ft) as a small tree or shrub, while the dwarf form (subspecies *nana*), clings to the ground and is restricted to mountains and rocky places. However, there are intermediate individuals and there may be 'no clear genetic distinction' between these two subspecies (Thomas *et al.*, 2007).

A slow-growing, aromatic evergreen species, juniper occurs naturally on a very wide range of soils from acid to base-rich, and can thrive on pure mineral soils with very low levels of nitrogen. It is also tolerant of extreme environmental stresses (drought, frost and waterlogging), although it is sensitive to high-intensity fire. It has been shown that respiration can continue as low as a temperature of minus 9°C (15.8°F), and photosynthesis down to nearly minus 5°C (23°F) – it is a truly hardy plant!

In some areas like the damp, north-facing slopes of Cumbrian hills juniper can form dense impenetrable masses. It has declined markedly in some areas such as the Sussex Downs, with populations fragmenting or disappearing altogether. There are thought to be several causes including burning, overgrazing of seedlings and shading under secondary woodland.

Juniper is dioecious with separate male and female trees, and is wind pollinated, the males shedding pollen from solitary cylindrical cones. The female flowers have three to six cone scales, which become fleshy, producing a berry-like cone containing up to six seeds. The cones take two to three years to mature (so that different-aged fruits can be found on the same branches) and eventually ripen to rather dry, but still aromatic, blue-black berries. As with other fruits dispersed by birds germination may be stimulated by passing through a bird's gut. The cones are also eaten by mice, which may destroy the seeds. In the soil the seeds may survive for 3–5 years before germinating, but they do not enter a long-term seed bank.

The uses of juniper

Juniper wood burns well with a fragrant smell and it produces almost no smoke; it was much used in former times as the undetectable fuel for illicit distilling. Excess felling for this purpose has been claimed as a reason for the scarcity of juniper in the Highlands of Scotland today. In some places, juniper branches

BELOW **With time and space juniper will slowly grow into a tree, as with this specimen in an extensive juniper stand at Glen Morriston in the Scottish Highlands.**

have been used as natural barbed wire placed along the tops of walls. 'Savin charcoal' was produced in the Lake District to make gunpowder, and the wood is good for smoking fish or meat.

Juniper berries have a sharp tang and are traditionally eaten with venison, or used to make chutneys and liqueurs. When crushed they give gin its flavour, and in the north of England the berries are sometimes used to vary the taste of bread and cakes.

The aromatic characteristic of juniper foliage and berries has been studied in some detail and juniper oil has been shown to contain

BELOW An ancient prostrate juniper growing at around 450m (1,500 ft) on Beinn Eighe, Wester Ross.

at least 149 different chemical constituents, many of them complex turpenes (which cause it to be unpalatable to some mammals but not red deer or rabbits). The oil has long been used for a wide range of medicinal purposes; it is known to have anti-inflammatory, diuretic and antiseptic (bacterial and fungal) properties. Medieval herbalists regarded juniper as a strong counter-poison with which to resist the plague, but its effectiveness for this is not confirmed. Culpeper recommends juniper berries for everything from the bites of venomous beasts to 'wind in any part of the body', and says that they should be taken to 'strengthen the brain'. The Somerset name, 'bastard-killer', derives from the traditional ingestion of the berries to procure an abortion; according to Vickery (1995), juniper pills were still marketed as 'The Lady's Friend' as recently as 1993.

Folklore

In country areas of Scotland and continental Europe, juniper is considered to be a powerful agent against witches and devils; sprigs hung above doorways on the eve of May Day keep away evil, and are burnt on Hallowe'en to ward off evil spirits, but the whole tree is not to be cut down. According to Thistleton-Dyer (1889), it is also supposed that 'juniper is potent in dreams' and that 'it is unlucky to dream of the tree itself, especially if a person be sick'.

BELOW Juniper fruits (not strictly berries) cluster on the stem, slowly changing from green to black during the three seasons they remain on the tree.

Juniper in the ecosystem

Juniper seedlings are suppressed by the winter grazing of deer, rabbits and mountain hares, to the extent that some juniper populations have declined, fragmented and even disappeared. (Juniper is relatively unpalatable like pine, but will be browsed in winter when nothing else is available.) Successful recruitment of young plants is limited to the periodic absences of rabbits (due to epidemics of myxomatosis), and deer fencing. Other measures to exclude browsing animals are being used at some Scottish sites. In the absence of browsing animals juniper 'is a characteristic invader of pasture', surviving in open woodland but not tolerating heavy shade.

In Europe ectomycorrhizae have occasionally been reported. In Britain and Ireland endomycorrhizae are more common, but there are no confirmed associations. Spectacular rashes of bright orange fruiting bodies like a line of swollen cornflakes are sometimes seen on the stems in Scotland and the north of England. These are the fruiting bodies of a parasitic rust, *Gymnosporangium clavariiforme*. A second fungus *Phomopsis juniperovora* causes needle and shoot dieback; originally found in America in 1920 it was first recorded in the UK in 1969.

In Scotland and the north of England juniper is widely dispersed by small birds for which the berries are an important source of winter food. In Upper Teesdale, Gilbert (1980) found that many bird droppings contained juniper seeds, although the species of bird involved had not been observed. Elsewhere in Europe, fieldfares and waxwings in particular take juniper fruits; the German name for fieldfare is Wacholderdrossel or 'juniper thrush'. Snow and Snow (1988), (working in the Chilterns) only observed juniper berries to be taken by thrushes and on one occasion by a robin.

A total of 64 invertebrates are recorded from juniper of which an unusually high proportion (30, or 47%) are restricted to the tree, and most of the others only occur on pine or yew. Among the juniper specialists are four gall-midges, one of which *Oligotrophus juniperinus* causes the small, bulbous 'whooping-cough-gall'. Among the 16 tiny moths recorded are beautiful, rarely seen species such as the juniper carpet moth, *Thera juniperata*, and the small juniper pug, *Eupithecia pusillata*. The caterpillars of the juniper webber moth, *Dichomeris marginella*, cause sufficient damage to the needles and branches to be listed as a pest by the Forestry Commission. In England, many of the specialised insects associated with juniper are threatened with local extinction due to the decline of the tree on the South Downs (Ward, 1973, 1977, 1981, 2004). The ecological strategy of juniper is as an extreme stress-tolerator. In mountain areas on thin soil, and sometimes on dry heathland or grassland, it can be a pioneer. It later forms dense, impenetrable thickets, which shade out other species, but which can effectively nurse both birch and rowan seedlings in areas where deer are abundant.

Research has shown that juniper stands in the Lake District are threatened by overgrazing (by sheep) and exhibit markedly reduced seed viability. The general decline of native juniper has been recognised and it is now a priority species in the UK Biodiversity Action Programme. Juniper stands are being mapped and recorded by botanists from Plantlife so that the fragmentation of populations can be arrested and existing areas conserved.

BELOW **Strange growths of the fungus *Gymnosporangium clavariiforme* on juniper, Glen Affric.**

BOTTOM **Juniper shield bug, *Cyphostethus tristriatus*, is common on cultivated juniper but also now recorded from native trees.**

LIMES *Tilia* spp.

Lime family: Tiliaceae
Small-leaved lime *Tilia cordata L.*
Large-leaved lime *Tilia platyphyllos Scopoli*
Common lime (hybrid) *Tilia* x *europaea*

Also known as: pry, lime is an altered form of the earlier lind, linden, lynde, lynd, line. Tilleul (French) derives from tilia (Latin). Other names include pisgwydden (Welsh) and crann-teile (Gaelic). Derivative place names: Lyndhurst, Lynsted, Linwood, Lindfield, Linsty Hall Wood etc.

Biological Flora: Pigott (1991)

Two species of lime, the small-leaved and large-leaved, are both native in Britain, both species having been much more abundant several thousand years ago. The most familiar lime is their hybrid, the normally sterile common lime. This occurs naturally in a few places where both parent species grow together, but along with both native species is widely planted (the trees survive heavy air pollution) in towns and the countryside. Common lime mostly originates from continental stock first brought from the Netherlands in the seventeenth century. The longest common lime avenue is at Clumber Park, Nottinghamshire. It was planted around 1840, is almost 3.2 km (2 miles) long and comprises 1,296 trees. Common lime is 'partially fertile' (Stace, 2010), occasionally producing viable seed.

The pollen record shows that the two native limes spread into southeastern England about 7,500 years ago (when there was still a land-bridge to Europe) and then into most of Wales and as far north as the Cheviot Hills (and possibly Fife according to Tipping, 2010) around 6,000 years ago, but they failed to cross to Ireland. *T. platyphyllos* was always less plentiful, and did not extend as far north or west. Over subsequent millennia both species declined in much of England being replaced in many places by beech or hornbeam.

Both native limes are very long-lived, lowland, densely gregarious trees common throughout the forests of Europe and occurring here on a wide range of soils. *T. cordata* is unevenly distributed, and only in well-defined lime areas, throughout most of England and Wales on richer soils, rarely reaching its full height (up to 38 m or 125 ft) except in a few ancient woodlands on sheltered sites. In the north of England it is rare in woodland; only coppice stools and some pollards can be found, and it does not occur in secondary woodland, and hardly at all in hedges. Some pure limewoods remain today such as Groton Wood in Suffolk, but they are few in number, and there is a suspicion that at least some such woods were originally planted.

Natural regeneration is thought to have been limited by temperature for many centuries (and this may partly explain the decline since about 6,000 years ago), as lime only produces fertile seed today in exceptionally warm summers, although it is tolerant of very low winter temperatures. Some ancient coppice stools survive in a few Cumbrian ravines, while stunted bushes ascend up

RIGHT The famous tree-house at Pitchford Hall, Shropshire, built in a large-leaved lime tree, *T. platyphyllos*.

to 600 m (2,000 ft) on cliffs such as Blakerigg and Whelter Crag (which suggests that at some time in the last century or two there were quite a lot of viable seeds blowing about in the Cumbrian air).

The seedlings are shade-tolerant but very palatable and are susceptible to browsing. The decline of lime, especially *T. cordata*,

is not well understood, but a combination of low seed viability and their palatability for browsers with the fact that the tree was relatively low value may provide part of the explanation in a landscape that became almost totally managed a few millennia ago. Lime trees do not sucker but will layer naturally, for example on

RIGHT Large-leaved lime is one of our scarcest trees; this old coppice stool is growing on a steep north-facing slope of the South Downs at Rook Clift in Sussex.

BELOW AND BOTTOM Bois de Mametz, near Albert on the Somme, France. During the First World War numerous woods were devastated by shellfire but both hornbeam and lime survive damage well, and within twenty years the woods had recovered. At the bottom is Mametz Wood today.

(For small leaved lime see pictures on p.16 and p.174.)

Ancient lime trees

Pigott and Huntley (1980–1989) mapped the occurrence of small-leaved lime, *Tilia cordata*, in northern England. They found that most populations were small, in all but a few localities every tree was very old, and there was apparently no production of new seedlings. Seeds collected from these populations were almost entirely infertile, contrasting with 30–50% fertility of seeds from trees in Worcestershire and much higher levels of fertility for populations in France. In the hot summer of 1976 the maximum fertility level increased to around 10%. They concluded that the primary cause of the failure of lime to regenerate was climatic, reducing the amount of viable seed below a threshold where all the seeds were consumed by predators.

They found aged lime coppice stools in the ravines of the southern Lake District (see Spirit of Trees no. 7), which had apparently survived but without successfully reproducing themselves for a very long time, well over 1,000 years. At one site, Linsty Hall Wood, the limes were apparently 'a conspicuous feature in the tenth century, as the name contains the Norse elements 'lind' and 'stigr', meaning 'lime-path'.

RIGHT **A thousand-year-old small-leaved lime coppice stool in Linsty Hall Wood in the Lake District.**

steep hillsides. The large-leaved lime, one of our scarcest native trees, is distinguished by star-shaped hairs in the angles of veins on the underside of the leaves. It grows to 34 m (112 ft) and is restricted to base-rich soils ascending to 400 m (1,300 ft) in Brecon, South Wales; today it is mainly found where seedlings have avoided browsing deer or sheep – on steep slopes and cliffs, although ancient coppice stools exist, such as at Rook Clift on the South Downs.

Lime trees are conspicuous in midsummer for their abundant yellowish flower clusters; pollen is shed from late June to the end of July (see p.14). The flowers are yellowish-white, the stamens exceeding the petals in length in *T. platyphyllos*, but only equalling them in *T. cordata*.

In woodland when limes are flowering, the emergent pale tops of the trees swarm with insects, especially bees and hoverflies; the nectar apparently intoxicates bees, which can be found helplessly struggling on the ground below. Researchers have suggested that a toxin in the pollen may be responsible.

ABOVE **Foliage carved by master wood-carver Grinling Gibbons. He worked mainly in lime as it can be sustain the most delicate work without cracking.**

Large populations of the lime aphid, *Eucallipterus tiliae*, can build up on the foliage in summer (especially on hybrid lime) and the rain of honeydew is a nuisance on pavements and parked cars. In woodland, the effect is to cause a build-up of nitrogen-fixing bacteria under the trees, effectively enriching the soil. For perhaps two millennia the small-leaved lime was a dominant species in the primeval woodlands of the English lowlands and was largely cleared as lime tended to grow on the most fertile soil. But which came first, the lime stands or the soil fertility?

Lime responds to coppicing and pollarding perhaps more vigorously than any tree except hazel. Pigott has estimated from measurements of soil erosion that some stools in deep valleys above Coniston Water may be over 1,000 years old, while at Silk Wood by Westonbirt Arboretum a stool 14.5 m (48 ft) in diameter has grown up into a ring of individual trees; its age has been estimated at anything up to 6,000 years. Lime trees are also able to survive severe mutilation: the Bois de Mametz on the Somme was devastated by bombardment in July 1916, but without being replanted the wood recovered, with many stems up to 25 m (82 ft) tall 50 years later. Today both the limes and hornbeams at Mametz are multi-stemmed – evidence of their violent history.

The uses of lime

Lime wood is creamy, soft, close and even-grained and very light. It has been a favourite with woodcarvers for centuries; Grinling Gibbons (1648–1721) used lime wood for his many fantastic friezes and altar-pieces in the form of sprays of flowers and fruit, such as those at Chatsworth House, and St James's Church, Piccadilly, 'so delicate that the flowers trembled when a carriage drove past'. Lime

wood was formerly used to make dug-out canoes and household articles such as bowls, ladles and cups, and chair-seats as, like elm, it does not split easily. During the Second World War native limes, particularly in the Wye Valley, were used in plywood for the airframe of Mosquito aeroplanes (see also ash, p.36).

Twigs and small branches can be woven like willow to make light and strong baskets and cradles, and pleached like hornbeam, but the main product from coppiced lime were the strong fibres of the underbark. Known as bast, this was used to make ropes and nets from as early as the Middle Stone Age (at least 5,000 years ago) right up until the last century in some parts of England, notably Devon, Cornwall and Lincolnshire. Church bell-ropes were traditionally made of lime fibres. In Russia rough cloth and sandals were made from lime bark, and worn by country people.

Fresh or dried lime flowers can be infused to make linden tea or tilleul, regarded as a calming drink for treating a variety of ailments, and they can also be fermented to produce wine. As with birch the sweet sap can be drawn off in the spring. The foliage and shoots are still cut for animal fodder in Scandinavia and some mountain areas of Europe, although not, apparently, in England or Wales, even though old pollards are found in some areas.

Both species were coppiced for various purposes including hop-poles (Kent and Sussex), and for charcoal; according to John Evelyn charcoal from lime wood is even better than that of alder for making gunpowder. In Dorset, children use lime leaves to produce an ear-splitting whistle, as with grass blades.

Folklore

Throughout Europe, many place names referring to lime trees date from the early period of settlement when they may have had spiritual significance. In Estonia, ancient limes were reputed to have been worshipped by the Baltic people even after their late conversion to Christianity, and in some places items of clothing are still attached to their branches, especially by women fearing infertility. The shade of a lime tree has long been a favourite trysting place of lovers, supposedly to lie on a bed of crushed, sweet-scented lime flowers. In Germany, dances are traditionally held under the spreading limbs of an ancient linden tree in the centre of old villages. These traditions do not seem to have reached England with Saxon invaders and there are very few folkloric associations of lime recorded here.

LEFT **Lime wood for woodcarvers – for sale at an agricultural show in Warwickshire.**

Lime in the ecosystem

In some parts of the country hybrid limes are frequently festooned with mistletoe (see p.67), but this parasite is much less common on native limes. The only mycorrhizal association with lime that is confirmed as producing above-ground fruiting bodies is ectomycorrhizal *Russula praetervisa*; in general lime has a 'surprisingly meagre mycota' (Spooner and Roberts, 2005), although 1,351 records are given in the Fungal Records Database of Britain and Ireland, putting lime tenth among native trees. Saprotrophic species specifically attacking dead lime are also few; the most conspicuous being the dark brown colonies of obscure fungi *Corynespora olivacea* and *Exosporium tiliae* that look like pieces of old felt rug.

Lime fruits are eaten by woodmice, and very few survive in the leaf-litter except those that fall later in cold autumn conditions. The seedlings are consumed by mice and bank voles, while young saplings and coppice shoots are eaten by roe deer, but not, apparently, by grey squirrels or rabbits (Pigott, 1985).

Only 162 species of plant-feeding invertebrate have been recorded from lime (of which just 24 (15%) are restricted to *Tilia*) but it is not clear why this should be so. In woodland, native lime trees rarely suffer from major attacks of insects at all; even infestations of the lime aphid, *E. tiliae*, are less frequent than on the hybrid common lime. Of the other foliage-eating species, the lime hawk moth, *Mimas tiliae*, is the most conspicuous; its large caterpillars are green with yellow stripes with a blue horn above the head. The more inconspicuous caterpillars of the rare scarce hook-tip, *Sabra harpagula*, are restricted to *T. cordata* in the southwest of England, and a beautiful brown leaf-hopper, *Pediopsis tiliae*, is also restricted to lime. Very few leaf-miners occur on lime; just seven species are recorded including the sawfly *Parna apicalis*, which first appeared in 2007, and now appears to be spreading quite rapidly on all species of *Tilia*. The lime mite, *Eotetranychus tiliarium*, causes bronzing and premature loss of leaves. Large colonies of sap-sucking woolly scale insects, *Pulvinia regalis* are a familiar sight on the dark bark of lime trees; related to aphids, this species is commonly seen on the trunks of horse-chestnut and other broadleaved trees.

Of 15 recorded galls the most frequently seen are the dense clusters of pointed yellow or red nail-galls on the leaves (particularly of hybrid lime) that look like tiny red bottles. These are caused by the gregarious mite *Eriophyes tiliae*, while the petiole-gall is caused by the midge *Contarinia tiliarum*. Common leaf-rollers (which cause the rolls to turn purplish) include the mite *Phytoptus tetratrichus* and the gall-midge *Dasineura tiliae*. Yellow blisters are caused by another mite, *Eriophyes leiosoma*.

The ecological value to woodland of lime litter, both leaves and twigs, which are rich in minerals and decay rapidly, has been established experimentally. Like beech, both lime species are forest competitors; in the most fertile soils they can overtop other trees. They are very long-lived, cast a deeper shade than both oak species and survive disturbance such as uprooting better than any other of our major forest trees. The seedlings and saplings are both shade-tolerant, and like those of hornbeam they are released into rapid growth by gaps in the canopy such as those caused by tree-fall.

BELOW Characteristic nail galls on common lime, caused by the mite *Eriophyes tiliae*.

BELOW The tiny weevil, *Byctiscus betulae*, one of the few beetles found on lime.

OAKS *Quercus* spp.

> **Beech family:** Fagaceae
> Common or pedunculate oak *Quercus robur L.*
> Sessile oak *Quercus petraea* (Mattuschka) Leibl.
>
> **Also known as:** darach (Gaelic), derry or dair (Irish), daur (Old Irish), derwen (Welsh). In ancient Irish law, oak was one of seven noble trees. Derivative place names include Accrington, Akenside, Aysgarth, Oakham, Little Oakley and Matlock. In Ireland, Derry, Darrary and many others.
>
> **Biological Flora:** Jones (1959)

Oaks are the major trees of the Atlantic deciduous forest of western Britain and the commonest trees of British broadleaved woodlands, although in fact they are less widespread (occur in fewer 10 km squares) than willows in the country as a whole (Kennedy and Southwood). The common or pedunculate oak is typically a tree of deep moist soils including heavy clay, while the sessile oak is more frequently a tree of drier sites including both acid soils and limestone. The two species frequently overlap and hybridise, so that many are difficult to identify with certainty. Both species will grow to around 42 m (138 ft) tall in sheltered situations on deep soil. They can also survive on mountainsides and ascend to around 550 m (1,800 ft) naturally (*Q. petraea* at Young Wood, Cumbria; *Q. robur* to 450 m/1,480 ft near Brecon). As with other trees such as Scots pine their altitudinal limit may have been artificially depressed by overgrazing by sheep and deer. Since earliest post-glacial times, oak has also been the predominant timber tree in Britain, spreading soon after the first group of trees (juniper, birch, hazel, aspen, willows etc.), and as early as the late Bronze Age it was frequently cut into planks to make trackways across marshland.

Pedunculate oak is the almost universal oak of eastern England, except in (pure) oakwoods, which are usually sessile oak. Sessile oak is more characteristic of the damper northern and western areas, especially on poorer, more acid soils, and is almost universal in Ireland. It is commonly the tree of old oakwoods. Both species are found widely in Europe, although they do not occur naturally any further north than northern Scotland. Pure oak forests occur in the west from Cornwall to Argyll, but at present oak appears to regenerate poorly in woodland (except where protected from deer). It is likely that, given time, oak would naturally be replaced on fertile soil in England by other trees such as ash, lime, hornbeam and beech. As Rackham (2006) points out, 'silvicultural treatment has favoured certain weakly competitive trees [such as] oak [for timber]; although present in many types of woodland it was the intervention of woodmen that made it the principal timber tree'. Both oak species are commonly found as a component of hedges, and together with ash are overwhelmingly the commonest hedgerow trees in England and Wales although much less so in Scotland. Oaks come into leaf as late as mid-May (see ash), but there are usually subsequent flushes of leaves, the

BELOW Giant oak pollard at Staverton Thicks, Suffolk.

RIGHT Sessile oak woodland high above Rigg Beck, Cumbria. At 500 m(1,700 ft) it is one of the highest natural oakwoods in Britain.

second usually being known traditionally as the lammas budding (supposedly coinciding with the Anglo-Saxon festival on 16 July in the old calendar, but often as much as six weeks earlier). This behaviour may be an adaptation enabling oak to survive early summer defoliation by caterpillars (see also hornbeam), an alternative strategy to that suspected of hawthorn (see p.85).

Oaks are monoecious, that is bearing separate male and female flowers. The male catkins and female spikes are small and pale green. The male flowers open and release pollen in early May until late June (only for a day or two on individual trees, see p.14) before the first leaves are fully grown. Some nectar is produced, attracting bees and some other insects, but pollination is largely by wind. Some self-pollination may occur although some authorities believe *Q. robur* is self-sterile (Jones, 1959).

Acorns are usually first produced after around 40 years, but sometimes as early as 20 years, and in some cases continuing for centuries, but the crop is erratic. Like beech, oaks tend to fruit abundantly only in mast years (when nearly 100,000 acorns can be produced on a single tree, and several million over the life of a tree). Masting occurs every six to seven years, the crop probably being influenced by similar factors as in beech, such as the late summer temperature determining whether masting will take place in the following season. In some non-mast years no acorns are produced at all.

Acorns are a prime example of what are termed recalcitrant seeds. Most acorns are only viable for a few weeks and can quickly be killed by drying or frost although some acorns will germinate after cold treatment, possibly because this releases them from dormancy. The synchronisation of acorn- and leaf-fall may result in hiding some acorns under leaf litter which may reduce predation as well as improving the germination rate. In damp conditions most acorns begin to germinate by putting out a strong vertical tap-root very soon after falling, though a shoot is not produced until the following spring. The substantial food source allows the young seedlings to become established, even under shade or in closed grassland, often when sheltered by thorny plants such as hawthorn or blackthorn. The tap-root seems to be an adaptation to frequent grazing, but young oaks are not very shade-tolerant – they do not survive under mature oaks or in other heavy shade. Humidity may encourage oak mildew, which weakens the saplings, and without sufficient light they may never develop.

The uses of oak

'To enumerate now the incomparable uses of this wood... the land and the sea do sufficiently speak of this excellent material; houses and ships, Cities and Navies are built with it.' (Evelyn). Although oak timber is the principal timber in surviving ships and buildings, it was the extensive use of oak bark for tanning (in the early nineteenth century) that made oakwoods such a valuable asset.

A century later tannin was being imported from cheaper sources abroad, including the huge acorn-cups of the Aegean oak,

LEFT Neglected oak coppice above Watersmeet, Devon.

BELOW LEFT The late Bill Hogarth MBE peeling oak bark in Black Beck Woods, south Cumbria.

BELOW RIGHT Oak bark after peeling before it is sent to specialist leather tanneries.

Q. macrolepis, although some bark was still produced in Cumbria. The late Bill Hogarth MBE, a coppice-wood merchant in the Lake District from the 1960s to the 1990s, claimed he spent three summer months every year cutting oak coppice and peeling the bark. Today native oak bark is in short supply; it is worth several hundred pounds a tonne to tanners of high-class leather. The peeled branches formerly went to make oak-swill baskets. Today, they are used to make rustic garden furniture.

For centuries oak was one of the most widely used hardwoods for interior joinery work and, being extremely durable, for most exterior purposes: fencing, mine timber, gates etc. Since it also bends well and is impermeable it is also used in contemporary boat-building. High quality oak has been imported from Europe since the thirteenth century (Oliver Rackham, pers. comm., 2009),

but British oak trees have been used for major carpentry such as cathedral roofs, shipbuilding, sea defences, bridges and railway sleepers. The turquoise staining produced by the ascomycete fungi *Chlorociboria* spp. is much valued in marquetry.

In Europe acorns have been used for food in times of famine although there are no records of this in Britain. Acorns are still sometimes eaten in Eastern Europe and Russia. In England they were used to feed pigs; oakwoods were prized for pannage rights for centuries.

Small globular marble galls, such as those produced by the gall-wasp, *Andricus kollari*, contain a high level of tannic acid and were used for dyeing and ink-making until the nineteenth century; originally the galls were imported but then the gall-wasp itself became established in Britain in the mid-nineteenth century.

Folklore

Folklore and traditions associated with the oak are legion, and the following gives no more than a hint of their range and diversity. The oak was sacred to many ancient peoples, including the ancient Greeks, the Norse and the Celts, who claimed it as the tree of their most powerful gods – Zeus, Thor and Dagda respectively. One of the five ancient trees of Ireland was an oak: the Oak of Mugna at Moone, Co. Kildare. The word druid may have originally meant 'oak man'.

Oak trees are often damaged by lightning (probably because in many places an oak is the tallest tree); as a result the oak was often associated with the gods of thunder. Saxon charters refer to specific oaks as boundary markers.

There are many sayings and customs symbolising both outer and inner strength; the significance of 'mighty oaks from little acorns grow' is not simply one of size, and the symbol of oak leaves on military or civil honours is used in more than one country. In England, the oak has traditionally been the tree symbolising the nation – the jingoistic lyrics of the patriotic song 'Hearts of Oak' (credited to Garrick and Boyce, 1759) being written nearly a century after John Evelyn bemoaned the 'notorious decay of our (oakwoods); nothing more fatally weakening the strength of this famous and flourishing nation'! The oak is also a national emblem of the Republic of Ireland, France, Germany and several other countries.

Enthusiasts such as the group Tree Spirit claim to feel the power of the tree just by standing close to or hugging the massive trunk of a great oak, and the psychological and spiritual benefits to some people should not be underestimated. The mystical strength of oak has long been employed in folk medicine: it is claimed, for instance, that rheumatism 'can be cured by walking round a large tree uttering appropriate incantations'.

There are numerous rhymes associating oaks with weather prediction. The most widespread are variations on the oak/ash theme (see p.36). In Dorset another couplet is added: 'If oak and ash leaves show together/we're surely in for awful weather.' Data compiled from records of the last 158 years indicates that ash is rarely before oak, and that oak (but not ash) responds to warmer spring temperatures by leafing first although this does not always result in a wetter summer (see www.naturescalendar.org.uk/findings/).

An old oak at Fort William in the Highlands was cut down in 1985, amid strong local protests, to make way for a new library. This tree, known as the Hanging Tree (a joug tree – see sycamore, p.136), was believed by local people to be inhabited by spirits, and subsequent unexplained incidents at the new library have been blamed on their awakening; some local residents are quite convinced that the new building is haunted.

The medicinal significance of oak has historically been associated with the epiphytes that commonly grow on it – mistletoe (very rarely) and the common polypody fern, *Polypodium vulgare*. However, Culpeper recommends various decoctions of leaves, inner bark and buds for 'staying all manner of fluxes [internal bleedings] in man or woman' and claims that powdered acorn

Oak Apple Day

In many parts of England 29 May is known as Oak Apple Day (also Shick Shack Day, Arbor Day), and is celebrated to commemorate the restoration of the monarchy in what was then Great Britain and Ireland in May 1660. Charles II was saved from the Roundheads by hiding in an oak tree when he fled after defeat at the Battle of Worcester in 1651, and as soon as he was restored to the throne in 1660 he declared the day (his birthday) a national holiday. Today Oak Apple Day is still celebrated at Aston on Clun (see black poplar, p.55), Northampton, Upton-upon-Severn, Marsh Gibbon (Buckinghamshire) and Membury (Devon). At Castleton, in Derbyshire, an effigy of a king bedecked with oak branches is paraded through the streets to the parish church.

Perhaps the most elaborate celebrations are at Great Wishford and Salisbury in Wiltshire, where there is a kind of beating-the-bounds exercise at which the villagers reaffirm their right to cut oak from local woods for fuel, fodder and other uses. To maintain this ancient right, the villagers are required to parade from their village to nearby Salisbury, carrying oak branches and 'nitches' (small bundles of hazel twigs), and to give the shout 'Grovely! Grovely! Grovely! All for Grovely!' in the nave of the cathedral. Today the annual parade is organised by the Oak Apple Club (established 1891). Oak branches are cut early in the morning and after the cathedral visit and traditional shout, there is a procession at the village followed by a fete including maypole dancing and general merrymaking (Frampton, 1992).

ABOVE The badge of the Great Wishford Oak Apple Club.

taken in wine acts as a diuretic and 'resists the poison of venomous creatures'. In Donegal the bark was boiled and the liquid used to treat soreness in horses' shoulders. A claimed remedy for diarrhoea is the drinking of warm milk into which a ripe acorn has been grated, while in Ireland it is claimed that ringworm can be cured by drinking water in which fresh oak leaves have been boiled.

Oak in the ecosystem

Oaks provide a substrate for many epiphytes: 65 species of mosses and liverworts, and 300 lichens are recorded from the trunks and branches especially in damp woodlands on the western side of Britain. Many fungal fruiting bodies that are known to be ectomycorrhizal have been found under oaks. Some are found under most beech family trees while others such as the oak milkcap, *Lactarius quietus*, are restricted to *Quercus* species. The strange but edible beefsteak fungus, *Fistulina hepatica*, occurs on old living oaks and on dead oak stumps. Other species are restricted to oak leaf-litter, including the tiny *Marasmius quercophilus*, while numerous specialist fungi degrade the dead wood and fallen timber. The (edible) rubbery black ascomycete *Bulgaria inquinans* is one of over a hundred different fungi found on rotting dead oak wood, including various bracket fungi (polypores) such as *Daedalea quercina* and *Inonotus dryadeus*, and the strange brown-speckled hen-of-the-woods, *Grifola frondosa*. Oak also hosts several rare fungi, which are specially protected, such as the oak polypores *Buglossoporus pulvinus* and *Piptoporus quercinus*. Healthy oak trees frequently suffer from dieback (in extreme cases producing typical 'stag's head' oaks. Dieback appears to be caused by a combination of factors, usually including water stress, but exacerbated by the damage caused by the jewel beetle, *Agrilus pannonicus*.

A serious disease of oak in North America called 'sudden oak death' (caused by a bacterium: *Phytophthora ramorum*) has been found infecting a few oaks in England but laboratory tests show that our oaks are much more resistant to it than American species. A further disease which has appeared recently is known as 'acute oak decline'. This causes dark fluid to exude from cracks in the bark and affects mature oaks of both native species. So far the bacterial pathogen has not been identified. These are just two of many potential new threats to oak, which may become more susceptible to new pathogens under stresses induced by changing climate (see Chapter 7, p.193).

Oak foliage is unpalatable or even toxic to some browsing mammals and the garden snail, *Helix aspersa*, but not to some deer. While oak is not its preferred food, a single roe deer can consume 0.5 kg (1 lb) of oak leaves per day. Mammals such as deer, squirrels, rabbits and woodmice destroy most of the acorns in non-mast years, although they may be overwhelmed in mast years.

ABOVE AND LEFT Grey squirrels kill acorns by eating out the embryo.

RIGHT A defoliated oak following an attack of green oak tortrix caterpillars, Queen's Wood, north London, May 2008.

LEFT Large caterpillars of the buff-tip moth, *Phalera bucephala*, a common foliage-feeder on oak and other broadleaves.

ABOVE Large cankers are thought to be caused by a bacterium *Agrobacterium tumifasciens*.

BELOW The native acorn weevil, *Cuculio glandum*, has an extraordinary long rostrum.

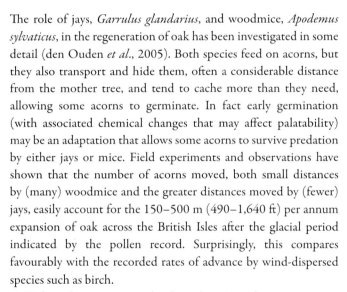

The role of jays, *Garrulus glandarius*, and woodmice, *Apodemus sylvaticus*, in the regeneration of oak has been investigated in some detail (den Ouden *et al.*, 2005). Both species feed on acorns, but they also transport and hide them, often a considerable distance from the mother tree, and tend to cache more than they need, allowing some acorns to germinate. In fact early germination (with associated chemical changes that may affect palatability) may be an adaptation that allows some acorns to survive predation by either jays or mice. Field experiments and observations have shown that the number of acorns moved, both small distances by (many) woodmice and the greater distances moved by (fewer) jays, easily account for the 150–500 m (490–1,640 ft) per annum expansion of oak across the British Isles after the glacial period indicated by the pollen record. Surprisingly, this compares favourably with the recorded rates of advance by wind-dispersed species such as birch.

Today oaks regenerate only where there is no dense tree canopy and even then usually in spurts resulting from mast years. Even when acorns do germinate and the seedlings become established, their success is by no means certain. Oak seedlings are attacked by the oak mildew fungus, *Microsphaera alphitoides*. Rackham believes that the natural regeneration of *Q. robur* in England has diminished in many woods over the last 150 years due to this pathogen, combined with the additional grazing pressure of deer and rabbits – especially where coppicing has ceased, causing many oaklings to struggle under heavy shade. Under lower grazing pressure, on colder, upland sites, the more shade-tolerant seedlings of *Q. petraea* survive better.

Is oak the tree with the richest insect fauna? Oak (two native species) certainly attracts a wide variety of plant-feeders, with 655 being recorded of which 185 (28%) are restricted to the genus, although *Salix* (19 species) has 839. Morris (1974) and Kennedy & Southwood suggest that the major factor in the high number of species recorded for oak may be the abundance of oaks across the entire country, but this is clearly not the whole story. Taking the measure they use (number of 10 km squares multiplied by their average frequency within squares) ash is in fact the most abundant tree in Britain, but the number of plant-feeding insects recorded from ash (155) (line 17, Table 4) is far less than those recorded for either oak or several other less widespread species.

Among the invertebrates recorded from oak, 250 are moths and butterflies, of which 63 are recorded only from *Quercus*, while many are restricted to oak and a few related trees like beech and

ABOVE Common silk-button galls, *Neuroterus numismalis*, covering oak leaves.

RIGHT Ramshorn gall, *Andricus aries*, another recent arrival.

BELOW Oak apples late in the season; earlier they are larger and cream-coloured, *Biorrhiza pallida*.

BELOW RIGHT The cardinal click-beetle, *Ampedus cardinalis*, found only on oak, ash and lime.

hornbeam. Virtually all those insects that feed on a wide range of broadleaved trees are sometimes found on oak; these include common defoliating species such as the oak tortrix, *Tortrix viridana* (mainly in England), and the winter moth, *Operophtera brumata*. In early summer these last two can strip the entire foliage from individual trees and severely damage whole oakwoods, especially if the trees are also under water stress, although most trees do usually recover with their second leafing. Oak tortrix moths lay the eggs in the uppermost branches and the caterpillars descend on silk threads, eventually reaching every part of the foliage. Epidemics tend to occur in groups of consecutive years, and are commoner in oakwoods than on oak trees in other situations.

Among common caterpillars found on oak are those of the lichen-mimicking merveille-du-jour, *Dichonia aprilina*, and many others which consume foliage or mine the leaves. Three species

of hairy, gregarious caterpillars can be a serious health threat, causing skin irritation and allergic reactions in some people. Those of the gypsy moth, *Lymantria dispar*, formerly common but extinct between 1907 and around 2008, are regarded as a pest in continental Europe. In the last few years, in spite of a government control programme, reintroductions (probably on imported timber and even egg-masses on the wheels of trucks) have resulted in the moth becoming re-established at several places in southeast England. These populations appear to be an Asian strain of the species. The browntail moth, *Euproctis chrysorrhoea*, is a gregarious species on oak, hawthorn or blackthorn, while the caterpillars of the oak processionary moth, *Thaumetopoea processionea*, an invader from southern Europe, defoliate whole trees as well as being a danger to health, being armed with sharp, barbed hairs. Over 100 colonies of this last species were removed from oak trees

111

in west London during 2008 alone; Plant Health Orders are now in place, which are aimed at keeping Britain a 'protected zone' by inspecting and not allowing the importation of any plants that may harbour infestations of this species. How successful this approach can be in the long run is a matter of some doubt.

Numerous different tiny moths mine oak leaves, some of which produce beautiful patterns on the leaves. Two of the commonest are *Phyllonorycter quercifoliella* and *P. messaniella*, which both produce small blotch mines on the leaves. The purple hairstreak, *Neozephyrus quercus*, a most attractive butterfly whose caterpillars feed on oak, tends to fly in groups above and around the upper canopy, both of solitary trees and in woodland.

Among over 200 species of beetle recorded from oak (although only five are restricted to *Quercus* species), two of the commonest are the extraordinary long-beaked acorn weevil, *Curculio glandum*, whose rostrum is as long as the rest of the beetle, and the shorter-beaked leaf-mining weevil, *Rhynchaenus quercus*. Acorns are frequently damaged by *C. glandum*, by the gall-wasp *Andricus quercuscalicis* and by caterpillars of the acorn moth, *Cydia splendana*; together these insects can kill up to 90% of the crop.

Oaks support over 50 species of gall on every part of the tree, more than on any other native species. Some of the commonest are caused by tiny gall-wasps, most of them restricted to oak, and they may have alternating generations each producing a different gall. Gall-wasps are responsible for the familiar oak-apple-gall, *Biorrhiza pallida*, several common spangle-galls, *Neuroterus numismalis*, and *N. quercusbaccarum*, ramshorn gall, *Andricus aries*, hedgehog gall, *Andricus lucidus*, currant-gall, the alternate generation of *Neuroterus quercusbaccarum,* and the more recently arrived knopper-gall, *Andricus quercuscalicis*. Most of these gall-wasps live in one host (e.g. oak) for part of the year, but then move to a different plant species – known as the alternate host – at another season. The alternate host for *A. quercuscalicis* is the introduced Turkey oak, *Q. cerris*. New species of gall-causers have arrived from Europe in recent years, and other new ones can be expected to arrive in the future.

Other insects specifically associated with oak include the leaf-hopper *Ledra aurita*, a carnivorous bronze ground-beetle, *Calosoma inquisitor*, which lives in the upper foliage feeding on caterpillars, and a small, rare, brown ant, *Lasius brunneus*, which nests in the heartwood of ancient oak trees. The oak bush cricket, *Meconema thallasinum*, is not restricted to oak but is found on other broadleaves as well. The plant-louse *Phylloxera glabra* is found mainly on *Q. robur*, while the oak slugworm (larva of the oak sawfly: *Caliroa annulipes*) is found on both species of oak and causes browning of the foliage in late summer without seriously affecting the overall health of the trees.

In spite of this vast array of insects feeding on the trees, oaks are rarely killed by these assaults, indeed the health of the trees may be little affected. One strategy of oak is to produce second spurts of leaf growth 'lammas budding' during a season, so that some foliage is always out of phase with the leaf-eating insects.

Ancient oak pollards such as those in many old wood-pastures may be 800 to 1,000 years old. They provide many other micro-habitats for insects in particular; many rare species of beetle (such as the purple click beetle, *Limoniscus violaceus*), flies and even spiders are restricted to these 'grandfather' trees. Britain has more of these veteran oaks than elsewhere in Europe because of the survival here of wood-pasture and deer parks. Old oaks are also found in long-established hedges but not in woodland, where mature trees have usually been harvested for timber, or coppiced for oak bark.

A good deal of the oak planted for timber is of selected (standardised) European stock and may not be genetically local at all. This is nothing new; in 1674 the Customs Commissioners recorded the import of 'two chests of trees and seeds coming from France for the King (Charles II)'s plantation at Windsor' (Roberts, 1997), but native oaks are genetically more diverse, resulting in varied growth-forms that are both more interesting and better for the local insect fauna, although they may not be as valuable as timber trees.

The ecological strategy of oak is complex but basically it is an ecological all-rounder (see p.27). At Wistman's Wood on Dartmoor some seedlings are produced in mast years and, protected from grazing sheep by the large boulders, are resulting in the gradual expansion of the wood. Some high altitude oakwoods in the Lake District (whose origin is not known, but may have been by planting) also appear to be increasing in area (Simon Webb, pers. comm., 2010). On fertile lowland soils oak does not naturally replace itself in dense woodland where it tends to be shaded out and overtaken by other trees, except where the canopy has opened as a result of tree-fall. On the other hand, neglected grassland with low grazing pressure (with nearby oak trees as a seed source) will often develop over a decade or less into secondary oak woodland – South Meadow on Hampstead Heath is one example. In the long run, and with a more unpredictable climate, the future of our oaks may depend on direct human influence; oak trees are frequently planted, but the removal of squirrels and deer from areas around existing oaks may, in the long run, be more successful.

PEARS *Pyrus* spp.

> **Rose family**: Rosaceae
> Wild pear *P. pyraster* L. Burgsd
> Cultivated pear (*P. communis* L.)
> Plymouth pear *P. cordata* Desv.
>
> **Also known as**: gellygen or peren (Welsh). Place names:
> Pyrford, Pirbright (pronounced pur-ford, pur-bright).

There are two species of wild pear in Britain, as well as the cultivated pear, but there is some doubt as to whether any of them are really native, and Stace (2010) even expresses doubt as to whether the wild pear and the domesticated pear are 'specifically distinct'.

Wild pear is found in England and Wales as an occasional solitary tree in ancient woodland (such as Hayley Wood in Cambridgeshire and Epping Forest) growing taller than the related crabapple, while the domestic pear has been been cultivated here for millennia.

Charcoal and carbonised pips of pear have been found at several Neolithic sites and are occasionally mentioned in medieval documents. Therefore, *P. communis* 'can be accepted as an archaeophyte' (Hill *et al.*, 2004), its establishment being probably due to ancient human migration. Worldwide over 1,000 cultivars of domestic pear are known, at least some of which (like apple varieties) have arisen here by chance genetic combination.

BELOW **Claimed to be the biggest wild pear tree in England at Cubbington, Warwickshire, it is now threatened by the proposed high-speed rail link to Birmingham.**

ABOVE LEFT Beautiful but foul-smelling blossom of the Plymouth pear tree, which attracts St Mark's flies as pollinators.

ABOVE RIGHT The small hard fruits of Plymouth pear that are only edible once they begin to ferment.

LEFT The bark of the Plymouth pear.

Pears are distinguished from other trees in the family Rosaceae such as rowan and cultivated apple, by the gritty, fibrous cells within the flesh of the fruit and (often but not always) the presence of spines on stems or shoot-tips. Like apple, pears are almost completely self-sterile, but after cross-pollination some domestic pears may produce viable seed, and some wild pear trees may have arisen from these pips.

Wild pear trees grow singly to at least 20 m (66 ft) and usually bear spines; in woodland, unlike crabapple, they can grow up into the canopy. In late April, before the leaves are fully grown, pear trees are covered with dense white blossom, which gives off a faint but sweet fragrance. The flowers are visited mainly by wasps and bees attracted by the nectar.

The Plymouth pear, found in hedges near Plymouth and at Truro, is one of our rarest trees. It does not grow as a single tree but suckers profusely, developing as a clonal thicket (see picture p.178) , and only reaching about 5 m (16 ft). The blossom appears together with the leaves. The earliest botanical record

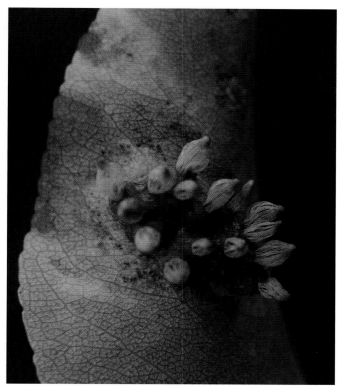

ABOVE The pear slugworm, *Caliroa cerasi*, a sawfly larva, common on pear and other fruit trees.

RIGHT The strange European pear rust, *Gymnosporangium sabinae*, an ascomycete fungus, not a serious pest.

in Britain dates from 1871 when the hedgerow trees were found near Plymouth by a local naturalist T. Archer Briggs. He sent them to J.B. Syme, Curator of the Botanical Exchange Club, who was unable to confirm their identity noting that the leaves and flowers were smaller than usual for a pear, and the fruit was much smaller: 'more like an elongated berry – it hardly deserves to be described as a pear at all'. He proposed to call it var. *briggsii* 'in the event of it being destitute of a name', but it has subsequently been accepted as a separate species, *Pyrus cordata* Desv.

In the early 1990s the known population of Plymouth pear was threatened by planned development near Plymouth airport and concern was raised that if the known hedges were damaged the tree could become extinct. Although absent from ancient woodland in the Plymouth area searches eventually revealed a small number of trees in other nearby hedges and some clones over 64 km (40 miles) away near Truro in Cornwall. DNA analysis established that, although superficially different, the Truro populations were genetically indistinguishable from the Plymouth trees and were thought to have originated as cuttings from the same clone.

Plymouth pear is common in Brittany and northern Portugal, where it occurs at woodland margins usually on acid soils up to an altitude of 1,100 m (3,600 ft). At Truro and Plymouth the soil of the hedgebanks where it is found (on granite) is also very acidic. Botanists at Kew have concluded that Plymouth pear was brought from Brittany as a hedging tree several hundred years ago (Jackson, 1995).

Plymouth pear flowers abundantly in early May (later than *P. communis*). The trees bear quantities of pale cream blossom, individual flowers having some pink on the flower buds and the outside of the petals. Unfortunately, the tree is best admired from a distance as, unlike the wild and domestic pears, the flowers of Plymouth pear give off a faint but quite disgusting smell, variously described as rotting scampi, soiled sheets or wet carpets. The rank odour attracts mainly flies, including St Mark's fly, *Bibio marci* (it first appears around St Mark's Day: 25 April), which otherwise are attracted to decaying plant matter. The smell does not appear to deter wasps and bees but may result in tainted honey.

As part of Kew's Species Recovery Programme, cross-pollination between the two populations produced viable seed in reasonable quantities. A new site was secured at Llanhydrock Garden some distance from the nearest pear orchard, where a new experimental population was established from seed. Satellite populations were also established at several botanic gardens, some as a result of micro-propagation, and the whole project has been claimed as a success.

The uses of pear

Pear wood is hard and fine-grained and is used for high quality turnery, when available. It is an acceptable substitute for box as a medium for wood-engraving and has been used for making musical instruments including bassoons, clarinets, flutes, recorders and harpsichords, for the hammers of pianos and – when stained black – as a substitute for ebony for violin finger-boards. Pear wood was sometimes used by Grinling Gibbons for his extraordinary carvings of leaves and flowers (see also lime).

Pear bark is known to have antibacterial action; Culpeper claimed that the flesh of wild pears are very effective if 'bound to green [i.e. fresh] wounds' preventing inflammation and effecting healing 'sooner... than others'.

A limited range of commercial pear varieties are grown in UK and Ireland, and sold as fresh fruit or used for perry or pear liqueur. As with apples, some old varieties are now conserved and promoted by enthusiasts; one that apparently originated in the Wolverhampton area is called Tattenhall Dick. The original tree has been lost but it survives as grafts on trees in orchards around the West Midlands.

Plymouth pear wood is little known, but as hedging the tree has a potential future in parks and gardens; as a result of the Recovery Programme grafts have been distributed to 15 other horticultural institutions. Although the fruits they produce will be of no interest (the result of cross-pollination with unknown other trees), these grafts are of value as back-up trees to the Recovery Programme.

Folklore

The Coalstoun pear is a lucky charm securely stored in a silver box at the house of the Laird of Coalstoun, near Haddington in Scotland. It is said to have been picked in the thirteenth century by a wizard who married a Coalstoun daughter, and has remained in the hands of the family ever since. In the seventeenth century the wife of the then laird 'tried to take a bite from the fruit', supposedly bestowing on the family a brief period of ill-fortune. The pear is said to have become as hard as rock' soon afterwards, perhaps preventing its destruction. In Ireland it is thought unlucky to bring pear blossom into the house in case it results in a death in the family.

Pears in the ecosystem

A small number of ectomycorrhizal fungi have been recorded for pear. Pear suffers from a serious fungal canker, *Nectria galligena mali*, which causes lesions on the stems and is a serious pest of pear orchards. Other cankers and rusts are common including the tongue fungus, *Taphrina bullata*, pear scab, *Venturia pirina*, and a powdery mildew, *Podosphaera leucotricha*. Perhaps the most extraordinary species affecting pear causes vivid orange-red stains on the upperside of the leaves associated with eruptive galls like a cluster of small volcanoes on the underside. The organism responsible is the (relatively harmless) European pear rust, *Gymnosporangium sabinae*, first recorded in 2005 but now spreading rapidly. Fireblight, caused by a bacterial pathogen, *Erwinia amylovora*, is also a major pest of pear orchards.

Like apple, pear foliage and fruit are palatable to a wide variety of insects, although far fewer (just 63 species) are recorded, only six being restricted to *Pyrus*, possibly because apple is grown much more widely. Common leaf-eaters like green oak tortrix, *Tortrix viridana*, and mottled umber, *Erannis defoliaria*, both feed on pear foliage, and several species of fruit tortrix mine the fruit. At least 16 species of micro-lepidoptera mine the leaves of pear, most of them also being found on apple. Several brown or green aphids of the genus *Anuraphis* use pear as their primary host-plant, while the pinkish-brown pear-bedstraw aphid, *Dysaphis pyri*, is a common pest of cultivated pear, damaging the leaves throughout the season. The pear and cherry slugworm, *Caliroa cerasi*, can cause serious damage to the foliage.

Several gall invertebrates are commonly found on pear and all are regarded as orchard pests. The pear midge, *Continaria pyrivora*, causes fruit to turn black and fall prematurely, while the pear leaf midge, *Dasineura pyri*, causes curling of the leaves. The pear leaf blister mite, *Eriophyes pyri*, causes pustules on the leaves. Other galls, known as black pear and similar to the pocket plums on blackthorn, are caused by another gall-midge, *Lestodiplosis pyri*.

The ecological strategy of pear species is difficult to assess as it is not clear what the 'natural' status of the trees is – in other words whether they would be here at all without human intervention. However, wild *Pyrus communis* is probably a shade-tolerant competitor, which can thrive in ancient woodland on good soil.

ROWAN *Sorbus aucuparia* L.

Rose family: Rosaceae

Also known as: mountain ash, care-tree, chitchat, rawn-tree (pronounced Rantry), sip-sap, quickbeam, quicken (Ireland), whitty tree, witch-wiggin, cuirn (Isle of Man), keirn, criafolen (Welsh), caorthann (Irish), caorrunn (Gaelic) and many other names.

Biological Flora: Raspe *et al.* (2000)

Rowan is a slender, densely branched, and often many-stemmed tree without a pronounced main trunk that can grow to around 21 m (70 ft) and is found throughout Britain and Ireland, first reaching its present range around 6,500 years ago according to pollen data.

Rowan is a fast-growing pioneer tree, which very occasionally suckers and grows as a clonal group, but more often occurs singly in rocky places where the seed has been dropped by birds. It favours well-drained acid soils but also occurs less frequently on the calcareous soils of limestone or chalk. Pure stands are rare; they may be the result of a succession from gorse due to the germination of seeds carried there by birds (Drennan Watson, pers. comm., 2010). Rowan is a relatively short-lived tree, supposedly with a maximum lifespan of 150 years, unless coppiced or pollarded; ancient pollards are found in various places such as the Stiperstones, Shropshire and at Geltsdale, Cumbria and there is at least one ancient rowan in Wistman's Wood on Dartmoor. Rowan ascends to 975 m (3,200 ft) in mountain areas and 'to a higher altitude than any other native tree apart from juniper and [mountain] willows' (Clapham *et al.*, 1989). It is found in the montane scrub zone at the upper limit of tree growth in the Cairngorms, but may be sensitive to salt spray and is not found in coastal scrub.

Rowan bark is silvery-grey and smooth, while the leaves are pinnate with usually five to seven leaflets each with 14–17 serrations on each side. The cream-coloured and sweet-smelling blossom occurs in dense inflorescences (usually about 250 hermaphrodite florets each 8–10 mm or about 1/3 in in diameter) in April–May,

BELOW **Mature rowan trees give splashes of colour in autumn to upland landscapes like this at Dartmoor, England.**

ABOVE Rowan in montane scrub at nearly 1,000 m (3,281 ft) Creag Fhiaclach, Cairngorms.

and is visited by a wide range of pollinating and nectar-collecting insects including beetles, moths, wasps and bees, the most frequent visitors being flies, such as St Mark's flies, *Bibio marci*, danceflies and hoverflies. Observations suggest that not all the blossoms are pollinated and yet by late July in mast years most trees are hung with abundant bunches of vivid reddish-orange berries, suggesting that unlike most rosaceous trees the flowers may be self-fertile.

At first the fruits contrast with the still-green leaves, but in autumn the foliage itself changes to orange and scarlet giving a striking effect that can contribute dramatically to the appearance of the landscape. The fruit, a two- to five-celled, berry-like pome, is a major source of food for some birds such as blackbirds and bullfinches, and in Scotland for migratory redwings. Rowan berries are too large for warblers to swallow and at the limit of

size consumable by robins. All these birds (apart from bullfinches, which eat the seeds) act as major dispersal agents for the tree, but dispersal by water has also been observed.

The seeds are characterised by deep dormancy and can require up to six months of stratification (or passage through the gut of a bird) for germination. The size and viability of seeds from trees growing at the highest altitude has been found to be reduced. The seeds are of unknown longevity but certainly remain viable in the seed bank for many years (Hill, 1979), rowan being one of the few native trees with seeds of such longevity.

Rowan coppices vigorously, and in some places has been successfully pollarded. The leaves are very palatable to the snail, *Helix aspersa*, and young growth is browsed by deer and sheep; deer culling in parts of the Cairngorms has resulted in rowan thriving and contributing to the tree-line 'moving up the mountain'. The seedlings are somewhat shade-tolerant and can grow up through juniper and especially gorse where deer grazing is heavy.

The uses of rowan

All parts of the tree are bitter and astringent; the bark has been used for tanning and to produce a black dye. The bitter berries contain tartaric acid before, and citric and malic acids after, ripening, as well as a sugar (sorbin) and the aromatic parasorbic acid. They are also rich in potassium. Medicinally the berries have been used to treat diarrhoea, as a gargle for a sore throat, and to treat scurvy. Although allegedly carcinogenic (Mabberley, 1997), the berries are used to make a tasty jelly. They have also been fermented to produce rowan perry and in Europe distilled to produce kirsch, while in Poland they are used to flavour vodka.

As with other species of *Sorbus*, the wood is tough and strong, with yellow sapwood and purplish heartwood. It has traditionally been used for handles of tools and also, when large enough, for planks and beams. Some varieties with decorative foliage and even a weeping habit are planted by horticulturalists, while var. *edulis* has sweet berries.

Folklore

The rowan is widely respected nearly everywhere for its protective power against all sorts of malign influences, witchcraft, spirits and bad luck, although this sometimes infuriates botanists, one of whom famously complained that 'accounts of this tree [are] seldom... unaccompanied by a more or less uninteresting [list] of superstitious usages respecting it'.

It is almost universally thought beneficial to have a rowan growing near to a house, and to tie up or carry parts of the tree to protect people and livestock. Cutting down rowan trees is not advised; in Ireland it is the home of good fairies, and scourge of evil ones and witches. Rowan twigs lighted on the morning of May Day 'produce smoke that will keep witches away'. Partly the protective qualities of rowan are thought to be due to the bright red berries – 'for there is no better colour against evil'.

An old Celtic name for rowan is fid nandruad or the wizard's tree, and in Ireland it plays a significant role in popular magic; 'it was hung in the house to prevent fire-charming, used to keep the dead from rising and tied as a collar on a hound to increase his speed'. Above all, rowan branches are regarded as the best protector of milk and they are hung in a byre to guard cows; this tradition is claimed to be of Viking origin (see also Fairy Trees, p.189).

In some places, pagan traditions associated with the tree have been Christianised; in Wales rowan trees are often found planted in churchyards, and people wear Easter crosses made of rowan wood.

Rowan in the ecosystem

There are few records of fungi specifically associated with rowan, and the number of fungal records is limited (see Table 5). A number of parasitic fungi attack the leaves, such as the rust *Gymnosporangium cornutum*, which produces orange-yellow swellings and horn-shaped projections on the undersides of leaves. Dark leaf-spots are caused by another parasitic fungus, *Septoria sorbi*. Fireblight, caused by the bacterium *Erwinia amyovora* has been reported to affect rowan. Rowan is very palatable to browsing animals, and this may limit its success in places where grazing pressure is intense; it is sometimes also debarked by cattle but appears to be tolerant of such damage. Rowan is occasionally host to mistletoe, *Viscum album* (see p.67).

Like other members of the genus *Sorbus*, rowan appears to be relatively unpalatable to herbivorous insects. Records of plant-feeding insects for all the *Sorbus* species (including whitebeam, wild service etc.) are limited to a total of 159, with only 24 being restricted to these trees. Other rosaceous trees like apple and hawthorn have far more. Two insects are attributed pest status by the Forestry Commission: larvae of a gall-wasp, *Torymus druparum,* damage the flowers and seeds of many rosaceous trees including rowan, while the rowan or wild service aphid, *Dysaphis aucupariae*, is the most damaging of at least 11 aphid species recorded from the tree. Rowan is the primary host of the fruit moth *Argyresthia conjugella* (also

found on apple), while the green caterpillars of the Welsh wave, *Venusia cambrica*, eat the leaves in August.

Seventeen leaf-mining micro-lepidoptera are recorded from rowan (mostly also from other *Sorbus* species), one of the most frequent being *Phyllonorycter sorbi*, whose activities cause a downward fold of the leaflet around the leaf-mine. Yellowish pustules on the leaf undersides are caused by a gall-mite, *Eriophyes sorbi*, while the flower buds are galled by a midge, *Continaria floriperda*.

Rowan appears to be equally at home in harsh conditions on poor soil in mountains and as an understorey component of dense woodland (occasionally reaching the canopy) on acid to neutral soils. Rowan is rarely present on limestone, and is thought to be limited more by its low seed viability and sensitivity to grazing than by climatic factors. It survives uprooting, damage and disturbance well. The seedlings can make use of the protection from grazing afforded by scrub and can be found in hedgerows or growing up through juniper or gorse.

BELOW The apple fruit moth, *Argyresthia conjugella*, found on rowan and other rosaceous trees.

BOTTOM Blotches on rowan leaves are caused by the mite *Phytoptus sorbi*.

SCOTS PINE *Pinus sylvestris* L.
var. *scotica* (Willd.) Schott

Pine family: Pinaceae

Also known as: fir, Scotch fir, guithais/guis (Gaelic), ochtach (Old Irish), giúis (Irish), pinwydden (Welsh). In ancient Irish law pine was one of seven noble trees. Derivative place names include Kingussie, Dalguise etc.

Biological Flora: Carlisle and Brown (1968)

Scots pine, *Pinus sylvestris*, is an evergreen coniferous tree of the pine family, which are mainly northern temperate trees but with some species growing on mountains even in the tropics. Vast expanses of forest across northern Europe to Asia are largely made up of *P. sylvestris*: the Siberian pine forests are the largest stands of any individual tree species in the world. The subspecies *scotica*, the Caledonian pine, is often pyramidal in shape, but *P. sylvestris* trees of continental origin and other growth-forms have been widely planted throughout these islands.

As a pioneer species Scots pine spread across Britain soon after the last glacial period, only preceeded by juniper, birch, aspen, hazel, holly and willow. The tree favours acid mineral soils but can grow on limestone and other base-rich sites. As the climate warmed, pine apparently became extinct around 5,500 years ago except in Scotland (and possibly at Kielder in Northumberland), being gradually overtaken by broadleaves such as oak, elm and lime. While the myth of a great Caledonian Pine Forest covering all of the Highlands within historical times has now been discounted (Rackham, 2006), the absence of fire together with the enormous increase in the numbers of deer (for visitors to shoot) has certainly prevented natural regeneration and much of the remaining forest has not regenerated itself for many years and is effectively moribund.

In Britain, Scots pine is recorded as growing to nearly 40 m (130 ft) (in sheltered parks) but more normally to about 30 m (100 ft). The characteristic features are the reddish or even orange colour of the bark on the upper part of the trunk, the paired blue-green leaves or needles and the resinous buds, the upper scales of which are free at the tips. In its Highland setting it is often a majestic tree, growing in a great variety of forms, which may be genetically determined – various authors have described between 9 and 18 major types, while plantations tend to be artificially uniform.

Scots pine has been planted in many areas of Britain and Ireland since the eighteenth century but mostly from European seed. Whatever its origin, Scots pine now forms naturally regenerating woods on acid lowland soils, particularly on the sandy Brecklands of East Anglia. In the eastern Cairngorms the native tree ascends to around 870 m (2,800 ft), and in southern Europe to over 2,200 m (7,200 ft). At its uppermost altitude Scots pine characteristically occurs in a semi-dwarf ('elfin') form, as part of the *krummholz* montane scrub; reduction of deer numbers in some places has already resulted in pines beginning to extend their range above the existing tree-line.

Like all pines, *P. sylvestris* is monoecious. The male flowers are yellow and are borne in dense clusters at the base of young shoots. The simple pollen grains have two wings, which make for wider wind dispersal (see p.14). Pollen is produced abundantly in May and June; of native trees only alder produces higher concentrations of airborne pollen. The female flowers are small cones, green at first and then gradually turning brown and maturing over three seasons so that there can be three different ages of cone on a single branch.

ABOVE Wind-weathered Scots pine, Beinn Eighe.

OPPOSITE A typical open pine woodland near Coylumbridge, Grampian.

The winged seeds are borne under the scales. Once released as a result of the alternate wetting and drying of the cones, the seeds can be carried by the wind for considerable distances, especially during dry and windy winter weather.

Pine seeds need fresh mineral soil (such as after fire) and good light to germinate. Once established the seedlings are sturdy and very frost-hardy. They are sensitive to shading, and drought, but unlike birch and rowan are too light-dependent to make use of juniper to 'nurse' the young seedlings. Once established they are suppressed but can survive the repeated winter browsing of their growing shoots by deer, although they then remain stunted and small. Where deer have been fenced out there is often spectacular establishment and regrowth.

Various groups such as Trees for Life and the RSPB are now successfully restoring and rejuvenating the pine forest by temporarily excluding deer to allow natural regeneration, in some places augmenting this by planting seedlings of pine, rowan, holly, aspen and other native species.

Except in dense stands, the mature pine trees do not usually form a complete canopy or cast a heavy shade (and in high latitudes most sunlight comes from a relatively low angle). Therefore, without overgrazing Scots pine is largely able to replace itself, although not usually on the same site except after fire (Oliver Rackham, pers. comm., 2009) or disturbance of the soil such as that caused by large mammals. Experiments with wild boar show that their activities in woodland can provide an excellent seedbed for pine (see p.197).

Preserved pine trees and pine stumps can still be found under the peat in many places, mostly dating from the Boreal period around 9,000 years ago, when climatic change resulted in inundation of the land in many areas, burying the trees. In some places, the remains of pine stumps can be found on the foreshore, where the sea-level rise drowned coastal forests.

The uses of Scots pine

The timber of Scots pine is one of the strongest softwoods and is widely used for interior construction purposes and joinery, and in Scandinavia for wood pulp (for paper). When treated with creosote, it can be used for exterior purposes such as telegraph poles, fencing etc. Pine lasts very well in wet conditions and was formerly used for waterwheels and for piles under buildings. In the eighteenth century, pine trunks were bored to make water-pipes. At Rothiemurchus in the Cairngorms a boring mill was established in 1770 and the wooden pipes were exported to London for domestic water schemes.

Pines can be pollarded although this is rarely done, but they are sometimes planted for windbreaks. In the Brecklands, rows of windbreak pines were subsequently lopped, resulting today in a series of stunted and irregular trees, seen especially on the A11 between Newmarket and Norwich. Like many pines, *P. sylvestris* can be tapped for resin, from which turpentine is produced; this is done commercially in Eastern Europe though not in the UK. Different physiological races produce various amounts and compositions of turpentine. (Most of the world's turpentine is produced from a different species, the American longleaf pine, *P. palustris*.) Other products from pine have included rope from the inner bark, tar from the roots and a reddish-yellow dye from the cones.

Medicinally, the steam from boiling fresh pine shoots, which contain aromatic turpenes like juniper, is said to relieve bronchial congestion, and pine essence is used with bath salts to combat fatigue, sleeplessness and skin irritations. Historically,

Scandinavian peasants used to grind up the inner bark to make bread, or to mix it with oats to make thin griddle cakes. Pine needle tea is recommended for vitamins A and C, but does not appear to be available commercially.

Folklore

In Celtic tradition pine is a positive tree, a symbol of renewal and of eternal life. Wordsworth extolled its virtues, especially when viewed in winter or by moonlight. Elsewhere there appears to be little folklore attached to Scots pines, but various researchers have traced the eighteenth-century planting of small groups of pines in several parts of England at prominent points along old drove-roads; some of these are still standing. The interpretation is that the dark evergreen foliage was visible from afar and so the trees acted as routemarkers. They may also have indicated the availability of accommodation for drovers and for their stock ('halfpenny fields'). One theory has it that there was a political context; the pines signified a safe house for Jacobite supporters in Protestant England. On Guernsey, pines are considered very unlucky indeed: planting pines is inadvisable as it 'may result in the loss of property'. It was even said you should not 'fall asleep under a pine tree or you (may) never wake up again'.

Scots pine in the ecosystem

Pines have a rich array of mycorrhizal relationships; young seedlings must establish these associations early in their development or they may not survive; commercial potting compost is often sterile and therefore unsuitable. Many of these fungi produce attractive fruiting bodies including edible species such as the cep or penny bun, *Boletus edulis*, the bay bolete, *B. badius*, the pine bolete, *B. pinophilus*, and slippery jack, *Suillus luteus*. Pine woods are rich in fungi of all kinds on live trees, dead timber, fallen cones or needles. Some are

very strange; the edible cauliflower fungus, *Sparassis crispa*, is parasitic on the roots, and the strange ear-pick fungus, *Auriscalpium vulgare*, grows on rotting cones. Two parasitic fungi are also a serious threat to commercial plantations of Scots pine: a bracket fungus (*Fomes*

OPPOSITE Planted Scots pines at Thirlemere in the Lake District.

TOP RIGHT The strange cauliflower fungus, *Sparassis crispa*, which grows on the boles of Scots pine trees.

MIDDLE RIGHT The well-camouflaged caterpillar of the pine looper or bordered white moth, *Bupalus piniaria*.

RIGHT The extremely hairy robber fly, *Laphria flava*, is a rare carnivorous fly restricted to native pinewoods. It predates on other insects catching them in mid flight.

123

ABOVE Mature pines with red deer; natural regeneration is
rare or non-existent under such grazing pressure.

(70 %) are restricted to the tree, the highest proportion of any native tree. Foliage-feeding caterpillars of the bordered white (also known as the pine looper: *Bupalus piniaria*) and the pine beauty moth, *Panolis flammea*, and also the larvae of the pine sawfly, *Diprion pini*, are considered serious pests in plantations, although in natural woodland they rarely do more than occasionally defoliate single trees that are probably already under environmental stress. The handsome green caterpillars of the pine hawk moth, *Hyloicus pinastri*, occur on (planted) pines in the south of England, while an attractive red and black click beetle (*Ampedus balteatus*) is now restricted mainly to the Highlands of Scotland. The largest native ladybird (*Anatis ocellata*), a red species with 20 spots, is also associated with pine forests and plantations where it feeds on aphids such as the pine woolly aphid, *Pineus pini*. Several insects such as the black pine beetle, *Hylastes ater*, the pine shoot moth, *Rhyacionia buoliana*, and the pine shoot beetle, *Tomicus piniperda*, and other wood-boring beetles and sawflies such as *Neodiprion sertifer* can cause enough damage to be regarded as economic pests, while a few tiny moths such as *Ocnerostoma piniariella* actually mine the pine needles.

Larvae of sawflies such as the horntail or 'wood-wasp', *Urocerus gigas*, tunnel in the wood of live trees but these also are usually trees already under stress. The grubs are parasitised by the spectacular giant ichneumon, *Rhyssa persuasoria*, which lays its eggs through the wood directly into the body of its host.

Pine twigs are sometimes deformed by the gall-mite *Trisetacus pini*, and other insects gall the needles (such as the gall-midge, *Thecodiplosis brachyntera*) or induce the development of sticky resinous masses on stems (pine resin-gall moth, *Retinia resinella*). A wide array of insects live in decaying pine timber. The extremely hairy robber fly *Laphria flava* attacks some of these larvae and is restricted to native pinewoods in Scotland. A related species (*L. gilva*) occurs in planted pinewoods in England. Another spectacular but extremely rare fly is the pine hoverfly, *Blera fallax* (black with a red abdominal segment), whose larvae depend on large rotting pine stumps. It is now restricted to a single site and is a Scottish BAP species in the Scottish Highlands.

The ecological strategy of the Scots pine is as a stress-tolerant pioneer, which develops as a stress-tolerant competitor. In fact some authors place Scots pine at the centre of the pioneer/stress-tolerator/competitor triangle (see p.27), as it is a resilient tree which can cope with a wide range of stresses and competition. In the Scottish Highlands (and in the vast forests across Russia), it is not overtopped by other species and it survives better than almost any other tree in harsh, cold conditions.

annosus) and the honey fungus, *Armillaria mellea*, which causes butt rot. Needle cast disease, which can be a serious cause of defoliation, is caused by another parasitic fungus, *Lophodermium seditiosum*.

A total of 297 species of plant-feeding insects and other invertebrates are recorded from living Scots pine trees, of which 209

SPINDLE-TREE *Euonymus europaeus* L.

Spindle family: Celastraceae

Also known as: (seventeenth century) as prick-timber, skewerwood, gatter, goat-bush, burning bush, bonnet-de-pretre, fusanum, fearas (Irish) and many other names.

Spindle is a small, stiff, understorey tree which grows to about 6 m (20 ft), but is perhaps most commonly seen in hedges. The foliage is not dense, and the bark is smooth and grey. A relatively recent arrival (not noticed in the pollen record earlier than 5,500 years ago), spindle is found on calcareous soils, such as on the chalk of the Chilterns, where it can be locally abundant, but also sometimes on clay or acid soils. The distribution is from the south and east as far north as the River Forth, west to include most of Ireland, ascending to 365 m (1,200 ft) in hill areas. Spindle coppices well and has long been managed in this way in Ireland.

The flowers are diminutive and greenish; pollination is by various small insects. The four-lobed fruits turn a spectacular bright pinkish-red, presumably leading to the French name 'bonnet-de-pretre' (although not all priests but only cardinals wear a scarlet biretta). When ripe, the fruits dehisce (burst) to reveal dark orange seeds each wrapped in a bright orange fleshy covering or aril.

BELOW **Mature spindle tree growing in an abandoned hedge near Henley-on-Thames.**

ABOVE The spectacular bright red fruits of the spindle tree almost look as if they are hand-painted.

ABOVE The dimutive green flowers of the spindle tree.

The uses of spindle

The name spindle indicates the use of this heavy straight wood for the traditional hand spinning of wool, although apparently this name was actually imported from the Netherlands. Butchers have long used spindle to make skewers, as it imparts no taste to the food. The stiff twigs were also used to make bows for violas, keys for the virginal, toothpicks, pipe-stems and bird-cages.

The seeds can be boiled to produce a yellow dye, which turns green when alum is added. The berries have a strongly purgative effect rather like those of buckthorn, but the seeds are generally thought to be poisonous. The fruits are fatal to sheep and the foliage is avoided by all browsers except goats, which are apparently immune to their effects, giving it the name goat-bush. When the fruits are macerated with vinegar the paste is a remedy for mange in horses and cattle, and the baked and powdered fruits were sometimes used to kill headlice.

The straight young shoots make excellent artists' fine charcoal; spindle wood has also been used to produce charcoal for gunpowder. Spindle is a decorative tree which is easily propagated from cuttings, and a number of varieties with different foliage are widely planted in gardens.

Folklore

In Buckinghamshire it is thought unlucky to bring spindle into a house; the local name being death-alder. The name *Euonymus* is associated with Euonyme, mother of the Furies, 'due to the plant's irritating properties'. Traditional stories involving accidental pricking of a finger on a sharp spindle are found in many European cultures, interpreted as part of an oral tradition referring to the loss of innocence.

Spindle in the ecosystem

The fruits of spindle are highly nutritious and are dispersed by several common birds including robin and blackbird, some of which may defend individual trees, but the poisonous seeds are not taken by seed-eaters such as finches.

Only 30 species of plant-feeding invertebrates have been recorded from spindle, of which just 10 are restricted to the tree. Spindle is a common food of aphids such as a brown subspecies of the common host-alternating *Aphis fabae*. In the south of England spindle can be heavily infested by the euonymus scale, *Unaspis euonymi*, a polyphagous pest of probable Asian origin, locally naturalised in

parts of southern England since its arrival in the 1950s, and now spreading northwards. These strange insects form sticky purplish masses on stems and leaves, under which they live, feeding on the spindle sap. Densities of one per square millimetre or 700 scales per leaf can occur, giving foliage of a whole tree a whitish look. The scale insects are browsed by the kidney-spot ladybird, *Chilocorus renipustulatus*, which has modified mouthparts enabling it to prise the female scale insect away from its protective scale.

Several moths are found on spindle, especially the gregarious spotted caterpillars of the spindle ermine, *Yponomeuta cagnagella*, which spin a silken web between leaves and which can completely defoliate the tree especially in hedges as can the white-with-black-spots looper caterpillars of the magpie moth, *Abraxas grossulariata*, normally found on currant bushes and recorded from several other broadleaved trees. The adult insect is a tiny white moth dotted black, like the caterpillars. Two gall-mites attack spindle, one, *Eriophyes convolvens,* rolling the upper side of the leaf, while the other, *Cecidophyes psilonotus,* causes an erineum or patch of hairs on the underside of leaves.

The ecological strategy of spindle is as a drought-resistant and shade-tolerant competitor, which tenaciously exploits the open habitats and woodland of dry calcareous soils.

TOP LEFT Encrustation of the recent invader, the Euonymus scale, together with its predator the kidney-spot ladybird, *Chilocorus renipustulatus*.

TOP RIGHT Leaf roll galls on spindle caused by the mite, *Eriophyes convolvens*.

ABOVE The magpie moth, *Abraxas grossulariata*, whose similarly marked caterpillars sometimes defoliate spindle trees.

STRAWBERRY TREE or ARBUTUS
Arbutus unedo L..

Heather family: Ericaceae

Also known as: caithne or gahiny (Irish), giving rise to place names in southwest Ireland such as Ishagahiny Lake (Arbutus Lake) and Doire na Caithne (Co. Clare) where it is now extinct. There is a word llwyn in Welsh meaning arbutus. In ancient Irish law, the tree is a 'commoner'.

Biological Flora: Sealy and Webb (1950)

The strawberry tree or arbutus is found on cliffs, rocky places and the edges of woodland in Killarney, scattered throughout Co. Kerry (where it ascends to around 230 m (750 ft)) and further north near Sligo near sea level. It has been widely planted and can withstand occasional frost. Pollen evidence quoted by Godwin (1984) indicates that it has been present in Ireland since at least 4,000 years ago and it may have reached Wales but if so no longer occurs naturally. It is also found in most parts of the Mediterranean. In Ireland it was formerly widespread in the southwest but has become scarce due to over-exploitation for charcoal. There has also been a suppression of fire, which may have affected it adversely and led to its being gradually shaded by taller trees (Oliver Rackham, pers. comm., 2009). Strawberry trees appear to be tolerant of salt spray (Sealy and Webb, 1950).

Strawberry trees grow to about 10–12 m (33–39 ft) on a range of soils including mineral soils down to very low pH (acid) in peaty conditions. The dark green, shiny leaves are elongated with a darker reddish serrated edge, and are paler underneath. They stay on the tree for about 15 months, giving the tree an evergreen appearance. The bark is reddish-brown and fibrous, peeling off in irregular thin shreds like that of yew. The base of the stem is apparently always swollen (possibly an adaptation to fire), and it is from this area that new buds are produced, especially after damage or cutting.

The small, creamy-white urn-shaped flowers are borne in dense inflorescences or flower clusters, and produce sweet nectar that attracts various pollinating insects, especially bees. Self-pollination is also thought to occur, although clusters of 25–50 flowers rarely produce more than 10 red, warty fruits that take a year to ripen. The tree is thus unusual in bearing both flowers and fruit simultaneously. The 'strawberries' are edible but have a weak

BELOW Full-grown Strawberry tree near Killarney, Ireland.

watery taste; the scientific name *unedo* means 'I eat one' (and no more!). The seeds germinate the following spring, but the viability is low at around 50%, increased when they have passed through the gut of birds. The seedlings can thrive on a wide range of soils, but are extremely susceptible to shading and frost. In southwest Ireland strawberry trees are largely restricted to rock crevices along the limestone shores of the Killarney lakes, where they naturally form more or less pure stands – though these have been disrupted by invasions of the alien *Rhododendron ponticum*, which has been much planted in the area.

The tree is very wind-resistant, and, like pine, fire-resistant, and may even be regarded as fire-dependent. Individual trees are often blown over, but new shoots appear with vigour all along the fallen stem. As a result, it is a very long-lasting tree, although its precise age is difficult to determine as the rotting of heartwood leaves no rings to count. Strawberry tree does not sucker like aspen but it coppices well especially after fire, and is fairly drought-resistant. A number of attractive dwarf cultivars are planted, although none is hardy.

The uses of the strawberry tree

Apart from its use for making gunpowder quality charcoal, the attractive wood varying from yellowish to deep reddish-brown has been used for inlay work, and the bark has been used for tanning. The leaves and root contain ethyl gallate, which is known to have antibiotic properties, but the full medicinal potential of arbutus has not been investigated. The 'strawberries' are eaten by birds, but it is claimed that they 'hurt the stomach and cause headaches' when eaten by humans. According to Grigson (1960), in the seventeenth century 'a decoction of the leaves and flowers was considered an excellent antidote against the plague and poisons'. The fruits contain around 15% sugar and 0.6% malic acid. They can be used to produce an inoffensive jam, while in Europe they are used to produce liqueurs: *medronho* in Portugal and liqueur à l'Arbouse in Corsica. The rumoured hallucinogenic effects of these beverages have not been substantiated.

Folklore

There is little folklore associated with arbutus, although the tree is the first of seven shrub or lower trees (less important than seven noble trees and seven peasant trees) listed among the ancient law of Ireland (see p.185).

Strawberry tree in the ecosystem

Very little is known about the biological associations of the strawberry tree in Ireland. There are only 16 fungal records in Britain where the tree is planted. Like the related heathers, it has a peculiar type of ectomycorrhizal association known as ericoid, which produces visible coral-like tubercles on the roots, some of the fungal filaments actually penetrating the root-cell walls. One of these produces the common, edible fungus called the deceiver, *Laccaria laccata*, named from its tendency to be very variable and hence difficult to identify with certainty.

So far only 10 species of plant-feeding invertebrates are recorded from strawberry tree (fewer than any other native tree), of which four are not found on any other native trees. Caterpillars of two diminutive moths, the small dark-yellow underwing, *Anarta cordigera*, and the broad-bordered white underwing, *A. melanopa*, are known from strawberry tree and the related bearberry, *Arctostaphylos uva-ursi*, while an aphid, *Wahlgreniella nervata,* is the only insect that is known to be restricted to *Arbutus unedo*.

Strawberry trees often grow at the edge of bogs or on rocks, and should be regarded as stress-tolerant pioneers. They survive disturbance well but only survive the arrival of trees such as oak and yew if subjected to occasional fires.

BELOW The deceiver, *Laccaria laccata*, an edible fungus associated with strawberry tree.

SWEET CHESTNUT *Castanea sativa* Miller

Beech family: Fagaceae

Also known as: Spanish chestnut, chestnut, but no names in Celtic languages. No place names in these islands are known to be associated with sweet chestnut.

Sweet chestnut, native to the Mediterranean region, was introduced to Britain probably two thousand years ago. It is often claimed that the chestnut was introduced by the Romans; chestnut charcoal has been identified from Roman sites across southeastern Britain. The scientific name may be derived from the town of Castania (now Kastania) in southern Greece, where it is particularly common. Over the last two millennia it has been widely planted in Britain and Ireland, especially in the southeast of England, and the Forest of Dean, as a coppice tree to produce fencing stakes. Unlike walnut which may have been introduced at around the same time, sweet chestnut has become completely naturalised (regenerating from seed in native woodland) in Kent and in the Channel Islands.

The trees are fast-growing, and can reach 35 m (115 ft), but often develop a twisted trunk and reach no more than 25 m (82 ft). Chestnut trees 'age' rapidly, and can often look older than they are, with deeply furrowed bark, prominent knot-holes and hollow trunks, all features which develop much earlier than in oaks. The natural habitat is on acid soil such as well-drained sandy loams; chestnut grows well on poor soils, even on steep slopes, and can form large pure stands in southern Europe. The flowers, in the form of catkins, are insect pollinated, and are largely self-sterile.

The nuts are eaten by squirrels, which may destroy the entire crop. Like acorns they have a short viability period; the seedlings are frost-sensitive and not very shade-tolerant.

Perhaps the most celebrated chestnut tree is the vast Tortworth Chestnut near Thornbury in south Gloucestershire, whose trunk was measured as having a circumference of over 50 ft (15 m) in 1720, and is still standing. Large plantations of coppiced chestnuts, often carpeted with bluebells in springtime, can be seen in Kent, while ancient coppice stools of 4.5 m (15 ft) or more can be found in some woods in Suffolk and Essex.

The uses of sweet chestnut

The timber is not as strong or long-lasting as oak, and develops cracks or 'shakes'. Chestnut timber has not been widely used in this country for buildings; there is a popular misconception that chestnut timbers roof Westminster Hall, but in fact the roof beams are oak (Rackham, 2006). Straight chestnut poles, cut every 12 years (Edlin, 1956) are still produced (on a coppice rotation) in Kent. They are used for supporting hops, and were formerly used for pit-props and for making barrels. Like hazel, chestnut is extremely splittable and is still popular in split form for fencing (chestnut paling), especially as it is resistant to rot, and it is also used for some furniture. Special chestnut tables and chairs are now being made in limited editions at Aconbury Wood, Duchy of Cornwall. Chestnut bark is sometimes used for tanning. Chestnut charcoal was probably used by the Romans for smelting iron and other metals in 'bloomeries', and may have been their primary motivation for planting the tree.

Sweet chestnut is a particularly rich source of tannin, which is present in large amounts in all parts of the tree. The bark is used for tanning leather, although it is apparently inferior for this purpose to oak tannin. There is a considerable industry in southern Europe to extract tannin from chestnut for various purposes including dyeing.

In some parts of southern Europe there is a long history of using ground chestnuts as a staple food. In Britain the crop of nuts is not usually of any commercial value (for use as food) and they are mostly imported from Spain. Roast chestnuts make a popular snack around

BELOW LEFT Sweet chestnut flowers and fruits.

BELOW Sweet chestnut trees take on an 'aged' appearance more quickly than most other trees. These are less than 100 years old, at Crowsley Park in Oxfordshire.

Christmas, and they can be used for stuffing game birds especially pheasant, while a particular variety (Marones) contains 15% sugar and is used to make marron glacé, the familiar French sweet

Folklore

There is little folklore associated with chestnut trees in this country. As fast-growing and impressive trees, they have become popular for planting when commemorating special events such as military victories, royal birthdays etc. (Altman, 1994).

Chestnut leaves have no odour but have an astringent taste due to high content of tannin. Culpeper recommended powdered nuts beaten with honey as a remedy for coughs 'and spitting of blood', while Grieve (1980) indicates that the leaves can be dried and later infused in boiling water to produce a medicine that is effective against 'irritable and excited conditions of the respiratory organs'. As a remedy for coughs this was apparently known in Sussex until at least the 1940s according to Vickery (1995). The application of a paste made of powdered chestnuts is supposedly a treatment for piles, and it is claimed that some gypsies carry some chestnuts in a small bag as a prophylactic.

BELOW Sweet chestnut coppice with bluebells, Mereworth, Kent.

Sweet chestnut in the ecosystem

Although it has not so far attacked trees in Britain, the chestnut-blight fungus, *Endothia parasitica*, is a serious pest of chestnut trees in North America and Europe, but in the past few decades the blight itself has been controlled by a virus so that it may cause only limited damage.

The high levels of tannin in bark and leaves protect chestnut against most foliage-eaters in Britain, although 112 mostly generalist (polyphagous) plant-feeding species have occasionally been recorded. Of these, just 16 (14%) are restricted to *Castanea*. A few moths seem to prefer chestnut to other broadleaved trees such as oak, and conservationists find that it is a useful addition to a woodland flora for some moth caterpillars – for example in years when there is major defoliation of oaks. There are very few leaf-miners, except for a few micro-moths that are found on numerous broadleaf trees, while apparently no gall species have so far been recorded on chestnut trees in Britain.

The ecological strategy of this species is as a competitor on poor, sandy soils, in sheltered places, outgrowing and shading out other species except oak, but the conditions in this country are not ideal for the natural performance of the tree.

SYCAMORE *Acer pseudoplatanus* L.

Maple family: Aceraceae

Also known as: faddy-tree, may, segumber, share, whistle-wood, wild fig-tree (Evelyn), sycamor wydden (Welsh), crann ban (Irish) and fior chrann (Gaelic), while the keys are known as chats, horse-shoes, knives-and-forks and locks-and-keys.

Biological Flora: Jones (1945)

Sycamore is a big, elegant tree thriving in open situations on all but the poorest soil types and growing to 30 m (100 ft) with a broad, spreading crown. On fertile soil it responds vigorously becoming a much-branched bushy tree, but in woodland it may become thin and strained in its effort to maximise light exposure, and in the long-term is probably shaded out. Sycamore tolerates both exposure and salt spray, ascending to nearly 500 m (1,600 ft) in some mountain areas. The most northerly wood in Britain is composed of (planted) sycamore at Baltasound on Unst, Shetland, where the trees still reach around 10 m (33 ft) in height. It is the fifth most common tree of broadleaved woodland, as recorded by the Botanical Society of the British Isles (BSBI) (www.bsbimaps.org.uk/atlas/) from more hectads (10 km squares) than any other tree, and is a common hedgerow tree in many western areas. Sycamore gradually exploits openings in many older woodlands on good soil, where it grows as a medium-age tree, longer living than birch or ash but not as long as oak or lime. It is susceptible to drought and may gradually give way in competition with ash (Morecroft *et al.*, 2008).

Sycamore occurs as a native tree in European mountains from the Pyrenees to the Balkans, thriving in harsh mountain conditions, but its origin in Britain is still a matter of controversy. Sycamore leaves are carved on St Frideswide's Shrine (dating from 1282) in Oxford cathedral, but Rackham and others argue that the absence of old Celtic or Saxon names for the tree suggests that it was absent from Britain in earlier times. It was thought to have been first

LEFT Spectacular autumn colours of a single sycamore tree on the banks of Coniston Water in the Lake District.

133

LEFT AND ABOVE This sycamore tree at Boot, Eskdale, has hardly changed in 60 years, since the monochrome photo was taken.

introduced into Scotland (earlier than in England) as early as the fifteenth century. Jones (1945) suggests that the earliest record is that of the sycamore avenues planted around Castle Methven, Perth, around 1487. Gerard (1597) refers to the tree as 'a stranger in England... especially planted for its shadowe sake'.

Ted Green (2005) believes that it was here long before this and has suggested that it should be renamed the 'Celtic Maple'. He points out that sycamore pollen may have been mistaken for that of field maple and quotes (unconfirmed) claims that charcoal and waterlogged wood found in Bronze Age and Iron Age burials are sycamore. Just because sycamore behaves (and is regarded by many country people) as a completely native tree is not evidence for its claimed native status. There is, however, an old name in Gaelic (fior chrann), which does suggest its ancient existence in Scotland, while the word sycamore actually comes from a different tree altogether, the biblical sycamore (a fig, *Ficus sycamorus*).

The bark, smooth when young, develops scales, which split off in large sections on old trees, and this characteristic probably explains why sycamore survives well under conditions of heavy air pollution and thus has been much planted in industrial towns. Sycamore is deep-rooted and responds vigorously to coppicing or pollarding.

A single tree of 19 m (62 ft), aged 48 years was investigated in detail (Jones, 1945). It bore 8,970 leaves with a total dry weight of the foliage of 3.3 kg (7¼ lb), compared with 12,000 leaves totalling just 0.9 kg (2 lb) on a 41-year-old field maple.

The flowers are borne in racemes containing up to 100 flowers, the earliest ones being male and opening first. They are mildly scented and produce nectar which attracts a variety of insects including bees, hoverflies and St Mark's flies, *Bibio marci*. Up to about 30 fruits are produced per raceme.

Sycamore seeds germinate in spring, especially in disturbed ground, and do not persist in the seed bank. The seedlings can grow very rapidly but are sensitive to drought, grazing and herbaceous competition. An invasive species, sycamore has become very unpopular with gardeners because of the mass germination of seeds in flower-beds, plant-pots and guttering, although relatively few of these seedlings survive for long. They are partly shade-tolerant (growing through low ground vegetation and even juniper scrub (Little Langdale)) but do not do well under the canopy of sycamore trees. If they do become established bud break is particularly early in saplings, before both the mature trees and that of competitors such as ash.

In open, disturbed ground sycamore saplings can rapidly out-compete other trees and shrubs; the tree is referred to as a 'weed' and some local councils claim to have 'declared war on the sycamore'. In nature reserves and ancient woodland it is frequently removed by land managers on the basis that it is an unwanted element in the local environment. Perhaps this view should be tempered by the knowledge that sycamore does support a wide range of associated species and provides a good supply of nectar and pollen for many insects, while the dead wood attracts many species of fungi.

The uses of sycamore

The light, even-grained wood of sycamore is a favourite with wood-turners for making bowls and plates, and since it does not taint food it is used for chopping boards and other kitchen utensils. Easy to work, it is carved to make small ornamental objects such as intertwined pairs of Welsh 'love-spoons' carved from a single piece of wood. The leaves may be dried and given to sheep in winter; in Cumbria sycamores are pollarded in hard winters and that season's twigs are eaten by sheep.

Folklore

Whether it is native or introduced, the folkloric associations of sycamore are surprisingly numerous. Country people, especially in Cornwall, have long gone 'faddying' on May Day, children making peweeps or whistles from sycamore twigs by sliding off the bark. At Helm Common, Kendal, a sycamore was a wishing tree; children would carry a stone to the tree where they would make a wish, then spit on the stone and add it to the stone wall nearby.

In Ireland a famous ancient sycamore marked the site of St Fintan's Well at Clonenagh, Co. Laois. Water found in a hollow of the tree was claimed to give relief to visitors with bad eyes and to cure various other ailments as well. It became a 'money tree', where the tradition was to hammer a coin into the trunk of the tree before taking the water and saying a prayer. By 1991 there were thousands of coins in the trunk. Unfortunately, the copper coins may have contributed to the tree's demise; just a few years later it collapsed and died.

The Aldenham trees

At the village of Aldenham in Hertfordshire, three sycamores grew from the grave of William Hutchinson (d. 1697) and his wife Margaret (d. 1706). They allegedly had declared their disbelief in the Resurrection and claimed that if trees grew from the grave 'the living would know there was a life after death'. This whole story was dismissed many years ago (Gibbs, 1928), and in any case would declared unbelievers have been buried inside the churchyard at all?

In fact Hutchinson is thought to have been a pious man who left money for the vicar to distribute among the poor of the parish at Christmas (this is still done). The aged trees were finally removed in the 1950s, and all that remains today is a few fragments of rotted stump, while the whole tomb is overgrown with ivy.

A similar story is told about the dying Lady Grimston at Tewin, also in Hertfordshire, above whose tomb a sycamore and an ash, each with seven stems, have grown up. Vickery comments, 'both of these graves are enclosed within substantial iron railings; they have been protected from mowing or grazing animals, thus encouraging the growth of trees'.

The persistence and extent of such legends is extraordinary; similar tales are known from many places including Passenham in Northamptonshire, Chislehurst in Kent, Cheshunt in Hertfordshire, Perivale in Middlesex and even Hanover, Germany (Westwood and Simpson, 2005).

BELOW The Aldenham tomb in 1934 (left) and in 1951 just after the sycamore trees are felled.

Elsewhere, sycamores have long been associated with death. There was a tradition in Scotland that feudal lords hanged their enemies on sycamore trees, which were known as 'dool trees' or 'joug trees'. In Wiltshire when a large sycamore tree blew down as recently as January 1938 it was considered an unlucky event; it had been referred to locally as a 'hanging tree'.

Sycamore in the ecosystem

Sycamore is susceptible to a fungal pathogen *Cryptostroma corticale*, which causes sooty bark disease. This can kill mature trees very quickly, especially when (as is quite frequent in urban situations) they are under water stress during hot summer weather. The common black tar-spot on sycamore leaves is caused by an ascomycete fungus, *Rhytisma acerinum*; it is sensitive to sulphur dioxide and occurs less frequently in urban areas or near other sources of atmospheric pollution. The parasitic toothwort, *Lathraea squamaria*, has been recorded from sycamore roots.

The most familiar insect associated with sycamore is the yellowish-green aphid *Drepanosiphum platanoides*, which is responsible for the deluge of sticky honeydew similar to that falling from lime trees. Vast numbers can occur, and they spread themselves out uniformly over the leaf surfaces. These insects have given the tree a bad name for centuries: 'the Honey-dew leaves... fall early, turn to a mucilage and (with their) noxious insects... contaminate and marr our walks, and therefore, by my consent, are to be banish'd from gardens and avenues' (John Evelyn). Though diminutive in size *D. platanoides* makes up in numbers: a single sycamore tree can be infested with over two million individual insects, 'equivalent in mass to a large rabbit' (Dixon and

LEFT In some places like Little Langdale in Cumbria sycamores have been pollarded for over a hundred years.

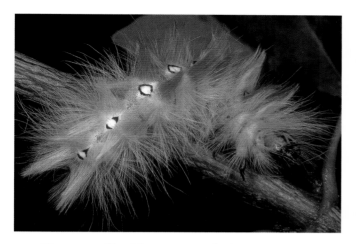

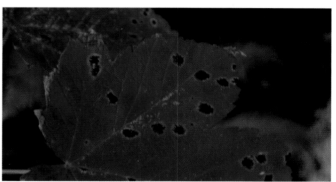

ABOVE Bizarre caterpillar of the sycamore moth, *Acronicta aceris*. The adult moth is a drab greyish colour.

ABOVE RIGHT Common red pustule galls on sycamore caused by the mite, *Aceria cephaloneus*.

RIGHT Blotches caused by the leaf fungus, *Rhytisma* sp., which is sensitive to air pollution. These leaves were photographed on the island of Lismore, Argyll.

Thieme, 2007). In summer the aphids collect in the lower canopy where leaf temperatures of midday can be 10°C (18°F) below those of the upper canopy. Damage to the foliage by aphids has been estimated to reduce the production of wood by 75% or more.

Sycamore foliage is very palatable and therefore susceptible to grazing mammals, and it also attracts many general broadleaf defoliators but few specialists. Just 22 of the 202 invertebrate species recorded from *Acer* species are restricted to sycamore. The bizarre caterpillars of the sycamore moth, *Acronicta aceris*, are bright orange, covered with dense tufts of orange hairs and bear a series of white-bordered black marks down their backs. These can occur in great numbers (and also on the foliage of field maple and horse-chestnut) but mainly in England south of a line from the Severn to the Humber. Disappointingly, perhaps, the orange colour fades at pupation; the adult is an unremarkable mottled grey moth.

Whitish blotches (felt galls) on sycamore leaves are caused by a gall-mite *Aceria pseudoplatani*, while the very common rashes of tiny red pustules on the upper leaf surface are caused by the gall-mite *Aceria cephaloneus* or (larger galls) *A. macrorhynchus*, while several gall-midges cause leaf-rolls and other distortions. At least eight species of insect mine sycamore leaves, varying from

simple blanked sections of leaf (the sawfly, *Heterarthrus aceris*) to beautifully intricate, tiny worm-like designs, *Stigmella speciosa*. Sycamore leaves decompose faster than most tree leaves, partly due to the coating of sugars from the aphids, which promotes bacterial and fungal growth on the dead leaf surface. As with lime leaves, this in turn promotes the activity of earthworms and nitrogen-fixing bacteria. In areas of poor soil and mountain areas the effect of sycamore is therefore to stimulate a rapid improvement of the soil fertility, reducing acidity and increasing organic content.

Mice 'avidly seek the seed and store [the seeds] in caches' (Jones, 1943), and may destroy a whole crop, while squirrels, crossbills and finches also eat the seeds. Rabbits apparently do not browse the foliage, although deer will do so, while grey squirrels attack the bark, often killing small trees.

Ecologically, sycamore has two different habits. It is an effective pioneer especially on lowland, nitrogen-rich soils, but it is short-lived and is ultimately overtopped by other species such as oak and ash (and probably beech and hornbeam) in relatively benign conditions. On the other hand, it is also a successful stress-tolerant competitor in harsher conditions. Its natural habitat is on mountain slopes, and it survives well in exposed places subject to cold and salt spray.

137

WAYFARING TREE *Viburnum lantana* L

> **Honeysuckle family**: Caprifoliacae
>
> **Also known as**: cobin-tree, coven-tree, dog-berry, dogwood, twistwood, whitten-tree and others; Grigson gives 17 names from as far north as Lancashire and Lincolnshire.
>
> **Biological Flora**: Kollman *et al.* (2002)

The wayfaring tree is usually no more than a shrub but it can grow to a densely branched 6 m (20 ft) tree in favourable situations on free-draining calcareous soils in sheltered but sunny, woodland-edge situations. It is native to the southern half of England (the northern limit of its European range) and in southern Wales, and with other *Viburnum* species has been widely planted elsewhere. On chalk downlands it is commonly found with hawthorn or within ash/field maple woodland, and in hedges. It is a lowland tree, only ascending to 285 m (935 ft) in Wiltshire, although it it is found above 2,000 m (6,500 ft) in Eastern Europe.

The characteristically paired, round, finely serrated, well-veined leaves and the twigs are felted with fine hairs. In autumn the

LEFT **Wayfaring tree in full blossom, Box Hill, Surrey.**

ABOVE Wayfaring tree blossom with visiting pollinator; a dance-fly, *Empis tesselata.*

ABOVE Wayfaring tree fruits showing the two colour fruit display advertising the berries to birds.

leaves turn a range of brilliant colours from orange through crimson to purple.

The attractive flat-topped inflorescences are creamy-white and give off a rather sickly aroma that attracts flies, especially hoverflies, as well as pollen beetles and bees. The flowers are self-fertile and usually set seed even if not visited by insects. The seeds do not survive long in the seed bank, while the seedlings are particularly shade-tolerant at first, but for onward growth are light-demanding. They are sensitive to waterlogging but recover well from drought.

The uses of wayfaring tree

The wayfaring tree has been widely planted by horticulturalists for the autumn colour of leaves and fruits, and because it attracts hoverflies (whose larvae eat aphids).

The wood is hard and dense-grained; it is used for the wooden pins holding together yokes for oxen, partly in a belief that it protects the cattle. The bark and leaves contain compounds with pharmacological potential including the bitter resin viburnin. According to Grigson, 'leaves and berries have been used to make a gargle, fasten the teeth, and settle the stomach. The crushed leaves to blacken the hair. You can eat the fruit when they go black, with no ill consequence, but also, I think, with no great pleasure'.

Historically, flexible young branches of wayfaring tree were used for binding sheafs and in wickerwork. The Neolithic 'Iceman' whose body emerged from an Austrian glacier was found to be carrying arrows whose shafts were made of viburnum wood.

Folklore

No particular tree lore is recorded as relating to wayfaring tree, except the name twistwood, which refers to its use for 'twisting into whip-handles'.

Wayfaring tree in the ecosystem

Few mycorrhizal fungi have been recorded from the tree; the national database gives just 20 fungal records. Wayfaring tree can be affected by honey fungus (see Table 7) and some parasitic fungi cause leaf-spots and mildew, but these are most frequently seen on cultivated trees in gardens rather than on wild trees or bushes. Dead branches are sometimes attacked by a saprophytic fungus, *Diplodia lantanae.* The leaves are unpalatable to both rabbits and deer and the tree can successfully colonise rabbit warrens.

As with other 'minor' trees, the plant-feeding insects associated with the wayfaring tree have received relatively little attention

ABOVE AND RIGHT The larva and adult of the viburnum beetle, *Pyrrhalta viburni*, which can completely defoliate wayfaring trees.

BELOW RIGHT Spectacular orange-tailed clearwing, *Synanthedon andrenaeformis*, found only on *Viburnum* spp.

and only 35 are recorded, 17 of them (49%) restricted to the tree. This small number may be partly due to the sparse and limited occurrence of the tree here; in Europe many other associated insects are known.

Among the more spectacular plant-feeders on viburnum is the orange-tailed clearwing moth, *Synanthedon andrenaeformis*, whose caterpillars bore into the stems. Three leaf-miners are recorded, one of which, *Phyllonorycter lantanella,* is specific to *Viburnum* species, but ordinary leaf-eaters are scarce, possibly due to the hairy leaves. One micro-moth, which curls leaves and feeds on them, is a scarce tortrix *Acleris schalleriana*. The complete skeletonisation of young leaves on whole bushes is sometimes achieved by the yellow and black grubs, and later in the season the pale brown furry adults, of the viburnum flea-beetle *Pyrrhalta viburni*. Two gall-midges, *Contarinia* spp., cause swollen flower buds, another, *Sackenomyia reaumurii*, causes pustules on the leaves, and the gall-mite *Eriophyes viburni* induces red pouch galls on the upper surface of the leaves, while aphids such as *Ceruraphis eriophori* curl the leaves.

A wide range of insects visit the flowers, of which by far the most frequent are small sap-beetles (Nitidulidae) and tiny pollen-feeding beetles (Scraptiidae). The fruits are a striking example of what Snow and Snow (1988) refer to as a two-colour fruit display. As they ripen in July the juicy fruits first become bright red but then within a week or two turn black, and within another

two weeks or so begin to shrivel. They interpret this as meaning that red phase advertises the site of future fruits for birds such as blackbird, robin and blackcap, the main seed dispersers, which then feed on some of the ripe black fruits in early August. These ripe fruits also attract small flies and ants.

The wayfaring tree is a short-lived light-demanding pioneer of dry calcareous soils; once surrounded by other trees it is shaded out by all except ash. Its place in a succession from grassland to woodland (on chalk or limestone) appears to be similar to that of hawthorn – its ecological strategy is that of a stress-tolerant pioneer, and it is gradually shaded out by taller trees.

WHITEBEAMS *Sorbus* spp.

Rose family: Rosaceae
(Common) whitebeam *Sorbus aria* L. Crantz
French hales, Devon whitebeam *Sorbus devoniensis* E.F.Warb.
Rock whitebeam *Sorbus rupicola* (Syme.) Hedl.
and other scarce whitebeams (*Sorbus* spp.)

Also known as: Common whitebeam is also known as
chess-apple, hen-apple, quickbeam, whittenbeam, white-rice,
white hazel, hoar withy and even wild pear tree (Derbyshire),
fionncholl (Irish), cerddinen (Welsh). The name whitebeam is
not recorded earlier than the eighteenth century (Grigson, 1960).

This is a group of very similar trees. The common whitebeam, *S. aria,* is generally very distinctive with a wide, dense crown, upward-sloping branches and smooth, dark grey bark growing to about 15 m (49 ft). The leaves are a silvery pale green when they first appear, contrasting well with the dark bark. Later, the green becomes brighter, although the downy undersides remain silvery, while in autumn the upper surfaces turn gold or russet.

ABOVE Characteristic pale, silvery buds of common whitebeam, Box Hill, Surrey.

BELOW Mature whitebeam on the chalk escarpment at Aston Rowant NNR, Oxfordshire.

Common whitebeam occurs naturally in woodland, scrub and heathland on a range of soils across southern England, as far north as Derby, perhaps most characteristically on base-rich soils such as chalk. It has been widely planted elsewhere as far north as Shetland, and it occasionally escapes from cultivation. It is generally a lowland tree, but it can be found at an elevation of 455 m (1,500 ft) in Upper Teesdale, where it may have been planted. Planted trees certainly thrive throughout these islands, and still produce viable seed as far north as Shetland.

French hales or Devon whitebeam, *S. devoniensis,* is locally frequent in north Devon as a hedgerow tree (up to about 8 m/ 26 ft), and is sometimes also found in woodland. It also occurs naturally in southeast Ireland and has become well established in Northern Ireland as an escape from cultivation.

Rock whitebeam, *S. rupicola,* is a small tree reaching about 2 m (6½ ft), which occurs as solitary individuals on limestone and basalt in north and west Britain and rarely in Ireland, ascending to 500 m (1,600 ft) in the Cairngorms. The creamy white flowers of whitebeams are small – 1.5 cm (½ in) across – and are borne in loose clusters on already swollen ovaries, appearing well after the leaves. The fruits are round, bright red and larger than many other berries like hawthorn and rowan. They are popular with birds and squirrels, having a better pulp to seed ratio than the otherwise similar rowan fruits, though they ripen later and do not stay as long on the tree. In Lancashire and Cumbria, the fruits are known as chess-apples (a name also used to refer to medlars: *Mespilus germanica*). The fruits of *S. devoniensis* are slightly larger and brownish, and were traditionally sold as fruit for eating in Devon markets, where they may still be found in good years.

Other whitebeams

Apart from Swedish whitebeam, *S.intermedia*, which is not a native tree, other reasonably widespread species of whitebeam include English whitebeam, *S. anglica* Hedl., a small tree found on

LEFT The rare rock whitebeam, *Sorbus rupicola*, growing on a limestone outcrop on the Isle of Skye.

BELOW Blossom of the rare Ley's whitebeam, *Sorbus leyana*.

limestone cliffs of the Avon Gorge at Bristol. The Lancashire whitebeam, *S. lancastriensis* E. F. Warb., is endemic to a small limestone area around Morecambe Bay. The bloody whitebeam, *S. vexans* E. F. Warb., and Somerset whitebeam, *S. subcuneata* Wilm., occur on sandstone and slates along the north Devon and Somerset coasts. The Arran service tree, *S. pseudofennica* E. F. Warb., Arran whitebeam, *S. arranensis* Hedlund., and the newly discovered Catacol whitebeam, *S. pseudomeinichii* Ashley Robertson, are only found on acid soils on the Isle of Arran.

All these rare trees are currently being studied and DNA analysis is being used to unravel their identities and track a rapidly changing situation. Many of the scarce species are polyploid, i.e. they have more than the normal (diploid) two sets of chromosomes. They reproduce apomictically, that is the seeds are not fertilised (and so have no genetic input from a paternal parent) and are thus direct copies or clones of the mother tree's chromosomes. To develop, they do require pollination to take place (to stimulate growth of the seeds) but not actual fertilisation of the ovum. In some cases cross-pollination between species has apparently led to fertilisation and then by apomixis these new entities have become fixed.

It seems that these scarcer species have originated from crossing between various combinations of the normal diploid trees such as rowan, common whitebeam, or wild service, with apomictic polyploids such as rock whitebeam, *S. rupicola*, or grey-leaved whitebeam, *S. porrigentiformis*. Physiologically these 'microspecies' are all slightly different, and as the climate changes some will inevitably be better suited than others. In 100 or 200 years some of these scarce trees may out-compete their parent species while others may have disappeared completely. There are already programmes to conserve and protect many of these species, however uncompetitive (and therefore rare) some of them are under present conditions – although of course conditions may change to their benefit. Under natural selection some would disappear naturally, but it is now realised that even uncompetitive species have genetic variability that could be of significance in the future. For example, if one of these 'microspecies' exhibited new resistance to a common orchard pest, such as apple and pear scab, *Venturia inaequalis*, it could be valuable for traditional plant-breeding. For this reason alone, conservation of these rare trees is worthwhile.

rocks and cliffs in southwest England, south Wales and very rarely at Killarney in Ireland; grey-leaved whitebeam, *S. porrigentiformis* E. F. Warb., which grows in similar places in southwest England and south Wales; and Irish whitebeam, *S. hibernica* E. F. Warb., which occurs at scattered sites across Ireland sometimes in woodland but most often in hedges.

Several other species of whitebeam with very restricted distributions are some of our rarest trees, and a number of these have only recently been described, mainly from the Avon Gorge, Cheddar Gorge and adjacent areas (Rich *et al.*, 2010).

Bristol whitebeam, *S. bristoliensis* Wilm., and Wilmott's whitebeam, *S. wilmottiana* E. F. Warb., are both endemic to the

The uses of whitebeam

As with most rosaceaous trees, whitebeam wood is even-grained and very hard. Whitebeam wood is white, and excellent for wood-turning and fine joinery. John Evelyn is said to have had one of his rooms panelled with whitebeam. In the past, the wood was used for gunstocks and for wood-engraving and before cast iron replaced it, for making cog-wheels and other hard-wearing machine parts. However, there is no record of it being planted or specially managed in England for this purpose.

Whitebeam fruits are edible especially once they begin to ferment. John Evelyn recommended mixing the pulp with new wine and honey to produce a beverage with the 'admirable effect to corroborate [settle] the stomach'.

Folklore

In Ireland, whitebeam (possibly the Irish whitebeam, *S. hibernica*) is said to be a symbol of a king's authority. There is also an old saying to the effect that the leaves of whitebeam curl up to show their silvery side to predict rain (Vickery, 1995), but otherwise there appears to be little or no recorded folklore associated with the trees.

Whitebeams in the ecosystem

Whitebeam, like some other rosaceous trees (but not *Prunus*), is susceptible to fireblight, *Erwinia amylovora*, which causes shrinking and blackening of tissues, eventually killing the tree, but few fungal species, either parasitic or mycorrhizal, are known to be specifically associated with these trees; just 48 are recorded in the Fungal Records Database of Britain and Ireland (compared with 344 for rowan).

The associated insect fauna is limited (most of the 182 species recorded for *Sorbus* species being from rowan, not whitebeams or wild service). Only one rare, tiny moth, *Argyresthia sorbiella*, appears to be restricted to whitebeam: the caterpillars feed on the shoots and flower buds. There are no published records of insects associated with *S. devoniensis* but the writer collected caterpillars of mottled umber, *Erannis defoliaria*, from a tree at Watersmeet, north Devon. Aphids, *Dysaphis aucupariae*, cause yellowish to reddish, rolled pseudogalls on the leaves, buds and shoots; inside the curled tissue the aphids are grey and bluish-green. The secondary host of these insects is usually plantain (*Plantago* spp.).

Yellowish pustules (erinea, or patches of hairs) on the undersides of whitebeam leaves are induced by tiny gall-mites; three forms are known from the commonest three *Sorbus* species (*Phytoptus sorbi* on rowan, *Vasates arianus* on whitebeam and *P. pyri* var. *torminalis* on wild service), but they also occur on other whitebeams (*S. devoniensis*, for example), although which species of gall-mite is involved is not known.

Whitebeam is a light-demanding, fast-growing competitor on well-drained calcareous soil. In dense beech–hornbeam woodland on flat ground it is probably shaded out, but on slopes of chalk or limestone it appears to hold its own – at places like Box Hill whitebeams stand out as silvery individuals in the darker woodland canopy. French hales is probably similar but occurring on a less base-rich soil. Rock whitebeam is a highly stress-tolerant pioneer, also on base-rich soil, and most of the others are light-demanding species requiring base-rich soil while a few thrive on acid soil.

ABOVE Foliage of Devon whitebeam, *S. devoniensis*, with leaf galls caused by an unidentified mite, probably *Vasates* sp.

ABOVE Caterpillar of common mottled umber, *Erannis defoliaria*, found on whitebeam, other rosaceous trees and also birch.

WHITTY PEAR or TRUE SERVICE TREE
Sorbus domestica L.

> **Rose family:** Rosaceae
>
> **Also known as:** service-tree, ceri or geri (Welsh). Place names: Porthceri, Fontigeri.

The whitty pear tree is superficially similar to the rowan (or whitty tree) in size and appearance, but it has a narrowly fissured rather than smooth bark. The attractive feathery foliage is serrated along only half the length of each leaflet, there being typically no more than seven points on either side, whereas in rowan there are more, usually 12 to 15. Unlike rowan, the whitty pear tree produces suckers and occurs in a clonal group like aspen or wild cherry.

The flowers, with pink-flushed petals, are larger and more conspicuous than those of rowan, and have five styles (instead of three to four). The shape of the whole inflorescence is pyramidal. The fruits are green, turning brownish, and usually less than 2 or 3 cm (1 in) long, but larger and longer than the 'berries' of rowan although smaller than cultivated pears.

S. domestica is characteristic of calcareous (lime-rich) soils, and is widely distributed in southern Europe, in North Africa and as far as the Middle East. According to the Worcestershire naturalist Norman Hicken, the first record of this 'ash-tree bearing pears' in Britain was in 1678, when Alderman Edmund Pitts reported a single *'Sorbus pyriformis'* tree growing in the Wyre Forest, near Bewdley. The tree was well known locally and a flowering branch was exhibited at the Worcestershire Naturalists' Club in 1855. In 1862 this tree was burnt down, but grafts were already flourishing elsewhere, and two trees in the grounds of Arley Castle (Worcestershire) were claimed to have been raised from seed. A descendant of the original tree was planted and grows near the original spot in the Wyre Forest today. Other specimens, some possibly descended from the original tree, are growing in a number of arboreta; the tallest individual, at 23 m (75 ft), grows at Claremont House in Surrey.

Until the mid-1990s the Wyre Forest tree was the only recorded specimen in Britain, raising the question as to whether it had been introduced, but even then some botanists believed that the tree could occur at places such as cliffs above the River Wye: 'If so, an interesting discovery is waiting to be made, and one that would

RIGHT Whitty pear, or true service tree, growing on soft calcareous cliffs on the bank of the river Severn near Sedbury, west Gloucestershire. (See also picture of fruits on p.201 and the tree p.193.)

confirm whether or not it is truly a native species' (Milner, 1992). When writing this sentence I was unaware that a clonal group of trees of an unidentified *Sorbus* species had already been found on almost inaccessible south-facing ledges of soft calcareous shale cliffs at Fontigeri on the Glamorgan coast. The trees were discovered by a local botanist, Marc Hampton, who eventually managed to collect both examples of foliage and some fruits, but the identity of these

trees was not established as *Sorbus domestica* L. until 1994 (Hampton and Kay, 1995). Subsequently, further trees were discovered a few miles along the coast at Porthceri; at Sedbury, near Chepstow; and finally a larger population was found at Horseshoe Bend on the River Avon at Shirehampton near Bristol.

The names of the first two sites in Welsh are Porthceri ('harbour of the service trees') and Fontigeri ('spring or well of the service trees'), both dating from at least the thirteenth and fifteenth centuries. This suggests the trees have long been known in the area (a different word, sorff, is used locally to refer to wild service trees, *S. torminalis.*)

The true service thrives in woodland on the rapidly shifting ground of the soft cliffs by suckering profusely and also by layering; some branches have sprouted roots where they touch the soil. Perhaps it is competes weakly with other trees except on such unstable ground, but it is clearly tolerant of salt spray and prospers on these south-facing slopes.

BELOW True service tree foliage infected by leaf wilt, probably *Venturia* sp.

BELOW RIGHT The creamy-white, lightly scented, inflorescence of the true service tree.

The uses of whitty pear

In continental Europe the fruit is sometimes used to make perry, but this tradition does not appear to be known on this side of the Channel.

Folklore

The origin of whitty is said to be the old English word witten (to know), meaning a wise tree, a stick of whitty offering stronger protective power than the related rowan. It was traditional in the Wyre Forest area to hang up bunches of the hard dry fruit 'to keep out witches'.

Whitty pear in the ecosystem

Few observations have yet been made about associations of *S. domestica* with other species in the wild. There are five fungal records from planted trees, and a fungal pathogen (*Venturia* sp. possibly *inaequalis*) infects the leaves of most of the cliff specimens in South Wales.

WILD CHERRY *Prunus avium* L.

Rose family: Rosaceae

Also known as: gean, crab-cherry, mazzard, merry-tree, merry, silín (Irish), ceiriosen (Welsh), craobh shirist (Gaelic).

Wild cherry – the scientific name means 'bird's cherry' – not to be confused with bird cherry, *Prunus padus* – occurs commonly in most parts of Britain, as far north as Caithness and Sutherland; however, there is the suggestion that in most parts of Scotland wild cherry is only associated with human habitation, and has all been planted (Wilson *et al.*, 1999). Wild cherry grows to 29 m (95 ft) with straight, upward-sloping branches, and is rarely overtopped. It is shallow-rooted and favours fertile, warm, south-facing sites on a wide variety of soils often, but not exclusively, at the edge of woodland. Numerous suckers are produced, so wild cherry nearly always occurs as a clonal group of trees.

The reddish-brown bark is smooth with characteristic horizontal lines of corky lenticels. In early April blossom covering the trees can light up the bare woodland 'like a troupe of towering brides in all their finery', while later 'the foliage is a fiery mix of yellow and crimson' (Mabey, 1996) and has inspired many writers since John Evelyn.

Bees are much attracted to the blossom, which provides both pollen and nectar early in the season and does not have the unpleasant aroma of the bird cherry. The flowers are completely self-sterile, like those of apple.

Wild cherry fruits, variously known as merries, mazzards and other local names, are black or dark red with relatively little flesh around the stone compared with cultivated varieties, but still sweet and good to eat. They are widely made into jams and jellies, unlike the smaller black fruit of *P. padus*, which is too sour to eat. Most birds that attack the fruit tend to eat the flesh alone. The stones are too large for small birds to manage but the cherries can be taken whole by woodpigeons and are also eaten by foxes. The seeds do not germinate immediately, even after passing through a bird's or a fox's gut, usually remaining dormant for at least a year, like the fruits of most native rosaceous trees.

BELOW **An ancient wild cherry tree at Loch an Eilein in the Cairngorms; most, if not all old cherry trees in Scotland are found at the sites of existing or abandoned dwellings.**

The uses of cherry

Cherry wood is reddish-brown in colour, has a fine, attractive grain, and is used for panelling and wood-carving. Cherry burls are much sought after by wood-turners for the richly patterned effects that can be produced, and smoking pipes were often made from cherry.

The bark, and especially the root bark, is collected for its medicinal properties. Dried and ground-up, its taste is aromatic and bitter; it contains an essential oil derived from hydrocyanic acid. In syrup or alcohol the powdered bark is used as a tonic, a sedative and to treat bronchitis, while the gum or resin is said to be good for the complexion. (The commercially available tinctures are made from a related North American species of cherry.)

John Evelyn recommends the 'darking' or wild cherry as 'excellent' for making wine, but Grigson, who refers to the blossom and the wood as 'virtuous', is less sanguine about the fruit. He dismisses it as 'only of use for the purposes of cherry brandy', and although the fruit used to be sold 'on the branch' around London, he quotes Gerard who says that 'they contain bad juice... [and] very soon putrify'. Culpeper recommends the juice of wild cherries for urinary complaints. Today wild cherry wine is produced by Moniack Wineries, and both jams and chutneys made with wild cherry are widely available.

Folklore

Cherry stones have been found in a Bronze Age crannog (loch dwelling) in Co. Offaly, Ireland. Various *Prunus* species are among the earliest domesticated plants apart from apple; cultivated cherries having both *P. avium* and the related *P. cerasus* (dwarf cherry) in their genetically complex ancestry.

In many places cherry blossom is widely appreciated and seen as uplifting and optimistic. As Houseman enthuses: 'Loveliest of trees, the cherry now /is hung with bloom along the bough'. In Ireland it has a romantic connotation being associated with youthfulness, beauty and love. In Japan cherry blossom (probably a hybrid of *P. avium* with *P. serrulata*) is known as 'sato zakura', a national symbol of peace; viewing cherry blossom is an old tradition associated with good luck and happiness, with a public holiday devoted to it. Cherry trees are regularly planted in memory of those who died at Hiroshima and Nagasaki. However, there are other traditions; in Somerset wild cherry blossom is thought to be particularly unlucky as decoration for a wedding, with associations of infertility or even future infidelity.

Wild cherry in the ecosystem

Some ectomycorrhizal fungi are recorded from wild cherry among just 202 records in the Fungal Records Database of Britain and Ireland. The tree is attacked by several parasitic fungi, which cause witches' brooms, *Taphrina wiesneri*, leaf scorch, *Apiognomonia erythostoma,* and 'shot-holes' in the leaves, *Blumeriella jaapii*, the last also being a serious pest of cultivated cherry in Europe. The powdery mildew *Podosphaera clandestina* also affects the leaves and

LEFT **Single clone of wild cherry trees, with many nearby suckers, Hampstead Heath, London.**

ABOVE LEFT Bark of wild cherry showing its characteristic horizontal lines of corky lenticels (pores).

ABOVE Cherry blossom attracts bees and flies in early April, when there are few other sources of pollen and nectar.

LEFT The tiny moth, *Phyllonorycter cerasicolella*, whose caterpillars commonly mine the leaves of wild cherry.

is a pest in orchards, the bacterium *Pseudomonas syringae* causes a disfiguring canker and dieback, while another fungus *Monilinia laxa* can cause blossom wilt.

The diversity of insects associated with cherries is fairly low: just 46, of which only 17 (37%) are restricted to *P. avium*. This compares with 159 species restricted to the related blackthorn, *P. spinosa*, and a total of 383 species recorded for all *Prunus* (although some of these may refer to introduced species). Some defoliating caterpillars can cause considerable damage, although wild cherry can sometimes be left unaffected when adjacent oak, hazel and hornbeam are stripped bare (Queen's Wood, north London, May 2008). The cherry blackfly, *Myzus cerasi*, induces the leaves to shrivel and curl inward producing sticky 'leaf nests' of these aphids, which can become covered with sooty moulds (ascomycete fungi). *M. cerasi* is regarded as a pest in cherry orchards and while common, it rarely does serious damage to wild trees. Another commercial pest is the cherry bark tortrix, *Enarmonia formosana*,

which commonly attacks ornamental cherries and which also occurs on wild cherry.

Leaf-mines in wild cherry leaves are excavated by at least five species of tiny moth, of which the commonest is an attractively marked brown and white species, *Phyllonorycter cerasicolella*; another is *Lyonetia clerkella* whose caterpillars excavate characteristically sinuous tunnels (also seen on birch). Other insects and mites cause actual galls, distorting leaves, buds or shoots; for example, the bright red or pink midrib pustules on leaves are caused by the mite *Eriophyes padi*, while boat-shaped galls on the leaf are due to another mite, *Aculus fockeui*.

The ecological strategy of cherry is intermediate. In woodland it is not overtopped by other trees although it may be susceptible to defoliating insect attack. It may set relatively little viable seed, but by suckering and forming a clonal group (like aspen) with the ability to reproduce vegetatively, it is probably immune to disturbance or destruction by storm or even fire.

WILD SERVICE TREE *Sorbus torminalis* L. Crantz

Rose family: Rosaceae

Also known as: wild service, chequertree, chequer-wood, hagberry or lezzory, cerddinen wyllt (Welsh). The fruits are sometimes called chequers (possibly due to their scarred appearance).

In England, at the northern edge of its European range (from the Mediterranean to Denmark and Poland), wild service is a medium-sized woodland tree (to 27 m/88 ft) that is common in the woods of southeast Essex and occurs naturally as far north as Westmorland and Yorkshire. It is a particularly elegant tree with a wide, umbrella-shaped

BELOW Wonderful autumn colours of a wild service tree at Hampstead Heath, London.

ABOVE LEFT AND ABOVE **Foliage and fruits of wild service at Leigh Woods, near Bristol.**

crown. In autumn the foliage often turns a spectacular yellowish-orange or bright scarlet and appears to glow in the sunlight.

Wild service is thought to be a relatively recent arrival (in geological time). It mainly thrives in lowland woods, and its altitudinal limit is around 300 m (1,000 ft). Service trees supposedly favour limestone or clay soils (Stace, 2010), but in Epping Forest at least are associated with the more gravelly, acidic soils (Lloyd, 1977). The tree's occurrence at exposed coastal sites in Wales suggests it is resistant to salt spray. Wild service trees produce suckers (which can be stimulated by coppicing) but only few of these develop into full-grown trees.

The foliage is rather shiny, the dark green leaves being similar to maple with five to nine pointed lobes and finely toothed margins. The small white faintly scented flowers with five petals, 20 creamy stamens and two styles are borne in inflorescences. They appear early in the season before the leaves are fully unfurled and, like those of other rosaceous trees, are pollinated by a variety of insects. The fruits are small, elongate brown berries containing bundles of gritty, fibrous cells similar to those in pear. Like those of other rosaceous trees, the seeds of wild service require prolonged cold to break their dormancy.

Wild service is regarded as an indicator of ancient woodland (historical time), but until recently the trees apparently produced little or no viable seed, being restricted by low summer temperatures. In the north London area, a local botanist, David Bevan, first discovered seedlings in the early 1990s at Coldfall Wood; since then they have started to appear in a number of London woods possibly due to warmer summers where the absence of deer allow them to develop unhindered. In France wild service sets more abundant seed and is common in secondary woodland in spite of the deer. Wild service responds well to coppicing and pollarding.

The uses of wild service

As with other species of *Sorbus*, the wood is hard, fine-grained and attractive. 'The timber of the sorb is useful for the joiner and of which I have seen a room curiously wainscotted; also for the engraver of wood-cuts... mill-spindles, pistol and gunstocks, and being of very delicate grain... looks beautifully and is almost everlasting' (Evelyn, 1664).

At Epping Forest there are numerous old wild service pollards; it appears to have been treated just like hornbeams and beech, with the pollarded branches used chiefly for firewood but possibly as 'tree hay' (fodder for animals).

The fruits are edible, if rather astringent, until overripe. They were popular with children in Essex, and sold in markets in Sussex and the Isle of Wight (Vickery, 1995). Before the use of hops the fruits were used to flavour beer, giving rise, some authors claim, to some public houses being called 'The Chequers'. Vickery reports that at The Chequers in Smarden, Kent, the inn sign was regularly garlanded with wild service fruits in the autumn (possibly over 100 years ago); the present owners still believe that the name is connected with the tree, but the garlanding tradition has been lost.

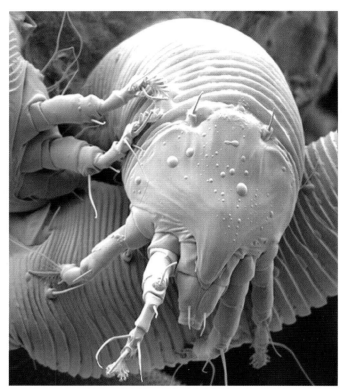

ABOVE Leaf pustules on wild service foliage caused by caused by the eriophyid mite, *Phytoptus pyri* var. *torminalis*.

RIGHT Electron micrograph (x400) of a typical eriophyid mite that causes leaf-galls on many native trees.

Folklore

Although there appears to be little folklore associated with wild service, it was thought to have certain health-giving properties – particularly its fruits, which in some areas are traditionally searched out by children. Grigson reports that more than a hundred years ago chequers were tied up in bunches and sold in the markets of Sussex and the Isle of Wight. While the scientific name *torminalis* is derived from tormina (colic), suggesting a traditional medicinal use, the herbalist Gerard had a poor opinion of the fruit for medicinal purposes.

Evelyn records that water distilled from the flower-stalks and leaves is recommended for various conditions including gripe, ear-ache, consumption (tuberculosis) and something he calls the 'green-sickness of virgins'.

Wild service in the ecosystem

There are few recorded associations with other organisms, either fungi or invertebrates; just 39 records in the Fungal Records Database of Britain and Ireland. Some organisms associated with other *Sorbus* species (rowan and whitebeam especially) are probably to be found associated with wild service, including rusts, mildews and scab. Of the very few plant-feeding invertebrates, including several leaf-mining caterpillars, recorded from wild service, just one species *Stigmella torminalis,* is restricted to this tree; most are found on other rosaceous trees like rowan, apple and hawthorn. Common leaf-eating caterpillars such as green oak tortrix, *Tortrix viridana*, and mottled umber, *Erannis defoliaria*, will feed on wild service foliage, and a hawthorn weevil, *Anthonomus chevrolati*, is known to attack the fruits.

A bluish-green aphid, *Dysaphis aucuparae*, causes leaves to become reddish and rolled or twisted; its alternate host is plantain, *Plantago* spp. Pustules commonly found on the leaves are caused by a variety of a common gall-mite: *Phytoptus pyri* var. *torminalis*. The tiny larvae of a sawfly *Torymus druparum* (also known from apple, pear and rowan) burrows through the flesh of the fruit and destroys the seed.

In England wild service is a weakly competitive woodland tree at the edge of its range; if climate change results in warmer summers it may spread and be more successful as viable seed production increases.

WILLOWS AND SALLOWS *Salix* spp.

Willow family: Salicaceae

Also known as: helygen (Welsh), saileach (Irish), seilleach (Gaelic).

Willows are some of the hardiest of woody plants, some species living in the extreme climate north of the Arctic Circle and extending further north than any other woody plant (as far north as Spitsbergen and the north of Greenland). They also ascend higher than most other flowering plants and some species are to be found at or near the summits of the highest Scottish mountains. Along with juniper and birch, some willow species (possibly *S. herbacea* and *S. reticulata*) were probably the first trees to recolonise the British Isles after the last glacial period. Our native willows range from tall trees, which can reach 30 m (100 ft) (white willow: *S. alba*), to dwarf shrubs growing close to the soil to survives now and wind, and down to tiny trees a few centimetres tall (*S. herbacea*).

Meikle (1984) and Stace (2010) list different numbers of willow species, of which at least 18 are accepted as native (see Table 1). They and other authors list many intermediate forms by giving them varietal or hybrid status. Separating these entities is very difficult; the trees are variable, hybrids occur regularly together with parent species and, to confirm their identification comparative material is needed from different times of the year. DNA studies to clarify the identities of all *Salix* species are continuing; the list I have used is that currently accepted at Kew Gardens (Irina Belyaeva, pers. comm., 2010).

BELOW Fine mature goat willow, *Salix caprea*, at Fortingall, Perth and Kinross.

All willows have some characteristics in common. Unlike poplars they rarely develop root suckers, but like poplars they are all dioecious, catkin-bearing trees with simple, usually alternate leaves. In some species such as goat willow and grey willow the flowers appear before the leaves. Willows are distinguished from poplars by the single outer scale that encloses the winter bud, the absence of a terminal bud on the branches, the thick waxy pollen and the presence of nectaries. By contrast, poplars have highly flexible petioles, produce naked pollen grains and no nectar, and are entirely wind pollinated. Willow catkins are also erect, unlike those of poplar.

The nectar attracts insects such as bumblebees (and even small birds such as the blue tit) as early as March, when few other food sources are available. While the heavier pollen grains of willow may not travel as far as poplar pollen, some wind pollination is thought to occur in most willows. Perhaps willows are still in the process of evolving from wind pollination to purely insect pollination.

After successful pollination mature female flowers produce large numbers of tiny wind-borne seeds (like those of poplars), with long woolly hairs that are carried in the breeze and can form drifts at the edge of waterways. For successful germination, the delicate short-lived seeds need fresh damp earth, gravel or mud to land on in the first few hours directly after maturing, except those of *S. pentandra* and some mountain willows that germinate the following spring (Skvortsov, 1999).

The seedlings are not shade-tolerant and the seeds generally do not survive in the seed bank. The increasingly managed nature of rivers and riverbanks means that, as with native black poplar, there is little successful reproduction of lowland willows by seed. However, nearly all species regenerate vegetatively with vigour; branches torn off by rivers in spate or rockfall tend to root where they land. Horticulturalists take advantage of this characteristic to propagate most species from cuttings, and osiers grow prodigiously when coppiced or pollarded (see p.179).

In the following account I have followed current research and grouped the willows as follows: Group A Non-alluvial willows: sallows, eared and bay willows; Group B Alluvial willows: long-leaved tree-willows; Group C Alluvial willows: osiers and basket willows and Group D Mountain and dwarf willows.

As the data given in Table 4a suggests, these groupings seem to be confirmed by the invertebrates associated with each group; many recorded insects are restricted to one or other of the four willow groups more than they are restricted to individual willow species.

GROUP A: Non-alluvial willows: sallows, eared and bay willows

> **Goat willow or sallow** *Salix caprea* L. (including two subspecies, ssp. *caprea* and ssp. *sphacelata* (Sm.))
> **Grey willow** or common sallow *Salix cinerea* L. ssp. *cinerea*
> **Rusty sallow** *Salix cinerea* L. ssp. *oleifolia* Mac.
> **Eared willow** *Salix aurita* L.
> **Dark-leaved willow** *Salix myrsinifolia* Salisb.
> **Bay willow** *Salix pentandra* L.

This group contains all 'non-alluvial' willows (Skvortsov, 1999), i.e. whose typical habitat is not riverbanks. These are much-branched trees growing on marshy ground, lake-margins, hedges or even in woodlands (*S. caprea* and *S. cinerea*). The first three species occur very widely throughout Britain and Ireland, the others most often

in the north of England and Scotland. The trees can reach 20 m (66 ft) in sheltered woodland but more often reach no more than about 5–8 m (16–26 ft) tall, often as round clumps, which may be 20 m (66 ft) across. Goat and grey willows readily hybridise with each other and with other willows.

The sallows are characteristically trees of base-rich soils, while eared willow occurs widely on acid soils, often in mountain areas where it grows as a shrub, but when not grazed can grow into a small tree of 3–4 m (10–13 ft) or more. Apart from bay willow all these trees can be found on mountains in the Highlands of Scotland where the subspecies *S. caprea* L. var. *sphacelata* (Sm.) Wahlenb. is recognised; this and the eared willow ascend to around 800 m (2,600 ft). The three sallows can all establish themselves on poor soil in disturbed areas including urban wastelands and railway land. They are regarded as representing the first stage in the succession of secondary woodland or the development of fen carr, but will usually give way to taller trees such as alder and birch as the habitat dries out.

Bay willow is a common willow of stream sides and on wet ground in lowland areas of northern Britain. It is probably not indigenous south of a line from Yarmouth to Aberystwyth, and is also rare or absent from northern Scotland, although it is found much further north in Scandinavia. It usually grows as a large shrub 5–7 m (16–23 ft) high but has been recorded as a tree of 17 m (55½ ft). As with most willows the (mildly fragrant) male catkins are popular with gardeners and this species has been widely planted outside its natural range; the absence of female trees in southern England may indicate that these populations have been planted and are of non-native origin.

GROUP B: Alluvial willows: long-leaved tree-willows

> **Crack willow** *Salix* x *fragilis* L.
> **White willow** *Salix alba* L. (including cricket bat willow: *S. alba* var. *caerulea*)

These two alluvial willows are the tallest of our willow trees, both growing to about 30 m (100 ft). Crack willow is so called because its brittle branches and twigs break cleanly from the trunk. Is it a native willow? Even its precise identity is unclear. 'The name crack willow is popularly attached to a complex group of tree-willows consisting of several distinct (genetic) segregates...' (Meikle, 1984). He explains that 'the status of *S.* x *fragilis* as a whole in Britain and Ireland must be regarded as dubious, since nowhere can it be said to form part of a natural, indigenous plant community'. Rackham (pers. comm., 2009) doubts this, as he has found that it is commoner than *S. alba* along streams in ancient woods. From genetic studies at Kew, willow researchers now regard crack willow as a hybrid between white willow and a newly described species *S. euxina* (Belyaeva, 2009).

White willow is a common tree of riverbanks in lowland areas of eastern England and Ireland, but is widely planted elsewhere. The cricket bat willow, *S. alba* var. *caerulea*, is a particularly vigorous, straight-trunked variety, which is claimed to have originated at Eriswell, Suffolk, in 1803, although Meikle states that the tree was already known in Norfolk as early as 1790. Most planted trees are females, as these are regarded as the best for making cricket bats.

OPPOSITE An unusually tall and tree-like eared willow, *Salix aurita*, in the Scottish Highlands.

BELOW Female catkins packed with tiny plumed fruits of white willow, *Salix alba*, near Salisbury in Wiltshire.

RIGHT A row of traditional crack willow pollards near Westbury on the Somerset Levels.

GROUP C: Alluvial willows: osiers and basket willows

> **Almond willow** *Salix triandra* L.
> **Common osier**, **basket willow** *Salix viminalis* L.
> **Purple willow** *Salix purpurea* L.

The trees in this second group of alluvial willows are all particularly fast-growing small trees whose natural habitat is the floodplain and gravel banks of rivers, streams and mountain torrents. They are tenacious and grow vigorously as is necessary to exploit such a shifting habitat.

Almond willow, *S. triandra*, is a small, bushy tree rarely reaching 10 m (33 ft) but growing very rapidly at first and when coppiced. It occurs widely in England but only as identifiable basketmakers' cultivars – its natural status is questionable. It is a particularly attractive and fragrant species – the twigs have a faint flavour of rose-water when chewed.

Similarly, basket willow or common osier, *S. viminalis*, occurs as a large bush but can grow into a 10 m (33 ft) tree on occasion. It has been widely planted, and as Meikle points out 'one rarely finds it except in an unnatural environment, and often as a relic of former cultivation'. In other words, like several other willows, it was probably introduced. Like other osiers it has been grown for basketry since ancient times; only in Russia is it thought to be

clearly indigenous, and it may have been brought to Western Europe by migrants in prehistoric times. Genuinely 'wild' populations of either this or almond willow have yet to be located in Britain or Ireland. Both these trees have very few associated invertebrates – a characteristic of many other introduced species.

Purple willow is a small tree, more often just a bush, but exceptionally grows to 5 m (16 ft) or so. According to Meikle, purple willow 'has a better claim to indigenous status than either almond willow or basket willow, being found in remote areas all over these islands, by streams or on damp hillsides'.

GROUP D: Mountain and dwarf willows

> **Creeping willow** *Salix repens* L.
> **Mountain willow** *Salix arbuscula* L.
> **Downy willow** *Salix lapponum* L.
> **Woolly willow** *Salix lanata* L.
> **Dwarf willow** *Salix herbacea* L.
> **Whortle-leaved willow** *Salix myrsinites* L.
> **Tea-leaved willow** *Salix phylicifolia* L.
> **Net-leaved willow** *Salix reticulata* L.
>
> **Biological flora**: Beerling *(S. herbacea)* (1998)

On the Scottish mountains, above the tree-line, there still linger remnants of an extensive sub-arctic montane scrub, 'which is now one of the rarest and most endangered habitats in the UK'

(Scottish Mountain Willow Research Group, 2005). The main woody components are small willow species, dwarf juniper and dwarf birch, together with common juniper and stunted pines, and, less frequently, other trees such as rowan. These willows are mostly very small trees, shrubs and woody ground-hugging plants such as the tiny dwarf willow, *S. herbacea*, which forms carpets 25 mm (1 in) tall on mountains in Britain and Ireland, usually between 610 m (2,000 ft) and 1,310 m (4,300 ft) but as low as 150 m (490 ft) in Shetland. This is not 'the world's smallest tree', as I claimed in 1992; in fact there are even smaller species growing to no more than 1 cm (½ in) in both North America (*S. nivalis*, *S. uva-ursi*) and the Himalayas (*S. serpyllum*).

Other small willows ascend to considerable altitudes (see Table 6). All are well adapted to extreme climatic conditions and acid, peaty soils, although some (such as *S. arbuscula*, *S. phylicifolia*, *S. reticulata* and *S. lanata*) are associated with base-rich soils on limestone (such as at Ben Lawers). Several are rare or very rare and few substantial populations of more than a few plants still exist.

The remaining isolated patches of both montane and coastal scrub are believed to be remnants of a once widespread vegetation type, whose reduction in the last few centuries is thought to have been caused largely by cutting for firewood, combined with greatly increased grazing pressure especially by deer and sheep preventing regrowth. Even the smallest species are naturally grazed by ptarmigans.

The main method of reproduction of these tiny trees is vegetative (suckers), but small catkins (bright red in *S. herbacea*) appear in most years. Even at high altitudes the catkins are visited by pollinators including bumblebees, small wasps and biting midges. In most mountain willows seed is produced irregularly depending on summer temperatures, but there is today very little natural regeneration, especially in the rarer species such as the woolly willow, *S. lanata*, which is now restricted to some of the most inaccessible ledges and cliffs.

Although these species were previously somewhat neglected, research is now being conducted with the aims of (1) clarifying species and hybrid definitions, (2) investigating factors limiting willow regeneration, (3) assessing genetic diversity within populations and (4) documenting the diversity of biological associations (especially with fungi, including myrorrhiza) of mountain willow populations.

The flowering, seed production, germination and seedling establishment all appear to be more or less problematic in at least some of these willows under present conditions, and all are adversely affected by overgrazing. Temporary fencing out of sheep and deer is being augmented by the planting of seedlings raised from locally collected seed. In some places where the diversity of the willow scrub has apparently diminished, some reintroductions are being attempted. Ultimately, the long-term future of these tiny trees will probably depend largely on a reduction in grazing pressure, see www.highlandbirchwoods.co.uk.

BELOW LEFT Downy willow, *Salix lapponum*, in fruit, Ben Lawers.

BELOW The tiny dwarf willow, *Salix herbacea*, which occurs at high altitude on most British mountains.

The uses of willow (see also pp.178–183)

Light and rather soft, willow wood is similar to that of poplar, but it is very variable and depends on the habit of the tree; crack willow wood becomes reddish or almost salmon-coloured when seasoned. Because of its lightness, willow wood was traditionally used to make Irish harps until about the nineteenth century, the laths for coracles and, more recently, for sport sailing boats, artificial limbs and toys. The wood from the cricket bat willow, S. *alba* var. *caerulea,* is largely exported to India and Pakistan in the form of blanks (clefts) from which the bats are actually made. For centuries fine willow stems have also been used to make high quality artists' charcoal.

Other uses of willow include bark for tanning, as an inferior alternative to oak bark. In Scandinavia, willow bark was sometimes ground-up and eaten mixed with oatmeal as a famine food. Loudon (1844) noted that willow down, the feathery covering of the seeds, was collected for stuffing mattresses, while crack willow has bright red roots from which a purplish-red dye can be extracted.

Dried willow foliage has long been used as winter fodder, and even cut and stored for this purpose. Willows have also been popular with beekeepers for centuries because they produce pollen so early in the spring, and the trees have at times been planted to attract insects.

The medicinal use of willow is ancient in origin. An infusion from the leaves was recommended in medieval times to ease the pain of various ailments, and in Wales willow twigs would be chewed for the same purpose long before the discovery of salicin. Salicylic acid, first extracted from willow bark in 1929 (see aspen, p.40), is the basis of aspirin having both analgesic and anti-inflammatory effects. Aspirin was one of the first drugs to come into worldwide usage, and still the most widely used drug today. Originally it was largely produced from natural sources but now it is synthesised, total production being over 100 billion tablets a year.

Folklore

There is an ancient tradition associating willow with grief and sadness that supposedly goes back to biblical times: when the Israelites found themselves enslaved near the waters of Babylon 'they wept, and hung their harps on willows' (Psalm 137). It is now thought that the trees referred to were probably the Euphrates poplar, *Populus euphratica*, but the association of willows with sadness has remained. Possibly due to the bitter taste of the leaves, willow also became associated with romantic grief; there is an English folk song that includes the lines: 'I often times have snatched at the red rose-bud/And gained aught but the willow-

LEFT **Cricket bat blanks being prepared from cricket-bat willow,** *Salix alba* **var.** *caerulea,* **at J S Wright & Sons near Chelmsford, Essex.**

tree'. According to Thistleton-Dyer (1889), 'it was customary for those who were forsaken in love to wear a garland made of willow'; willows frequently appear in poems of lost love, and in Shakespeare's *Hamlet* Ophelia drowned herself next to a willow.

Pussy willow has its own folk associations. The (male) flowering branches are sometimes used instead of palms to celebrate Palm Sunday, and in some places country people wear sprigs of pussy willow in their lapels around the same time of year – although like other folk customs this may now have completely died out.

In Ireland the sally (goat willow) has power against enchantment, and it is still regarded as lucky to take a sally rod with you on a journey. On St Patrick's Day a sallow twig would be charred then used 'to mark the sign of the Cross on everyone's arm'. Willow (probably sallow) twigs hung by the door would keep away marsh witches. A peeled 'sally rod' placed round a milk churn would ensure good butter, and another brought into the house on May Day was definitely good luck and potent against the Evil Eye.

The crack willow has also been called 'the widow's willow'. This is claimed to be due to its tendency to drop branches without warning onto unsuspecting husbands.

Willows in the ecosystem

In spite of the bitter taste, most willows are sometimes browsed by sheep, deer, rabbits and hares. Commercial growers have to fence out these herbivores, or use particularly bitter species such as purple willow to make a woven living fence to keep them out. Commercial willow beds (see p.179) make a rich semi-wetland habitat that provides shelter for a wide range of birds and small mammals, insects and other invertebrates.

A number of fungi are associated solely with lowland willows, including the pale *Lactarius aspideus*, which grows in muddy places under the trees, and the large cushion-like grey bracket fungus, *Phellinus ignarius*, on the tree trunks. There are over 3,900 records of fungi associated with *Salix* species in the Fungal Records Database of Britain and Ireland, more than for any other native tree genus except *Betula*.

Mountain willows also have a number of fungi associated with them; even the tiny dwarf willow, *S. herbacea*, has been found to

have two *Laccaria* species, three *Boletus* species. and two *Russula* species associated with it.

Old trees and dead wood are attacked by several fungi such as the blushing bracket, *Daedalopsis confragosa*, the willow bracket, *Phellinus igniarius*, and the orange-brown jelly-fungus *Exidia recisa*. Black canker, *Physalospora miyabeana*, is a parasitic fungus that attacks willows, while various leaf scabs, *Venturia* spp., are also common. The tar-spot or black rust occasionally affecting willow leaves is caused by the ascomycete fungus *Rhytisma salicinum*, and a variety of orange rusts attack the leaves of all willows, even the smallest mountain species.

A bacterial infection of willow *Erwinia salicis* known as 'watermark', can cause serious damage to commercially grown tree-willows such as cricket bat willows, and as yet no effective remedy has been found.

Most willows are extremely palatable to insects. A total of 839 invertebrates are listed as being associated with willows – more than any other tree including oak and of these 314 are restricted to *Salix* species (see Tables 4 and 4a). Particularly bitter-tasting species such as purple willow have fewer, as do two of the three willows of uncertain origin and status: *S. x fragilis* and *S. triandra*. Goat willow alone has 360 species recorded (129 or 36% restricted to the tree) while four others each have more than 100. There are far fewer species from both the mountain willows and the species thought to have been introduced.

RIGHT Fruiting bodies of the ectomycorrhizal fungus; the willow milk-cap, *Lactarius aspideus*.

ABOVE **Purple emperor butterfly,** *Apatura iris,* whose caterpillars live on goat willow foliage.

ABOVE RIGHT AND RIGHT **Sawflies** such as *Pontania acutifoliae* are responsible for many blister galls on willow leaves, especially crack willow.

The star of this vast assemblage of invertebrates is the elusive, canopy-inhabiting purple emperor butterfly, *Apatura iris,* whose main food plant is goat willow. According to Oates (2008) 'no British insect has received such interest or adulation'. Since 2001 it has been the subject of its own 'master tree project' to map places where it can be seen (see www.ukbutterflies.co.uk). Other striking species include the eyed hawkmoth, *Smerinthus ocellata,* on crack willow, and the lunar hornet clearwing, *Sesia bembiciformis,* on grey willow; this extraordinary black and yellow striped moth can be mistaken for a hornet, but is in fact harmless.

The Forestry Commission (Bevan, 1987) lists a number of species as defoliating pests (primarily tree-willows: groups A and B), including the strange twin-tailed larvae of the spectacular puss moth, *Cerura vinula,* three sawflies, *Nematus* spp., seven species of leaf beetle, Chrysomelidae, and the impressive poplar longhorn beetle, *Saperda carcharias.* Another longhorn, *S. populnea,* causes the 'timberman' gall of the main stem tissues in goat willow and less often in other species. Among the most common beetles are the wood-boring osier weevil, *Cryptorhynchus lapathi,* the brown willow beetle, *Gallerucella lineola,* and some beautiful metallic

beetles such as the blue willow beetle, *Phratora vulgatissima,* and the (reddish-brown) willow leaf beetle, *Lochmaea caprea.*

Willows support more gall species than any other tree, although a single oak tree may have more species than a single willow, while an individual elm tree may have fewer species but support the greatest number of actual galls. Some of the bud-galls on willow catkins (including on mountain willows) are caused by midges (*Rabdophaga salicis, R. rosaria* etc.), and others by mites (Eriophyoidea) whose identities await scientific clarification. The common red pustules on the leaves of various willow species are all caused by sawfly larvae (*Pontania bridgmanii* only on Group A and *P. proxima* usually on group B). Even mountain willows are attacked, small globular galls on the dwarf willow, *S. herbacea,* being caused by its own tiny sawfly *P. herbaceae.*

Strange deformities on the stem commonly seen on willows of both groups A and B are caused by a tiny mite *Stenacis triradiatus,* but recent research suggests that the effect of the mites is compounded by a viral infection which they carry.

On almond willows the most serious pests are the button-top midge, *Rabdophaga heterobia,* the bright orange rust *Metalampsora amygdalinae* and aphids including one of the largest in the world, the giant willow aphid, *Tuberolachnus salignus*. Common osier is attacked by another orange rust, *M. epitea*, and by different aphids including the willow-carrot aphid, *Cavariella aegopodii*, and the black willow aphid, *Pteracomma salicis*. The damage caused to all these trees by aphids is considerable – they kill the shoots and drain the sap. As with other aphids, in order to get enough protein they have to ingest far more sugar than they need, the excess leaking out as honeydew, which attracts many other insects including both predators and parasites. Aphids also act as vectors for plant viruses. From a purely ecological point of view these pests and infections may be seen as contributing to the natural succession to woodland that willows initiate, and enhance that process by debilitating the trees. That does not suit willow growers, whose activities effectively halt the process for commercial purposes. As in most other crops, the genetic diversity of commercial willows is very low (whole fields may be derived from cuttings and are genetically uniform), so they are particularly susceptible to epidemics of one sort or another.

The ecological strategy of lowland willows is as stress-tolerant pioneers of highly unstable riverbeds and disturbed, damp and even waterlogged ground. As the trees can be relatively short-lived they occupy a stage in the succession from wetland to woodland, often as some of the first woody species. Group A are stress-tolerant competitors of a wider range of habitats. The mountain willows are extreme stress-tolerators, and some are particularly susceptible to grazing.

LEFT Strange deformities of the flowers of goat willow caused by the mite *Stenacis triradiatus* apparently exacerbated by a viral infection carried by the mite.

BELOW LEFT The giant willow aphid, *Tuberolachnus salignus*, is one of the largest aphids in Britain.

BELOW Leaf-roll galls are common on crack willow, and are cause by midges of the genus *Rabdophaga*.

YEW *Taxus baccata* L..

Yew family: (Gymnospermae): Taxaceae

Also known as: English yew, iubhar (Gaelic), ibar (Old Irish), iúr (Irish), ywen (Welsh), palm tree (Kent). Derivative place names: Ifield (West Sussex), Newry (and many others in Ireland).

Biological Flora: Thomas and Polwart (2003)

The yew is perhaps our most mysterious and sacred tree. Many writers have affirmed that it has had immense spiritual significance for millennia, and yews are our oldest living trees.

Taxus baccata occurs naturally in Ireland and England, across Europe to central Asia and the Himalayas. There is some dispute about its natural northern limit but it may be native even in the north and west of Scotland where it occurs today on some sea-cliffs such as on Lismore and Bernera islands. Dickson (1994) has suggested that yew is not native to Scotland, but there are some

LEFT The famous old yew at Crowhurst in Surrey, complete with door.

post-glacial pollen records of yew from the western parts of the Highlands (H. J. B. Birks, pers. comm., 2009), and remote sea-cliffs seem an unlikely place for the tree to have been planted. But, as a revered tree in Ireland, yews may have been taken to Scotland and planted in prehistoric times.

The yew typically occurs in woodland on a wide range of soils but especially on well-drained calcareous soils in sheltered locations, where the trees can grow to 20 m (66 ft). Yews occur on cliffs, including sea-cliffs, on neutral or alkaline rock, and ascend to 425 m (1,400 ft) in England and 470 m (1,500 ft) on Purple Mountain, Kerry (and at much greater altitudes in Europe). Yews are particularly slow-growing but are highly shade-, salt- and even drought-tolerant, and they are relatively immune to atmospheric pollution. On steep chalk or limestone slopes yew can form 'remarkably species-poor woodland' (Thomas and Polwart, 2003), with a closed, very dense canopy that excludes most other plants. The trees also produce a toxin in the soil that discourages most competitors, including its own seedlings, except scattered individuals of whitebeam, ash and box, the only other trees found in yew woodland.

The most extensive yew woods are on chalk at Kingley Vale, on the South Downs near Chichester. Reenadinna Wood at Killarney is believed to be hundreds of years old but it is thought that at least some pure yew woods are not ancient and may have arisen on abandoned agricultural land or in places where grazing suddenly ceased, for example when rabbit populations were wiped out by myxomatosis. Relatively soon after the last glacial period very large yew trees grew in many places; enormous (post-glacial) bog yews preserved in the peat for many thousands of years have been unearthed in East Anglia and the Bog of Allen, Co. Offaly, Ireland.

The heartwood of very old yews tends to rot away leaving a hollow trunk, making it difficult to date ancient specimens. Yew will also layer and sometimes, when a ring of branches have all touched the ground and rooted, the result is a circle of yew trees around the spot where the original tree stood.

Flowering is from February to April, when copious clouds of pollen are released by the slightest breeze from the small, yellow, male cones. Pollination is by wind, although honeybees have been

RIGHT **Possibly the oldest living tree in Europe: the Fortingall yew as it is today.**

163

Ancient yew trees

In the village of Fortingall, Glen Lyon, Perthshire, near groups of ancient 'druid' stones, there is the living hulk of a vast yew tree, known to have had a circumference of 16 m (52 ft) in 1769. Local tradition has it that funeral processions passed through the arch made by the ancient tree.

All yew trees of a really great age are hollow, so ring-counting has been impossible. Based on measurements of trees for which there are known planting dates, it has been calculated that for the first 500 years the girth of a churchyard yew increases on average by 1.1 cm (just under half an inch) per year to approximately 5.5 m (18 ft). Some grow very much more slowly; the ancient tree at Totteridge in north London is still 8 m (26 ft) in girth, just as it was in 1677. The great hollow yew at Crowhurst in Surrey apparently only grew from 9 m (30 ft) in girth in 1630 to 9.4 m (30 ft 9 in), between 1850 and 1991; it is little more than this today.

Many ancient yews are found growing on what are known to be ancient burial sites dating from the Neolithic, Celtic and Saxon periods. The yew at Ashbrittle in Somerset is growing on a Neolithic barrow. At Tandridge in Surrey the foundations of the original Saxon church were constructed over and around the roots of an ancient yew that is still thriving today; the foundations could be seen in the crypt until this was sealed. The tree has hardly changed in nearly 1,500 years.

The position of church buildings in relation to the ancient trees has been documented and interpreted as follows: where the church is west or east of the yew the site is Celtic, where north or northeast of it, Saxon, and where south of the yew, Neolithic.

At Fortingall in Perthshire there are historical records of a 'samhain' (autumn) festival when a communal bonfire was burnt on a Bronze Age tumulus known as the Mound of the Dead. The occurrence of ancient yews at burial grounds in Ireland was recorded as long ago as the year 1184 by Geraldus Cambrensis, although there are very few ancient yews known in Ireland today.

The past neglect of some of the most important of these trees is almost unbelievable.

The ancient tree at Ankerwyke, on the north bank of the Thames at Runnymede, was forgotten for decades. Two hundred years ago the Thames ran on a more southerly course, so that Runnymede was on the same bank as the sacred yew, under which oaths were declared and holy ceremonies held in medieval times. This tree may even mark the site where the Magna Carta was signed by King John in 1215; the site would have been chosen for its ancient spiritual significance and, as some researchers

TOP AND ABOVE The yew tree at Iffley Parish Church, Oxford, as it was in 1900 as shown in an old postcard and as it is today.

have claimed, the only place the king's sincerity could be trusted. Yet in modern times this extraordinary ancient tree was not protected, and it was completely overgrown with scrub when it was discovered by Alan Meredith, a yew researcher, early in 1992. Only since then has the tree been properly protected and cherished.

observed visiting the flowers and collecting pollen. Even though the trees are relatively scarce, atmospheric pollen counts put yew in the top 10 plants for average pollen abundance. Yew trees are normally dioecious, the male tree bearing small, yellow, pollen-bearing cones, while the female flowers are simple fleshy pink arils each with a single ovule in the centre. The arils are cup-shaped and sticky, and stay on the tree for a whole year before they ripen. The sex ratio of yew trees varies, and it has been observed that some trees change sex over a period of years.

The seeds are dispersed by birds and as a result sometimes germinate in the crook of branches or high up on old pollards. The seedlings are successful pioneers in disturbed areas on bare soil, where they can be associated with juniper and hawthorn, but gradually (over centuries) grow up to shade out the other species and become pure yew stands. Yew seedlings can establish themselves in woodland where they are shade-tolerant, but they are susceptible to grazing by deer. Yew itself will coppice (and pollard) but it is too slow-growing for this to be worthwhile, although some ancient yews appear to be pollards. Yew can be propagated from cuttings (and layered branches), as well as from seed.

In the nineteenth century an unusual fastigiate form of yew was found on a hillside near Florencecourt in Northern Ireland. Replanted in the grounds of a large estate the original (female) tree can still be seen; propagated from cuttings this form has been much planted in churchyards and cemeteries as Irish yew: *T. baccata* var. *fastigiata*. The first male fastigiate trees were discovered in Sussex in 1927. Numerous other cultivars are known.

The uses of yew

Yew wood is one of the densest of coniferous woods but it is also very elastic and was traditionally used for longbows, spears and also dagger handles; Neolithic longbows have been found preserved in the peat in Somerset and at the Carrifran valley in the Scottish borders. The world's oldest artefact of wood was a yew spear around 150,000 years old, found near Clacton, Essex, and another, dating from about 90,000 years ago, was found in Germany between the ribs of a fossilised straight-tusked mastodon, *Hesperoloxodon antiquus*.

Eighth-century Irish manuscripts refer to yew's 'noble artifacts', domestic vessels being commonly made of yew at that time. In the medieval period several English kings encouraged the military use of yew wood. In the 1400s Edward IV proclaimed that 'every Englishman should have a bow made of yew or, ash or laburnum' (the last presumably from wood imported from Europe) and various monarchs decreed a general planting of yew for this purpose

BELOW AND BELOW LEFT The Ankerwycke Yew today and an engraving of King John signing the Magna Carta underneath next to it in 1215.

(Thomas and Polwart, 2003) although it is thought that bows were in fact always made from imported yew wood. Yew longbows and spears are claimed as the key to various military successes from the Battle of Crecy in 1326 to the siege of Devizes in 1645.

The dark, reddish-brown colour of the wood and the irregularities of the ring structure result in most attractive surfaces on turned objects and veneers, although the colour has a tendency to fade with time. As an external timber yew is said to make fence posts that 'will outlive a post of iron'. Yew pegs were used as fastenings for Neolithic trackways on the Somerset levels, while John Evelyn recommends yew wood for 'parquet-floors, cogs of mills, posts to be set in moist ground, bowls, pins for pulleys, and for drinking tankards'. In the seventeenth century yew wood was used for the body of lutes. In recent times a specialised art form has developed in Ireland by turning and polishing carefully dried, fossil bog yew.

Taxin (a complex mixture of alkaloids) is present in all parts of the yew except the aril; it was first discovered in the bark of the Pacific yew, *T. brevifolia*, in America. In 1978, experiments showed that taxin was mildly effective at treating leukaemic mice. It was subsequently found that several related compounds (known collectively as taxol) had anti-cancer properties, and as demand for yew bark exploded there was an unsustainable worldwide assault on standing yews. More recent studies showed that taxol is also effective against several species of pathogenic fungi and some bacteria. Luckily, long before the total destruction of naturally growing yew trees, a way was found to produce taxol from yew foliage using a fermentation process, and today all medicinal taxol is produced in this way.

Folklore

Yews are taken to be symbols of immortality in many traditions, yet at the same time they can also be seen as omens of impending doom, although paradoxically the trees are also accepted as places of sanctuary. For centuries yew branches were carried on Palm Sunday and at funerals in England; the custom still persists in parts of rural Ireland, where it was also said that yew was 'the coffin of the vine' as wine barrels were thought (mistakenly) to be made of yew staves.

The spiritual significance of the yew is thought to have been very great in pre-Christian times and, while yew trees occur near churches throughout Britain and Ireland, in certain parts of the country some of these trees are truly ancient, pre-dating both existing churches and Christianity itself. Yew trees have also been planted in churchyards since medieval times. A popular explanation of this was that, since the foliage was poisonous to stock, the trees would discourage farmers from allowing their cattle to enter consecrated ground.

Yew branches (or sometimes other evergreen branches) are traditionally used in 'topping-out' ceremonies when the highest (wooden) beam in a building is erected. It is said that the lullaby 'Rock-a-bye-Baby' originated at Ambergate, Derbyshire, when a group of eighteenth-century charcoal burners hollowed out the bough on a nearby yew tree to make a crib for a baby.

Yew in the ecosystem

Despite popular opinion, yew is rarely toxic to larger mammals; indeed the trees are particularly susceptible to browsing by roe deer, *Capreolus capreolus*. On the limestone pavement at Gait Barrows National Nature Reserve in Lancashire, deer have pruned yews down to no more than small humps close to the ground, while most other saplings remain untouched. Yew foliage is also browsed and the bark stripped by rabbits, hares and grey squirrels, but the tree is tolerant of repeated browsing or pruning (and so is an excellent tree for topiary). Cattle and sheep are occasionally poisoned by eating yew, but it is suggested that if fed small quantities over time they are able to build up an immunity to the toxins. It has been suggested that the swelling of the lower parts of the trunk of yew trees is caused by repeated nibbling by browsing animals.

The familiar red 'berries' (known locally as snotty-gogs or snottle berries in parts of England) are attractive to birds (especially blackbird and thrushes), small mammals and even ants, which all consume the fleshy aril and disperse the seeds. Snow and Snow (1988) list 10 birds as feeding on the berries, of which some – the greenfinch, great tit and others – eat the seed, as do woodmice. To humans the fleshy part is edible, if unappetising, although the seeds are indigestible but probably harmless. In different parts of the country there are stories and memories of children eating the berries without ill-effect.

A few fungal fruiting bodies are typically found under yew trees; the commonest decay fungus associated with yew is chicken-of-the-woods, *Laetiporus sulphureus*, whose yellow or orange fruiting bodies can sometimes be seen emerging from the live tree while the rest of the fungus is decomposing the heartwood.

Yew foliage may be palatable to some mammals but it is attacked by very few (32) plant-feeding invertebrates, of which seven (22%)

ABOVE Artichoke galls on yew are caused by a gall-midge, *Taxomyia taxi.*

ABOVE Male flowers of yew produce copious pollen.

ABOVE *Suillus tuidentatus,* an edible fungus found under yew on chalky soils.

are restricted to the tree. Only holly, box and strawberry tree have fewer recorded species.

The yew big-bud mite, *Cecidophyopsis psilaspis,* is a common gall-former found on yew, and in northern Europe is regarded as a commercial pest causing chronic bud mortality throughout the crown of the tree. The yellow gall-midge, *Taxomyia taxi,* is not uncommon, causing the growth of a common artichoke-gall, while the yew scale, *Parthenolecanium pomeranicum,* damages the foliage and excretes honeydew that is colonised by sooty moulds. The black vine weevil, *Otiorhynchus sulcatus,* is attracted by volatile compounds produced by yew leaves, while new shoots can be ring-barked (and killed) by the caterpillars of the red-barred tortrix moth, *Ditula angustiorana.*

Yew is a tree ecologically similar to box, a highly defensive, chemically armoured, slow-growing competitor as part of a shade-tolerant understorey in woodland on base-rich soils, but which can shade out other species under certain conditions, and can resist the arrival of all other trees except ash. Yew is almost indestructible and is protected from most insect and other attacks by the toxins in its leaves. The tree vigorously reproduces itself vegetatively, naturally layering, sprouting from damaged parts and surviving uprooting strongly.

The seedlings, which are able to germinate and become established on bare rock (especially limestone) and even under dense (non-yew) shade, must be considered stress-tolerant pioneers.

BELOW Yew grazed by roe deer at Gait Barrows Nature Reserve, north Lancashire.

5 Managing native trees and tree products

NEARLY EVERY SORT OF NATIVE TREE IN BRITAIN produces valuable items of food, medicine, fuel, fodder or material for construction large and small. In the last two hundred years many 'natural' items have been replaced with cheap manufactured alternatives made of metals and more recently plastic, while unique chemicals are now synthesised. At the same time society has become urbanised; the traditional ways of managing trees and obtaining their products have been allowed to decline and die. The value of trees themselves seemed diminished. This trend has now been arrested; under the threat of climate change the true value of all aspects of trees is coming to be re-evaluated, starting with the products we get by managing trees sustainably. How far public policy is influenced by this change is another question altogether.

The sustainable management of trees for their diverse products is of course an ancient human activity. There may have been continuous human occupation of the forests of Europe for many millennia, and even in Britain, while the present forests are only as old as the retreat of the ice-sheet, they must have been substantially influenced by human activity for at least half that time.

We now know the original wildwood, the 'natural vegetation' (whether or not it consisted largely or even partly of closed canopy forest), substantially disappeared several millennia ago; the pollen record shows major changes not all of which have been convincingly explained. Our Neolithic ancestors and their animals are thought to have contributed hugely, but as Rackham has pointed out in relation to the Elm Decline, human activity is an inadequate explanation – put simply the manpower was not available to create such massive changes. Natural processes must have been largely the cause, but exactly what these were is not fully understood. At the same time human migrants evidently not only brought some new trees, such as

OPPOSITE Gnarled trunks of an aged wild cherry tree at Henley-on-Thames, Buckinghamshire.

RIGHT Tapping birch sap in the Scottish Highlands at Moniack Castle to make the increasingly popular silver birch wine.

fruit trees and willows, but also a familiarity with various techniques for managing trees and harvesting their products.

The earliest written records give some indication about how trees were used and valued (see Brehon Law, p.185). Domesday records reveal that in England more woodland must have been cleared before the eleventh century than has been cleared since, and that by then nearly every parcel of woodland was very carefully managed, and its value well established. As Rackham puts it, 'for (at least) a thousand years England has had less woodland than most European countries and has taken correspondingly more care of its woods'.

Even before humans built shelters, the first use of wood must have been as a source of fuel, and everywhere trees have been used for this purpose, especially in cold northern lands like Britain and Ireland. There are even traditional rhymes, setting out the values of the various trees as firewood:

> *Beechwood fires are bright and clear,*
> *If the logs are kept a year;*
> *Chestnut only good they say,*
> *If for long it's laid away;*
> *Make a fire of elder tree,*
> *Death within your house shall be.*
> *But ash new or ash old,*
> *Is fit for Queen with crown of gold.*
> *Birch and fir logs burn too fast,*
> *Blaze up bright and do not last;*
> *It is by the Irish said*
> *Hawthorn bakes the sweetest bread;*
> *Elmwood burns like churchyard mould —*
> *E'en the very flames are cold.*
> *But ash green or ash brown,*
> *Is fit for Queen with golden crown.*
> *Poplar gives a bitter smoke,*
> *Fills your eyes and makes you choke;*
> *Apple wood will scent your room,*
> *With incense-like perfume.*
> *Oaken logs, if dry and old,*
> *Will keep away the winter's cold;*
> *But ash wet or ash dry*
> *A king shall warm his slippers by.*
>
> (ANON)

While it makes a good verse, the detail is unconvincing; ash is generally regarded as satisfactory rather than spectacular, and hornbeam, one of the best fuel woods, is not even mentioned!

ABOVE **An old traditional orchard outside the city of Durham.**

In recent times trees and tree products have been largely neglected by successive governments. Apart from fuelwood (until the last two centuries) the major product from native trees has always been timber, and its production on a commercial scale was the prime purpose of the UK's Forestry Commission (FC), set up after the First World War. For many years the FC (like the Irish Forestry Service) concentrated on maximising timber output. It planted introduced fast-growing species, mostly from North America, such as Sitka spruce and lodgepole pine, in large blocks with no regard for local ecology or landscape amenity value. Smaller and lesser plantations of some native trees such as oak has always been part of its activity, although as with the spruce and pine, this was often done using introduced seed. More recently the Forestry Commission's approach has broadened to include other purposes of trees and woodland such as amenity, landscape value and even conservation – in spite of the previous damage done to biodiversity by its planting policies.

It is claimed that many natural woods both (publicly and privately owned) are 'protected for conservation', but often this means neglect, while deer numbers increase without constraint, preventing natural regeneration by eating all tree seedlings. Woodlands that were formerly working woods have largely stagnated, their canopy closed over, managed cycles of change arrested. Even where traditional management has been restored, for example to promote the habitat for rare butterflies, I know of no case where this has been done as part of a plan to restore a complete working wood.

Britain currently imports charcoal to a value of over £35 million per annum; the restoration of the charcoal industry could potentially replace all of this. High quality leather tanners find that their demand for oak bark far outstrips actual supply; again, this could be produced from native trees; in fact extensive oak coppice is now neglected and abandoned for want of skilled woodsmen to make use of it, while tanners have to import oak bark from elsewhere in Europe.

The policies of successive governments have been to neglect all non-timber products from trees; since these areas have not been part of the Forestry Commission's remit there is no 'home' for such matters. Charcoal production in some parts of the country has been restored by enthusiasts but with little or no official help. In many countries willow production is officially encouraged and backed by research and training, but not in the UK. Basketmakers have to grow their own withies. There is some experimental use of fast-growing varieties to produce biomass for power generation (see p.182), but at the same time vast amounts of existing woody biomass is wasted, much of it going into landfill. It is astonishing that tree surgeons have to pay to dispose of their trimmings. Similarly, neither fruit-tree growing nor beekeeping are publicly supported. All fruit tree research has now effectively ceased at the government's chief horticultural research station at East Malling, while apiculture has been removed from the curriculum of agricultural colleges. The scope for development and reinvigoration of many neglected countryside industries involving trees and tree products, is enormous.

Fruit trees and orchards

The domestication of fruit trees may have preceded the development of the first cereal crops (barley and wheat, in western Asia) in the mountains of central Asia around 10,000 years ago. Carbonised pips at least 8,500 years old have been found at Catal Hüyük in Turkey, and in excavations of prehistoric lake settlements of a similar age in Switzerland remains of both crabapples and a larger fruit, possibly a cultivated apple, have been found. In Britain it is known that the Romans brought their own popular varieties of fruit trees, as did other migrants such as the Huguenots in more recent times.

The reason why there is such a diversity of fruit trees like apple (derived from the Almaty apple, *Malus sieversii*) – and why every individual grown from a pip is genetically unique – is due to their almost complete self-sterility. They have co-evolved with insect pollinators to the point where cross-pollination is obligatory for sexual reproduction to take place. As a result the trees are genetically very variable because every fertilised seed or pip has a chance combination of genes from two different parents, and so no apple tree breeds true. The selective advantage that results from these diverse offspring means that the trees are adaptable to changing conditions and local variations of soil, humidity and temperature. These are features that are probably characteristic of species that have diversified in mountain areas with mosaics of

RIGHT The ancestor of cultivated apples, *Malus sieversii*, from central Asia, here growing at Reading University Arboretum.

small areas each having different ecological conditions. Pears and cherries are similar to apples in their genetic strategy. The cultivated pears of Europe are derived from *Pyrus pyraster*, the wild pear, and two other species, *P. korschinskyi* and *P. heterophylla*, while in the Far East cultivated pears are varieties of a different species, the Chinese pear, *P. serotina*.

In many cultivated varieties apples and pears can still develop without the pollen fertilising the ovule – although in this case the pip is sterile or even, in some cases, absent. Where fertilisation does occur and the pips are viable, they may give rise to varied offspring, the majority of which will prove of little value or interest. Occasionally one of these sports produces good fruit, and it may then be transplanted to an existing garden or orchard. This is the origin of 'new' varieties, which must be considered native having arisen (by chance) locally. When additional trees with the same characteristics are required, then propagation has to be vegetative – by cuttings or the ancient art of grafting. Cuttings from desired trees can be grafted on to related rootstock – usually the common wild species or a related rosaceous species such as hawthorn. Every commercial fruit farm is like this, rows and rows of identical trees of the selected variety, all created by grafting cuttings from an original tree (or its descendants vegetatively multiplied) on to a different rootstock.

Many of the recorded and existing varieties were named after their discoverers or owners. Henry VIII employed fruiterers to search Europe for good varieties with which to establish orchards such as that at Hampton Court (now lost). Perhaps due partly to the royal family's interest, fruit growing became very popular; according to Keith Thomas (1983), there were so many orchards in Norwich that it was described as 'either a city in an orchard or an orchard in a city, so equally were houses and fruit-trees planted'. Every local area, even village, proudly cherished its own varieties, and many would be on sale at local markets. Today fruit growing has largely become standardised, with just a few commercial varieties being grown in vast commercial orchards, and the trends in European food legislation threaten to curtail the number of varieties even more.

The dangers of reducing this genetic diversity and paying too little attention to conservation are clear: pests and diseases thrive on monocultures, especially those that are genetically uniform, and with climate change and global travel unfamiliar pests are a constant threat. Even cider manufacturers are using fewer and fewer varieties of apple – indeed they now import apple concentrate. Local varieties of cider apples are scarcely in demand at all, and traditional orchards, formally such an important and well-loved element in the country landscape, have gradually disappeared. For some years up to 1988, the government gave grants for the grubbing-up of old orchards, without any reservation, and the original trees of old varieties may have been lost.

Perhaps the most celebrated apple variety in England is Bramley's Seedling, named after Matthew Bramley, who once owned the cottage in Southwell, Nottinghamshire, where the original tree still stands bearing fruit. Bramleys now constitute over 90% of the cooking apples produced in the UK, with some 135,000 tonnes being produced annually from about 28,000 acres of fruit trees. As with other varieties of fruit tree, all Bramley apples come from the grafted progeny of the original pippin. Botanists from Nottingham University, using modern micro-propagation techniques, have now effectively cloned the Bramley apple, and these are claimed to maintain the true nature of the

Traditional fruit varieties - a disappearing heritage

Paul Hand, the 'apple detective' of Bees and Trees, 1991 *(Spirit of Trees*, no. 6)

We are still losing old varieties like Onibury Pippin and Shropshire Ladies' Fingers – if we hadn't found those particular trees we could have lost those varieties forever. It's important to keep as many varieties as possible – they taste different and they have unique genetic material that may be useful for breeding programmes in the future. Things like late flowering, frost resistance and resistance to different diseases – these traits are all very valuable. There are still people alive, round here, who remember orchards as they used to be (70–80 years ago) when there were 20 or 30 varieties of apple in a local market that people would pick and bring in. Those days are gone – today we have just nine varieties grown commercially in this country – the fantastic variety of fruit is just in people's gardens and in remnants of old orchards.

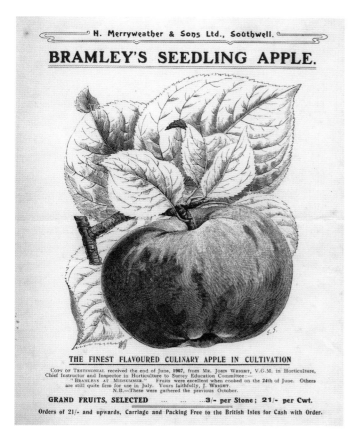

ABOVE, ABOVE RIGHT AND BELOW RIGHT
Advertisement in *Merryweather's Catalogue*,
c. 1920. The original Bramley's Pippin tree
with the owner, Nancy Harrison, and the tree
itself today.

fruit better than cuttings or descendants of cuttings.

The Bramley apple had its origin in about 1809. Mary Ann Brailsford (then a young girl) planted the pips of an apple she had enjoyed, and saw it grow into a tree. In 1846 her parents sold the cottage to Matthew Bramley, landlord of the White Lion in Easthorpe, who lived there until his death in 1871. In 1857 Henry Merryweather, a local nurseryman, met a gardener with a basket of fine apples from the tree. Impressed, he asked to have cuttings for grafting, which Bramley agreed to, on the condition he called them 'Bramley's Seedling'. Merryweather found the apples sold well. He planted many acres with the grafted trees, and exhibited the apples at the Royal Horticultural Society where they won a first-class certificate in 1893.

The taste of apples

The sharp taste of apples is due to the presence (greater in the skin than the flesh) of polyphenols, including the red flavonoids, and related to both the pale yellow anthocyanins and tannin. These are chemicals that protect the fruit against diseases and herbivores. In humans, their antoxidant activity protects against cancer, heart and artery problems. Traditional apple varieties tend to have a higher polyphenol content; they are sharp to taste and go brown rapidly when sliced open. Modern varieties tend to be sweeter with lower polyphenol levels; their food value and taste has been compromised to increase their 'marketability', in particular their shelf-life. Royal Gala and Fuji apples have particularly low phenol contents; this can be as little as a quarter of that of some old varieties such as Blenheim Orange or the French Calville Rouge d'Automne.

Coppicing

A mass of roughly equal, straight branches can be obtained from some trees such as hazel and willows when they are cut at or just above ground level at regular intervals of a few years. This ancient practice, which may have originated in the Neolithic period, is known as coppicing, from the Old French *couper* to cut. The origins of this technique are not recorded but for millennia it has been used as a way of managing many sorts of tree sustainably. In England and Ireland the trees are usually hazel, oak, lime, alder, elm, hornbeam, maple, ash, sweet chestnut and even rowan, crabapple and birch. When individual trees such as oak, lime or maple are allowed to grow to full height (for timber) among the coppice stools, this is known as coppice-with-standards.

Coppice stools need protection from browsing animals for the first year or two, and in Britain's woodland today this is often a problem owing to the greatly increased numbers of deer. In former times deer numbers were smaller, and domestic animals would be kept out by shepherds or herdsmen. The length of time between cuttings (the coppice cycle) varies according to the tree species and the products required: ash for tool handles – four to seven years; hazel for pottery crates or barrel hoops and oak for bark-peeling – 7 to 10 years; birch for broom handles – 10 to 15 years; and alder for clogs or oak for peeling – 20 to 25 years.

Not only were such cycles sustainable, the process has the effect of greatly prolonging the life of the individual trees. Ancient hazel, elm and lime coppice stools in England have been estimated to be over 1,500 years old – more than 10 times the normal span of uncoppiced hazel. As they say in Cumbria, 'if you want wood, you have to cut wood'. Abandoning coppiced woodlands too long between cuts ultimately condemns many of the stools, especially when taller 'standards' such as oaks are allowed to shade out an area – the coppice thrives on being cut, but can rapidly succumb to shading and browsing by deer. It has been estimated that in

BELOW Neglected hornbeam coppice with oak standards in north London, recently reworked for the first time in over 50 years.

BELOW Very few pure lime coppice woods still exist. This is Groton Wood near Lavenham, Suffolk.

RIGHT Traditional charcoal-burning in the New Forest in the 1920s, a labour-intensive method involving continuous monitoring of the burn.

the mid-nineteenth century the textile industry in England was using an incredible 1,500 million bobbins annually, about half of which were made from coppiced birch and alder, especially from the Lake District. A single large cotton mill in Stockport is said to have used about 10 million bobbins at any one time, with a replacement rate of about 350,000 per week. Other industrial uses for wood were similarly voracious. In the early nineteenth century a major constraint on the production of hops in Kent was the availability of poles from 12-year-old coppiced chestnut. In the 1830s 100,000 acres of coppice on this rotation were needed to supply the 25 million new poles required per annum.

During the early part of the Industrial Revolution the main fuel used in the production of iron was charcoal; very large areas in Shropshire (near Ironbridge) and in south Cumbria were given over to coppice woods solely to supply this industry, until coal took over as the main fuel. Demand for coppice wood (including willow) peaked around 1850, with firewood, charcoal, rough baskets for coal and hoops for barrels all requiring large quantities.

Thereafter firewood and charcoal were overtaken by coal and all the woodland industries began to decline, probably due more to a migration of workers to towns than a reduction in demand for the products. Timber was imported from Europe, undercutting local prices, especially in the large towns and seaports; other products were replaced by mass-produced items, often made from imported raw materials. Fewer clogs were worn, wire-netting replaced hurdles, coal fires warmed homes. Gradually, further changes meant gas or electricity were used domestically instead of firewood, and demand for charcoal slumped only to be revived in recent years for barbecues and restaurant cooking.

Woodland industries did not disappear completely. In the 1920s a survey carried out by Fitzrandolph and Hay (1977) revealed a wide range of woodland products still being made by individual craftspeople in rural workshops for local use. Charcoal was produced in some places, alder clogs were still being made, hazel and birch faggots were used for sea defences, oak bark was in demand from the tanners, and makers of swill baskets and tool handles still needed small ash poles. (All this was in addition to the uses to which timber from standard trees was put, such as furniture making from beech and elm in the Chilterns.) In some areas there was still a small-scale trade in some coppice products, but they found that the market for most coppice-wood industries was almost at a point of no return.

In Cumbria, where thousands of artisans once made vast quantities of charcoal for local industry, birch fenders for ships, quantities of industrial baskets and panniers, many of these rural industries had already died out before the Second World War. But some traditions survived, and a few woods were maintained as working coppices.

What makes hazel such a popular coppice wood?

Walter Lloyd, a charcoal and tent-peg maker from Finsthwaite near Ulverston, 1991 (*Spirit of Trees*, no. 4)

First of all it grows very fast, on good ground. When you grow it, the stools or root-stocks can be very close together so when it's time for cutting you really have a mass of poles, a lot of weight. And then it's very easy to work, it splits beautifully. You can split or cleave it with a billhook or whatever. It almost comes apart in your hand when you do it the right way. It bends beautifully like on a hurdle, it goes round a corner without losing its strength. But the only thing is once you've started coppicing hazel you must go on, you must cut it, once you leave it too long it will [decline and eventually] die, it'll get shaded out by the other trees. It really saddens me to see so much derelict hazel coppice that's been left so long it's no good any more. *[In fact much 'derelict' hazel coppice could be resuscitated by careful management involving cutting and the removal of taller shading trees.]* There's actually a terrific potential from coppice woods. Traditionally the coppice made a vast number of different products, but so many of them got taken over by plastic. Now people want to get back to real things made out of real wood

from real trees. Take wooden tent-pegs; I can make them out of oak or ash coppice and sell them at 25p a time. Marquee hirers buy a terrific number, they buy them by the thousand. The army buys them by the hundred thousand, and one or two big camping firms order a quarter of a million at a time. Then there's the Red Cross... Well, as you can see, the demand is astronomic for things like that. You can make 200 to 600 tent-pegs out of oak in a day depending on your equipment and how skilled

you are, but then of course you don't want to be doing just tent-pegs all day long, it would soon get boring and there's many other things to make. Take thatching spars, made out of hazel coppice; 20 million of them are being used in a year at present; there isn't enough woodland left to be coppiced, to meet these demands, because people have forgotten how to do it.

BELOW Walter Lloyd tending his iron charcoal clamps.

The late Bill Hogarth MBE, master woodsman, speaking in 1991 (*Spirit of Trees*, no. 4)

In the early autumn I cut hazel; most of the things I use hazel for you need the sap out – net stakes for the inshore fisheries, thatching spars, hurdles, walking sticks and so on. Birch too, now the leaves are coming off I cut birch with the sap out to make next year's besoms [birch brooms]. Then in the summer, when the sap rises, it's the oak-peeling season. I peel oak for about three months in the summer: that's a very good earner, it all goes to the specialist tanneries where they make the highest class leather, and what's left, the peeled wood, goes to make rustic furniture, or it's swill wood, for making oak-swill baskets. There's something to do here every month of the year.

After these interviews were made and the film on their work was shown by Channel 4, Bill Hogarth and Walter Lloyd each received hundreds of letters of interest. Subsequently Bill Hogarth reckoned that at least a hundred people around the country had started making a living from managing coppice woodland

and selling coppice products. Today, coppicing courses are now increasingly popular and run by various organisations including the Greenwood Trust at Ironbridge, and in Cumbria by the Bill Hogarth MBE Memorial Apprenticeship Trust, www.coppiceapprentice.org.uk.

ABOVE The late Bill Hogarth MBE with some of his many products from coppice woodland.

LEFT Detail of hazel hurdle; as flexible as willow when freshly cut, hazel makes a strong fence once it has dried out.

BELOW Ancient ash pollard, Hatfield Forest – an old estate with extensive woodland pasture.

Pollarding and wood-pasture

Pollarding is the technique of cutting trees at a height of about 2.5–3 m (8–10 ft) on a regular basis, but whereas coppicing is done in the winter, pollarding is often done in the summer. In medieval times a major product of pollarding was fodder or 'tree hay' or 'greenhew' (leafy branches, especially of elm, stored for use as winter fodder), in addition to the production of wood for fuel, tools etc. The practice, which can still be seen in Norway and parts of Eastern Europe, dates here from at least Anglo-Saxon times as a way to combine tree production with grazing for animals on a sustainable basis. This was known as wood-pasture – grassy pastureland for grazing animals, wild or domesticated, dotted with large, often very old, frequently cut pollards.

At Muker in Yorkshire, Muir (2000) has found seventeenth-century court documents recording payments for greenhew, which show that it was regarded as a valuable resource. Other trees managed in this way most frequently were oak and ash, less frequently lime, beech, holly, hawthorn, maple and aspen, and in some areas alder, although it is not clear that all of these would have been used for fodder.

Ancient pollards

Like coppice stools, pollards can be very long-lived. The practice has fallen into disuse in the last two centuries, but relics of ancient wood-pasture dating back hundreds of years still survive in many parts of the country such as Windsor Park (oaks and beeches), Burnham Beeches, Hatfield Forest (mainly hornbeams, maples, oaks, hawthorn and others), Stiperstones (holly and rowan), Geltsdale

177

in Cumbria (alder) and Stourhead, Wiltshire (sweet chestnut). Where they are still standing these ancient pollards are impressive relics, as is apparent in Rackham's description (1986) of Staverton Park in Suffolk: 'an awesome place of Tolkienesque wonder and beauty. The mighty and bizarre shapes of oaks of unknown age rise out of a sea of tall bracken or else are mysteriously surrounded by rings of yet mightier hollies. Some of the birches and rowans, as well as the hollies, are nearly the largest recorded in the kingdom. Overshadowed giants moulder in the twilit shade or lean half-fallen against other giants. Big hollies and birches are rooted high in the crotches of oaks; [there is] an atmosphere of timeless decay' (see picture p.10).

Ancient pollards are an extremely rich habitat for lichens, mosses and specialised insects. Many of our rarest beetles and flies occur in such trees and nowhere else so conserving the trees is very important. Recent investigations of ancient pollards in several countries have revealed numerous previously unknown insects.

Apart from wood-pasture, many old pollards can be found in hedges, in farmland as boundary markers, and along water-courses (pollard willows or poplars). There are probably more ancient pollards in England than anywhere else in Western Europe, partly due to the survival of large estates and the preservation of 'traditional parkland', although widespread pollarding was largely abandoned before the Enclosure Acts in the late eighteenth and early nineteenth centuries (Muir, 2000).

As a result of renewed interest, pollarding has been restarted at a number of places where it had been discontinued long ago. Neglected pollards tend to become top-heavy and may ultimately collapse outwards, while restarting pollarding after a long gap has not always been successful. It is now understood that the process must be done very carefully, single limbs being cut at intervals of several years to give the entire tree time to survive the stresses and microbial attack (Read, 1991).

Shredding

Another way of managing trees to produce fodder is called shredding. The side branches are cut off at intervals to use for fodder, leaving just the top tuft to grow naturally. The effect is to produce exceptionally tall and thin trees. These are common in France, and although never popular in Britain shredded trees can be seen in some places such as north of Dundee in Scotland.

BELOW Plymouth pear clone growing in an abandoned hedge near Plymouth airport. It may have been introduced into Britain as a hedging tree.

Hedges

Another long-established use for wild trees is to make hedges. The earliest hedges may have been remnants of wildwood, but the technique of planting trees in lines to make a living barrier is also a very old one. Trees that layer well and coppice vigorously obviously make good hedges, and thorny species like hawthorn and blackthorn have long been popular where the control of grazing animals was a primary purpose. Some hedges in England are more than 500 years old and these are often very diverse with 10 or more woody species. Some of these hedges date from piecemeal enclosures between 1450 and 1650, while many more originated during Enclosures of Commons between 1750 and 1850. A formula to estimate the age of a hedge based on the average number of woody species in a 30 yard section of hedge produces an age which is roughly 100 years per species. However, as Pollard *et al.* (1974) have pointed out, such an approach is not reliable; there have been periods when mixed hedges originated, while at other times mostly single species hedges (usually hawthorn) were planted. Hedgelink campaigns for the conservation and restoration of hedges, many thousands of miles of which have been lost in the past few decades especially in areas of the south and east of England where arable farming predominates (www.hedgelink.org.uk).

Willow growing: withy and osier beds

Most willows respond vigorously to accidental damage, as their natural habitat is the floodplain of rivers. This characteristic has been used for thousands of years to manage willows, either coppicing or pollarding them, to produce young stems for basket-weaving, and indeed some types of willow were apparently brought here for the purpose several millennia ago.

One- or two-year-old willow twigs (or 'withies') are extremely flexible when fresh, and become strong and firm when dried. The technique of weaving them into baskets was known to the ancient Egyptians, the Greeks and the Romans, while the ancient Gaulish God Esus is portrayed as a woodcutter, often of willow, as in a stone bas relief at the Musée de Cluny, Paris. The oldest known baskets found in Upper Egypt have been carbon dated at about 10,000 years. In England fragments of wickerwork from wild willow dating from more than 2,000 years ago have been found preserved at the Glastonbury lake village site.

Local willow growing for basket-making has traditionally been done in low-lying areas all over these islands, but especially on the Somerset Levels, west Lancashire, the Trent Valley, in some parts of East Anglia, and in Ireland around Lough Neagh, in the Dublin area and in Connemara. Until the early twentieth century, much of the Thames riverbank above Hammersmith was used for osier beds on both sides of the river; gradually the areas were drained for vegetable growing and today all that is left is a small osier bed on Chiswick Eyot, which was still cut regularly until 1935. The cutting has recently been revived by amateur enthusiasts of the Old Chiswick Preservation Society.

The species of willow most frequently cultivated for baskets are *Salix triandra* (almond willow), *S. viminalis* (basket willow) and *S. purpurea* (purple willow), and some hybrids of these species. In

BELOW Traditional withy-processing such as bark-stripping is still a labour-intensive activity in Somerset: Tom David at Stoke St Gregory.

BELOW Modern withy harvesting on Somerset Levels.

Basket willows: whites, browns and buffs

One-year-old willow rods or 'withies' are traditionally cut by hand. If sold in this form with the bark still on they are known as 'browns'. The majority of rods are peeled to make the more valuable 'whites' – these are cut in the spring and peeled directly or 'pitted', that is they are left over the winter with their ends in about 15 cm (6 in) water before being peeled. 'Buffs' are boiled for eight hours in large tanks so the rods become stained with tannin before being stripped. Today the rods are peeled using a rotating drum powered by an electric motor or tractor. Peeled rods are dried in the sun before being bundled up by hand for sale, often tied with a withy 'tie'. *Salix triandra* rods can be used to produce good quality whites or buffs. Coarse work, such as agricultural baskets or the tidal fish-traps that are still in use on the River Severn, are made from unpeeled brown rods often from pollards. *S. purpurea* produces finer rods, and was once used to make whites of high quality for fancy baskets, especially around Mawdesley in Lancashire. Today *S. purpurea* is more often used in the brown form, and is much in demand from artistic basketmakers. The red- and orange-stemmed cultivars of *S. alba* and *S. fragilis* are particularly used for river and sea defence work in the Netherlands and Belgium. There is

ABOVE The centuries-old tradition of withy-growing on the Somerset Levels only declined in the early twentieth century.

also a tradition of using thin willow shoots to tie agricultural crops such as vines or hops; old willow stools kept and cut for this purpose can still be seen in the Vale of Evesham.

In former times baskets were used to carry light or perishable goods of all kinds such as fish, fruit, meat and vegetables. For heavier goods like coal, clay or bricks, heavy duty willow baskets or oak-swill baskets were used. During the First World War the demand for containers of all kinds increased enormously at the same time that

imports from the continent were once more unavailable. Special panniers were needed to transport food, medical and military supplies and even individual artillery shells on horseback or by mule to the front.

ABOVE Withies are used for making a wide range of baskets. The different colours are produced by the different treatment of cut stems.

LEFT In the First World War special baskets were made to carry single artillery shells and other miltary items.

fact there are very many varieties and hybrids that go under names such as 'Whissender', 'Noir de Villaines' and 'Champion' – each with slightly different colour and weaving characteristics. The best quality baskets are made from *S. triandra* stems; on the Somerset Levels, 80% of the willows are a single variety known as 'Black Maul'.

Basket willows are grown in rows about a metre apart, and the 'withies' are cut at or near ground level every year – a version of short-rotation coppicing. They are traditionally cut by hand with a small sickle, and trimmed as close to the stool as possible so that they grow straight. Some willow growers now use mechanical harvesters, but, as traditional growers will tell you – the stools still should be trimmed by hand. Cutting is every year between November and early April, traditionally after cattle have been allowed into the willow beds for a week or so to 'clean' them by eating the weeds without damaging the flexible willow stems.

Walking through a withy bed in late summer is a breathtaking experience, enveloping the walker completely in a magical, waving, rustling and ever-moving tumult, with beautiful light effects and occasional glimpses of wildlife such as shy marshland birds, grass snakes and voles.

Some stems are left for two years to produce the 'sticks' from which stronger items such as chair legs are made. Many withy beds are 40 to 50 years old, and a good withy bed lasts a willow-growing family for two generations or more. Serious infestations of rust or other pests sometimes make it necessary for willow growers to replant their withy beds, but this occurs infrequently – partly because the varieties in use have been selected to resist common diseases.

The great expansion of the willow industry in England was in the early nineteenth century. Large-scale drainage of the Somerset Levels made possible a major expansion of commercial growing; this spread to various other parts of the country in response to demand, peaking in around 1900, when local production began to be challenged by cheaper, mass-produced imports. In Ireland, between 1766 and 1806 the Dublin Society gave grants to landowners to encourage commercial tree-planting of all types; a few of these 'sally gardens' still survive in Co. Dublin today. Willow growing in England and Ireland has declined almost to zero; some of the history can be seen at Coates' Willows and Wetlands Centre at Stoke St Gregory near Taunton in Somerset.

The importance of cultivated willow

As a result of the First World War the significance of willow as a strategic raw material was recognised. A National Willow Collection was established at Long Ashton Research Station near Bristol (since moved to Rothamsted Research Station). However, the collection is very limited in scope and today funding has been cut to the point where the entire collection may be lost, and there is little chance of it becoming more representative. This is short-sighted; willows are genetically very variable and a full programme to collect and conserve genetic resources of willow here and throughout Europe for breeding purposes (for rapid growth, rust resistance etc.) should be supported (see Chapter 7).

At the same time that the National Collection was being put together, the actual use of willow baskets began to decline in favour of cheap wooden boxes and, later, plastic containers. Many traditional uses died out and the whole industry declined. In 1925 over 6,000 acres of willows were being grown commercially, but this had dropped to 2,000 by 1953, and just 250 by 1992. There was a minor revival of demand during the Second World War as panniers were required for pack animals and for airborne transport. Today there are very few traditional growers left, although withy beds cut by hand can still be found on the Somerset Levels. There has been a resurgence of willow use which is set to continue, as both the aesthetic quality and sustainable nature of basketwork has been rediscovered. Today willow for baskets is grown mainly in small withy beds by the users themselves.

Other commercial uses of willows

For centuries withies have been used to bind and strengthen riverbanks and prevent scouring and erosion, and for sea defences. In Holland willow mattresses have been used in dykes to protect the polders, and for storm protection of low-lying coastal areas. In the 1980s willow mattresses were used to stabilise the sea bed for deep-water port construction at Port Talbot in Wales, and for harbour improvements at Zeebrugge in Belgium and Dunkirk in France.

Steep mountain slopes, such as those near ski runs, have been stabilised using willow mattresses, whose full potential for holding soil and preventing landslips even in harsh climatic conditions is now being appreciated. With increases in erratic weather, this use may become more important to prevent landslips especially in hill areas. Willows establish easily and, as they can be planted much closer together than poplar, they are particularly suited as quick-growing windbreaks. For reducing exterior noise pollution, paired woven 'hurdles' of live willow can be erected about a metre apart, and the gap between them filled with earth. This creates a 'willow wall', an effective structure for reducing noise and air pollution

coppiced willow. Experimental work at Rothamsted Research has concentrated on breeding high-yielding rust- and insect-resistant varieties of willow optimal for UK conditions, usually involving foreign willows crossed with common osier, *Salix viminalis*. These hybrids can produce up to 20 stems from a single rootstock, each growing 3–4 m (10–13 ft) in a season. Biomass yields already average more than twice that obtained 10 years ago, and further improvements in both yield and reliability are being sought.

In 2008 about 7,000 hectares were planted with willows, producing around 70,000 tonnes of dry biomass. The plan is for this to be increased to upwards of 1 million tonnes by 2020, partly by increasing yields to an average 15 tonnes per hectare per annum on a two-year rotation. There are currently no plans in the UK to use biomass from willow or poplar to make biofuel (ethanol); elsewhere there are programmes to produce GM (genetically modified) trees with reduced lignin supposedly for the same purpose. The whole programme to produce biomass specially should perhaps be regarded with some scepticism, as there are large quantities of woodland trimmings and garden waste available already, most of which is not used for energy generation and goes into landfill.

New uses for trees: phytoremediation

Polluted or contaminated land occurs as a result of industrial processes at sites of former factories, chemical works and stores, tanneries, munitions test-sites etc. The main forms of contamination are caused by (toxic) heavy metals or by organic compounds such as solvents and fuel oils. In recent years it has been found that some trees are able to grow on these heavily contaminated substrates, absorbing or immobilising the poisonous elements or breaking down the toxic organic compounds. Experiments have shown that willows and poplars (including aspen) can both be used for phyto-remediation, a 'low-tech' approach that probably works as a result of the activity of their mycorrhizal associates. At Mugdock near Glasgow a well-developed poplar woodland now grows on land that was badly contaminated by an old alkali works. The treatment of sewage has also been successfully achieved using a succession of beds containing first reeds, *Phragmites* spp., then willows. Most elements, even heavy metals, are required in small quantities by plants for normal growth, but

caused by motorway traffic. Comparable in cost to concrete walls, they are graffiti-proof, will not crack, corrode or break down and require little maintenance, becoming even stronger as they age. This technique is used widely in the Netherlands and Belgium, but not so far in the UK.

New uses for trees: energy from biomass

Biomass is the term used for organic material derived from any living organisms; in the context of energy generation this means waste plant material. As part of the Renewables Obligation, a government scheme to reward the use of sustainable energy sources, biomass 'has a major contribution to make'. It is already used as part of the fuel in many large power stations (8% of all renewables in 2008) and biomass is increasingly used for small-scale local power generation. Theoretically, various materials can be used: forestry thinnings, energy crops, agricultural residues (straw etc.), food waste, industrial waste, household waste and short-rotation metals in particular become toxic at higher concentrations. In acid conditions contaminated with these elements, few plants will grow. Such barren sites are easily eroded by rain and wind, as a result of which the contaminants can become widely spread. Experiments have shown that strains of some common willow species such as the sallows and common osier, but also native poplars, aspen, alder, sycamore and even birches will grow on contaminated soil and develop a complete vegetative cover (phyto-stabilisation). Once willows (or other trees) have stabilised the ground, then soil erosion is reduced or halted altogether and leeching of pollutants is reduced. Leaf-litter builds up and other plants arrive, brought by birds etc., so that a succession towards normal woodland is started. As the organic content of the soil increases, some elements such as lead and copper become immobilised by becoming attached to organic compounds.

Some plants (including various species growing naturally on metalliferous volcanic soils) are known as hyperaccumulators. They are capable of accumulating (to levels of more than 100 times normal) potentially toxic elements, slowing their growth but 'possibly providing protection against fungal and insect attack' (Pulford and Watson, 2002).

Willows and poplars are not hyperaccumulators, but they will concentrate heavy metals in their wood and bark, where they are effectively immobilised, and the stems can then be removed from the site. The trees' normally rapid growth is hardly affected even when the soil is very acid, and they can be used to extract specific elements such as cadmium, a common, but poisonous urban soil pollutant. Short-rotation coppicing is used to remove the wood containing the metal. When soil contamination is high, the growth of these trees may be impaired, but potentially this approach could be used not just to clean soil but even to obtain cadmium. Alder is known to accumulate gold in its tissues (assuming there is gold in the adjacent soil or water) so it has even been suggested that some of these trees could be used for 'phyto-mining', the sustainable extraction of gold or rare elements from soil or rock waste.

The processes and mechanisms by which these contaminants are neutralised are not well understood, but it is clear that among the genetic diversity of common willow and birch species there are individuals or strains that are particularly effective. This may be due to a greater rate of acclimatisation to the pollutants, rather than any genetically transmitted tolerance. The role of mycorrhizal associations is probably critical, but in some cases this is mysterious because in other contexts copper compounds are effective general fungicides, so why are the trees' mycorrhizal associates not affected? Some researchers have suggested that in certain cases specific mycorrhizal associations may confer an increased resistance to toxic levels of metal ions in the soil.

LEFT Willows bred for maximum growth; biomass trial at Rothamsted Research Station.

6 The folklore of trees

SACRED TREES ARE FOUND IN EVERY COUNTRY, in all spiritual traditions, and there is almost universal respect for trees as individual living things. For some people their first response to a tree is a spiritual one, although the idea of talking to trees or 'communing with nature' is still considered by some a bit eccentric. Individual trees are at the very centre of certain civilizations. To many indigenous peoples all over the world, certain trees are sacred; they are revered as totem poles, their ancestral sacred groves are their holiest places. This was also clearly the case throughout much of Europe, and in these islands, particularly in Ireland, many centuries ago (Lucas, 1962–3). The following account is heavily weighted towards Ireland because folklore associated with trees has survived much better there than elsewhere in these islands.

The folklore of trees divides opinion; some people dismiss most of these 'beliefs' as so much superstition, especially when they are thought to be factually erroneous or 'ill-founded', whereas groups such as Tree Spirit (www.treespirit.org.uk) take this whole subject very seriously indeed. I have taken an open-minded view; many people I have met during the writing of this book and the making of the films '*Spirit of Trees*' still believe in these ideas without needing any further discussion. Clearly, ill-founded or not, these beliefs about trees are an important part of our understanding of the place of trees in our culture – which is a dynamic phenomenon in itself.

ABOVE Villagers of Great Wishford dancing at Salisbury Cathedral with oak branches and hazel 'nitches' for their annual shout.

OPPOSITE The wishing tree at Nunnington Hall, Yorkshire, is an example of a 'new' tradition being created; visitors tie a piece of coloured material to this apple tree and make a wish.

Ancient laws of Ireland

According to the eighth-century Brehon Law (Neeson, 1991) the following trees were considered valuable property for landowners and penalties were specified for anyone who damaged them. Noble trees: oak, hazel, holly, yew, ash, pine, apple; commoners: alder, willow, hawthorn, rowan, birch, elm, (possibly) wild cherry; lower orders: blackthorn, elder, hazel, spindle, aspen, arbutus, juniper.

Brehon Law also specified the four seasons and later texts specify the great festivals which celebrated them. The start of the warm half of the year was celebrated at Beltaine, or May Day.

Rag trees

In many parts of the world selected trees, often at sacred sites such as next to holy wells (Ireland), at springs or in sacred groves, are known as 'prayer trees' or 'rag trees'. Fragments of cloth or garments are tied to the branches as offerings, a custom that can be found in many countries from Russia to Ethiopia, and at scattered places throughout Britain (Harte, 2008, and pers. comm. 2010). In Scotland one of the most celebrated is the Clootie Well on the Black Isle north of Inverness. At Paphos in Cyprus, a terebinth tree, *Pistacia terebinthus*, that grows from the ancient underground chapel dedicated to Ayia Solomon, a local early Christian martyr, is continually festooned with offerings from people hoping for cures for particular ailments; local informants suggest that today most supplicants are young and female.

ABOVE Pilgrims visiting Abbey Well at Ballyshannon, tying rags to the ash tree and taking the holy water.

RIGHT Fans of Marc Bolan (lead singer of T-Rex) have turned this sycamore tree into a shrine; his car hit the tree and he was killed in 1973.

At Barnes Common in south London, the pop musician Marc Bolan was killed in a car crash in 1973. The sycamore that his car hit is regularly bedecked with flowers, fan letters and other memorabilia. The site is now leased on a long-term basis by T-Rex Action Group (TAG) and a memorial plinth has been added (Clayton, 2008).

Oak and yew trees are believed to have been at the spiritual centre of Celtic, Anglo-Saxon and druidic cultures in Britain and Ireland; the best estimates for the age of the Fortingall yew put its origin very early in the human settlement of Scotland. We have little idea about whether it was planted or not. The tradition of planting a rowan (or 'roden') tree near a habitation to ward away evil spirits also has a long history; old roden trees survive in Scotland in places where there is nothing left of the dwelling but a few scattered stones. We may have forgotten or lost the traditions and beliefs of our distant (pagan) ancestors but it seems that some of the actual trees they revered are still here with us.

The Crucifixion on a wooden cross is claimed as a link between trees and Christian witness. The fact that trees were revered in many parts of the world long before Christianity arrived has caused inevitable ambiguities that have been resolved in various ways. Early Christian missionaries were generally hostile to the sacred trees of paganism: as late as the eleventh century the Church in England made it an offence to build a sanctuary around a tree, while most holy wells were Christianised.

In Ireland every holy well in Ireland has an attendant tree, an association that can be traced back to the earliest written records and must pre-date Christianity. There may be around 3,000 holy wells today, many of which have significant trees associated with them. Lucas (1963) made a random survey of 210 wells, and found that by far the commonest associated trees were 'whitethorn' (hawthorn) (103) and ash (75), which together made up 85% of the total, the others being oak (7), willow (6), elder (5), holly (4), rowan (3), alder (3), elm (2), yew (1) and fir (1). He identifies the surprising frequency of ash – an important timber tree in a much deforested country – as a testimony to the sacred character of these trees: 'for nothing else would have saved them from use as fuel or timber in a country as starved of wood as Ireland... where the winning of semi-fossil bog-timber developed into a major rural industry'.

Many holy wells survive in England, Scotland and Wales, but the traditional association with significant trees is found only rarely. Harte (2008) has surveyed holy wells in England but hardly mentions any associated trees, while Shepherd (1994) visited holy wells in and around Bradford and noted that 'ash is the tree most frequently found next to wells in Yorkshire' while 'hawthorn, rowan and elder are also embedded in British [sic] folklore and are often found at wells'. In Wales, Jones (1992) cites wells being associated with hawthorn, elder, ash, oak, holly and yew trees and observed that 'the ragged remnant of

tree–well association can be recognised, in what was formerly a widespread custom'.

Historically (and still today in much of rural Ireland), there was believed to be a connection between trees and healing, with fertility, revival and rejuvenation; the long life of trees being one constant in an unpredictable and dangerous world. Sacred groves were revered by many local cultures (as they are in many parts of the world today) and in Ireland they were frequently the sites for the inauguration of kings. Once Christianity gained acceptance these places were secured for the new faith (and many of the trees felled) by becoming the sites for churches, just as churches were built next to yew trees elsewhere. Today there are relatively few surviving folk traditions centred on trees in England, Scotland or Wales.

Folklore of trees in Ireland

In Ireland, sacred trees have been defined as those that are 'treated with a certain reverence which normally protects them from wilful damage or cutting' (Neeson, 1991). Examples include celebrated trees such as the Big Bell Tree in Co. Tipperary and the Red Cross Tree and the Monument Tree of Co. Meath. At places like Ballykumber in Co. Offaly, ash trees (or ancient stumps) associated with holy wells were claimed to have special properties; anyone in possession of even the smallest fragment would be protected from drowning (Mac Coitir, 2003). Large numbers of Irish emigrants crossing the Atlantic provided themselves with chips or twigs of these trees; some people still carry them today.

In Ancient Greek mythology, Orestes, fleeing from the Furies, found sanctuary under Apollo's laurel, and there are other stories of trees offering sanctuary right up to the present time. In Ireland yew trees offered sanctuary in pre-Christian times; the tradition was apparently transferred to churches during the process of Christianisation of sacred sites, dates and customs.

Five legendary trees of Ireland

Name of tree	Species	Probable site	County
Bile Tortan	Ash	Ard Breccain	Co. Meath
Eo Mugna	Oak	Ballaghmoon	Co. Kildare
Eo Rossa	Yew	Oldleighlin	Co. Carlow
Craeb Daithi	Ash	Forbill	Co. West Meath
Bile Uisnigh	Ash	Usnagh	Co. West Meath

All these trees were felled or died around the 7th century

The spiritual and earthly power of kings or chieftains in ancient Ireland is thought to have been closely related to sacred trees and groves; their survival a vital adjunct to a chiefly or royal residence. There are numerous accounts in early Irish manuscripts of such trees being destroyed in times of conflict: 'it seems that the crowning insult which could be inflicted on an enemy was the desecration (and destruction) of the sacred tree or trees at the inauguration place of his kings' (Lucas, 1963).

Many place names in Ireland can be traced to anglicised versions of Irish-language words denoting big or important trees such as bile (probably meaning ash, anglicised as vill or villa), dar (oak) and skeagh (thorn). Some examples are Drumaville in Co. Donegal, Billy in Co. Antrim and Skeagh in Co. Cork.

Although ancient yew trees are very scarce in Ireland today – the only two with girths of over 6 m (19½ ft) are at Bunclody in Co. Wexford and Glencormac in Co. Wicklow (Tree Council of Ireland, 2005) – there are many references to yew trees in ancient chronicles and in fairy tales. According to a typical one of these tales, Oilean an luir (Island of Yew) is an enchanted isle with a yew tree growing on it. A fisherman from Gola began to cut a sacred tree to make curach ribs (for boat-building) when a violent storm arose. A local man shouted to him to abandon the wood or he would be drowned. No sooner had he done so than the lake calmed down 'until it was as smooth as the page of a book'. Since then no one has ever gone back to gather curach ribs there (Mac Coitir, 2003).

BELOW The Great Ash of Leix, an ancient tree that finally disappeared in the early nineteenth century.

Folklore Great ash of Leix

Fairy trees

In Ireland there is a widespread belief that the 'little people' live in or near fairy trees (usually fairy thorn or hawthorn or rowan): they must at all costs be respected (Evans, 1972). According to an eighth-century hymn, the Irish worshipped the gods of the sidh (the modern 'fairy faith') until St Patrick converted them. The pagan gods became 'the fallen angels', not good enough for heaven but, on the other hand, not bad enough for hell.

Fairy legends are still told in Ireland and most of them are set in the ancient past. Fairy-lore has largely lost its hold on the people, but vestiges of the old traditions remain, often in connection with sacred sites on the landscape, such as fairy trees and glens and lone trees. There are many tales about fairy trees causing misfortune to those that damage or destroy them; new roads have been diverted to avoid them. It was widely believed that the DeLorean car factory in Belfast failed because a fairy tree had been removed to make way for it. Under certain circumstances appeals to the spirits to move have been 'successful'.

At Shanveen in the Blue Stack Mountains, Co. Donegal, a local man, the late Jimmy Burke, had two fairy trees growing on his land. One of these, a small rowan, still grows on an isolated pile of rocks, in the middle of a bog.

If you damaged the tree you could wake up in the morning and find your hair gone; I do go in the field where it is but I would never touch it or have anything to do with it. If you interfered with the tree, or tried to cut it, you can be sure something would come upon you.

This particular fairy tree has a scar on its trunk from an attempt by three youths to cut it down and destroy it in the 1940s.

They were trying to break it, but they weren't able to, though they did split it and trampled on it. But the next day the tree was up again and it's been growing away ever since.

LEFT AND BELOW Jimmy Burke's fairy tree – a rowan growing on a pile of stones, and Jimmy Burke himself.

May festivals in England and Ireland

The May festivals are particularly associated with milk and dairy products, which were the staple items of the diet in Ireland before the introduction of the potato. The productivity of the cows being of prime importance, many folk traditions concerned the health and well-being of cows (trees being symbolic, or providing actual fodder), while the failure of cows to produce milk yield was commonly ascribed to supernatural forces. Part of the tradition of Beltaine also involves boundary marking with sprigs of rowan or quicken tree, again aimed at protecting stock from 'magic'.

Folklorists, including those of the former Irish Folklore Commission have documented these traditions from all over Ireland and recognise four main forms (Lysaght, 1991). The traditions and where they are found are listed below, though the traditions coexist in some areas.

1 The May bough tradition is found exclusively in the south and west of Ireland (Munster).

2 The May bush tradition is more recent in origin. It is followed in certain parts of the east, centre and northwest of the Republic and in parts of west Ulster. (This tradition is thought to have been introduced from England.)

3 The May flowers tradition is the most widespread and is found in the centre and west (Leinster and Connacht) as well as parts of Ulster.

4 The maypole tradition is found predominantly in the centre (Leinster) and on the east coast of Ulster.

The May bough consists of the small branch of a newly leafed tree (hazel, elder, rowan or ash, but not hawthorn) that is collected on May morning and brought into the house unadorned, and placed over the door, on window-sills or over the fire. May (hawthorn)

BELOW The may-bush, a springtime tradition in some parts of Ireland, is erected at the gate by a farmer to protect the cows and dairy products for the following season.

BELOW Arbor Day being celebrated under the black poplar at the village of Aston-on-Clun, Shropshire.

Money trees

The 'money tree' at Clonenagh, Co. Laois, stood outside a graveyard a few miles from Portlaoise on the road between Dublin and Limerick. An old sycamore pollard, it was associated with the nearby holy well of St Fintan. Pilgrims would tie clothing on the tree for luck, and it became customary for travellers to hammer a coin into the bark for luck. However, the effect of copper from these coins together with the mutilation of the tree by souvenir hunters apparently took its toll and the tree collapsed over 10 years ago.

Other celebrated money trees with similar traditions are known from below Malham Cove in North Yorkshire, near Bovey Tracey on Dartmoor, on the Degnish Peninsula in Argyll, and on an island in Loch Maree, Wester Ross.

RIGHT The old money-tree at Clanenagh (now fallen) on the Dublin to Limerick road, Co Laois, Ireland.

blooms are not brought into the house as this is widely thought to be unlucky even in England. In Co. Cork branches of sycamore, known as 'summer tree', are used as the May bough.

In contrast the May bush is usually a small whitethorn (hawthorn) bush in full leaf that is cut on May Eve and decorated with yellow and blue May flowers (picked on May Eve). Yellow flowers such as primroses, cowslips or marsh marigolds signify the purity of the milk, while blue flowers such as bluebells signify the Virgin Mary. Wayside shrines to the Virgin Mary may also be decorated. The shells of eggs that were laid on Good Friday may also be added. The May bush is then set up, usually in front of the house, to be ready for May morning, when it will – according to Lysaght (1991) – 'reaffirm boundaries at the boundary-less time between the seasons, and protect the milk and the dairy products at that particular time'. The May bush stays on show for a week or two, or until all the flowers have withered.

May flowers are typically yellow, with blue probably only added during the early nineteenth century when the association of May celebrations with the Virgin Mary seems to have first become established. May flowers frequently include elder leaves, while

the maypole tradition (more celebratory and less protective in emphasis) of dancing around a recently cut straight timber pole is the only one also seen today in England.

In Cheshire in the early nineteenth century groups known as May-birchers would distribute tree branches on doorsteps according to a code based on a rhyme:

NUT (hazel) for a slut,

PEAR if you're fair,

PLUM if you're glum...,

ALDER (pronounced 'owler') for a scowler.

HAWTHORN which did not rhyme with anything, counted as a general compliment.

(Vickery, 1995).

7 Our native trees – the future

STUDIES OF THE COUNTRYSIDE OF BRITAIN AND IRELAND over millennia reveal a wide range of dynamic changes, many of them due to human activities. These have resulted in an enormous loss of native trees so that both Britain and Ireland have less tree cover, even including plantations, than almost anywhere in Europe (though tree cover has increased somewhat, mainly due to planting, over the last century).

Except where they have been planted as specimen trees or to mark boundaries, the vast majority of existing native trees have been managed more or less intensely at some time. Both the objectives and the methods of management have changed. Traditional woodland management declined once wood was superseded by coal and later by gas, so that by the Second World War in many areas it had disappeared altogether. Trees were no longer seen as productive of anything except timber for construction or pulp for paper.

Enhancing the role of trees as part of the landscape, for public amenity and for conservation, is now promoted as a major objective. Organisations such as the Woodland Trust and county Wildlife Trusts manage trees and woodland primarily for these purposes. Invasive and alien species are discouraged and native species encouraged and even planted, although not always from locally sourced seed, in a management regime that is basically interventionist. Tree-planting has become almost a fetish, as if it alone can undo some of the losses of trees in the past. Of course much tree-planting is of a commercial nature, concentrating on fast-growing introduced conifers, with the sole aim of maximising the profit for landowners or investors. The watchwords are speed and quantity; the products are timber and woodchips.

OPPOSITE A fine whitebeam at Watersmeet, Devon, now regarded not as French hales, *S. devoniensis,* but a separate species *S. admonitor* (so-called as the type-specimen is growing next to a 'NO PARKING' sign! (Rich et al. 2010).

RIGHT Heavily grooved bark of an old (planted) true service tree at St Annes's Hospital, north London.

There is another way of appreciating trees. On a still day, stand by the trunk of a great tree and pause, look up at the canopy and watch the almost imperceptible movements or absolute stillness, and keep watching. Trees offer something else, not profit or box-ticking or publicity, but something intangible hinted at by the old-fashioned term 'communing with nature'. Trees are part of the living world which, given time and tranquility arouse our sense of wonder and peace – it is this sort of appreciation that motivates so many people to become naturalists and others to just enjoy visiting the countryside. Walking among trees can be a form of spiritual renewal. In *Spirit of Trees*, no. 8, Dick Warner sensed this in the presence of the giant redwoods of California – but it isn't necessary to go so far afield.

You can start by looking at every tree. Close observation reveals that, like people, every tree is different, not just in its shape and structure, but also in its response to the seasons, its precise flowering period, its relationship with other plants and animals. Seedlings differ in their rates of growth, the colour and shape of their leaves, their susceptibility to infections or insect attack. Some

would say that each one has its own personality. This is all due primarily to their genetic identity, the DNA that determines their characteristics including the potential to respond to environmental influences, whether from the elements, from other organisms like fungi or insects, or to human activity.

A study of trees shows that, under natural circumstances, they follow a strategy to maximise their genetic diversity as a species or as a population. Wind-pollinated trees allow their pollen to be scattered as widely as possible in space and time, while many insect-pollinated species are self-incompatible ensuring out-crossing. But why, you might wonder? Would it not be better for trees to be more similar? How can it be advantageous for some trees to grow irregularly and misshapen, while others are tall and thus clearly get more light and grow bigger? Why do some produce less or later pollen, while some individuals regularly produce earlier leaf-break

BELOW Scots pine seedlings can colonise pure mineral soil or even bare rock, as here near Contin in the Scottish Highlands.

and as regularly are defoliated by caterpillars? The advantage is that the maximum diversity means the best possible response, collectively, to whatever conditions prevail, over the lifetime of the trees. This is an arboreal equivalent of 'covering all bases'. Every tree is different, and every group of trees is different from every other group.

There is a consensus among scientists that we are facing major changes in our environment in both the short and long term. The climate may change slowly, but it seems as if the weather may change too (storms becoming more frequent and of greater severity), affecting trees very much. Inevitably those individuals that are better equipped to cope will thrive, whereas others may be at a disadvantage, but exactly how these changes will impact on populations of trees may be much more complex than at first appears.

The 'heat island' effect in large towns may give some indication of the effect of future changes, by elevating air temperatures a few degrees in all seasons. Most urban trees are planted, many of them being alien species or cultivated varieties which may be already better adapted to these changing conditions, for example by surviving water stress better. Trees such as the tree of heaven,

Ailanthus altissima, the Indian bean tree, *Catalpa bignonoides*, and holm oak, *Quercus ilex*, already seem to be at a competitive advantage in the larger urban areas, their seedlings out-competing those of native trees (at least in the absence of browsing deer).

'The most recent predictions for the UK suggest increased temperatures (especially in the southeast) and changes in rainfall patterns, wind speed and variability, cloud cover, and humidity' (Broadmeadow and Ray, 2005). There are likely to be direct effects on all native trees. So which of our trees are likely to be most affected?

Here are a few predictions: in the south, beech is likely to suffer increased drought stress and risk of windthrow on shallow soils; trees such as small-leaved lime, whitebeam and wild service may be able to reproduce by seed more successfully and spread northwards (and to greater altitudes); while some species such as box and midland hawthorn may suffer competitively against more vigorous species. The possible indirect effects are far more complex and unpredictable. Increased air turbulence and frequency of storm events leading to windthrow may adversely affect some trees to

RIGHT AND BELOW RIGHT Blossom and seedling of wild service, a native tree that is likely to benefit from warmer summers, especially where deer populations are low such as in and around towns.

BELOW A lost cache of acorns abandoned by the mice that collected them, germinating in a grassy bank. Without intervention perhaps one will survive.

the benefit of others that survive uprooting better. More disturbed ground is likely to be created in which the seeds of pioneer trees (if available) such as birch, ash, goat willow and sycamore will be moved greater distances and then germinate and prosper. In some woods, where coppicing has been reintroduced after a long gap (such as Coldfall Wood in north London), some of these trees have begun to appear in woods where they did not grow before, along with aliens such as Norway maple, *Acer platanoides*, seeding from street trees.

Beechwoods have been managed to become substantially pure stands in the past, but they may now become infiltrated by newcomers. Under drought stress trees may be weakened so they become more susceptible to disease and to herbivores including plant-feeding insects. The changed conditions may affect numbers of deer (outside towns), squirrels and even mice. In woodland seed production and seedling predation may increase so that masting (which may occur more frequently) may become more significant. But then there may be additional stress due to summer drought or higher temperatures affecting existing trees – especially beech and oak – opening the way to invasive species, both native and introduced, and the net result may be for some woodland to be converted into scrub before many trees can become re-established. Different assemblages of trees will be favoured, especially once the seedlings are established.

TOP RIGHT Gypsy moth, *Lymantria dispar*.

BELOW Gregarious caterpillars of the oak processionary moth, *Thaumetopoea processionea*.

BOTTOM RIGHT Pest control officers destroying nests of oak processionary moths.

Many plant-feeding insects have already been observed to be extending their range north and west from continental Europe, and we can expect others to arrive from further afield; serious pest species such as oak processionary moth, *Thaumetopoea processionea*, and gypsy moth, *Lymantria dispar*, are likely to spread. Infestations may become even more serious and possibly lethal, as can be seen with the very high incidence of the leaf-miner *Cameraria ohridella*, together with the bleeding canker, *Pseudomonas syringae* pv *aesculi*, on horse-chestnut trees. A potentially lethal threat to native ash trees is the emerald ash borer, *Agrilus planipennis,* which originates in China and has already been found at ports on imported timber (see Exotic Pest Alerts at www.forestresearch.gov.uk/).

Perhaps even more threatening are the alien pathogens whose appearance is 'increasing in tempo' as importation of exotic species of trees from other parts of the world increases, carrying new diseases and pests with them. Viruses and bacteria evolve quickly and new strains appear frequently on cultivated species that are closely related to native trees. Rackham (2008) has suggested that the 'globalisation of plant diseases' may be the single most serious threat to our native trees and this may be exacerbated by the direct effects of climate change. The Forestry Commission regularly issues lists of 'top threats' (mostly affecting trees grown for timber), and even more disturbingly 'threats not yet present'.

New fungi may also be introduced. Native species (including mycorrhizal fungi) may suffer in the increased summer temperatures, while their fruiting bodies may become scarcer in hotter, drier conditions, limiting their dispersal and adversely affecting trees and various fungivorous insects. Britain is one of the most important countries in Western Europe for veteran trees and their suite of specialised insects, but these hotspots like Windsor Park, Moccas and Hatfield Forest are relatively small and isolated. The veteran trees may be particularly vulnerable to higher temperatures and water stress.

It is predicted that not only will climatic changes be considerable but they may also happen relatively quickly, favouring opportunist (pioneer) species of all sorts (including planted aliens) and skewing the environmental context in their favour. This process has already been documented by Grime (2007) for the Sheffield area, where he has noted a general eutrophication (nutrient enrichment) of all habitats over the past few decades caused by pollution, particularly airborne nitrogen compounds. This process is expected to continue and, together with climatic instability, have the overall effect of reducing diversity and simplifying communities. Trees would be affected to different extents; ash, birch, goat willow, elder and sycamore being likely beneficiaries, while others, such as beech, yew, lime, wild service, juniper and wild cherry and even oak, may suffer.

Planting trees or natural regeneration?

There is a popular view that any problem concerned with trees is best solved by planting more of them. One problem with tree-planting is that it is often not matched by tree-caring. Many planted trees are allowed to die because we are not very good at protecting and cherishing the trees we already have. Surveys show that the commonest cause of tree death in towns is damage at the base caused by mowers and strimmers.

Various 'new woodlands' are promised by several organisations including the National Forest Company operating in the English Midlands where eight million trees have so far been planted (late 2010), most of them native broadleaves from (fairly) local sources. There is some merit in this; we could do with more trees on good land (instead of on drained peat-bogs) so that we have to import less timber – and of course growing trees certainly absorb carbon. More trees can also be planted in towns, although these tend not to be native species. Introduced species do not contribute to the normal life of native woodland and planting these trees does not lead to the development of natural woodland. Tree cover, yes, but natural woodland is a complex ecosystem of native trees with many components including quantities of old, decaying wood, rich leaf mould and a diversity of plants, animals and fungi. Woodland arises and develops by natural regeneration (if it's allowed to do so) within and around the edges of existing woodland, and it takes time to do it. For newly planted plots like the National Forest it is understood that it will take several decades to become recognisable as real woodland when natural regeneration will take over from active planting.

There are some special places where I think tree-planting of native trees is both advisable and even necessary, such as where local seed sources have diminished or disappeared completely. In the Highlands natural regeneration is now being promoted by excluding (and in some places culling) deer; at high altitude around the existing tree-line this has resulted in some trees like Scots pine and rowan 'moving up the hill'. In some deforested areas organisations such as Trees for Life (www.treesforlife.org.uk) have planted seedlings raised from selected seed sources. At the same time they are experimenting with wild boar to try to re-create better conditions within existing woodland for natural regeneration; wild boar disturb the ground and create the natural seedbeds suitable for Scots pine to germinate.

In the Carrifran Valley a spectacular project aims to reforest an almost totally deforested valley with native species of (relatively) local provenance, re-creating the flora that clothed the valley 5,000 years ago (www.carrifran.org.uk; Ashmole & Ashmole, 2009). On some mountains montane scrub is being revived or even re-created by special planting. There are other special cases, but in general, given the chance, native trees will plant themselves.

The natural processes, which resulted in Britain becoming a substantially wooded land after the last glacial period, can still work. Given an adjacent seed source and restricted grazing, land in most parts of Britain will grow trees. All that is needed is to give nature, and natural succession, a chance. Unfortunately it is rarely as simple as that. It is rare to find places where natural regeneration is actively encouraged, apart from places where trees become established through neglect of previously managed land, and there, especially in urban areas, sycamore tends to dominate unless checked.

BELOW **Carrifran valley, site of a brave experiment to recreate an ancient forest.**

Introduced squirrels and deer (in the absence of their natural predators) are a major problem. Squirrels kill acorns before burying them, and damage young beech and mature hornbeam, while deer graze seedlings of most native trees wherever they can find them. Estimates vary but there could be as many as two million deer on the British mainland. In lowland areas outside towns, the regeneration of trees nearly everywhere is adversely affected by deer numbers uncontrolled by predators (although more than 74,000 deer may be killed each year in road accidents). In the Highlands until a few years ago there was hardly a single stretch of unfenced pine forest which was regenerating because in the winter deer ate every seedling. The threat of deer is recognised even by bodies that promote deer: 'There is increasing evidence of some [sic] negative impacts of deer... across the country' (Deer Initiative, 2004).

Why is natural regeneration so much better than planting? One major reason is that it promotes the normal process of natural selection. When a birch tree drops thousands of seeds, just a few survive to seedling stage – fewer still to become saplings, while just one or two may reach maturity. In many years, none do. The selection process to fit the offspring precisely to the local environment is brutally fierce. By planting trees (of other provenance) already grown to sapling stage in a nursery (and so avoiding early selection pressure), we may be introducing genetic material that is not well suited to the area or the particular site. If these trees then grow to maturity, their subsequent cross-pollination with local trees may effectively dilute the native stock and even affect the ability of the entire population to adapt and survive. On the other hand, careful selection of planted material (such as aspen from widely separated clones) may enable sexual reproduction, when it does occur, to be more effective by increasing the viable seed in both abundance and genetic diversity.

Our native trees have already been affected by past planting policy. Some native trees have been replaced by alien relatives, even 'lookalikes' such as *Crataegus rhipidophylla* used as hedging instead of native hawthorn. For centuries the stock (of both seeds and saplings) used for the planting of trees such as oak has been selected primarily for timber production (and often insect or disease resistance) and was frequently of foreign provenance. Some foresters approve of this; I have heard it said that 'selected continental oaks will improve the quality of local trees'. Indeed, EC rules require the use of commercially approved seed – and until recently there were no approved seed sources for oak in the UK. These rules were drawn up for the benefit of timber producers with

no consideration of the conservation issues (other than to deter insects altogether!) – or even local climatic conditions. Many insects are particularly choosy; we may find it difficult to separate the two oak species or the two tree birches but a lot of plant-feeders depend on one and not the other. If mature trees did not interbreed there would be no problem, but there is nothing to stop the wind carrying pollen from imported trees to local trees. This is why there is a potential threat from GM trees, which have been 'improved' by adding alien genes from very different organisms with unpredictable effects. There is already evidence that pollen contaminated by agricultural chemicals or derived from genetically modified crops may be contributing to the decline of honey bees (Bioscience Resource, 2008), and this affects plants of all sorts, not just insect-pollinated trees.

Changing the genetic make-up of native tree populations does not just affect the trees; many associated organisms can be affected too. Wild trees often have alien relatives in gardens nearby, and these can be a source of unsuitable pollen, quite apart from alien pests and diseases. Unlike wild populations, most cultivated plants are genetically very similar ('superior' oak, a single apple variety, English elm), and so they are extremely susceptible to new infections or pests. Wild populations may have sufficient diversity to be resilient, and this diversity should be conserved as a major priority.

Wild populations of many of our native trees are now small and fragmented, and in some cases, such as the large-leaved lime or aspen, substantially reduced from their earlier distribution. How much of their genetic diversity has already been lost? As selective pressures on our native species change, will our trees be able to respond?

The forestry industry is preparing itself for coping with these changes, and I suggest that other interests concerned with native trees should follow their lead. We need more information about the genetic diversity of all our trees, not just those of interest to timber producers.

Some limitations to genetic diversity derive from past human actions. Widespread forest clearance over several millennia may have led to restrictions in native species to marginal-site types, especially for lowland species such as lime, and possibly affecting rowan and aspen as well. In recent centuries the planting of common trees such as oak and hawthorn from non-indigenous stock has resulted in the impoverishment of local wild populations. Seed of mixed parentage can be poorly adapted to local conditions resulting in low seed viability, and low seedling survival, thus causing restrictions to natural regeneration, and resulting in increased dependence on planting. In Europe the effects of this have sometimes been dramatic; a major decline of alder in Germany has resulted from the widespread planting of frost-sensitive trees from coastal Belgium.

In Britain black poplar has been widely planted, but 'past selection of cuttings from a small number of "prime" male black poplars, a dioecious native tree, has virtually eliminated females (which were considered a nuisance because of their production of large quantities of seed fluff) and has narrowed the genetic base of the species' (Ennos *et al.*, 2000). This absence of females has effectively prevented sexual reproduction.

Paradoxically, in other species there is the opposite problem. Ennos *et al.* have suggested that 'levels of adaptive variation for date of bud burst [are] insufficient within Scottish [birch] populations to allow adaptation to predicted rates of climatic warming'. The implication is that birch stock from outside the UK may be required to accelerate adaptive change in native birch trees, whether for commercial forestry or for any other purpose.

Conserving genetic resources for the future

Conserving all plant genetic resources is now an urgent global issue. There are two basic approaches available; seed banks (*ex situ* conservation) where seeds are stored at low temperatures, and *in situ* conservation, that is conserving plants where they grow naturally.

Seed banks have been promoted since the 1930s when the pioneer Russian plant scientist N.I. Vavilov first began to make collections. In the 1940s and 1950s collections of major crop plants were built up around the world and plant breeders rapidly improved the quality and productivity of grains such as wheat and rice; the Green Revolution resulted from crossing some dwarf Japanese varieties of wheat with others that responded to added nitrogen.

BELOW **Male native black poplar in flower, Cotswold Water Park, Cirencester.**

Tree seeds of many species are now held in seed banks around the world. But for some trees seed banks are inappropriate. Acorns are almost impossible to store for long. For trees such as apple and pear (which do not breed true) it is not the seed that needs to be preserved but living examples of the varieties or cultivars; for all these trees collections of plants or field gene banks can be maintained, but high quality 'mother trees' growing in the wild should also be identified and protected.

For a few native trees there are well-established national collections (field gene banks); these include collections of willow at Rothamsted, poplar at Farnham, box at Ickworth Park, fruit trees (apple, pear and cherry) at the Brogdale Trust, Faversham, and hornbeam at the Beale Arboretum (Hadley Wood). These collections are limited mainly to cultivated varieties; so far little or no attempt has been made to collect samples from many of the wild populations of these trees, although one exception is the small collection of wild crabapples maintained at East Malling Research Station.

In recent years the limitations of seed banks have been recognised; they preserve the seed from a particular moment, and as conditions change these seeds held in cold storage will

ABOVE RIGHT Dr N I Vavilov, the famous Russian scientist who made the first collections of cultivated plant varieties, including trees.

RIGHT A whole range of food products from native trees are commercially available, from silver birch wine to hazelnut butter.

BELOW The tasty fruits of whitty pear, a potential new orchard crop.

be different from the seed from naturally evolving and adapting populations. The idea of conserving genetic resources of wild plants *in situ* by locating a number of autochthonous stands (i.e. of local origin) has been developed by the forestry industry, and separate surveys of such stands of the main timber trees in Scotland, Wales and England have been made (Wilson *et al.*, 1999; Wilson and Jenkins, 2001; Wilson and Samuel, 2003). There are tentative moves to extend this approach with regard to particular species for wider conservation reasons (the Aspen Initiative, Juniper BAP in Scotland etc.); this work should be given a major priority, whatever the presumed future use of the trees concerned. Small isolated populations, and trees where individuals are widely scattered and scarce (like holly, aspen and rock whitebeam in the Highlands, the unique whitebeams of Arran etc.), particularly need protecting and conserving.

Native trees must be the subject of active and informed conservation, and their use encouraged – ideally for more than one purpose. We use wood today far less than we should; the carbon in it has been extracted from the atmosphere, and while we are concentrating efforts at reducing carbon emissions we should be putting a similar effort into finding ways to sequestrate more carbon by producing and keeping more trees and wood. Trees are valuable not just because of their direct environmental effects and because their products are useful; as Rackham points out, the more valuable the tree the more effort is put into conserving and managing it. And the full range of natural habitats with their full complement of animals and plants are worth conserving in themselves. Do we want an impoverished future planet? Or a richer one?

The documentation and protection of existing stands of *all* native trees is most urgently needed for the trees and for the full complement of their associated plants, animals and fungi. Some progress has been made with the Ancient Woodland Inventory, which lists ancient woodland sites (www.magic.gov.uk/info/awreadme.html), but urgent consideration should be given to a more comprehensive approach to: (1) locating especially very

The genetic diversity of our native trees

Until recently this topic had hardly been investigated; the few studies available were summarised by Ennos *et al.* (2000), but further investigation of possible land races of some species would be valuable, especially for highly variable species such as birch.

ASH genetic diversity low but occurs widely and regularly produces abundant seed. Conclusion: not currently under threat and no action needed, but needs further study.

ASPEN there is considerable local variation (up to 20 different clones within a single wood) but regionally little difference; only some clones from southern Scotland being in any way different from the rest. Conclusion: attention is needed to improve the size and variability of particular populations by cross-pollinating between clones.

BEECH variability was low – hardly surprising since England was known already to be at the edge of the European distribution of the species. Conclusion: perhaps beech conservation is more critical in other parts of Europe.

BLACK POPLAR populations of the true native black poplar (*P. nigra ssp. betulifolia*) were very scarce, even as low as around 2,000 trees derived from at least two ancestral sources. Conclusion: active conservation of native populations is vital.

JUNIPER as with aspen, considerable genetic diversity was found (in Scottish studies) within even small populations, but relatively little between populations, suggesting that the fragmentation and isolation of populations has occurred only recently. Conclusion: where possible protect and rejoin fragmented populations.

OAK (2 spp.) in both species most populations were genetically similar but in East Anglia pedunculate oaks differed in their ancestry from those elsewhere, suggesting that they were of different parentage. Conclusion: the conservation of pedunculate (common) oaks in East Anglia should be given a high priority, as should conservation of trees that resist mildew better (generally sessile oak). Small isolated populations should be given special priority.

ROWAN limited studies suggested that overall genetic diversity was not very great and diminished northwards. Bacles *et al.* (2004) found that in southern Scotland even where rowan populations consist of small numbers of widely spaced individuals this had not resulted in the loss of genetic diversity, due to the combination of self-incompatibility, insect pollination and bird dispersal.

SCOTS PINE in Scotland it was found that there had been two distinct genetic sources (from southwest Ireland and from mainland Europe) but that there was a good deal of variation between and among different populations. Conclusion: many different populations in the Highlands should be conserved. (To this should be added that a full investigation of the 'self-sown' Kielder Forest trees should be undertaken.)

WILLOWS, HOLLY AND HAZEL all widespread, but little studied.

old living individual trees, particularly pollards and ancient coppice stools (Ancient Tree Hunt has made good progress but various native species are severely under-represented); (2) halting and reversing the fragmentation of stands (such as juniper); (3) documenting and conserving coastal and montane woodland and scrub; (4) documenting and conserving the best examples of assemblages of native trees in woodlands; (5) for all of the above documenting the associated plants, animals and fungi found with the trees; and (6) assessing other possible seed sources to augment native seed where the genetic diversity may be too narrow (such as birch, see above). Perhaps it is wishful thinking that the documentation of particularly elegant examples, or 'elite stands' of our native trees is attempted. I hope some of the trees photographed for this book might come into this category, but other tree-enthusiasts may beg to differ and work to preserve their own favourites.

But that is not the whole story either; we still have many traditions and beliefs involving trees that are part of the culture of these islands. Our native trees provide a very real link to the past; it was with real pride that the late Bill Hogarth pointed out that certain woods were last cut by his father, or even his grandfather, on known dates. Similar historical information is available on many large estates. Because of their longevity, real work with trees requires several generations of people. Ancient trees and woodlands have seen many human generations; the most ancient may connect us directly with the very earliest times when humans first recolonised the land after the last glacial period. The long-term view does not play well with short-term political or financial ends, but sooner or later we will have to regain that view, if we are to bequeath a living planet to future generations. Whatever we can do at a local level should perhaps keep that bigger picture in mind.

BELOW The northernmost natural birch and oak woodland in Britain, Loch a' Mhuillin, near Scourie, Sutherland. Remote trees like this should be conserved as a priority for their genetic potential.

TABLE 1 Checklist of native and naturalized trees
Taxonomic order (according to C. Stace, *New Flora of the British Isles*, 3rd ed., 2010)

'	not an accepted single species	
[ ]	a cultivated tree	

Within Britain and Ireland		C	catkins
[I]	native to Ireland only	N	nectar
[S]	native to Scotland only	S-S	self-sterile
[E]	native to England only	FO	foul odour
*	max height in metres; (mostly) from Johnson (ed.), *Champion trees of Britain and Ireland*, 2003	NR	not recorded (pollinated by flies)

Pollination		Distribution:	
Insects:		W	wind
H	bees and wasps (Hymenoptera)	w	water (including rainwater)
D	flies (Diptera)	b and B	birds (small and large)
C	beetles (Coleoptera)	m and M	mammals (small and large)
A	no pollination required (apomictic)		

Common name	Latin name	Max height*	Family	Pollination	Fruit	Dispersal
Alder	Alnus glutinosa (L.) Gaertn.	40	Betulaceae	wind C	'cone'	W, w
Alder buckthorn	Frangula alnus Miller	6	Rhamnaceae	insects	berry	B
Apple, domestic	[Malus domestica]	NR	Rosaceae	insects	apple	B, M
Ash	Fraxinus excelsior L.	37	Oleaceae	wind	key (achene)	W, ?m
Aspen	Populus tremula L.	24	Salicaceae	wind	2-valved plumed capsule	W
Beech	Fagus sylvatica L.	42	Fagaceae	wind	Nut with hard cupule	W, B
Birch, downy	Betula pubescens Ehrh.	24	Betulaceae	wind C	Winged fruit	W, w, m, b
Birch, Dwarf	Betula nana L.	1	Betulaceae	wind C	Winged fruit	W
Bird cherry	Prunus padus L.	19	Rosaceae	insects (esp D)	cherry	B, m
Black poplar	Populus nigra L. var. betulifolia	33(?)	Salicaceae	wind C	2-valved plumed capsule	W
Box [E]	Buxus sempervirens L.	11	Buxaceae	insects (D, H)	simple	?W, w
Buckthorn	Rhamnus catharticus L.	6	Rhamnaceae	insects	berry	B
Crabapple	Malus sylvestris (L.) Miller	10	Rosaceae	insects (D, H: bees) often S-S	apple	B, M
Elder	Sambucus nigra L.	11	Caprifoliaceae	small flies	drupe	B
Elm, English	'Ulmus procera Salisb.'	33	Ulmaceae	wind, ?insects	2-wing key	W
Elm, Plot's, Exeter, Huntingdon, etc.	'Ulmus plotii Druce' and other Ulmus 'spp.' are all considered strains of U. minor	30	Ulmaceae	wind, ?insects	2-wing key	W
Elm, smooth-leaved, East Anglian	Ulmus minor Miller	31	Ulmaceae	wind, ?insects	2-wing key	W
Field maple	Acer campestre L.	25	Aceraceae	small insects (D?)	1-seed keys	W, (m)
French Hales (see Whitebeam, Devon)		20				
Hawthorn	Crataegus monogyna Jacq.	15	Rosaceae	insects (D, H: bees, C)	berry	B, m
Hawthorn, Midland	Crataegus laevigata (Poiret) DC	10	Rosaceae	insects (D, H: bees, C)	berry	B
Hazel	Corylus avellana L.	12	Betulaceae	wind	nut	B, m,
Holly	Ilex aquifolium L.	23	Aquifoliaceae	?insects	berry	B
Hornbeam	Carpinus betulus L.	32	Betulaceae	wind	Winged fruit	W, b, m
Juniper	Juniperus communis L.	16	Cupressaceae	wind	berry	B
Lime, common	Tilia x europaea	36	Tiliaceae	insects (esp H: bees)	nut	W, m
Lime, large-leaved	Tilia platyphyllos Scop.	34	Tiliaceae	insects (esp H: bees)	nut	W, m
Lime, small-leaved	Tilia cordata Miller	38	Tiliaceae	insects (esp H: bees)	nut	W, m
Oak, pedunculate	Quercus robur L.	37	Fagaceae	wind	acorn (M)	B, m
Oak, sessile	Quercus petraea (Mattuschka)	42	Fagaceae	wind	acorn (M)	B, m
Pear, wild pear	Pyrus communis L. & P. pyraster	15	Rosaceae	insects (D, H) some selfing	pear	B, M
Plymouth pear	Pyrus cordata Desv.	4-5	Rosaceae	insects (D) (Bibionidae) FO	(small pear)	?b
Rowan, mountain ash	Sorbus aucuparia L.	(18) 21*	Rosaceae	insects (various) or self-pollinated.	berry	B
Sallow, rusty	Salix cinerea L. ssp. oleifolia Mac.	10	Salicaceae	wind C	2-valved plumed capsule	W
Scots pine [S]	Pinus silvestris L.	36	Pinaceae	wind	cone	W
Service-tree, Arran	Sorbus pseudofennica E.F.Warb.	7	Rosaceae	insects /A	berry	B
Silver birch	Betula pendula Roth	30	Betulaceae	wind C	winged	W, w, m, b
Spindle	Euonymus europaeus L.	10	Celastraceae	insects	Fleshy capsule	B
Strawberry tree (Arbutus) [I]	Arbutus unedo L.	11	Ericaceae	insects/self	berry	?b
Sweet chestnut	Castanea sativa Miller	35	Fagaceae	insects (H)	Nut with prickly cupule	B, M
Sycamore	Acer pseudoplatanus L.	30	Aceraceae	insects (H)	1-seed keys	W, (m)
Wayfaring tree	Viburnum lantana L.	6	Caprifoliaceae	insects/self	berry-like fruit (drupe)	B
Whitebeam	Sorbus aria (L.) Crantz	23	Rosaceae	insects	berry	B
Whitebeam, Arran [S]	Sorbus arranensis Hedl.	7.5	Rosaceae	insects/A	berry	B
Whitebeam, Bloody	Sorbus vexans E.F.Warb.	10	Rosaceae	insects/A	berry	B
Whitebeam, Bristol	Sorbus bristoliensis Wilm.	15	Rosaceae	insects/A	berry	B

Whitebeam, Catacol [S]	Sorbus pseudomeinichii Ashley Robertson	4	Rosaceae	insects/A	berry	B
Whitebeam, Cheddar	Sorbus cheddarensis L.Houston & Robertson	7	Rosaceae	insects/A	berry	B
Whitebeam, Devon	Sorbus devoniensis E.F.Warb.	20	Rosaceae	insects/A	berry	B
Whitebeam, English	Sorbus anglica Hedl.	3	Rosaceae	insects/A	berry	B
Whitebeam, Gough's Rock	Sorbus rupicoloides T.C.G.Rich & L.Houston	7	Rosaceae	insects/A	berry	B
Whitebeam, Grey-leaved	Sorbus porrigentiformis E.F.Warb.	5	Rosaceae	insects/A	berry	B
Whitebeam, Irish	Sorbus hibernica E.F.Warb.	6	Rosaceae	insects/A	berry	B
Whitebeam, Lancashire	Sorbus lancastriensis E.F.Warb.	5	Rosaceae	insects/A	berry	B
Whitebeam, Least	Sorbus minima (Ley) Hedl.	4	Rosaceae	insects/A	berry	B
Whitebeam, Leigh Woods	Sorbus leighensis T.C.G.Rich	10	Rosaceae	insects/A	berry	B
Whitebeam, Ley's	Sorbus leyana Wilm.	3	Rosaceae	insects/A	berry	B
Whitebeam, Llangollen	Sorbus cuneifolia T.C.G.Rich	5	Rosaceae	insects/A	berry	B
Whitebeam, Llantony	Sorbus stenophylla M.Proctor	8	Rosaceae	insects/A	berry	B
Whitebeam, Margaret's	Sorbus margaretae M.Proctor	6	Rosaceae	insects/A	berry	B
Whitebeam, No Parking	Sorbus admonitor M.Proctor	20	Rosaceae	insects/A	berry	B
Whitebeam, Rock	Sorbus rupicola (Syme) Hedl.	6	Rosaceae	insects/A	berry	B
Whitebeam, round-leaved	Sorbus eminens E.F.Warb.	6	Rosaceae	insects/A	berry	B
Whitebeam, Doward	Sorbus eminentiformis T.C.G.Rich	15	Rosaceae	insects/A	berry	B
Whitebeam, Scannel's	Sorbus scannelliana T.C.G.Rich	5	Rosaceae	insects/A	berry	B
Whitebeam, Ship Rock	Sorbus parviloba T.C.G.Rich	8	Rosaceae	insects/A	berry	B
Whitebeam, Somerset	Sorbus subcuneata Wilm.	18	Rosaceae	insects/A	berry	B
Whitebeam, Stirton's	Sorbus stirtoniana T.C.G.Rich	5	Rosaceae	insects/A	berry	B
Whitebeam, Symond's yat	Sorbus saxicola T.C.G.Rich	5	Rosaceae	insects/A	berry	B
Whitebeam, thin-leaved	Sorbus leptophylla E.F.Warb.	3	Rosaceae	insects/A	berry	B
Whitebeam, Twin Cliffs	Sorbus eminentoides L.Houston	9	Rosaceae	insects/A	berry	B
Whitebeam, Watersmeet	Sorbus admonitor M.Proctor	16	Rosaceae	insects/A	berry	B
Whitebeam, Welsh	Sorbus cambrensis M.Proctor	8	Rosaceae	insects/A	berry	B
Whitebeam, White's	Sorbus whiteana T.C.G.Rich & L.Houston	10	Rosaceae	insects/A	berry	B
Whitebeam, Wilmott's	Sorbus wilmottiana E.F.Warb.	6	Rosaceae	insects/A	berry	B
Whitty Pear, true service tree	Sorbus domestica L.	30	Rosaceae	insects/A	berry	B
Wild cherry	Prunus avium (L.)	31	Rosaceae	insects S-S	cherry	B, M
Wild service	Sorbus torminalis (L.) Crantz	27	Rosaceae	insects/A	berry	B
Willow, almond	Salix triandra L.	10	Salicaceae	wind C	2-valved plumed capsule	W
Willow, basket	Salix viminalis L.	10	Salicaceae	wind C	2-valved plumed capsule	W
Willow, bay	Salix pentandra L.	18	Salicaceae	wind C	2-valved plumed capsule	W
Willow, crack	Salix x fragilis L.	25	Salicaceae	wind C	2-valved plumed capsule	W
Willow, creeping	Salix repens L.	2	Salicaceae	wind C	2-valved plumed capsule	W
Willow, dark-leaved	Salix myrsinifolia Salisb.	4	Salicaceae	wind C	2-valved plumed capsule	W
Willow, downy	Salix lapponum L.	1.5	Salicaceae	wind C	2-valved plumed capsule	W
Willow, dwarf	Salix herbacea L.	<10cm	Salicaceae	wind C	2-valved plumed capsule	W
Willow, eared	Salix aurita L.	3	Salicaceae	wind C	2-valved plumed capsule	W
Willow, goat	Salix caprea L.	19	Salicaceae	wind C	2-valved plumed capsule	W
Willow, grey	Salix cinerea L. ssp. cinerea	15	Salicaceae	wind C	2-valved plumed capsule	W
Willow, mountain	Salix arbuscula L.	<1	Salicaceae	wind C	2-valved plumed capsule	W
Willow, net-leaved	Salix reticulata L.	<20cm	Salicaceae	wind C	2-valved plumed capsule	W
Willow, purple	Salix purpurea L.	5	Salicaceae	wind C	2-valved plumed capsule	W
Willow, tea-leaved	Salix phylicifolia L.	5	Salicaceae	wind C	2-valved plumed capsule	W
Willow, white	Salix alba L.	33	Salicaceae	wind C	2-valved plumed capsule	W
Willow, whortle-leaved	Salix myrsinites L.	<50cm	Salicaceae	wind C	2-valved plumed capsule	W
Willow, woolly	Salix lanata L.	1.5	Salicaceae	wind C	2-valved plumed capsule	W
Wych elm	Ulmus glabra Hudson	37	Ulmaceae	wind, insects S-S	2-wing key	W
Yew	Taxus baccata L.	28	Taxaceae	?insects	berry (p)	B

Orange-fruited whitebeam (*Sorbus croceocarpa* P.D.Sell); broad-leaved whitebeam (*S. latifolia* (Lam.), Swedish whitebeam (*S. intermedia* (Ehrh.) and Mougeot's whitebeam (*S. mougeotii*) are regarded as naturalised introductions.

Walnut (*Juglans regia* L.), horse-chestnut (*Aesculus hippocastanum* L.), tree of heaven (*Ailanthus altissima*), etc., are omitted as being introductions and/or not fully naturalised in the sense that they do not, generally, occur outside plantations and gardens and so do not compete directly in natural plant communities (unlike sycamore which invades even ancient woodland).

TABLE 2 Biological characteristics of native and naturalized trees
Adapted (with permission) from Rackham (2006, pp.12–13) with additions by the author.

(1) Gregariousness
1 solitary
2 in groups due to seedfall
3 gregarious due to suckering

(2) Coppicing 0–4
0 unsuccessful to widely
4 practised

(3) Pollarding 0–4
0 unsuccessful to widely
4 practised

(4) Preference for woodland
0 not found naturally in woodland
1 occasionally
2 often
3 usually
4 only found in woodland

(5) Occurrence in field hedges
0 virtually never
1 occasional
2 frequent
3 widespread
T1 occasional 'hedgerow tree'
T2 frequent 'hedgerow tree'
T3 very common 'hedgerow tree'
C especially on base-rich soils

(6) Palatability to grazing animals 1–4
1–4 unpalatable to extremely palatable
D especially grazed by deer

(7) Leaves used as fodder (historically)
0 not used
1 sometimes used
2 often used

(8) Suckers
0 never
1 occasionally
2 frequently

(9) Survives uprooting
1 (does not survive to
–4 thrives on uprooting - see Chapter 7 *Our native trees - the future*)

(10) Sequence: leaves & flowers
L leaves first
F flowers first
sim simultaneous
cat flowers are catkins

(11) Flowering strategy
M monoecious (Male & female flowers on the same tree)
D dioecious (male and female flowers on different trees).
(h) hermaphrodite flowers male and female flowers separate but on the same tree
(d) self-compatible (otherwise probably or definitely self-sterile)
(s)

(12) Masting
X a mast tree (mast years)
x individual trees are masting
F/FF fruiting variable/very variable but not recognised as a masting tree
O not a masting tree
? evidence not available

(13) Seed size
Number of (cleaned) seeds per kilo (from Grime et al.1988, quoted by Thomas, 2000). Blank = not recorded.

(14) Normal seed viability
1 low
to 4 high
W a few days/weeks
S 1–2 seasons later (growers use stratification)
* may survive long-term in the seedbank (in many trees seed viability can vary from year to year and there is evidence that in some species (e g pine) younger trees produce seed with a higher viability).

Tree	Latin name	(1) Greg.	(2) Coppice	(3) Pollard	(4) Woods.	(5) Hedges	(6) Palat.	(7) Leaves as fodder	(8) Suckers	(9) Survive uproot	(10) Sequence	(11) Flowering strategy	(12) Masting	(13) Seed size	(14) Seed viability
Alder	Alnus glutinosa	2	4	2	1	0-1T2	1	–	0	2	L (cat)	M (d)	?V	770,000	4 (W) S
Alder buckthorn	Frangula alnus	1	?2	?2	2	1?	2	?	0	?	L	M (h)	V		2-3 (?S)
Ash	Fraxinus excelsior	2	4	4	0	3T3 C	4	2	0	2	F (cat)	D	X	14,000	4 W or S
Aspen	Populus tremula	3	0	0	3		1	1	2	1	F (cat)	D	X	8m	1 (rare)
Beech	Fagus sylvatica	3	3	1	2	1T2	3	1?	0	3	Sim.	M	V	4,500	3 S
Birch	Betula spp.	2	3	1	2	2T1	3	1	0	1	F (cat)	M (d) (s)	?V	5.9m	4 S
Black poplar	Populus nigra	1 (-2)	3	4	0	2-3	2	?	0	2	F (cat)	D	?X		1 (rare)
Blackthorn	Prunus spinosa	3			0		3	1?	3	3	F	M (h)	F		2? W
Box	Buxus sempervirens	2	?1	?1	0	0	2	0	2	2	L	M (h)	?		3 S
Buckthorn	Rhamnus cathartica	3	?2	?2	2	1T1 C	2	0	0	?	L	D	V		2 S
Cherries	Prunus avium/padus	3	1	0	3	1 (-2) T1	3	1?	2	3	L	M (h)	X	?100	2 W
Chestnut	Castanea sativa	2	4	4	2	0	0	0	0	4	L	M (h) (?s)	V		1 S
Crabapple	Malus sylvestris	1	2	1	2	1T2	3	1?	0	3	L	M (h)	?		2 S
Elder	Sambucus nigra	1	?1	?2	1	2T1	2	1?	0	4	F	M (h)	?V		2 S
Elm	U.minor &U.procera	3	4	4	2	3T2	4	2	2	4	F	M (h or u)	1		1
Field maple	Acer campestre	1	4	2	2	2T2 C	3	1?	0	4	F (cat)	M (h) (s)	?X		3 (W) S
Goat willow	Salix caprea	1–2	4	2	1	1T2	4	1?	0	4	F	D	?O		4
Hawthorn	Crataegus monogyna	2	3	2	0	3T2	1	1	0	4	F (cat)	D	X		4 S
Hazel	Corylus avellana	2	3	4	1	3CT1	4D	1	(1)	3	F (cat)	M (d)	X	1,200	4 W/S
Holly	Ilexaquifolium	1	3	4	1	1T2	4D	1	0	4	L	D	V	125,000	4 S
Hornbeam	Carpinus betulus	2	4	3	3	2T1	2	1?	0	3	L	M (d)	?	28,000	4 S
Juniper	Juniperus communis	1	0	0	4	?0	1	0	0	4	L	M (d)	?O		3 S
Lime	Tilia cordata	2	4	4	4	1-2T1	2	1	1	?	L	M	?	32,000	2 S
Midland hawthorn	C.laevigata	1	3	0	4	1?	4	1?	0?	?	M	M	?		2 S
Oak	Quercus petraea	1–2	3	2	2?	2T3	1	1	0	3	Sim (♂ cat)	M	X	400	2 W
Oak	Q.robur	1–2	3	3	0?	2T3	1	1	0	3	Sim (♂ cat)	M	?O	290	2 W*
Osier	Salix viminalis	1	4	4	–	?	0	0	0	4	F (cat)	D	?O		
Pear	Pyrus spp.	1	2	1	3	1T1	3	1?	1	2	F	M(h)(s)	V		1 S
Rowan	Sorbus aucuparia	1 (-3)	3	3	2	1-2T1	2?	1?	0	2	Sim	M (h)	?O	5,000	3 S
Scots pine	Pinus sylvestris	2	0	0	4	0T1	2D	0	0	1	–	M (d)	?O	200,000	3 ?
Spindle	Euonymus europeus	?2	?1	?1	4	2T1	2	–	0	?	Sim	M (h)	V		2 S
Strawberry tree	Arbutus unedo	?1	3	?2	?	?	?	1?	0	?	L	D	?		?S
Sycamore	Acer pseudoplatanus	2	4	4	1	2T2	2	2	0	4	Sim	M	?O	3,300	4 S
Tree willows	Salix alba/fragilis	2	4	4	–	1T1	4	1	4	4	F (cat)	D	?		3 S
Wayfaring tree	Viburnum lantana	2	3	3	1	1C	4	0	0	3?	Sim	M (h)	?		2 (?)
Whitebeam	Sorbus aria	1	3	?	2?	1C	3	1?	1	?	L	M (h)	?V		3 S
Wild service	S.torminalis	3	3	3	4	2T3	3	1?	2	?	L	M (h)	?V		2(+) S
Wych Elm	Ulmus glabra	1	4	0	4	1	4	2	0	4	F	M(h or u)	?V	73,000	S
Yew	Taxus baccata	1	2	2	3	1	1D	0	0	4	Sim	D	?		S

* At least some *Q. robur* acorns have dormancy which is broken by extended cold weather (the author's experimental observation).

TABLE 3 Seedling characteristics; response to various factors

Mineral soil means unweathered soil or bare rock

O   susceptible (seedlings are relatively uncompetitive)
X   thriving (seedlings are relatively competitive)
XX especially successful

Tree	Latin name	Establishing on mineral soil	Effect of waterlogging	Effect of drought	Effect of shade	Effect of browsing (by deer etc.)	Competition with other plants
Alder	Alnus glutinosa	X	X	O	X	X	O
Alder buckthorn	Frangula alnus						
Ash	Fraxinus excelsior	X	X	X	X	O	X
Aspen	Populus tremula	X	O	X	O	O	
Beech	Fagus sylvatica	X		X	XX	X	
Birch	Betula spp.	X	X (b.pubescens)	O	X	O	
Black poplar	Populus nigra		X	OO	O	O	O
Blackthorn	Prunus spinosa			X	X		X
Box	Buxus sempervirens			X	XX		O
Buckthorn	Rhamnus cathartica				X		
Cherries	Prunus avium/padus			X	X		
Chestnut	Castanea sativa		?O	X	X		X
Crabapple	Malus sylvestris				X		X
Elder	Sambucus nigra	O			X	X	X
Field maple	Acer campestre			X	X		
Goat willow	Salix caprea	X	X		X		X
Hawthorn	Crataegus monogyna	X			O	X	XX
Hazel	Corylus avellana			X	X	O	X
Holly	Ilex aquifolium	X	O	O	XXX	X	
Hornbeam	Carpinus betulus				XX		O
Juniper	Juniperus communis	X			X	O	
Lime	Tilia cordata	X			X	O	X
Midland hawthorn	C. laevigata				XX		
Oak	Quercus petraea	X		X	X	O	X
Oak	Q. robur	X		X	X	O	X
Osier	Salix viminalis	X	X	O			
Pear	Pyrus spp.				X		
Rowan	Sorbus aucuparia	X	X	X	X		O
Scots pine	Pinus sylvestris	X	X	X	O	X	
Spindle	Euonymus europeus				X		
Strawberry tree	Arbutus unedo	X			O		
Sycamore	Acer pseudoplatanus			X	X	O	X
Tree willows	Salix alba/fragilis	O	X				
Wayfaring tree	Viburnum lantana	O			X		X
Whitebeam	Sorbus aria			X	X	?O	
Wild service	S. torminalis				X	O	
Wych elm	Ulmus glabra				X	O	
Yew	Taxus baccata	X	X	X	X		

TABLE 4 Herbivorous insects associated with native and naturalized tree genera
Figures given are species recorded from the tree(s) given. The figure in brackets is the number of invertebrates restricted to that tree

(1) to
(7) figures from PIDB database (www.brc.ac.uk/dbif) updated last in 2007–2008
(8) totals with (in brackets) species restricted to the genus and this figure as % of totals. Four trees with highest percentage of plant-feeders restricted to them in **bold**
(9) total insects (i.e. excluding mites, column (1)) recorded by Kennedy & Southwood (K&S) (1984) (blank cells mean no figures given)
(10) psocoptera records from foliage: Savile, R (pers. comm.) National Barkfly Recording Scheme

* records include those where genus of host but not species is recorded
X Scots pine with 185 out of 257 species (72%) has the highest proportion of invertebrates restricted to the genus, while trees such as lime, ash, rowan and beech all have fewer than a quarter of recorded (i.e. specialised) invertebrates restricted to that genus

Common name	Tree genus	(1) Acari mites	(2) Coleoptera beetles	(3) Diptera flies	(4) Hemiptera bugs	(5) Hymenoptera wasps, sawflies etc.	(6) Lepidoptera moths	(7) Thysanoptera thrips	(8) Total (PIDB data)*	(9) Total insects (K&S)	(10) Psocoptera barklice
Willows	1 *Salix* (all spp.)*	15 (10)	178 (30)	50 (39)	129 (74)	111 (67)	351 (91)	5 (3)	839 (314-37%)	450	20
Oak	2 *Quercus* (2 spp.)	6 (3)	206 (5)	17 (15)	104 (41)	65 (57)	251 (63)	6 (1)	655 (185-28%)	423	42
Birch	3 *Betula* (3 spp.)	7 (4)	139 (14)	11 (9)	72 (25)	52 (24)	317 (62)	7 (4)	606 (143-24%)	334	23
Hawthorn	4 *Crataegus* (2 spp.)	9 (4)	80 (8)	7 (5)	60 (13)	17 (5)	233 (22)	1 (1)	407 (58-14%)	209	32
Aspen/Poplar	5 *Populus* spp. (2 spp.)	8 (5)	109 (14)	27 (19)	59 (27)	35 (10)	135 (31)	8 (5)	381 (111-29%)	188	6
Blackthorn/cherries	6 *Prunus* spp. (3 spp.)	10 (6)	74 (9)	6 (6)	48 (10)	18 (9)	211 (30)	4 (-)	371 (70-19%)	153	19
Alder	7 *Alnus* *	9 (5)	89 (5)	7 (5)	68 (7)	28 (10)	110 (15)	4 (1)	315 (48-15%)	141	13
Hazel	8 *Corylus* *	9 (3)	84 (7)	6 (6)	57 (7)	18 (3)	134 (5)	3 (-)	311 (31-10%)	106	16
Scots pine	9 *Pinus sylvestris*	2 (1)	146 (95)	16 (16)	44 (28)	17 (17)	68 (48)	4 (4)	297 (209-70%)	172	36
Elm	10 *Ulmus* (3 'spp'.)	11 (10)	76 (6)	13 (9)	63 (18)	9 (2)	108 (20)	4 (1)	284 (66-23%)	124	16
Crabapple	11 *Malus* (2 spp.)	12 (1)	51 (-)	5 (3)	57 (11)	6 (1)	139 (14)	1 (-)	271 (30-11%)	118	15
Beech	12 *Fagus*	5 (5)	122 (20)	15 (12)	3 (3)	4 (1)	83 (14)	2 (1)	234 (56-24%)		34
Sycamore/maple	13 *Acer* spp (2 spp.)	15 (13)	41 (3)	9 (8)	50 (21)	5 (3)	81 (25)	1 (-)	202 (73-36%)	43	6
Rowan/whitebeams.	14 *Sorbus* (15+ spp.) *	6 (4)	41 (1)	3 (2)	33 (2)	20 (8)	83 (5)	- (-)	186 (21-11%)	58	9
Pears	15 *Pyrus* (2 spp.)	8 (-)	44 (1)	4 (3)	39 (10)	8 (-)	66 (2)	2 (-)	171 (16-9%)		4
Lime	16 *Tilia* (2 spp. + hybrid)	4 (3)	36 (1)	8 (7)	36 (2)	3 (1)	72 (9)	3 (1)	162 (24-15%)	57	12
Ash	17 *Fraxinus*	5 (4)	49 (5)	8 (5)	29 (9)	8 (4)	51 (10)	5 (1)	155 (38-41%)	68	17
Hornbeam	18 *Carpinus*	6 (2)	46 (2)	4 (4)	27 (2)	3 (-)	68 (4)	1 (-)	155 (14-9%)	51	0
Sweet chestnut	19 *Castanea*	1 (-)	45 (3)	1 (1)	25 (7)	3 (-)	40 (5)	- (-)	112 (16-14%)		
Juniper	20 *Juniperus* *	4 (1)	7 (2)	6 (4)	18 (4)	3 (2)	24 (16)	2 (1)	64 (30-47%)	32	11
Buckthorn	21 *Rhamnus*	2 (2)	3 (-)	3 (2)	10 (4)	- (-)	28 (1)	- (-)	46 (9-20%)		0
Elder	22 *Sambucus*	2 (1)	8 (1)	9 (9)	6 (2)	2 (-)	10 (4)	3 (2)	41 (17-41%)		22
Wayfaring tree	23 *Viburnum* *	2 (2)	4 (2)	4 (4)	12 (5)	3 (-)	10 (4)	- (-)	35 (17-49%)		2
Spindle	24 *Euonymus* *	1 (1)	2 (-)	1 (1)	15 (3)	- (-)	16 (7)	- (-)	35 (12-34%)		2
Alder buckthorn	25 *Frangula*	- (-)	1 (1)	2 (2)	5 (2)	- (-)	25 (2)	- (-)	33 (7-21%)		
Yew	26 *Taxus*	4 (3)	3 (1)	2 (1)	10 (2)	- (-)	13 (-)	- (-)	32 (7-22%)		35
Holly	27 *Ilex*	- (-)	12 (-)	1 (1)	11 (1)	- (-)	8 (-)	- (-)	32 (2-6%)	10	17
Box	28 *Buxus*	2 (2)	1 (-)	2 (2)	12 (4)	- (-)	- (-)	- (-)	17 (8-47%)		4
Strawberry tree	29 *Arbutus*	- (-)	- (-)	- (-)	5 (3)	- (-)	5 (1)	- (-)	10 (4-40%)		

Specificity to host varies; while many invertebrate plant-feeders are restricted to trees, most of the mites are host-specific, as are most flies and some wasps but many others especially moths and beetles include large numbers of polyphagous species (i.e. they feed very widely on plant hosts)

NB= while there have been new records for many tree species since the ITE database was published, some trees have been studied more than others; sweet chestnut has around 36 new Lepidoptera recorded although none is restricted to this tree

TABLE 4a Herbivorous insects and mites on willows, in groups

First figure is for total records, figure in brackets is the number restricted to that species (or in group totals, for that willow group)

		Willow group	Mites (Acari)	Beetles (Coleoptera)	Flies (Diptera)	Bugs (Hemiptera)	Wasps, sawflies (Hymenoptera)	Moths (Lepidoptera)	Thrips (Thysanaptera)	Total interactions*
Goat willow	Salix caprea	A	4 (1)	39 (9)	24 (3)	41 (3)	25 (5)	227 (108)	–	360 (129–36%)
Grey willow	S. cinerea	A	4 (1)	32 (8)	20 (1)	37 (2)	27 (2)	91 (8)	–	211 (22–10%)
Eared willow	S. aurita	A	3 (-)	13 (-)	21 (-)	20 (2)	24 (3)	30 (4)	–	111 (9–8%)
Bay willow	S. pentandra	A	2 (-)	7 (1)	7 (1)	5 (1)	10 (3)	4 (1)	–	35 (7–20%)
Total for group A			**7 (2)**	**52 (18)**	**34(9)**	**47 (19)**	**50 (20)**	**171 (86)**	**–**	**361 (154–43%)**
White willow	S. alba	B	6 (1)	18 (1)	16 (-)	24 (8)	15 (-)	68 (7)	–	147 (17–12%)
Crack willow	S. x fragilis	B	4 (-)	18 (3)	11 (-)	20 (-)	19 (3)	19 (2)	–	91 (8–9%)
Total for group B			**6 (1)**	**27 (9)**	**16 (0)**	**31 (11)**	**25 (5)**	**75 (12)**	**–**	**180 (38–21%)**
Purple willow	S. purpurea	C	3 (1)	9 (1)	18 (2)	20 (2)	8 (2)	6 (-)	1 (-)	65 (8–12%)
Almond willow	S. triandra	C	2 (-)	4 (-)	11 (2)	11 (-)	5 (1)	7 (-)	–	40 (3–8%)
Basket willow	S. viminalis	C	2 (-)	22 (3)	11 (1)	17 (5)	25 (6)	37 (7)	1 (-)	115 (22–19%)
Total for group C			**4 (1)**	**24 (2)**	**21 (4)**	**32 (7)**	**30 (9)**	**41 (5)**	**1 (1)**	**153 (29–19%)**
Creeping willow, dwarf willow, etc.	S. repens etc.									
Total for Group D		**D**	**4 (0)**	**17 (2)**	**17 (1)**	**27 (6)**	**27 (13)**	**51 (15)**	**1 (1)**	**144 (38–26%)**
Total for all willows*			**15**	**176**	**49**	**131**	**110**	**353**	**5**	**839**

* records include those where genus of host but not species is recorded

TABLE 5 Fungal associations and insects associated with dead/decaying wood

(1) FRDB: Fungal Records database of the British Isles www.fieldmycology.net/FRDBI/FRDBI.aspd
(2) *Micro-fungi*, Ellis & Ellis (1997). *Microfungi on land plants*: scale:
 * poor, to ***** very rich
(3) *Macrofungi*, Spooner & Roberts (2005): scale as for (1)
(4) Alexander, K. (2002) insects associated with timber, living and decaying

		(1) No of fungal records	(2) Micro-fungi	(3) Macro-fungi	(4) Flies (Diptera)	(4) Moths (Lepidoptera)	(4) Beetles (Coleoptera)
Alder	*Alnus*	1138	**	**	3	1	11
Ash	*Fraxinus*	12	***	*	25	3	47
Aspen	*Populus tremula*	374	**	*	(20) 37*	2	6
Beech	*Fagus sylvatica*	3347	****	***	88	6	103
Birch	*Betula* spp.	1095	***	***	39	8	50
	B. pendula	460					
	B. pubescens						
Black poplar	*P.nigra*	161	*	*	15	1	6
Bird cherry	*Prunus padus*	80					
	All *Prunus* spp.		*	**	1	0	4
Blackthorn	*Prunus spinosa*	391	**				
Box	*Buxus*	143	**	*6			
Buckthorn	*Rhamnus cathartica*	-	**	*			
Crabapple	*Malus* spp.	250	*	*	3	2	5
Elder	*Sambucus nigra*	551	*	**	3		
Elms	*Ulmus* spp.	1780	**	**	37	6	34
Field maple	*Acer campestris*	401	***	*	1	0	8
Hawthorn	*Crataegus*	1468	**	*	3	0	17
Hazel	*Corylus*	1839	**	*	2	2	7
Holly	*Ilex*	567	**	*	2	0	1
Hornbeam	*Carpinus*	644	*	*	4	0	7
Juniper	*Juniperus*	100	**	*	-		
Lime	*Tilia* spp.	1351	*	***	5	1	3
Oak	*Quercus* (2 spp.)		****	*****	45	7	151
	Q.petraea	701					
	Q.robur	1521					
Pear	*Pyrus* spp.	158	*	*	-	0	5
Rowan	*Sorbus aucuparia*	344					
	All *Sorbus* spp.		*	*	-?	0	3
Scots pine	*Pinus sylvestris*	1833	*****	*****	33	2	94
Spindle	*Euonymus*	-	*	*			
Strawberry tree	*Arbutus unedo*	16	*	*			
Sycamore	*A. pseudoplatanus*	1404	**	*	2	2	8
Wayfaring tree	*Viburnum lantana*	20	***	*			
Willows	*Salix* spp.	3960	***	****	15	3	25
Yew	*Taxus*	679	*	*	2		
	All native trees				(352)	(46)	(595)

* updated figure (Rotheray, pers. comm.)

TABLE 6 Maximum recorded altitudes (in UK) for native trees

Figures based on Ashmole (2006), Gilbert, D. (pers. comm.), Clapham et al. (1991), Webb, S. (pers. comm.), Preston et al. (2002) and BSBI website

* presumably planted (outside area of its natural distribution)
M occurs in montane scrub
C occurs in coastal scrub

Tree genus/species	Max altitude in metres and site [ ] = exceptional record	Montane/ Coastal scrub
Acer campestre	380 Llanthony, Brecon	no
Acer pseudoplatanus	580 Dowgang Hush, Cumbria	C possibly
Alnus	547 Argyll (above Clova)	no
	470 Garrigill, E. Cumbria	
Arbutus	230 Killarney, Ireland	C
Betula pendula	600 'Highlands'	
Betula pubescens	774 Coire of Bonhard/685 Hilton Fell	C, M
Betula nana	850 Glen Cannich	
Buxus	330 Cwmsymlog lead mine	no
Carpinus	380* Great Mell Fell, Cumbria	no
Corylus	776 Coire of Bonhard	C; M possibly
Crataegus monogyna	610 Melmerby High Fell, Cumbria	C; M possibly
Euonymus	400 Malham	No
Fagus	650* Garrigill, E.Cumbria	No
Frangula alnus	[450* The Arch, Cardigan]	
Fraxinus	840 Cairn Mairy, Glen Lyon	C possibly
	585 Cwm Idwal, Caerns.	(limestone)
Ilex	776 Coire of Bonhard	C; M possibly
Juniperus	1200 Ben Macdui	C, M
Malus spp.	440 Peithnant	No
Pinus sylvestris	1160 Cairn Lochan	C, M
Populus tremulus	776 Coire of Bonhard	C, M

Tree genus/species	Max altitude in metres [ ] = exceptional record	Montane/ Coastal scrub
Prunus avium	400* Garrigill, E Cumbria	No
Prunus padus	650 Dove Crag, Westmorland	C?, M?
Prunus spinosa	500* Crossfell, Cumbria	no
Quercus petraea	550 Young Wood, Cumbria	C possibly
Q. robur	450 Talgarth, Brecon	C
Rhamnus cathartica	380 Malham Tarn, Yorks.	No
Salix purpurea	440 E Allandale, Northumberland.	
Salix x fragilis	410* Allandale, Northumberland.	
Salix caprea	776 Coire of Bonhard	C
Salix cinerea	845* Great Dun Fell, Westmorland	No
Sambucus	470 Nenthead, Cumbria	
Sorbus aria	455 Teesdale	
S. aucuparia	900 Helvellyn, 870 Beinn Dearg	C?, M
S. rupicola	667 Allt Coire Cisteachan	no
S. domestica	(lowland)	C
S. torminalis	338 Craig-y-rhiw	no
Taxus	470 South Kerry, Ireland	C
Tilia cordata	550- Whelter Crag, Cumbria	M (Cumbria)
T. platyphyllos	400 Brecon	no
Ulmus glabra	530 Atholl	C (e.g. Lismore), M?
Viburnum lantana	(lowland)	no

Mountain willows/ species	Max altitude in metres and site [ ] = exceptional record
Salix arbuscula	1032 Creag Meaghaidh
S. aurita	790 Ben Lawers
S. herbacea	1310 Ben Nevis
S. lanata	1035 Ben Alder
S. lapponum	1125 Lochnagar
S. myrsinifolia	940 Stob Binnien
S. myrsinites	1025 Coire Cheap
S. phyllicifolia	1039 N Loch Avon
S. repens	855 Atholl
S. reticulata	1125 Ben Lawers

TABLE 7 Main diseases/causes of ill-health in common native trees when planted
(based on Strouts & Winter, Diagnosis of ill-health in trees, 1994)

1   honey fungus: *Armillaria* spp. (uncommon in street trees)   X susceptible   R resistant
2   phytophthora root disease: *Phytophthora* spp.
3   other root diseases: *Ganoderma* spp.
4   fireblight: *Erwinia amylovora*
5   nectria canker: *Nectria galligena/ditissima*
6   leaf and shoot aphids/mites etc.: various
7   leaf miners: various
8   other problems and new threats

	Tree genus	1	2	3	4	5	6	7	8
Alder	*Alnus*		X						Undiagnosed die-back. Leaf skeletonization by leaf beetles *Chrysomela aenea*
Apple/Pear	*Malus/Pyrus*	X			?X	X			Apple scab: *Venturia* spp.
Ash	*Fraxinus*	R				X			Bacterial canker *Pseudomonas syringae* ssp. *savastanoi*. Ash bud moth: *Prays fraxinella*
Beech	*Fagus*	R	X	X		X	X	X	Beech bark disease *Nectria coccinea*
Birch	*Betula*	X		X			X		Leaf rusts *Metalampsoridium* spp. Witches brooms *Taphrina turgida/betulina*
Box	*Buxus*	?							Rusts: *Puccinia buxi*, *Cylindrocladium buxicola*
Cherries, blackthorn	*Prunus*	X	X				X		Bacterial canker *Pseudomonas syringae*, cherry leaf scorch: *Apiognomonia erythrostoma*, cherry leaf spot: *Blumeriella jaapi*, blossom wilt: *Monilinia laxa* Silver-leaf: *Chondrostereum purpureum*
Elms	*Ulmus*								Dutch elm disease: *Ophiostoma novo-ulmi*
Field maple, sycamore	*Acer*	X				X	X		*Verticillium dahliae* wilt
Hawthorn	*Crataegus*	R	X		X	X	X		
Holly	*Ilex*	R							
Hornbeam	*Carpinus*	R							
Juniper	*Juniperus*	R					X		*Phomopsis juniperovora* (canker)
Lime	*Tilia*	R	X	X			X		Scale insects: *Pulvinaria regalis*
Oak	*Quercus*	R		X			X	X	Potential threats: sudden oak death (*Phytophthora ramorum*), acute oak decline
Poplar, aspen	*Populus*								Leaf rusts: *Metalampsoridium* spp.
Rowan	*Sorbus aucuparia*	X							
Scots pine	*Pinus*	X				X	X		Needle cast diseases: *Lophodermium seditiosum* et al.
Sweet chestnut	*Castanea*		X						
Wayfaring tree	*Viburnum*								Viburnum leaf-beetle: *Pyrrhalta viburni*
Whitebeam, wild service	*Sorbus aria*				X				
Willows	*Salix*	X					X		Leaf rusts, Willow scab: *Venturia* spp.
Yew	*Taxus*	R	X						(Unexplained) branch death

TABLE 8 Occurrence of tree species according to two national surveys of mainland UK
Figures in brackets are for trees where it is clear that areas outside their natural distribution i.e. planted are included

(1) BSBI maps: No. of 10 km squares recorded
(2) Countryside Survey: No of 10 km squares (out of 591) recorded
(© Database Right/Copyright NERC – Centre for Ecology & Hydrology)
(3) Countryside survey zones; from: R.H. Haines-Young *et al.* (2000)

Total UK	(1)	(2)	(3) 1 East lowland England	2 West lowland England	8 lowland Wales	4 lowland Scotland	3 upland England	9 upland Wales	5 intermediate /islands Scotland	6 upland Scotland
Hawthorn	3499	420	96	94	93	76	67	82	20	8
Ash	3517	402	97	89	82	79	56	71	23	8
Willows	*	377	75	76	89	73	39	65	42	34
Oak	*	368	84	85	88	62	48	63	22	14
Sycamore	3576	354	76	81	77	83	6	55	20	7
Birch	*	276	44	46	52	60	39	63	36	39
Alder	3465	245	38	49	73	46	41	59	16	17
Elder	3499	239	74	61	32	43	28	33	3	3
Beech	3238	237	51	57	55	59	33	31	9	3
Blackthorn	3275	219	64	49	79	17	6	51	3	
Hazel	3407	213	37	53	70	22	22	67	8	7
Rowan	3362	211	11	21	23	57	50	73	39	53
Scots pine	(2955)	194	35	39	20	46	(39)	(25)	22	30
Elm	(3091)	164	54	40	27	33	15	10	3	3
Field maple	1875	161	70	39	32	3		16	3	
Holly	3288	149	20	46	50	8	31	40	7	
Poplars	*	127	48	35	20	6	13	6	7	2
Lime	(2352)	101	37	21	13	(21)	6	4	7	3
Apple	?2099	73	20	25	14	5	9	6	1	
Crabapple	2668	70	13	16	13	10	4	37	1	2
Wild cherry	2656	62	13	15	16	11	6	16	1	2
Sweet chestnut	(1940)	59	17	21	13	6	4	2	1	
Hornbeam	(1642)	50	19	13	7	(3)	(4)	(6)	(3)	
Yew	2257	28	6	10	7	2	6	2		2
Aspen	2781	25	4	4	9	2	2	10	3	3
Whitebeam	(1503)	14	3	1	4	(5)	(2)	(2)	(3)	
Juniper	1298	13		2						8
Buckthorn	1031	11	7				6			
Bird cherry	(1769)	10			2	3				
Pear	(895)	9	2	4	2	3		2		
Spindle	1912	7						2		
Box	1222	3							(1)	(2)

TABLE 9 Trees in hedges: by hedge length and as emergent 'hedge trees'
From National Countryside Survey (mainland UK) © Database Right/Copyright NERC– Centre
for Ecology & Hydrology
www.countrysidesurvey.org.uk/archiveCS2000/index.htm

Species	Frequency by hedge length	Hedge trees	Hedge trees by region*					
			1	2	8	4	3	9
Hawthorn	1	110	32	39	17	8	3	11
Ash	2	1347	637	510	43	17	50	90
Oak	3	1203	454	616	39	8	17	69
Hazel	4	11	3	6	1			1
Willow	5	90	35	30	14		5	6
Sycamore/field maple	6							
sycamore only		175	39	95	6	9	2	24
field maple only		92	69	15	6			2
Cherry/blackthorn	7	20	8	8	2			2
Birch	8	24	3	11		1	1	7
Alder	9	47	13	18	2		9	5
Beech	10	62	8	26	7	18	2	
Elder	11	6	1	2	2			1
Rowan	12	16		6		1	4	6
Holly	13	66	11	42	3	1	2	7
Elm	14	82	17	50	3	12		
Poplars incl aspen	15	13	7	4		1		1
Lime	16	24	5	15		3		
Crabapple/Malus sp.	17	44	26	12	6			
Scot's pine	18	7	1	6				
Hornbeam	19	6	3	3				
Buckthorn	20							
Whitebeam/other Sorbus spp.	21	1	1					
Sweet chestnut	22	2	2					
Yew	23	2		2				
Pear	24							
Box	25							
Non-native species		15	6	4	4			1
Unspecified conifer		10	7	3				
Unspecified broadleaf		8	4	3	1			
Mixed (native) broadleaf		4		1				3
Aspen		1			1			
Viburnum		1			1			
Grand total			1392	1527	159	78	95	237

* Region numbers as for previous table (Upland Scotland and intermediate/islands Scotland omitted)

Glossary

ACHENE A small, dry, non-dehiscent fruit developed from a single carpel containing a single seed.

AGROFORESTRY A method of land use based on the integration of trees and shrubs within crop or livestock production systems. Carefully selected and managed trees can increase soil fertility, control erosion, provide shade and protect crops from livestock and adverse weather, as well as conserving water.

ALLUVIAL Transported by water, sedimentary, pertaining to riverbeds.

ARBUSCULAR MYCORRHIZAE Fungi associated with plant roots and penetrating the cell wall so that they grow inside the root cells of the host plant.

ANCIENT WOODLAND Woodland that has stood on the same land for at least the last 400 years without being felled.

ANGIOSPERM Flowering plant *see also* Gymnosperm.

ANTHER The apical part of a stem that produces pollen or microspores. (Male sex organ of the plant.)

APOMIXIS (apomictic) Reproduction without fertilization; development of a viable ovule without union with male gamete (pollen), but with genetic characteristics of mother plant only. Frequent in plants such as bramble, *Rubus fruticosus*, hawkweeds, *Hieracium* spp., and rosaceous trees, *Crataegus* and *Sorbus*. Apomictic abilities can be inherited through crossing; for example apomixis is known to occur after crossing of common *Sorbus* spp. specifically with *S. rupicola*, producing 'microspecies', which produce apparently normal flowers with pollen and ovaries and which then breed true.

ARBORICULTURE The cultivation of trees in order to produce individual specimens of the greatest ornament, for shelter or any other primary purpose apart from the production of timber.

ARCHAEOPHYTE A non-indigenous plant which arrived before 1500 (see p.9).

ARIL A fleshy or hairy outgrowth of a seed or ovule, i.e. unlike 'normal' fruits where the fruit is made up of expanded ovary walls (see Yew p.162).

ASCOMYCETE A very numerous group of fungi (including yeasts, mildews and *Pennicillium*) that produce microscopic fruiting bodies of diverse shapes, but unlike typical basidiomycetes (mushrooms and toadstools).

BAP Biodiversity Action Plan: a contemporary conservation category.

BASE-RICH Referring to soils, lime-rich, with a high pH value, typically found on chalk, limestone etc. and the opposite of acid, peaty soils.

BASIDIOMYCETE The most familiar group of fungi typically producing fruiting bodies such as mushrooms, toadstools, truffles and bracket-fungi.

BIOMASS The total mass of organisms (plant, animal and fungi) measured by volume, dry-weight or standing crop.

CALCAREOUS Lime-rich, usually referring to soil originating from limestone, chalk or similar underlying rock.

CARR Damp or marsh woodland that is usually dominated by alder.

CATKIN A pendulous inflorescence modified for wind pollination (though sometimes insect pollinated).

CELLULOSE An organic polysaccharide (containing carbon, hydrogen and oxygen only) manufactured by plants and used as the main structural element in trees.

CLONE, CLONAL Genetically identical. Some trees grow as clonal groups by producing suckers all from one rootstock (e.g. aspen, wild cherry).

COASTAL SCRUB Low-growing salt-resistant woody vegetation that develops on sea cliffs and slopes facing the sea, especially found on west-facing coasts.

COPPICE/COPPICING A form of woodland management in which trees are cut back down to ground level regularly (every few years) to encourage growth of shoots from the base. The resulting thicket is termed a copse or a coppice.

COTYLEDONS The leaf-like parts of seeds that that contain stored food. Flowering plant classification is based on distinguishing those with one cotyledon, like grasses (monocotyledons), or two as in beans or acorns (dicotyledons).

DENDROCHRONOLOGY Dating of wood from the pattern and sequence of tree rings.

DICOTYLEDON *see* cotyledon.

DIOECIOUS PLANTS (including trees) in which the female and male reproductive organs grow on different individuals (as opposed to monoecious plants, where they are found on the same plant), such as in poplars and yew.

DIPLOID The (normal) state of having paired chromosomes.

DORMANCY (in seeds) Characteristic state that requires special conditions (such as

a period of extreme cold) before they will germinate.

DOZED A term used by woodworkers to describe wood that has veins or patterns of darkened wood passing through it due to (past) infection by fungi.

DRUPE Fleshy fruit containing one or more seeds each separately enclosed in a hard endocarp (the pip of an apple).

ECTOMYCORRHIZA Fungi closely associated with roots of plants, including trees, but not penetrating the root cells.

ENDEMIC Restricted to the particular country, island or area where it occurs naturally.

ENDOMYCORRHIZA *see* arbuscular mycorrhizae.

EPIPHYTE Living on the exterior surface of a plant, but using it only for support such as mosses and lichens on trees.

ERINEUM Patch of hairs on a leaf or stem, induced by the presence of gall-mites, which live amongst them.

FASTIGIATE A tree with almost vertical branches close to the stem, resulting in a pyramidal or conical form, e.g. Irish yew or hornbeam street-trees.

GALL To gall is to provoke the development in plants of special tissue which then feeds and protects the gall-causer. Galls are the structures produced in this way, such as oak-apples.

GENUS A rank in the taxonomic hierarchy, meaning a group of similar species, denoted by a Latin name starting with a capital letter. The binomial naming system was standardised in 1753 by a Swedish botanist Linnaeus, in his *Species Plantarum*.

GLOMEROMYCOTA *(Glomerales)* A large group of little-known fungi which apparently pass their whole lives within the soil and are thought to be widely associated with the roots of plants in mycorrhizal relationships.

GLUCOSIDE A complex molecule derived from glucose attached to another molecule.

GRAFTING A horticultural method of plant propagation in which a segment (the scion) of the plant to be propagated is inserted into another plant (the stock) in such a way that their vascular tissues fuse allowing growth of the grafted segment.

GREGARIOUS A tree which tends to occur in groups (often a clone of ramets).

GYMNOSPERM One of two important

divisions of seed-bearing vascular plants, with seeds not enclosed in an ovary, i.e. fruit and typically borne on cones, e.g. conifers. (*See also* angiosperm.)

HAPLOID Having a single set of chromosomes as in a pollen grain or an (unfertilised) ovum.

HEARTWOOD The central wood of trees consisting of dead cells. The properties of this wood (darker colour, resistance to decay, greater density) make it more highly prized for furniture manufacture and other uses.

HEMI-PARASITIC Form of living in which part of nutrition is obtained from another organism. Mistletoe is an example; it is parasitic on the trees it grows on, but also manufactures its own organic matter from the atmosphere with chlorophyll.

HOLOCENE Approximately the last 12,000 years, i.e. the millennia since the most recent glacial period.

INFLORESCENCE Any flowering structure consisting of more than one flower. Rowan or whitebeam flowers form an inflorescence, while a daffodil is a single flower.

INVERTEBRATE Animals without an internal backbone: insects, spiders, mites, worms, etc.

KEY The common name given to the winged seeds found on some trees, e.g. ash, sycamore.

KEYSTONE SPECIES Species that interact with many other species in an environment and whose removal would destabilise that environment. Classically used for organisms whose significance is much greater than its biomass would suggest, but used here to include trees (although the term is generally going out of common use).

KRUMMHOLZ The dwarfed and sometimes flattened trees that are found above the normal tree-line on mountains. They tend to grow low to the ground and are thus able to withstand strong winds and snowfall.

LENTICEL Loose aggregation of airy cells which act as pores in the bark or on the skin of fruits.

LIGNIN A dark brown organic chemical compound which strengthens wood and may make up as much as one third of its total weight.

MAST, MASTING A year (of irregular frequency) when fruiting of a tree is particularly high, determined usually by conditions (temperature etc.) in the previous summer when flower-buds are being set down. In trees like oak (and very commonly among trees in tropical forests) where most or all seeds in low production years are consumed by predators, masting may be a strategy which has evolved to effectively overwhelm predators, allowing a periodic pulse of regeneration to occur.

MICROSPECIES *see* apomixis.

MONOCOTYLEDON *see* cotyledon.

MONOECIOUS PLANTS in which the female and male reproductive organs are found on the same plant (*see* dioecious).

MONTANE SCRUB Term used to describe the low-growing woody vegetation that develops at and above the tree-line on mountains, often including krummholz trees.

MYCORRHIZA Specialised fungi which are associated with the roots of most plants including trees; in exchange for minerals and salts they receive organic sugars manufactured by the plants which they break down releasing the energy they need for life.

NATIVE TREE A tree not originally introduced by human agency, growing on a site it occupies as a result of natural, i.e. non-human processes.

NEOPHYTE A non-indigenous plant which arrived since 1500 (see p.9).

NATURALISED (and fully naturalised) Growing naturally in an alien environment, usually when planted or protected. Fully-naturalised means reproducing naturally and competing with a native flora in natural plant communities (e.g. sycamore but not, so far, walnut).

OSIER Species of willow used for basket-making.

OVULE The female reproductive unit and its protective and nutritive tissue, which develops into the dispersal unit or seed after fertilization.

PALAEOBOTANY Study of plant life of the geological past.

PERICARP Fruit wall (sometimes fleshy) developed from the outer part of the ovary.

PHYTOPHAGOUS Plant-feeding (as of insects).

PLEACHING Training of tree species into decorative shapes; particularly hornbeam and lime.

POLLARDING Method of tree-management in which the main trunk of a tree is cut at about 2.5–3 m (8–10 ft), and the resulting branches are then cropped on a regular rotation of a few years. Pollarding stimulates the production of numerous shoots and results in a characteristic tree shape of a short, thick trunk with a mass of small branches at the top.

POLLEN The male reproductive spores of seed plants, which are produced in vast numbers, usually in pollen sacks (anthers) borne on the stamens.

POLLINATION The transfer of pollen grains from the male reproductive organs, stamens, to the female reproductive organs, style and ovary, in seed plants.

POLYGAMOUS The condition of bearing male, female or hermaphrodite flowers on the same plant.

POLYPHAGOUS Herbivorous insects that feed on a wide range of plants, such as the caterpillars of many common moths.

POLYPLOID A state of having more than the normal two sets of chromosomes, usually in multiples, e.g. tetraploid (4x) and hexaploid (6x), frequently found in cultivated plants.

POME Fleshy false fruit such as apple, where the fruit (core, including the seeds) is surrounded by additional fleshy tissue derived from the receptacle (base) of the flower.

RACEME/RACEMOSE Inflorescence (often conical in outline) in which the main axis continues to grow so that the youngest flowers are apical, e.g. buddleia, bird cherry.

RADIOCARBON DATING Method of determining the age of organic material. When plants incorporate atmospheric carbon (from carbon dioxide) it contains a proportion of a carbon isotope (carbon-14) that is present in the atmosphere at the time. When the tree or other organism dies, this carbon-14 decays at the known rate so that by measuring the amount left the (approximate) age of the organic material can be estimated. First developed by Walter Libby at the University of Chicago in 1949, since then it has been developed to become more accurate. For wood such as oak it has been calibrated precisely, using dendrochronology.

RAMET Stem which is part of a clone; a sucker.

RECALCITRANT SEED Seeds that are highly sensitive to desiccation (unlike other seeds) and that often have a very limited period of viability, e.g. oak.

RUDERAL Weed or pioneer species, exploiting disturbed habitats such as landslips, river banks etc.

SAMARA (disused term) Type of achene or nut in which the wall of the fruit (the pericarp) is produced to form a membranous wing to aid dispersal by wind (e.g. acer). The term is now being replaced by the term 'winged fruit'.

SAPROTROPHIC, SAPROPHAGE, SAPROPHYTE Specialised to derive nutrition from dead and decaying plants.

SERE, SERAL The ecological succession of habitat development, usually changing from 'simple' (low diversity) to more 'complex' (higher diversity), but dependant upon environmental factors such as temperature, rainfall etc.

SILVICULTURE The management and exploitation of trees in forests.

SPECIES A group of organisms, which make up a single actual or potential successful breeding population. It is the main unit of biological classification below genus and is referred to by the second part in the Latin binomial naming system.

SPORE Tiny reproductive cell of lower plants or fungi.

STAMENS Male part of flower that bears anthers, which produce pollen.

STANDARD Tree grown to full stature, usually for timber.

STOOL Ground level base of a coppiced tree such as willow or hazel.

STRATIFICATION The practice of placing seeds between layers of moist sand or peat and exposing them to low temperature. This treatment is necessary for those seeds that need a period of chilling before germination can begin.

STYLE Female part of flower that receives pollen.

TAXONOMY The principles and practice of classification, especially of living organisms.

WILDWOOD Prehistoric forest.

WITHY One- or two-year-old willow shoots cut for basket-work.

WOOD PASTURE A traditional form of agroforestry. Grazing pasture dotted with trees (oak, beech, hornbeam etc.) that are pollarded for winter fodder, firewood and small timber.

Acknowledgements

Many people have helped me in writing this book generously giving their time and wisdom and I would like to thank them all. In particular Oliver Rackham, George Peterken and Alan Stubbs, David Bevan and Charles Turner, all saw the entire text at some stage in the process and made extensive valuable comments. I am particularly indebted to David Bevan, Mark Broadmeadow, Keith Kirby, George Peterken, Alan Stubbs and Drennan Watson for suggestions and comments regarding chapter 7.

Many others helped correct errors, add expert comment and generally improve the text with reference to particular sections. Several specialists have given me the benefit of up-to-date research: Dr Tim Rich, National Museum of Wales (whitebeams); Dr Irina Belyaeva, Royal Botanic Gardens, Kew (willows); Dr Peter Hollingsworth and Dr Max Coleman, Royal Botanic Gardens, Edinburgh (elms); E. and Ms V. Emmet (aspen), Diane Gilbert and Marc Hampton. Many others have helped with particular sections or answered specific questions and made various suggestions and corrections; these include Keith Alexander, Philip Ashmole, Max Barclay, Janet Boyd, Jonathan Briggs, Alistair Broun, Jill Butler, Jonathan Coate, John Clarkson, Gerwyn Clegg, Barney Davies, Prof. Tim Dixon, Brian Ecott, Ian Evans, Diana Gilbert, Peter Gosling, Ted Green, Philip Grime, Paul Hand, Marc Hampton, members of the Highland Biological Recording Group (in particular Ian Evans, Ken Glass and Tamara Weston), Andrew Jackson, Roger Key, Keith Kirby, Emily Ledder, Walter lloyd, William Macalpine, Liz Manley, Ed Mills, Bill Morris, Mike Morris, Lisa Norton, Rebecca Oaks, Caroline Oates, Colin Plant, Ian Pulford, Tim Rich, David Roy, Rachel Sanderson, Michael Scott, Alan Shepley, John Southey, Brian Spooner, Peter Thomas, Ian Tubby, Ted Tuddenham, Roy Vickery, David Wainhouse, Drennan Watson, Peter Wise-Jackson and Pat Wolseley and Claire Wood, to all of whom I would like to express my gratitude.

Any errors that remain are my own responsibility.

Picture Credits

Unless indicated otherwise all images are copyright Edward Milner/ACACIA Environment.

CHAPTER 2 p.13 bottom © Peatlands Centre; p.14 © NHMPL; p.15 Lisa Wilson © NHM.

CHAPTER 3 p.17 top Roger Griffith/Wikipedia; p.19 © Teresa Morris; p.21 © Stuart Roberts; p.22 bottom right © B. Holland; p.27 Mercer Design © NHM.

CHAPTER 4 p.31 bottom © Glyn Williams; p.32 left © S. Buchan/Flickr; p.34 top © B. Holland; p.34 middle Lubomir Hlasek; p.34 bottom © Roger Key; p.36 © Imperial War Museum; p.38 top right UKM/Ian Kimber; p.39 © Alan Watson; p.40 top © E. Emmett; p.41 bottom left © Alan Watson; p.41 bottom right © Roger Key; p.44 © High Wycombe Museum; p.45 middle © Jean-Marc Moingeon; p.47 © Neil Mackenzie; p.50 top left, middle and bottom © Roger Key; p.51 © Alan Watson; p.53 top © UKM/Ian Kimber; p.60 right © T. Bantock; p.65 © Illustrated London News; p.67 bottom left © Pietro Niolu; p.67 bottom right and middle © Roger Key; p.70 top © UKM/Ian Kimber; p.76 © Royal Botanic Gardens Edinburgh; p.77 top © Jean-Marc Moingeon; p.77 bottom right © Roger Key; p.78 top © T. Bantock; p.78 middle © Rob Edmunds; p.80 top right © National Trust Photo Library; p.81 middle right © Lubomir Hlasek; p.81 bottom right © Rob Edmunds; p.83 bottom right © M. Massie; p.85 bottom © Somerset Museum, Taunton; p.88 left © Jean-Marc Moingeon; p.88 right © David Bevan; p.89 top right and middle and p. 93 bottom © Roger Key; p.99 top © Alan Watson; p.99 bottom © T. Bantock; p.101 top left © Imperial War Museum; p.104 bottom right, p.110 middle right, p.111 bottom right and p.115 top left © Roger Key; p.119 top © UKM/Ian

Kimber; p.123 top and middle © Alan Watson; p.123 bottom © Peiter Gordijn/Flickr; p.127 top left © Michael Kirby; p.127 bottom © Roger Key; p.129 © Killarney National Park; p.130 © Jean-Marc Moingeon; p.135 © J. Southey; p.137 top left © Roger Key; p.140 top left © Adam Cheeseman; p.140 top right © Albert de Wilde/Flickr; p.140 bottom right © UKM/Paul Harris; p.142 left © A. Broun; p.142 right © M. Hampton; p.143 © Graeme Walker; p.144 bottom right and p.149 bottom left © UKM/Ian Kimber; p.146 bottom left M. Hampton; p.152 top right © Central Science Laboratory; p.154 © I. Balaevna; p.157 bottom left © Neil Mackenzie; p.159 © Jean-Marc Moingeon; p.160 top left © Butterfly Conservation; p.160 bottom right © Jens Kopelke; p.161 bottom left © Roger Key; p.165 bottom left © British Museum; p.167 top right © Jean-Marc Moingeon.

CHAPTER 5 p.173 top left © Roger Merryweather; p.175 and p.180 bottom right © Museum of English Rural Life; p.180 bottom left © Imperial War Museum.

CHAPTER 7 p.196 left and bottom right © Christophe van der Eecken/Science Photo Library; p.196 top right © UKM/Ian Kimber; p.201 top right © Vavilov Institute, St Petersburg.

NHM = Natural History Museum, London
UKM = UK Moths

Every effort has been made to contact and accurately credit all copyright holders. If we have been unsuccessful, we apologise and welcome correction for future editions and reprints.

References

NB Website addresses are subject to change.

REGULARLY CITED

Evelyn, J. 1664. *Sylva: a Discourse of Forest Trees* (facsimile of 5th edn., 1979). Stobart and Son Ltd., London.
Rackham, O. 1986. *The History of the Countryside*. Dent, London.
Rackham, O. 2001. *Trees and Woodland in the British Landscape*, 2nd edn. Orion Press, London.
Rackham, O. 2003. *Ancient Woodland – Its History, Vegetation and Uses in England*, 2nd edn. Edward Arnold, London.
Rackham, O. 2006. *Woodlands*. Collins New Naturalist, London.
Rackham, O. 2008. Ancient woodlands: modern threat. *New Phytologist* 180:571-586.

CHAPTER 1 INTRODUCTION (AND GENERAL REFERENCES)

Bradshaw, A. 1994. *Ancient, Interesting and Unusual Trees of Cumbria*. Cumbria Broadleaves, Bowness-on-Windermere.
Clapham, A. R., Tutin A. G. and Moore D. M. 1991. *Flora of the British Isles*, 3rd edn. Cambridge University Press.
Colebourn, P. 1982. *Hampshire's Countryside Heritage: Ancient Woodland*. Hants. County Council.
Collis, J. S. 1951. *The Triumph of the Tree*. Country Book Club, London.
Deakin, R. 2007. *Wildwood: A Journey through Trees*. Hamish Hamilton.
Elves, H. J. and Henry, A. H. 1913? (reissued 1969). *The Trees of Great Britain and Ireland*. Royal Forestry Society.
Gerard, J. 1597. *Historie of Plants*. London.
Gosling, P. 2007. *Raising Trees and Shrubs from Seed. A Practice Guide*. Forestry Commission, Edinburgh.

Grigson, G. 1960. *The Englishman's Flora*. J.M Dent & Sons, London.
Grime, J. P., Hodgson, J. G. and Hunt, R. 2007. *Comparative Plant Ecology; a Functional Approach to Common British Species*, 2nd edn. Cambridge University Press.
Hageneder, F. 2000. *The Spirit of Trees*. Floris Books, Edinburgh.
Hageneder, F. 2001. *The Heritage of Trees*. Floris Books, Edinburgh.
Hageneder, F. 2005. *The Living Wisdom of Trees*. Duncan Baird. London.
Harris, J. G. S. 1989. *Trees and the Law*. Arboricultural Association.
Hibberd, B.G. (ed.). [date?] *Urban Forestry Practice*. Forestry Commission Handbook No. 5.
Hill, M. O., Preston, C. D. and Roy, D. B. 2004. *PLANTATT: Attributes of British and Irish Plants: Status, Size, Life History, Geography and Habitats*. Centre for Ecology and Hydrology, NERC.
Hilliers Nurseries, 1981. *The Hillier Colour Dictionary of Trees and Shrubs*. David & Charles, Newton Abbot.
Hodge, S. A. 1991. *Urban Trees – A Survey of Street Trees in England*. Forestry Commission Bulletin No. 99, HMSO.
Innes, J. L. 1990. *Assessment of Tree Condition*. Forestry Commission Field Book No. 12.
Johnson, O. (ed.) 2011. *Champion Trees of Britain and Ireland*. Royal Botanic Gardens, London.
Johnson, O. and More, D. 2006. *Tree Guide: The Most Complete Field Guide to the Trees of Britain and Europe*. HarperCollins, London.
Kent, D.H. 1975. *The Historical Flora of Middlesex*. Ray Society, London
Law, B. 2001. *The Woodland Way*. Permanent Publications, Hants.
Law, B. 2008. *The Woodland Year*.

Permanent Publications, Hants.
Loudon, J. C. 1844. *Arboretum et Fruticetum Britannicum*. London.
Mabberley, D. J. 1997. *The Plant-book: A Portable Ddictionary of the Vascular Plants*. Cambridge University Press.
Mabey, R. 1996. *Flora Britannica*. Sinclair-Stevenson, London.
Miles, A. 1999. *Sylva: the Tree in Britain*. Ebury Press.
Milner, J. E. D. 1992. *The Tree Book*. Collins and Brown, London.
Mingay, G. E. (ed.). 1989. *The Agrarian History of England and Wales Vol. VI 1750–1850*. Cambridge University Press.
Mitchell, A. 1991. *A Field Guide to the Trees of Britain and Northern Europe*. HarperCollins.
Morton, A. 1986. *The Trees of Shropshire*. Crowood Press, Marlborough.
Morton, A. 2004. *Tree Heritage of Britain and Ireland*. Crowood Press, Marlborough.
Neeson, E. 1991. *A History of Irish Forestry*. Lilliput Press, Dublin.
Pakenham, T. 1997. *Meetings with Remarkable Trees*. Pheonix, London.
Perring, F. H. and Walters, S. M. 1976. *Atlas of the British Flora. Botanical Society of the British Isles*, 2nd edn. Wakefield.
Peterken, G. 1992. *Woodland Conservation and Management*. Chapman & Hall.
Peterken, G. F. 1996. *Natural Woodland: Ecology and Conservation in Northern Temperate Regions*. Cambridge University Press.
Peterken, G. F. 2008. *The Wye Valley*. Collins New Naturalist No. 105.
Preston, C. D., Pearman, D. A. and Dines, T. D. 2002. *New Atlas of the British Isles and Irish Flora*. Oxford University Press.
Ratcliffe, D. 2002. *Lakeland*. Collins New

Naturalist, London.
Rich, T, Houston, L, Robertson, A and Proctor, M. 2010. *Whitebeams, Rowans and Service Trees of Britain and Ireland*. BSBI Handbook No 14.
Sinden, N. 1989. *In a Nutshell: A Manifesto for Trees and A Guide to Growing and Planting Them*. Common Ground, Bristol Press.
Stace, C. 2010. *New Flora of the British Isles*, 3rd edn. Cambridge University Press.
Strutt, J. G. 1822. *Sylva Britannica*. London.
Tansley, A. G. 1939. *The British Islands and their Vegetation*. Cambridge University Press.
Tree Council of Ireland. 2005. *Champion Trees; A Selection of Ireland's Great Trees*. Tree Council of Ireland, Dublin.
Tudge, C. 2006. *The Secret Life of Trees*. Penguin Books, London.
Vera, F. W. M. 2000. *Grazing Ecology and Forest History*. CABI Publishing, Wallingford.
Vera, F. W. M. 2002. The dynamic European forest. *Arbor. J.* 26: 179–211.
Vickery, R. 1995. *Dictionary of Plant-Lore*. Oxford University Press, Oxford
Webb, D.A., Parnell, J, and Doogue, D. 1996. *An Irish Flora*. Dundalgan Press, Dundalk.
White, Gilbert. 1789 (1990 edn.). *A Natural History of Selbourne*. Penguin, London.
White, J. 1995. *Forest and Woodland Trees in Britain*. Oxford University Press, Oxford.
Whone, H. 1990. *Touch Wood: A Journey Among Trees*. Smith Settle, W. Yorks.

WEBSITES
Botanical Society of British Isles (maps)
www.bsbimaps.org.uk
www.britishbugs.org.uk

British Leafmines www.leafmines.co.uk
Butterfly Conservation www.ukbutterflies.co.uk
Coleopterist www.coleopterist.org.uk
Dipterists' forum www.dipteristsforum.org.uk
Ecoflora www.ecoflora.co.uk
www.fruitforum.net
Fungal Records Database for British Isles www.fieldmycology.net/FRDBI/FRDBI.asp
ITE database www.brc.ac.uk
Northern Ireland Fungus Group www.nifg.org.uk
PLANTATT database www.ceh.ac.uk
Plant Gall Society www.british-galls.co.uk
Tree Register of British Isles (TROBI) www.treeregister.org
UK Moths www.ukmoths.org.uk

CHAPTER 2 THE HISTORY OF OUR NATIVE TREES
Birks, H. J. B. 1989. Holocene isochrone maps and patterns of tree-spreading in the British Isles. *J. Biogeograph.* 16: 503–540.
Coles, J.M. and Orne. B J. 1981. The sweet track 1980. *Somerset Levels Papers* 7: 6-12. Somerset Levels Project, Taunton.
Godwin, H. 1984. *History of the British Flora – A Factual Basis for Phytogeography*. Cambridge University Press.
Robinson. W. J. et al. 1990. Some historical background on dendrochronology. In: E.R Cook and L.A. Kairiukstis, 1990. *Methods in Dendrochronology: Applications in the Environmental Sciences*. Springer, USA.
Vera, F. W. M. 2002. The dynamic European forest. *Arbor. J.* 26: 179–211.

CHAPTER 3 TREES IN THE WEB OF LIFE

Alexander, K. N. A. 2002. *The invertebrates of living and decaying timber in Britain and Ireland: a provisional annotated checklist*. English Nature Research Reports No. 467, Peterborough.
Alexander, K., Butler, J. and Green, T. 2006. The value of different tree and shrub species to wildlife. *British Wildlife* 18: 18–28.
Baldwin, I. T. and Schultz, J. C. 1983. Rapid Changes in Tree Leaf Chemistry Induced by Damage: Evidence for Communication between Plants. *Science* 221 (No. 4607): 227–229.
Bevan, D. 1987. *Forest Insects: A Guide to Insects Feeding on Trees in Britain*. Forestry Commission Handbook No. 1, HMSO.
Bioscience Resource Project, 2008. Bee learning behaviour affected by consumption of Bt Cry1Ab toxin. www.bioscienceresource.org/news/article.php?id=35
Brzeziecki, B. and Kienast, F. 1994. Classifying the life-history strategies of trees on the basis of the Grimian model. *Forest Ecology and Management 69: 167–187.*
Buchmann S.L. & Nabhan, G.P. 1995. *The Forgotten Pollinators*. Island Press.
Buczacki, S. and Harris, K., 1983. *Collins Shorter Guide to the Pests, Diseases and Disorders of Garden Plants*. Collins, London.
Burdekin, D. A. 1979. *Common Decay Fungi in Broadleaved Trees*. Arboricultural Leaflet No. 5, HMSO, London.
Chambers, V. H. 1946. An examination of the pollen loads of *Andrena*: the species that visit fruit trees. *J. Anim. Ecol.* 15: 9–21.
Collis, J. S. 1951. *The Triumph of the Tree*. Country Book Club, London.
Corbet, S. A. 1990. Pollination and the weather. *Israel Journal of Botany*. 39: 13–30.
Deer Initiative 2004. *Deer on our Roads: Counting the Cost*. The Deer Initiative, www.thedeerinitiative.co.uk.
Dixon, T. and Thieme, T. 2007. *Aphids on Deciduous Trees*. Naturalists' Handbook 29. Richmond Publishing, Slough.
Edwards, P. J. and Wratten, S. D. 1985. Induced plant defences against insect grazing; fact or fiction? *Oikos* 44: 70–74.
Ellis, M. B. and Ellis, J. P. 1997. *Microfungi on Land Plants* (enlarged edn.) Richmond Publishing, Slough.
Emmet, A. M. (ed.) 1988. *A Field Guide to the Smaller British Lepidoptera*. BENHS, London.
Emmet, A. M. and Heath, J. (eds.) 1992. *Moths and Butterflies of Great Britain and Ireland. Vol. 7 Part 2*. Harley Books, Colchester.
Frost, C. J., Mescher, M. C., Carlson, J.E. and de Moraes, C.M. 2008. Plant defense priming against herbivores: getting ready for a different battle. *Plant Physiology* 146: 818–824.
Greig, B. J. W., Gregory, S. C. and Strouts, R. G. 1991. *Honey Fungus*. Forestry Commission Booklet No. 100, HMSO.
Grime, J. P. 1979. *Plant Strategies and Vegetation Processes*, 2nd edn. John Wiley and Sons.
Grime, J. P., Hodgson, J. G. and Hunt, R. 2007. *Comparative Plant Ecology; a functional approach to common British species*, 2nd edn. Cambridge University Press.
Hardy, P. B., Sparks, T. H., Isaac, N. J. B. and Dennis, R. L. H. 2007. Specialism for larval and adult consumer resources among British butterflies: implications for conservation. *Biol. Conserv*. 138: 440–452.
Hicken, N. E. 1971. *The Natural History of an English Forest*. Nicholls, London.
Hodder, K. H., Bullock, J. M., Buckland, P. C. and Kirby, K. J. 2005. *Large Herbivores in the Wildwood and Modern Naturalistic Grazing Systems*. English Nature Research Reports No. 648.
Kennedy, C. E. J. and Southwood, T. R. E. 1984. The number of species of insect associated with British trees: a re-analysis. *J. Ecol.* 53: 455–478.
Kirby, P. 2001. *Habitat Management for Invertebrates: A Practical Handbook*. RSPB/JNCC. Peterborough.
Kirby, K. J. 2003. *What might a British Forest-landscape Driven by Large Herbivores Look Like?* English Nature Research Report No. 530.
Matthews, J. D. 1955. The influence of the weather on the frequency of beech mast years in England. *Forestry* 28: 107–116.
Paine, R. T. 1969. A note on trophic complexity and community stability. *American Naturalist* 103: 91–93.
Peterken, G. 1992. *Woodland Conservation and Management*. Chapman & Hall.
Peterken, G. F. 1996. *Natural Woodland: Ecology and Conservation in Northern Temperate Regions*. Cambridge University Press.
Peterken, G. F. 2008. *The Wye Valley*. Collins New Naturalist No. 105.
Proctor, M. and Yeo, P. 1973. *The Pollination of Flowers*. William Collins Sons & Co.
Redecker, D. 2005. *Glomeromycota: Arbuscular Mycorrhizal Fungi and their Relatives*. www.tolweb/Glomeromycota
Redfern, M. and Shirley, P. 2002. *British Plant Galls: Identification of Galls on Plants and Fungi*. FSC, Shrewsbury.
Side, K. C. 1955. A study of the insects living on the wayfaring tree. *Bull. Amat. Ent. Soc.* 14: 3–50.
Smith, R.M and Roy, D. B. 2008. Revealing the foundations of biodiversity: the database of British insects and their foodplants. *British Wildlife* 20 (1):17-25
Snow, B. and Snow, D. 1988. *Birds and Berries*. T. & A. D. Poyser, Staffs.
Southwood, T. R. E. 1961. The number of species of insect associated with various trees. *J. Anim. Ecol.* 30: 1–8
Spooner, B. and Roberts, P. 2005. *Fungi*. Collins New Naturalist, London.
Stokoe, W. J. 1944. *The Caterpillars of the British Butterflies*. Frederick Warne, London.
Stokoe, W. J. 1948. *The Caterpillars of British Moths: 1st Series – Sphingidae to Brephidae*. Frederick Warne, London.
Stokoe, W. J. 1948. *The Caterpillars of British Moths: 2nd Series – Geometridae to Hepialidae*. Frederick Warne, London.
Strouts, R. G and Winter, T. G. 1994. *Diagnosis of Ill-health in Trees*. Forestry Commission Research for Amenity Trees No. 2. TSO.
Thomas, P. 2000. *Trees: their Natural History*. Cambridge University Press.
Winter, J. G. 1983. *Catalogue of Phytophagous Insects and Mites on Trees in Great Britain*. Forestry Commission Booklet No. 53.

WEBSITES
Ancient Tree Forum www.woodlandtrust.org.uk/ancient-tree-forum/
Ecoflora www.ecoflora.co.uk

CHAPTER 4 PORTRAITS OF NATIVE TREES

Alder (*Alnus glutinosa*)
Allen, D. 1990. Alder in folk medicine. *Plant-Lore: Notes and News* 15: 66.
Bennett, K. D. and Birks, H. J. B. 1990. Postglacial History of alder (*Alnus glutinosa* [L.] Gaertn.) in the British Isles. *Science*, 5: 123–133.
Grigson, G. 1960. *The Englishman's Flora*. J.M Dent & Sons, London.
Grime, J. P., Hodgson, J. G. and Hunt, R. 2007. *Comparative Plant Ecology; a Functional Approach to Common British Species*, 2nd edn. Cambridge University Press.
Mabberley, D. J. 1997. *The Plant-book: A Portable Dictionary of the Vascular Plants*. Cambridge University Press.
McVean, D. N. 1953. *Alnus glutinosa* (L.) Gaertn. *Biological Flora of J. Ecol.* 41: 447–466.
Neeson, E. 1991. A *History of Irish Forestry*. Lilliput Press, Dublin.
O'Suilleabhain, S. 1942. *The Handbook of Irish Folklore*. Educational Company of Ireland Ltd., Dublin.
Vickery, R. 1995. *Dictionary of Plant-Lore*. Oxford University Press, Oxford.

Alder buckthorn (*Frangula alnus*)
Godwin, H. 1943. *Frangula Alnus* Miller. *Biological Flora of J. Ecol.* 31(1): 77–92.
Link, J.A. 1889. Beobachtungen am Kuckuk. *Orn. Monatsschr.* 14: 439-453 (quoted by Snow and Snow, 1988).
Pearson. F.G.O. 1945. The utilization of alder buckthorn. *Forestry* 19 (1): 95–96.
Snow, B. and D. 1988. *Birds and Berries*. T. & A. D. Poyser, Staffs.

Ash (*Fraxinus excelsior*)
Grime, J. P., Hodgson, J. G. and Hunt, R. 2007. *Comparative Plant Ecology; a Functional Approach to Common British Species*, 2nd edn. Cambridge University Press.
Lucas, A. T. 1963. The sacred trees of Ireland. *J. Cork Historical and Archaeological Society*, 68: 16–54.
National Countryside Survey (mainland UK) 2007. NERC– Centre for Ecology & Hydrology. http://www.countrysidesurvey.org.uk/archiveCS2000/index.htm
Spray, M. 1981. Holly as a fodder in England. *Agric. Hist. Rev*. 29(2): 97–110.
Wardle, P. 1961. Fraxinus Excelsior L. *Biological flora of J. Ecol.* 49: 739-751.
White, G. 1789 (1990 edn.). *A Natural History of Selbourne*. Penguin, London.

WEBSITES
Botanical Society of British Isles. www.bsbimaps.org.uk
www.druidry.org
Tree Register of the British Isles (TROBI) www.treeregister.org

Aspen (*Populus tremula*)
Cosgrove, P., Amphlett, A., Elliott, A., Ellis, C., Emmett, E., Prescott, T. and atherstone, A. Watson. 2005. Aspen: Britain's missing link with the boreal forest. *Brit. Wildlife* 17(2): 107–115.
Glass, D. 2008. A survey of aspens on Dunnet Head. *Bull. Caithness Field Club* 7(4): 8–12.
Jones, E.W. 1945. *Acer* L. *Biological Flora of J. Ecol.* 32: 215-219.
MacGowan, I. 1991 (revised 1997). *The Entomological Value of Aspen in the Scottish Highlands*. Malloch Society Report.
Mackenzie, N. 2010. *Ecology, Conservation and Management of Aspen: A Literature Review*. Scottish Native Woods, Aberfeldy.
Worrell, R., Gordon, A. G., Lee, R. S. and McInroy, A. 1999. Flowering and seed production of aspen in Scotland during a heavy seed year. *Scottish Forestry* 72: 27–34.

WEBSITES
Scottish aspen group www.scottishaspen.org.uk
Trees for Life www.treesforlife.org.uk

Beech (*Fagus sylvatica*)
Crispin, T. 1992. *The English Windsor Chair*. Alan Sutton.
Foley, M. and Clarke, S. 2005. *Orchids of the British Isles*. Griffin Press/RBG Edinburgh.
Godwin, H. 1984. *History of the British Flora – A Factual Basis for Phytogeography*. Cambridge University Press.
Hilliers Nurseries. 1981. *The Hillier Colour Dictionary of Trees and Shrubs*. David & Charles, London.
Matthews, J. D. 1955. The influence of the weather on the frequency of beech mast years in England. *Forestry* 28: 107–116.
Rackham, O. 2006. *Woodlands*. Collins New Naturalist, London.
White, G. 1789 (1990 edn.). *A Natural History of Selbourne*. Penguin, London.

Birches (*Betula* spp.)
Ashmole, P. 2006. The lost mountain woodland of Scotland and its restoration. *Scottish Forestry* 60: 9–22.
Atkinson, M. D. 1958. *Betula pendula* Roth (*B.verrucosa* Ehrh.) and *B. pubescens* Ehrh. *Biological Flora of J. Ecol.* 80: 837–870.
Ennos, R., Worrell, R., Arkle, P. and Malcolm, D. 2000. *Genetic Variation and Conservation of British Native Trees and Shrubs: Current Knowledge and Policy Implications*. Forestry Commission Technical Paper 31, Edinburgh.
De Groot, W. J., Thomas, P. A. and Wein, R. W. 1997. *Betula Nana* L and *Betula Glandulosa* Michx. *Biological Flora of J. Ecol.* 85: 241–264.
Mather, A.S. 1990. *Global Forest Resources*. Belhaven Press, London.
Mac Coitir, N. 2003. *Irish Trees: Myth, Legend and Folklore*. The Collins Press, Ireland.
Vickery, R. 1995. *Dictionary of Plant-Lore*. Oxford University Press, Oxford.

Bird cherry (*Prunus padus*)
Leather, S. R. 1996. *Prunus padus* L. *Biological Flora of J. Ecol.* 84: 125–132.
Gregor, W. 1889. Some folk-lore on trees, animals and river-fishing from the north-east of Scotland. *Folk-lore Journal* 7: 41–44.
Snow, B. and Snow, D. 1988. *Birds and Berries*. T. & A. D. Poyser, Staffs.
Vickery, R. 1995. *Dictionary of Plant-Lore*. Oxford University Press, Oxford.

Black poplar (*Populus nigra* ssp. *betulifolia*)
A'Hara, S., Samuel, S and Cottrell, J. 2009. The role of DNA-fingerprinting in the conservation of the native black poplar. *Brit. Wildlife* 21(2):110-115.
Barnes, G., Dallas, P & Williamson, T. 2009. The black poplar in Norfolk. *Quarterly Journal of Forestry* 103 (1):31-37.
Cooper, F. 2006. *The Black Poplar: Ecology, History and Conservation*. Windgather Press, Oxford.
Hobson, D. D. 1991. The status of *Populus nigra* L.in the Republic of Ireland. *Watsonia* 18: 303–305.
Rackham, O. 1986. *The History of the Countryside*. Dent, London.

Blackthorn (*Prunus spinosa*)
Kirby, K. J. 2003. *What Might a British Forest-landscape Driven by Large Herbivores Look Like?* English Nature Research Report No. 530.
Phillips, R. 1983. *Wild Food*. Pan Books, London.
Vera, F. W. M. 2002. The dynamic European forest. *Arbor. J.* 26: 179–211.

Box (*Buxus sempervirens*)
Grundy, L. 1998. *The Box Hill Book of Box*. Friends of Box Hill, Dorking.
Staples, M. J. C. 1970. A history of box in the British Isles. *Boxwood Bulletin* 10: 18–23, 34–37, 55–60.
Evelyn, J. 1664. *Sylva: a Discourse of Forest Trees*. (facsimile of 5th edn. 1979), Stobart and Son Ltd., London.
Vickery, R. 1995. *Dictionary of Plant-Lore*. Oxford University Press, Oxford.

Buckthorn (*Rhamnus cathartica*)
Godwin, H. 1943. *Rhamnus Cathartica* L. *Biological Flora of J. Ecol.* 31(1): 69–76.

Crabapple (*Malus sylvestris*) **and domestic apple** (*Malus pumila*)
Juniper, B. and Mabberley, D. 2006. *The Story of the Apple*. Timber Press.
Phillips, R. 1983. *Wild Food*. Pan Books, London.
Rackham, O. 2006. *Woodlands*. Collins New Naturalist, London.
Snow, B. and Snow, D. 1988. *Birds and Berries*. T. and A. D. Poyser, Staffs.
Vickery, R. 1995. *Dictionary of Plant-Lore*. Oxford University Press, Oxford
Wilkes, J. H. 1972. *Trees of the British Isles in History and Legend*. Frederick Muller.

WEBSITES
www.fruitforum.org
www.mistletoe.org.uk

Elder (*Sambucus nigra*)
Atkinson, M.D. & Atkinson, E. 2002. *Sambucus nigra* L. *Biological Flora of J. Ecol.* 90:895-923
Howkins, C. 1994. *Elder – The Mother Tree of Folklore*. Chris Howkins Publications, Addlestone, Surrey.
Snow, B. and Snow, D. 1988. *Birds and Berries*. T. & A. D. Poyser, Staffs.
Vickery, R. 1995. *Dictionary of Plant-Lore*. Oxford University Press, Oxford.

Elms (*Ulmus* spp.)
Coleman, M. 2000. Application of RAPDs to the critical taxonomy of the English endemic elm *Ulmus plotii* Druce. *Bot. J. Linn. Soc.* 133: 241–262.

Coleman, M. (ed.). 2009. *Wych Elm.* Royal Botanic Garden, Edinburgh.
Gil, L., Fuentes-Utrilla, P., Soto. A., Cervera, M. T. and Collada, C. 2004. English elm is a 2,000-year-old Roman clone. *Nature* 431: 1053.
Goodall-Copestake, W. P., Hollingsworth, M. L., Hollingsworth, P. M., Jenkins, G. I. and Collin, E. 2004. Molecular markers and ex situ conservation of the European elms (*Ulmus* spp.). *Biological Conservation.* 122: 537–546.
Fleming, A. 1997. Towards a history of wood pasture in Swaledale (North Yorkshire). *Landscape History* 19: 57–73.
Fleming, A. 1998. *Swaledale, Valley of the Wild River.* Edinburgh University Press.
Lees, E. 1874a. Notes on remarkable elms. *Gardeners Chronicle.* June 30, 790–791.
Lees, E. 1874b. Notes of old and curious Wych elms. *Gardeners Chronicle.* July 25, 102–103.
Muir, R. 2000. Pollards in Nidderdale: a landscape history. *Rural History* 11: 95–111.
Rackham, O. 1986. *The History of the Countryside.* Dent, London.
Richens, R. H. 1983. *Elm.* Cambridge University Press.
Spray, M. 1981. Holly as a fodder in England. *Agric. Hist. Rev.* 29(2): 97–110.
Vickery, R. 1995. *Dictionary of Plant-Lore.* Oxford University Press, Oxford.
Wilkinson, G. 1978. *Epitaph for the Elm.* Hutchinson.

Field maple (*Acer campestre*)
Jones, E.W. 1945. *Acer campestre L. Biological Flora of J. Ecol.* 32: 239-252.
Vickery, R. 1995. *Dictionary of Plant-Lore.* Oxford University Press, Oxford.

Hawthorns (*Crataegus* spp.)
Edwards, P. J. and Wratten, S. D. 1985. Induced plant defences against insect grazing; fact or fiction? *Oikos* 44: 70–74.
Lucas, A. T. 1963. The Sacred Trees of Ireland. Journal of the Cork Historical and Archaeological Society. 68: 16–54.
Tansley, A. G. 1939. *The British Islands and their Vegetation.* Cambridge University Press, London.

Hazel (*Corylus avellana*)
Howe, J. 1991. *Hazel Coppice; Past, Present and Future, the Hampshire Experience.* County Planning Dept., Hampshire County Council, Winchester.
Lucas, A. T. 1962-3. The sacred trees of Ireland. *Journal of the Cork Historical and Archaeological Society.* 68: 16–54.
Rackham, O. 1986. *The History of the Countryside.* Dent, London.
Oaks, R. and Mills, E. 2010. *Coppicing and Coppice Crafts.* Crowood Press, Marlborough.
Rackham, O. 2006. *Woodlands.* Collins New Naturalist, London.

Holly (*Ilex aquifolium*)
Howkins, C. 2001. *Holly – A Tree for All Seasons.* Chris Howkins Publications, Surrey.
National Countryside Survey (mainland UK) 2007. Database Right/ Copyright NERC– Centre for Ecology & Hydrology. http://www.countrysidesurvey.org.uk/archiveCS2000/index.htm
Peterken, G & Lloyd, P.S. 1967. *Ilex aquifolium L. Biological Flora of J Ecol.* 55: 841-858.
Radley, J. 1961. Holly as a winter feed. *Agric. Hist. Rev.* IX: 89–92.
Rackham, O. 2006. *Woodlands.* Collins New Naturalist, London.
Spray, M. 1981. Holly as a fodder in England. *Agric. Hist. Rev.* 29(2): 97–110.

Hornbeam (*Carpinus betulus*)
Spooner, B. and Roberts, P. 2005. *Fungi.* Collins New Naturalist, London.

Juniper (*Juniperus communis*)
Dearnley, T.C and Duckett, J.G. 1999. Juniper in the Lake District National Park. A review of condition and regeneration. *Watsonia* 22:261-267.
Gilbert, O. L. 1980. Juniper in Upper Teesdale. *J. Ecol.* 68: 1013–1024.
Thistleton-Dyer, T. F. 1889. *The Folklore of Plants.* London.
Thomas, P.A., El-Berghathi, M and Polwart, A. 2007. *Juniperus communis L. Biological Flora of J. Ecol.* 95:1404-1440.
Vickery, R. 1995. *Dictionary of Plant-Lore.* Oxford University Press, Oxford.
Ward, L. K. 1973. The conservation of juniper. 1. Present status of juniper in southern England. *J. appl. Ecol.* 10: 165–188.
Ward, L. K. 1977. The conservation of juniper. The associated fauna with special reference to southern England. *J. appl. Ecol.* 14: 81–120.
Ward, L. K. 1981. The demography, fauna and conservation of *Juniperus communis* in Britain. In: H. Synge (ed.). *The Biological Aspects of Rare Plant Conservation,* pp. 319–329. John Wiley, London.
Ward, L. K. 2004. The local extinction of a gall fly, *Schmidtiella gemmarum* Rubs. (Diptera. Cecidomyiidae), on a declining *Juniperus communis* colony. *Ent. Gaz.* 55: 269–275.

WEBSITES
www.plantlife.org.uk

Limes (*Tilia spp.*)
Halliday, G. 1997 (reprinted 1998). *A Flora of Cumbria.* Centre for North-West Regional Studies, University of Lancaster.
Pigott, C. D. 1981. The status, ecology and conservation of *Tilia platyphyllos* in Britain. In: H. Synge (ed.) *Biological Aspects of Rare Plant Conservation.* J. Wiley and Sons.
Pigott, C. D. 1985. Selective damage to tree seedlings by bank voles. *Oecologia,* 67: 367–371.
Pigott, C. D. 1991. *Tilia cordata,* Miller. *Biological Flora of J. Ecol.* 79: 1147–1207.
Pigott, C. D. and Huntley, J. P. 1980–1989. Factors controlling the distribution of *Tilia cordata* at the northern limits of its geographical range. *New Phytol* 81: 429–441; 84: 145–164; 87: 817–839; 112: 117–121.
Spooner, B. and Roberts, P. 2005. *Fungi.* Collins New Naturalist, London.
Stace, C. 2010. *New Flora of the British Isles,* 3rd edn.. Cambridge University Press.
Tipping, R. 2010. *Bowmont: an Environmental History of the Bowmont Valley North Cheviot Hills, 10000 BC to 2000 AD.* Society of Antiquaries of Scvotland, Edinburgh.

WEBSITES
Fungal Records Database of Britain and Ireland www.fieldmycology.net/FRDBI

Oaks (*Quercus* spp.)
Crawley, M. J. and Akhteruzzaman, M. 1988. Individual variation in the phenology of oak trees and its consequences for herbivorous insects. *Functional Ecology* 2: 409–415.
Crawley, M. J. and Long, C. R. 1995. Alternate bearing, predator satiation and seedling recruitment in *Quercus robur* L. *J. Ecol.* 83: 683–696.
Den Ouden, J., Jansen, P. A. and Smit. R. 2004. Jays, mice and oaks: predation and dispersal of *Quercus robur* and *Q. petraea* in NW Europe. In: P.M. forget et al. (eds.) *Seed Fate: dispersal and seedling establishment.* CABI International, Wallingford.
Frampton, G. 1992. *Grovely! Grovely! Grovely! And All Grovely! The history of Oak Apple Day in Great Wishford.* Quacks Books, York.
Giles, A. 1990. The Grey Old Men of Moccas. *Tree News* (Sept issue).
Howkins, C. 2006. *Oak, the Lightning Tree.* Chris Howkins Publications, Addlestone, Surrey.
Jones, E.W. 1959. *Quercus L. Biological Flora of J Ecol.* 47:169-222.
Kennedy, C. E. J. and Southwood, T. R. E. 1984. The number of species of insect associated with British trees: a re-analysis. *J. Ecol.* 53: 455–478.
Morris, M. G. 1974. *Oak as a habitat for insect life.* In: M.G. Morris and F.H Perring (eds.). *The British Oak: its History and Natural History.* BSBI/E.W.Classey, Faringdon.
Rackham, O. 2006. *Woodlands.* Collins New Naturalist, London.
Roberts, J. 1997. *Royal Landscape: Gardens and Parks of Windsor.* Yale University Press.

WEBSITES
Tree Spirit www.treespirit.org.uk
www.naturescalendar.org.uk/findings/

Pear (*Pyrus pyraster*), Plymouth pear (*P. cordata*) and cultivated pear (*P.communis*)
Briggs, T. R. A. 1870. *Annual Report.* Annals of the Botanical Exchange Club, London.
Hill, M. O., Preston, C. D. and Roy, D. B. 2004. *PLANTATT: Attributes of British and Irish Plants: status, Size, Life History, Geography and Habitats.* Centre for Ecology and Hydrology/ NERC.
Jackson, A. 1995. The Plymouth Pear – the recovery programme for one of Britain's rarest trees. *British Wildlife Mag.* 6, No. 5: 273–278.
Stace, C. 2010. *New Flora of the British Isles* (3rd edn.). Cambridge University Press.

Rowan (*Sorbus aucuparia*)
Bacles, C. F. E., Lowe, A. J. and Ennos, R. A. 2004. Genetic effects of chronic habitat fragmentation on tree species: the case of *Sorbus aucuparia* in a deforested Scottish landscape. *Molecular Ecology* 13: 573–584.
Clapham, A. R., Tutin A. G. and Moore D. M. 1991. *Flora of the British Isles,* 3rd edn. Cambridge University Press, Cambridge.
Hill, M. O. 1979. The development of a flora in even-aged plantations. In: Ford, E. D., Malcolm, D. C. and Atterson, J. C. (eds.), *The Ecology of Even-aged Forest Plantations* pp. 175–192. NERC, Institute of Terrestrial Ecology.
Hill, M. O., Preston, C. D. and Roy, D. B. 2004. *PLANTATT: Attributes of British and Irish Plants: status, Size, Life History, Geography and Habitats.* Centre for Ecology and Hydrology/ NERC.
Howkins, C. 1994. *Rowan, the Tree of Protection.* Chris Howkins Publications, Surrey.
Mabberley, D. J. 1997. *The Plant-book: A Portable Dictionary of the Vascular Plants.* Cambridge University Press.
McAllister, H. A. 1986. *The Rowan and its Relatives.* Ness Botanic Gardens, Liverpool University.
Raspe, O., Findlay, C. and Jacquemart, A-M. 2000. *Sorbus aucuparia L. Biological Flora of J Ecol.* 88: 910–930.

Scots pine (*Pinus sylvestris*)
Carlisle, A and Brown, A. H. F. 1968. *Pinus sylvestris L. Biological Flora of J. Ecol.* 56: 269–306.
Edlin, H.L. 1961. The wild pines of Kielder Forest - are they truly native? *J. of For. Comm.* 30: 38-44.
Rackham, O. 2006. *Woodlands.* Collins New Naturalist, London.
Watts, K. 1989. Scots pine and droveways. *Wiltshire Folklife* 19: 3–6.

Spindle-tree (*Euonymus europaeus*)
Kirby, M. 2008. The ladybird, the scale and the spindle – a highly specialised relationship. *British Wildlife* 19 (3) 193–196.

Strawberry tree or Arbutus (*Arbutus unedo*)
Dixon, T. and Thieme, T. 2007. *Aphids on deciduous trees.* Naturalists' Handbook 29. Richmond Publishing, Slough.
Godwin, H. 1984. *History of the British Flora – A Factual Basis for Phytogeography.* Cambridge University Press.
Grigson, G. 1960. *The Englishman's Flora.* J.M Dent & Sons, London
Sealy, R. J. 1949. *Arbutus unedo. J. Ecol.* 37: 365–388.
Sealy, R. J. and Webb, D. A. 1950. *Arbutus unedo L. Biological Flora of J. Ecol.* 38: 223–236.
Webb, D. A. 1948. Some observations on the arbutus in Ireland. *Irish Naturalists Journal* 9: 198–203.

Sweet chestnut (*Castanea sativa*)
Altman, N. 1994. *Sacred Trees.* Sierra Club, San Francisco.
Edlin, H. L., 1956. *Trees, Woods and Man.* Collins New Naturalist Series, London.
Grieve, M. 1980 (reprint from 1931 edn.) *A Modern Herbal.* Penguin, London.
Howkins, C. 2003. *Sweet Chestnut: History, Landscape, People.* Chris Howkins Publications. Addlestone, Surrey.
Rackham, O. 2006. *Woodlands.* Collins New Naturalist, London.
Vickery, R. 1995. *Dictionary of Plant-Lore.* Oxford University Press, Oxford.

Sycamore (*Acer pseudoplatanus*)
Dixon, T. and Thieme, T. 2007. *Aphids on Deciduous Trees.* Naturalists' Handbook 29. Richmond Publishing, Slough.
Gerard, J. 1597. *Historie of plants.* London.
Gibbs, Rev. R. 1928. *William Hutchinson of Delrow.* Aldenham Parish Magazine (October issue).
Green, T. 2005. Is there a case for the Celtic Maple or the Scots Plane? *British Wildlife* 16: 184–188.
Jones, E.W. 1945. *Acer Pseudo-Platanus L. Biological Flora of J. Ecol.* 32: 220–237.
Morecroft, M.D., Stokes, V.J., Taylor, M.E. and Morison, J.I.L. 2008. Effects of climate and management history on the distribution and growth of sycamore (*Acer pseudoplatanus* L.) in a southern British woodland in comparison to native competitors. *Forestry* 81 (1): 59-74.
Westwood, J. and Simpson, J. 2005. *The Lore of the Land.* Penguin Books, London.

Wayfaring tree (*Viburnum lantana*)
Kollmann, J. and Grubb, P. J. 2002. *Viburnum lantana* L. and *Viburnum opulus* L. (*V. lobatum* Lam., *Opulus vulgaris* Borkh.). *Biological Flora of J. Ecol.* 90: 1044–1070.
Snow, B. and Snow, D. 1988. *Birds and Berries.* T. & A. D. Poyser, Staffs.

Whitebeam (*Sorbus* spp.)
Grigson, G. 1960. *The Englishman's Flora.* J.M Dent & Sons, London
Rich, T.C.G. & Proctor, M.C.F. 2009. Some new British and Irish *Sorbus* L. taxa (Rosaceae). *Watsonia* 27:207-216.
Rich, T, Houston, L, Robertson, A and Proctor, M. 2010. *Whitebeams, Rowans and Service Trees of Britain and Ireland. BSBI Handbook No 14.*
Sell, P. D. 1989. The *Sorbus latifolia* (Lam.) Pers. aggregate in the British Isles. *Watsonia* 17: 385–399.
Vickery, R. 1995. *Dictionary of Plant-Lore.* Oxford University Press, Oxford.

Whitty pear, true service (*Sorbus domestica*)
Hampton, M. and Kay, Q. O. N. 1995. *Sorbus domestica* L. new to Wales and the British Isles. *Watsonia* 20 (4): 379–384.
Milner, J. E. D. 1992. *The Tree Book.* Collins and Brown, London.

Wild cherry, gean (and cultivated cherry) (*Prunus avium*)
Wilson, S. McG., Malcolm, D. C. and Rook, D. A. 1999. Locating natural populations of Scottish native trees. *Scott. Forestry* 53(4): 215–224.
Mabey, R. 1996. *Flora Britannica.* Sinclair-Stevenson, London.

Wild service (*Sorbus torminalis*)
Evelyn, J. 1664. *Sylva: a Discourse of Forest Trees* (facsimile of 5th edn., 1979). Stobart and Son Ltd., London.
Lloyd, E. G. 1977. The wild service tree *Sorbus torminalis* in Epping Forest. Lond. Nat. 56: 22–28.
Roper, P. 1993. The distribution of the wild service tree, *Sorbus torminalis* (L.) Crantz, in the British Isles. *Watsonia* 19:209-229.

Stace, C. 2010. *New Flora of the British Isles*, 3rd edn. Cambridge University Press.
Vickery, R. 1995. *Dictionary of Plant-Lore*. Oxford University Press, Oxford.

Willows (*Salix* spp.)
Beerling, D. J. 1998. *Salix herbacea* L. *Biological flora of J. Ecol.* 86: 872–895.
Belyaeva, I. 2009. Nomenclature of *Salix fragilis* L. and a new species, *S.euxina (Salicaceae). Taxon 58 (4): 1344-1348.* 1344-1348.
Bevan, D. 1987. *Forest Insects: A Guide to Insects Feeding on Trees in Britain.* Forestry Commission Handbook No. 1.
Brendall, T. 1985. *Willows of the British Isles.* Shire Natural History.
Loudon, J. C. 1844. *Arboretum et Fruticetum Britannicum.* London.
Meikle, R. D. 1984. *Willows and Poplars of Great Britain and Ireland.* BSBI Handbook No. 4.
Newsholme, C. 1992. *Willows*. Batsford, London.
Oates, M. 2008. The myth of the master tree – mate-location strategies of the purple emperor butterfly. *British Wildlife* 19: 330–337.
Scottish Mountain Willow Research Group. 2005. *Biodiversity, taxonomy, genetics and ecology of sub-arctic willow scrub.* Royal Botanic Garden, Edinburgh.
Skvortsov, A. K. 1999. *Willows of Russia and Adjacent Countries* (English trans. of Russian text, Moscow, 1968). University of Joensuu, Finland.
Stace, C. 2010. *New Flora of the British Isles* 3rd edn.. Cambridge University Press.
Stott, K. G. (updated by B. Braster, R. Parfitt, S. Wynter, and R. Youdale) 2001. *Cultivation and Use of Basket Willows*. Basketmakers Association/IACR Long Ashton Research Station. Leaflet, 28 pp.
Thistleton-Dyer, T. F. 1889. *The Folklore of Plants.* London.

WEBSITES
www.irishharps.net
Montane Scrub Action Group www.nts.org.uk and www.snh.org.uk.
Scottish Mountain Willow Research Group www.scottishbirchwoods.co.uk
www.ukbutterflies.co.uk

Yew (*Taxus baccata*)
Chetan, A. and Brueton. D. 1994. *The Sacred Yew*. Penguin, Arkana.
Cornish, V. 1944. *The Churchyard Yew and Immortality.* Frederick Muller, London.
Dickson, 1994. J. H. The yew tree (Taxus baccata L.) in Scotland: native or early introduction or both? *Scottish Forestry* 48(4): 241–261.
Nelson, E. C. 1981. The nomenclature and history in cultivation of the Irish yew, *Taxus baccata "fastigiata". Glasra* 5: 33–44.
Snow, B. and Snow, D. 1988. *Birds and Berries.* T. & A. D. Poyser, Staffs.
Thomas, P. A. and Polwart, A. 2003. *Taxus baccata* L. *Biological flora of J. Ecol.* 91: 489–524.
Williamson, R. 1978. *The Great Yew Forest.* Macmillan.

WEBSITE
Ancient yew documentation project www.ancient-yew.org

CHAPTER 5 MANAGING NATIVE TREES AND TREE PRODUCTS
Armstrong, L. 1978. *Woodcolliers and Charcoal Burning.* Coach Publishing House.
Ltd. Weald and Downland Open Air Museum, Kent.
Baker, H. 1986. *The Fruit Garden Displayed.* Royal Horticultural Society, Wisley.
Barratt, M. 1983. *Oak Swill Basket Making in the Lake District.* Barratt.
Common Ground. 1989. *Orchards; A Guide to Local Conservation.* Common Ground, Bristol.
Crispin, T. 1992. *The English Windsor Chair.* Alan Sutton.
Culpeper, N. undated. *Culpeper's Complete Herbal* (facsimile edn.). Foulsham, London.
Edlin, H. L., 1966. *Trees, Woods and Man.* Collins New Naturalist Series, London.
Edlin, H. L., 1970. *Collins Guide to Tree Planting and Cultivation.* William Collins and Co., London.
Edlin, H. L., 1973. *Woodland Crafts of Britain.* David and Charles, London.
Edwards, I. 2009. Versatility and utility: uses of elm past and present. In: M. Coleman, (ed). 2009, *Wych Elm.* Royal Botanic Garden, Edinburgh.
Fleming, A. 1997. Towards a history of wood pasture in Swaledale (North Yorkshire). *Landscape History* 19: 57–73.
Fitzrandolph, H. E. and Hay, M. D. 1977 (reprint of 1926–27 edn.). *Rural Industries of England and Wales (Vols 1 and 2).* Oxford University Press.
Grieve, M. 1931 (reprint 1980). *A Modern Herbal.* Penguin, London.
Mabey, R. 1996. *Flora Britannica.* Sinclair-Stevenson, London.
Mabey, R. 1972. *Food for Free – A Guide to the Edible Wild Plants of Britain.* William Collins Sons and Co. Ltd.
Mitchell, P. L. 1989. Repollarding large neglected pollards: a review of current practice and results. *Arboriculture* 13: 125–142.
Morgan, J and Richards, A. 2002. *The New Book of Apples: the definitive guide to apples including over 2000 varieties.* Ebury Press, London.
Muir, R. 2000. Pollards in Nidderdale: a landscape history. *Rural History* 11: 95–111.
Oaks, R. and Mills, E. 2010. *Coppicing and Coppice Crafts.* Crowood Press, Marlborough.
Phillips, R. 1983. *Wild Food.* Pan Books, London.
Pollard, E., Hooper, M.D. and Moore, N.W. 1974. *Hedges.* Collins New Naturalist.
Pulford, I. D. and Watson, C. 2002. Phytoremediation of heavy metal-contaminated land by trees – a review. *Environment International* 29: 529–540.
Rackham, O. 1986. *The History of the Countryside.* Dent, London.
Read, H.J. (ed.). 1991. *Pollard and Veteran Tree Management.* Proceedings of a Meeting at Burnham Beeches. Corp. of London.
Read, H.J. 2008. Pollards and pollarding in Europe. *British Wildlife.* 19:250-259.
Roach, F. A. 1985. *Cultivated Fruits of Britain: Their Origin and History.* Basil Blackwell.
Royal Horticultural Society. 1981. *Manual of Trees and Shrubs.* Hillier Press.
Savill, P. S. 1991. *The Silviculture of Trees used in British Forestry.* CABI International.
Shepley, A. (ed.). 2001. *Bill Hogarth MBE: Coppice Merchant.* Wood Education Programme Trust, Staveley, Cumbria.
Thomas, K. 1983. *Man and the Natural World.* Penguin, London.

WEBSITES
www.biomasssenergycentre.org.uk
Hedgelink www.hedgelink.org.uk
Renewables Obligation www.ofgem.gov.uk

CHAPTER 6 THE FOLKLORE OF TREES
Altman, N. 1994. *Sacred Trees.* Sierra Club, San Francisco.
Bord, J and Boyd, C. 1986. Sacred *Waters: Holy Wells and Water Lore in Britain and Ireland.* Paladin, London.
Clayton, A. 2008. *The Folklore of London.* Historical Publications, London.
Evans, E. E. 1972 (reprinted from first edn. 1957). *Irish Folkways.* Routledge and Kegan Paul, London.
Fife, H. Undated. *The Lore of Highland Trees.* Famedram Publishers.
Frazer J. G. 1933 (abridged edn. 1991). *The Golden Bough – A Study in Magic and Religion.* Papermac Publishers.
Giorno, J. 1985. *The Man who Planted Trees.* Chelsea Green Publishing Co., London.
Graves, R. 1990. *The White Goddess.* Faber and Faber, London.
Gregor, W. 1889. Some folk-lore on trees, animals and river-fishing from the north-east of Scotland. *Folk-lore Journal* 7: 41–44.
Grigson, G. 1987. *The Englishman's Flora.* J.M Dent & Sons, London.
Harte, J. 2008. *English Holy Wells – a Sourcebook.* Heart of Albion Press, Wymeswold.
Healy, E. 2001. *In Search of Ireland's Holy Wells.* Wolfhound Press, Dublin.
Hole, C. 1984. *A Dictionary of British Folk Customs.* Paladin, London.
Hope, R. 2000. *Devon and Cornwall's Holy Wells.* Oakmagic Publications, Church Stretton.
Howard, A. 1987. *Countryways – The Four Seasons.* Countryside Books/TVS.
Howkins, C. 1993. *Trees and People in Surrey and Beyond.* Chris Howkins Publications, Surrey.
Howkins, C. 1994. *A Dairymaid's Flora.* Chris Howkins Publications, Addlestone, Surrey.
Jackson, A. 1996. A Celtic Mystery. *Tree News*, Autumn 1996, 14–15.
Jones, F. 1992. *The Holy Wells of Wales.* University of Wales Press, Cardiff.
Jones Joyce, P. W. 1901. *The Origin and History of Irish Names of Places,* 7th edn. Longmans, Green and Co.
Kelly, F. 1976. The Old Irish Tree List. *Celtica* 11: 107–124.
Logan, P. 1980 (reprinted 1992). *The Holy Wells of Ireland.* Colin Smythe Ltd., Gerrard's Cross.
Lucas, A. T. 1962-3. The sacred trees of Ireland. *Journal of the Cork Historical and Archaeological Society*, 68: 16–54.
Lysaght, P. 1991. Verdure customs and their distribution in Ireland. *International Folklore Review* 8 :75-82.
Mac Coitir, N. 2003. *Irish Trees: Myth, Legend and Folklore.* The Collins Press, Ireland.
Macleod, Rev. Dr. N. and Dewar, Rev. Dr. D. 1893. *Dictionary of the Gaelic Language.* John Grant, Edinburgh.
Mills, A. D. 1999. *Dictionary of English Place-names,* 2nd edn. Oxford University Press.
Neeson, E. 1991. A *History of Irish Forestry.* Lilliput Press, Dublin.
O'Connor, F. 1991. *Kings, Lords and Commons.* Gill and Macmillan, London.
O'Heochaidh, S., NiNeill, M. and O'Cathain, S. 1977. *Fairy Legends from Donegal.* University College Press, Dublin.
Opie, I. and Opie, P. 1959. *The Lore and Language of Schoolchildren.* Oxford University Press.
Powell, T. G. E. 1958. *Ancient Peoples and Places 6 – The Celts.* Thames & Hudson.
Quiller-Couch, M. 2009 (original 1894). *Ancient and Holy Wells of Cornwall.* General Books.
Sant, J. 1994. *Healing Wells of Herefordshire.* Moondial, Bodenham.
Shepherd, V. 1994. *Historic Wells in and Around Bradford.* Heart of Albion Press, Wymeswold.
Simpson, J and Roud, S. 2000 (reprinted 2003). *Oxford Dictionary of English Folklore.* Oxford University Press.
Smith, A. H. 1970. *English Place-Name Elements.* English Place-Name Survey, Vols 25, 26, EPNS, University of Nottingham.
Tree Council of Ireland. 2005. *Champion Trees: A Selection of Ireland's Great Trees.* TCI , Dublin
Thistleton-Dyer, T. F. 1889. *The Folklore of Plants.* London.
Thomas, K. 1983. *Man and the Natural World.* Penguin, London.
Trubshaw, B. 1990. *Holy Wells and Springs of Leicestershire and Rutland.*
Vickery, R. 1979. *The Holy Thorn of Glastonbury.* Toucan Press, St Peter Port.
Vickery, R. (ed.). 1985. *Unlucky Plants.* Folklore Society, London.
Vickery, R. 1995. *Dictionary of Plant-Lore.* Oxford University Press, Oxford.
Westwood, J. and Simpson, J. 2005. *The Lore of the Land.* Penguin Books, London.
Wilkes, J. H. 1972. *Trees of the British Isles in History and Legend.* Frederick Muller.

WEBSITES
Tree Spirit www.treespirit.org.uk

CHAPTER 7 OUR NATIVE TREES – THE FUTURE
Ashmole, M. and Ashmole, P. 2009. *The Carrifran Wildwood Story.* Borders Forest Trust & John Muir Society.
Bacles, C. F. E., Lowe, A. J. and Ennos, R. A. 2004. Genetic effects of chronic habitat fragmentation on tree species: the case of *Sorbus aucuparia* in a deforested Scottish landscape. *Molecular Ecology* 13: 573–584.
Bioscience Resource Project. 2008. Bee learning behaviour affected by consumption of Bt Cry1Ab toxin. www.bioscienceresource.org/news/articlephp?id=35.
Broadmeadow, M. (ed.) 2002. *Climate Change: Impacts on UK Forests.* Forestry Commission, Edinburgh.
Broadmeadow, M. and Ray, D. 2005. *Climate Change and British Woodland.* (Information Note 69). Forestry Commission, Edinburgh.
Ennos, R., Worrell, R., Arkle, P. and Malcolm, D. 2000. *Genetic Variation and Conservation of British Native Trees and Shrubs: Current Knowledge and Policy Implications.* Forestry Commission Technical Paper 31, Edinburgh.
Deer Initiative, 2004. Deer on our Roads: Counting the Cost. The Deer Initiative. www.thedeerinitiative.co.uk.
Grime, J. P., Hodgson, J. G. and Hunt, R. 2007. *Comparative Plant Ecology; A Functional Approach to Common British Species,* 2nd edn. Cambridge University Press.
Haines-Young, R.H., et al. 2000. *Accounting for Nature: Assessing Habitats in the UK Countryside.* DETR, London
Hemery, G. E. 2008. *Trees and Climate Change.* www.nicholson-nurseries.co.uk/ClimateChange/climatechange01.htm
Hubert, J. and Cottrell, J. 2007. *The Role of Forest Genetic Resources in Helping British Forests Respond to Climate Change.* Forestry Commission Information Note No. 86.
Kennedy, C. E. J. and Southwood, T. R. E. 1984. The number of species of insect associated with British trees: a re-analysis. *J. Ecol.* 53: 455–478.
Ledig, F. T. 1988. The conservation of diversity in forest trees. *Bioscience,* 38: 471–480.
Miller, R. 2008. Gypsy moth *Lymantria dispar* (L.) (Lep: Lymantriidae) female in Central London. *Entomologist's Rec. J. Var.* 120: 172.
Rackham, O. 2008. Ancient woodlands: modern threat. *New Phytologist* 180:571-586.
Rich, T, Houston, L, Robertson, A and Proctor,M. 2010. *Whitebeams, Rowans and Service Trees of Britain and Ireland.* BSBI Handbook No 14.
Wilson, S. McG and Jenkins, R. 2001. Identifying local seed origins for Welsh native tree species. *Q. J. of Forestry* 95 (3): 201–208.
Wilson, S. McG, Malcolm, D. C. and Rook, D. A. 1999. Locating natural populations of Scottish native trees. *Scott. Forestry* 53(4): 215–224.
Wilson, S. McG and Samuel, C. J. A. 2003. Genetic conservation of native trees. In: *Forest Research Annual Report and Accounts 2002-2003*: pp. 56–61. Forest Research, Edinburgh.

WEBSITES
Forestry Commission www.forestry.gov.uk/forestry/INFD-6ABL5V
National Forest Co. www.nationalforest.org
HM Government's interactive map site www.magic.gov.uk/info/awreadme.html

TABLES
Alexander, K. N. A. 2002. *The invertebrates of living and decaying timber in Britain and Ireland: a provisional annotated checklist.* English Nature Research Reports No. 467, Peterborough.
Ashmole, P. 2006. The lost mountain woodland of Scotland and its restoration. *Scottish Forestry* 60: 9–22.
Clapham, A. R., Tutin A. G. and Moore D. M. 1991. *Flora of the British Isles,* 3rd edn. Cambridge University Press.
Ellis, M. B. and Ellis, J. P. 1997. *Microfungi on Land Plants* (enlarged edn.) Richmond Publishing, Slough.
Haines-Young, R.H., et al. 2000. *Accounting for Nature: Assessing Habitats in the UK Countryside.* DETR, London
Preston, C. D., Pearman, D. A. and Dines, T. D. 2002. *New Atlas of the British Isles and Irish Flora.* Oxford University Press.
Spooner, B. and Roberts, P. 2005. *Fungi.* Collins New Naturalist, London.
Strouts, R.G. and Winter, T.G. 1994. *Diagnosis of Ill-health in Trees.* TSO, London.